All that glitters...

Even the stars

All things precious...

Even your life

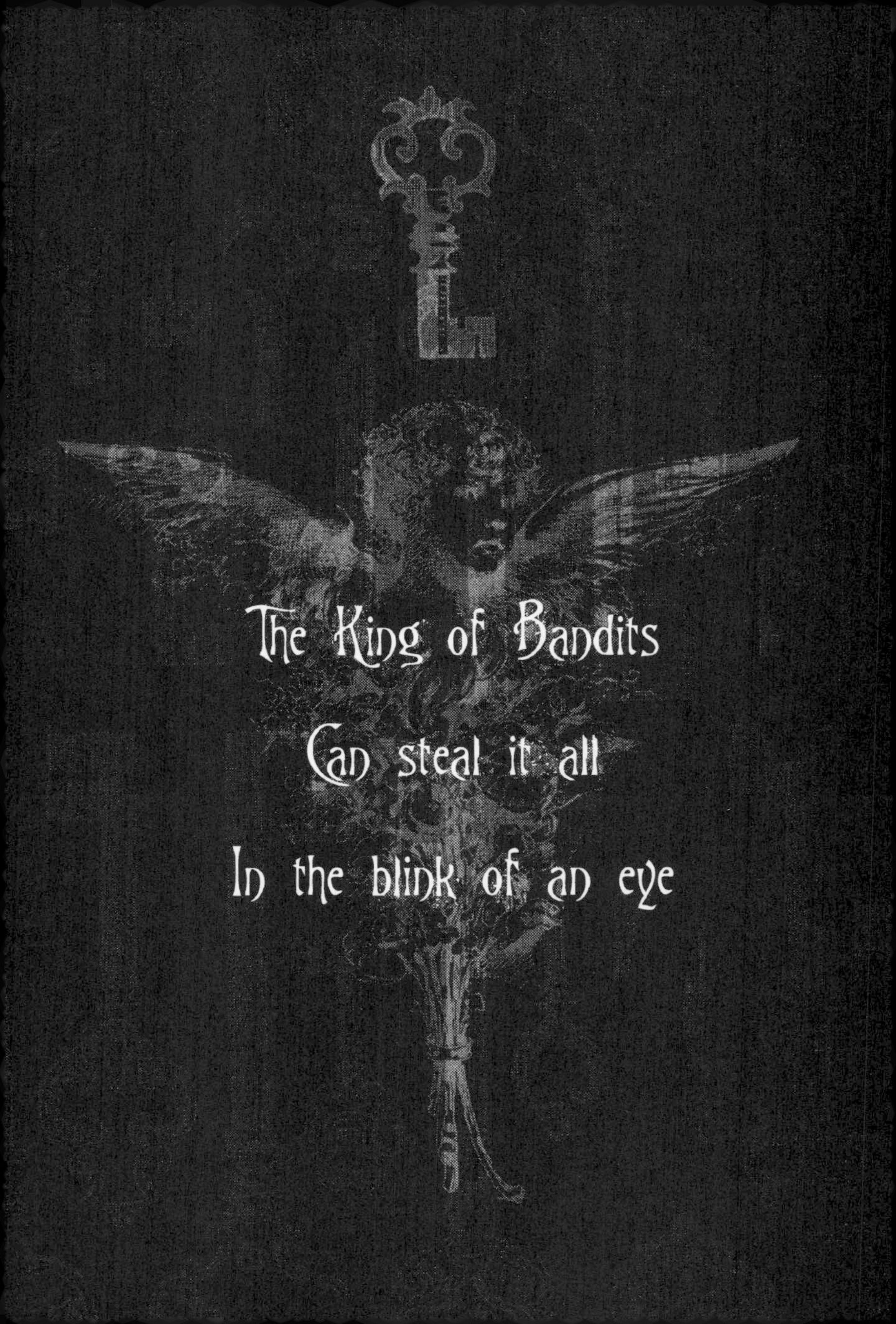
The King of Bandits
Can steal it all
In the blink of an eye

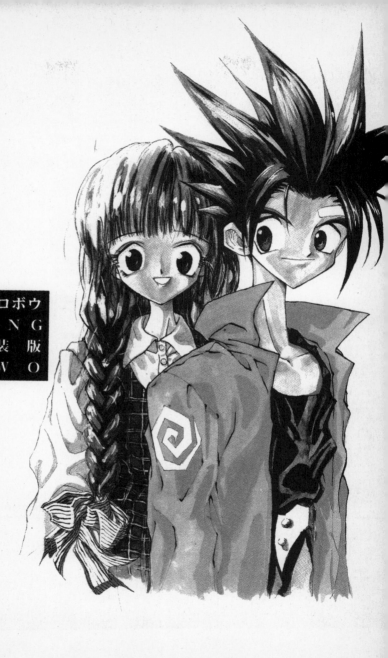

王ドロボウ
JING
新装版
TWO

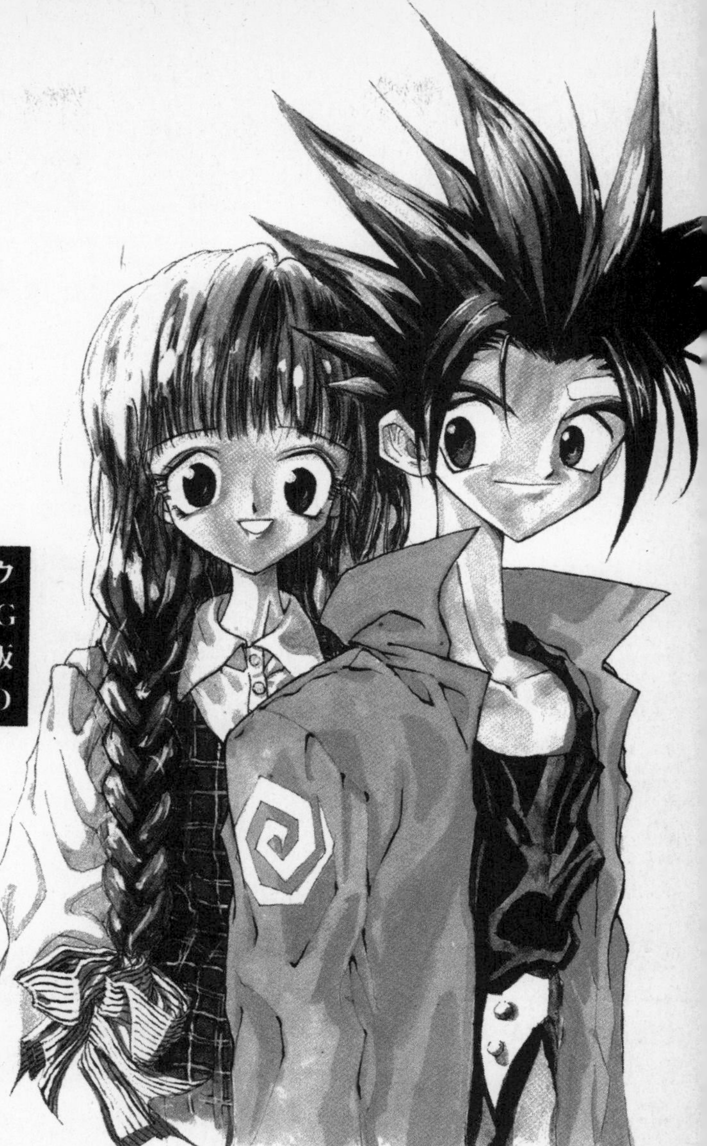

ALSO AVAILABLE FROM  TOKYOPOP®

MANGA

.HACK//LEGEND OF THE TWILIGHT*
@LARGE (December 2003)
ANGELIC LAYER*
BABY BIRTH*
BATTLE ROYALE*
BRAIN POWERED*
BRIGADOON*
CARDCAPTOR SAKURA
CARDCAPTOR SAKURA: MASTER OF THE CLOW*
CHOBITS*
CHRONICLES OF THE CURSED SWORD
CLAMP SCHOOL DETECTIVES*
CLOVER
CONFIDENTIAL CONFESSIONS*
CORRECTOR YUI
COWBOY BEBOP*
COWBOY BEBOP: SHOOTING STAR*
CYBORG 009*
DEMON DIARY
DIGIMON*
DRAGON HUNTER
DRAGON KNIGHTS*
DUKLYON: CLAMP SCHOOL DEFENDERS*
ERICA SAKURAZAWA*
FAKE*
FLCL*
FORBIDDEN DANCE*
GATE KEEPERS*
G GUNDAM*
GRAVITATION*
GTO*
GUNDAM WING
GUNDAM WING: BATTLEFIELD OF PACIFISTS
GUNDAM WING: ENDLESS WALTZ*
GUNDAM WING: THE LAST OUTPOST*
HAPPY MANIA*
HARLEM BEAT
I.N.V.U.
INITIAL D*
ISLAND
JING: KING OF BANDITS*
JULINE
KARE KANO*
KINDAICHI CASE FILES, THE*
KING OF HELL
KODOCHA: SANA'S STAGE*
LOVE HINA*
LUPIN III*
MAGIC KNIGHT RAYEARTH*

MAGIC KNIGHT RAYEARTH II* (COMING SOON)
MAN OF MANY FACES*
MARMALADE BOY*
MARS*
MIRACLE GIRLS
MIYUKI-CHAN IN WONDERLAND*
MONSTERS, INC.
PARADISE KISS*
PARASYTE
PEACH GIRL
PEACH GIRL: CHANGE OF HEART*
PET SHOP OF HORRORS*
PLANET LADDER*
PLANETES*
PRIEST
RAGNAROK
RAVE MASTER*
REALITY CHECK
REBIRTH
REBOUND*
RISING STARS OF MANGA
SABER MARIONETTE J*
SAILOR MOON
SAINT TAIL
SAMURAI DEEPER KYO*
SAMURAI GIRL: REAL BOUT HIGH SCHOOL*
SCRYED*
SHAOLIN SISTERS*
SHIRAHIME-SYO: SNOW GODDESS TALES* (Dec. 2003)
SHUTTERBOX
SORCERER HUNTERS
THE SKULL MAN*
THE VISION OF ESCAFLOWNE*
TOKYO MEW MEW*
UNDER THE GLASS MOON
VAMPIRE GAME*
WILD ACT*
WISH*
WORLD OF HARTZ (November 2003)
X-DAY*
ZODIAC P.I. *

For more information visit www.TOKYOPOP.com

*INDICATES 100% AUTHENTIC MANGA (RIGHT-TO-LEFT FORMAT)

CINE-MANGA™

CARDCAPTORS
JACKIE CHAN ADVENTURES (November 2003)
JIMMY NEUTRON
KIM POSSIBLE
LIZZIE MCGUIRE
POWER RANGERS: NINJA STORM
SPONGEBOB SQUAREPANTS
SPY KIDS 2

NOVELS

KARMA CLUB (April 2004)
SAILOR MOON

TOKYOPOP KIDS

STRAY SHEEP

ART BOOKS

CARDCAPTOR SAKURA*
MAGIC KNIGHT RAYEARTH*

ANIME GUIDES

COWBOY BEBOP ANIME GUIDES
GUNDAM TECHNICAL MANUALS
SAILOR MOON SCOUT GUIDES

080503

KING OF BANDITS

VOLUME 2 OF 7

STORY AND ART BY
YUICHI KUMAKURA

Los Angeles • Tokyo • London

Translator - Kong Chang
English Adaptation - Carol Fox
Copy Editors - Paul Morrissey and Bryce Coleman
Retouch and Lettering - Brian Bossin
Cover Layout - Gary Shum

Editor - Jake Forbes
Managing Editor - Jill Freshney
Production Coordinator - Antonio DePietro
Production Manager - Jennifer Miller
Art Director - Matt Alford
Editorial Director - Jeremy Ross
VP of Production - Ron Klamert
President & C.O.O. - John Parker
Publisher & C.E.O. - Stuart Levy

Email: editor@TOKYOPOP.com
Come visit us online at www.TOKYOPOP.com

A  Manga

TOKYOPOP Inc.
5900 Wilshire Blvd. Suite 2000
Los Angeles, CA 90036

ISBN: 1-59182-177-0

First TOKYOPOP® printing: August 2003

10 9 8 7 6 5 4 3 2
Printed in the USA

JING: KING OF BANDITS TWO
CONTENTS

The Story so Far...

Jing, greatest of thieves, is in hot pursuit of his latest prize – the Clockwork Grape of Adonis. With his trusty "sidebird" Kir by his side, the troublesome twosome sneak past the temporally tempestuous city guards, but trouble is right on their heels. Adonis is a city ruled by the clock, where breaking schedule is a crime punishable by death. Jing and Kir stumble upon one such execution – the lovely young Mirabelle is set to be beheaded in the town square. Kir upsets the execution and saves the girl, but the commotion attracts Mastergear, the sinister ruler of Adonis. When last we saw our heroes, they were locked in mortal combat with Mastergear and his foxy companion Sherry. Now, let us return to the heist.

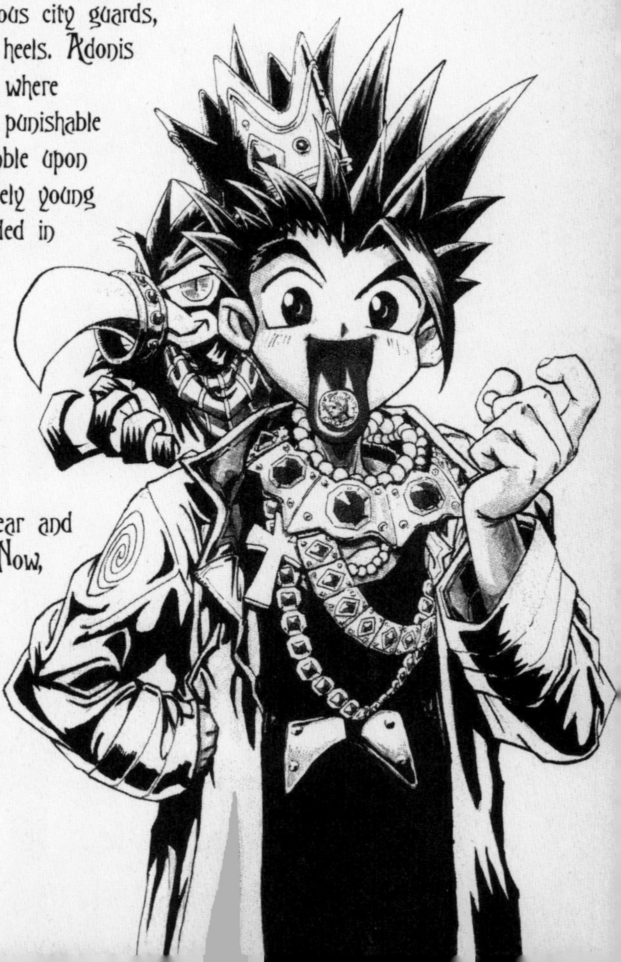

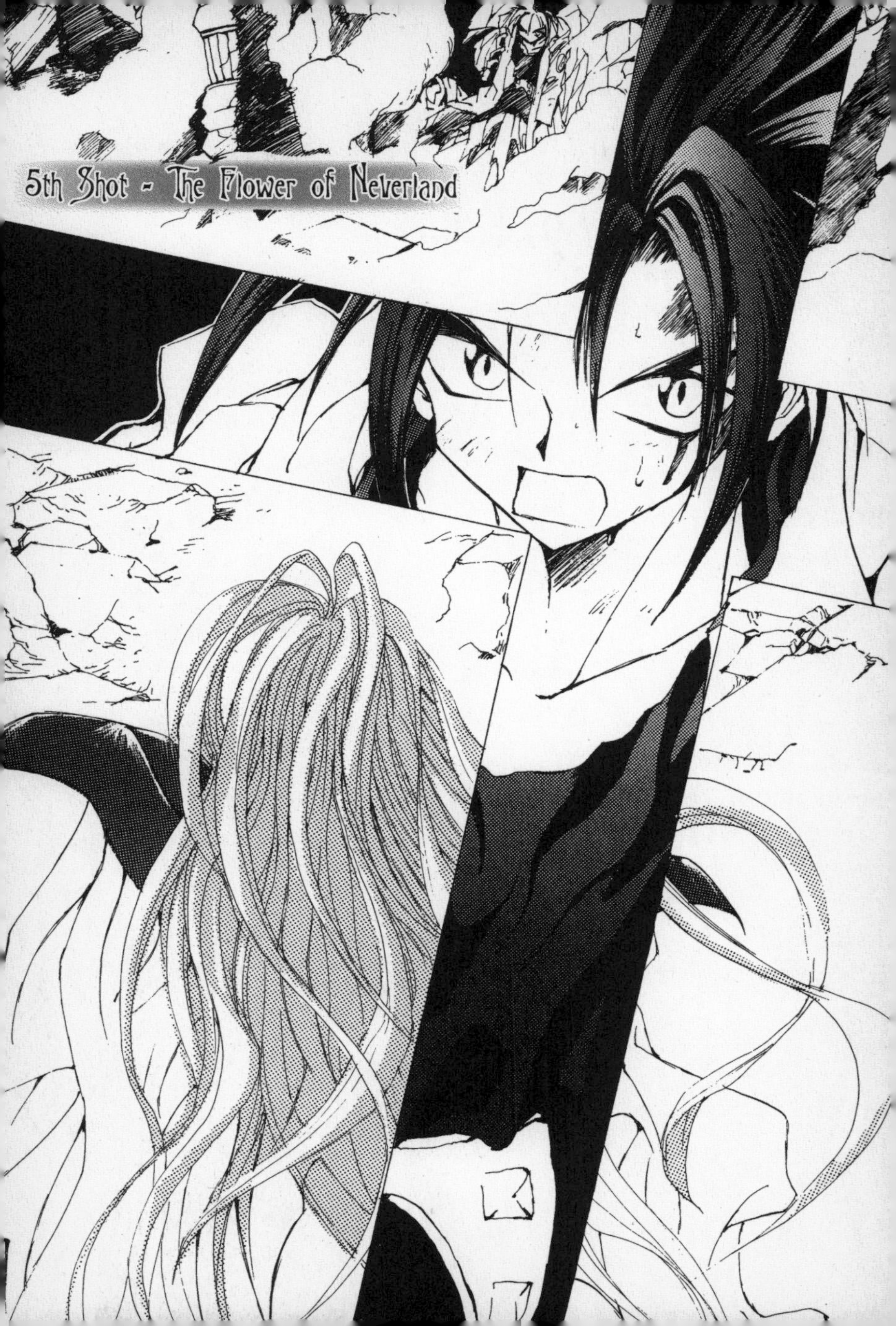
5th Shot - The Flower of Neverland

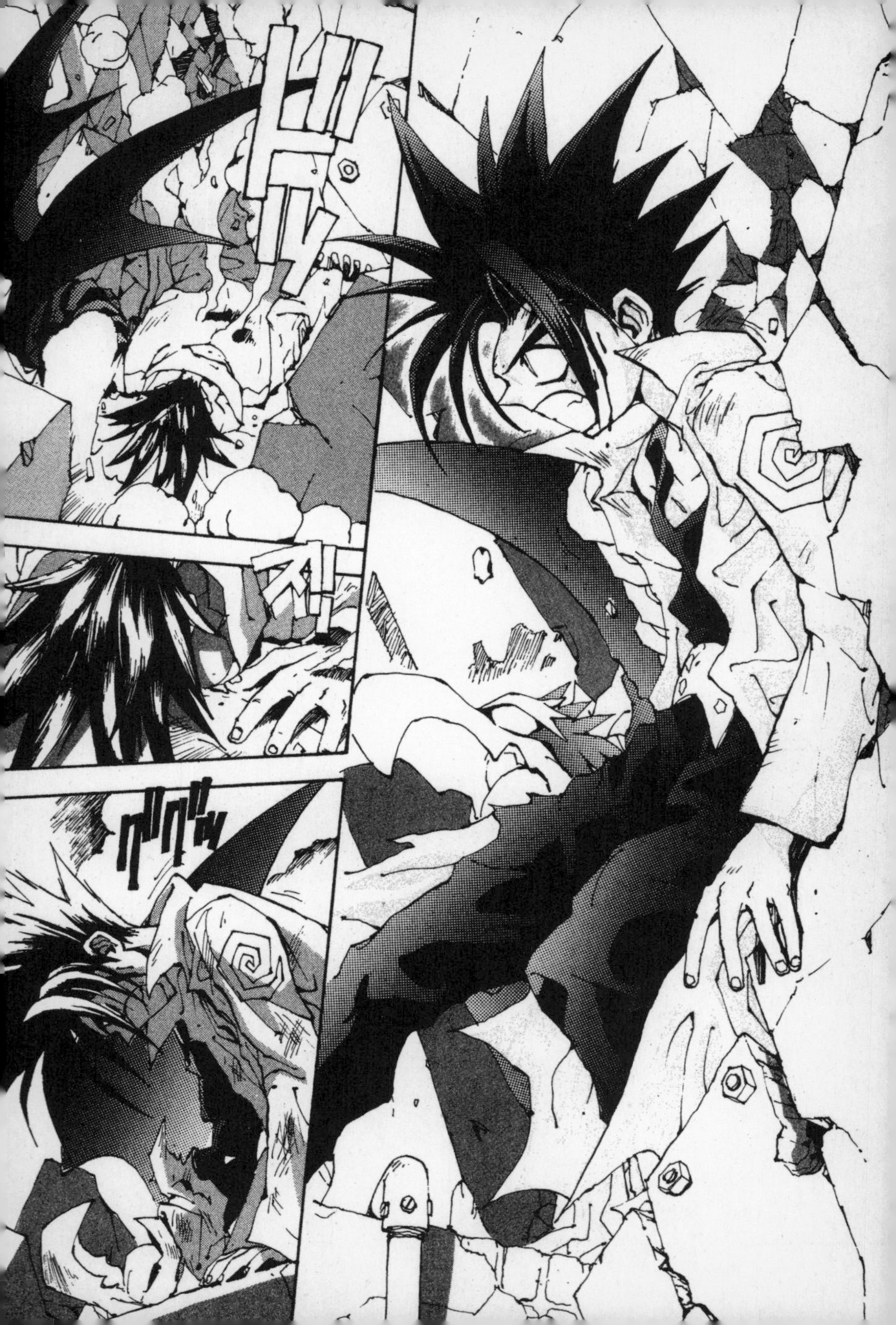
ドッ
ズ

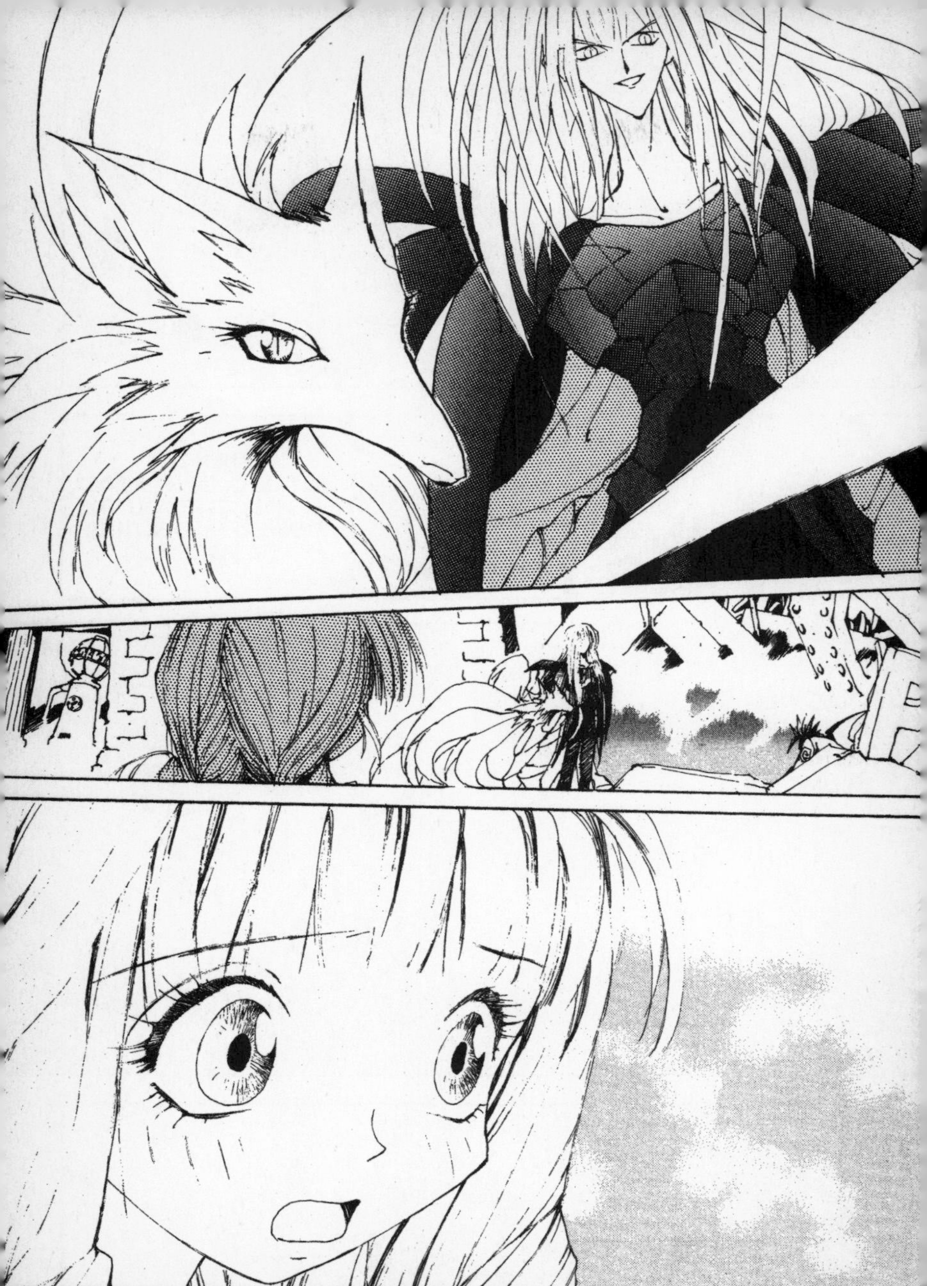

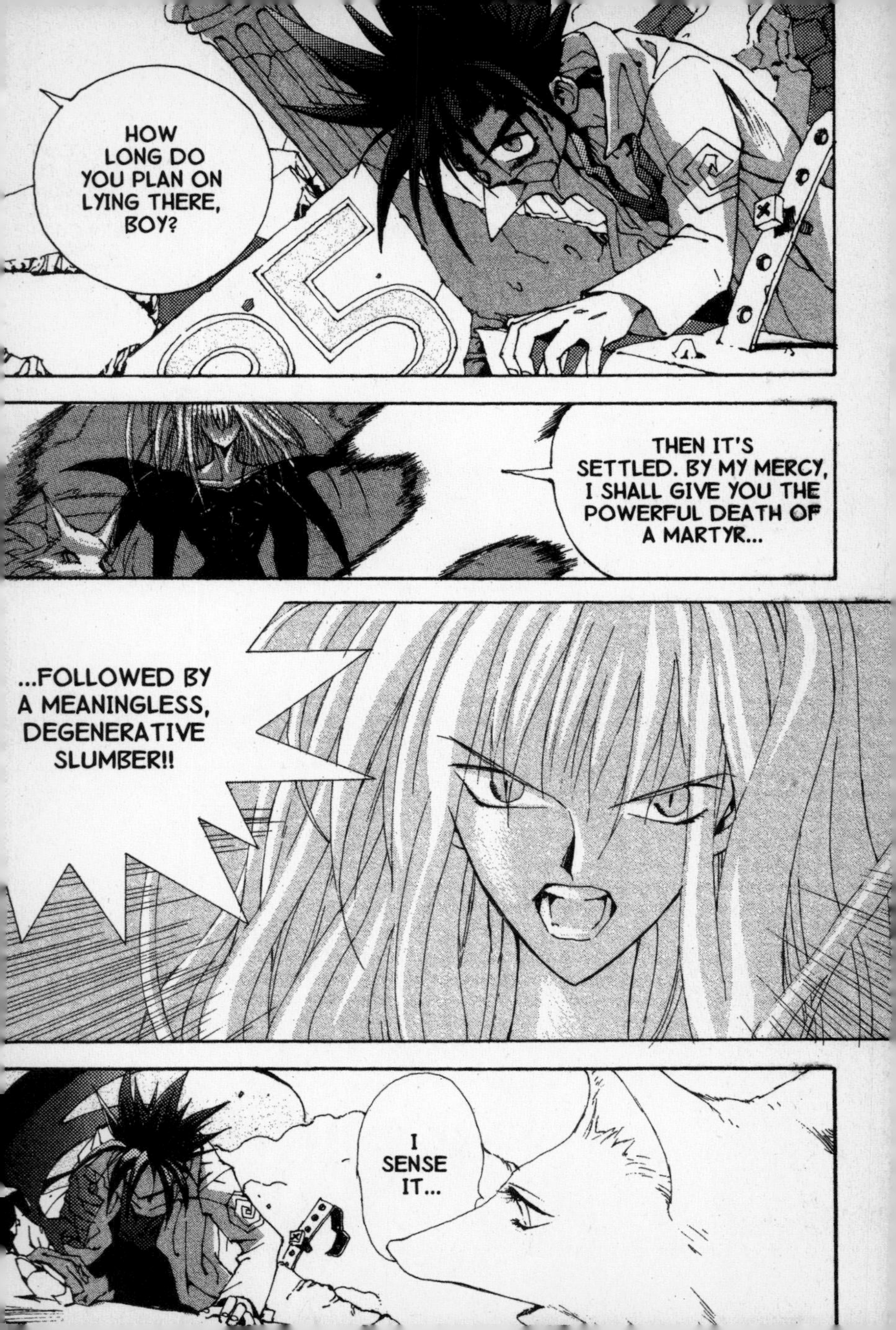
HOW LONG DO YOU PLAN ON LYING THERE, BOY?
THEN IT'S SETTLED. BY MY MERCY, I SHALL GIVE YOU THE POWERFUL DEATH OF A MARTYR...
...FOLLOWED BY A MEANINGLESS, DEGENERATIVE SLUMBER!!
I SENSE IT...

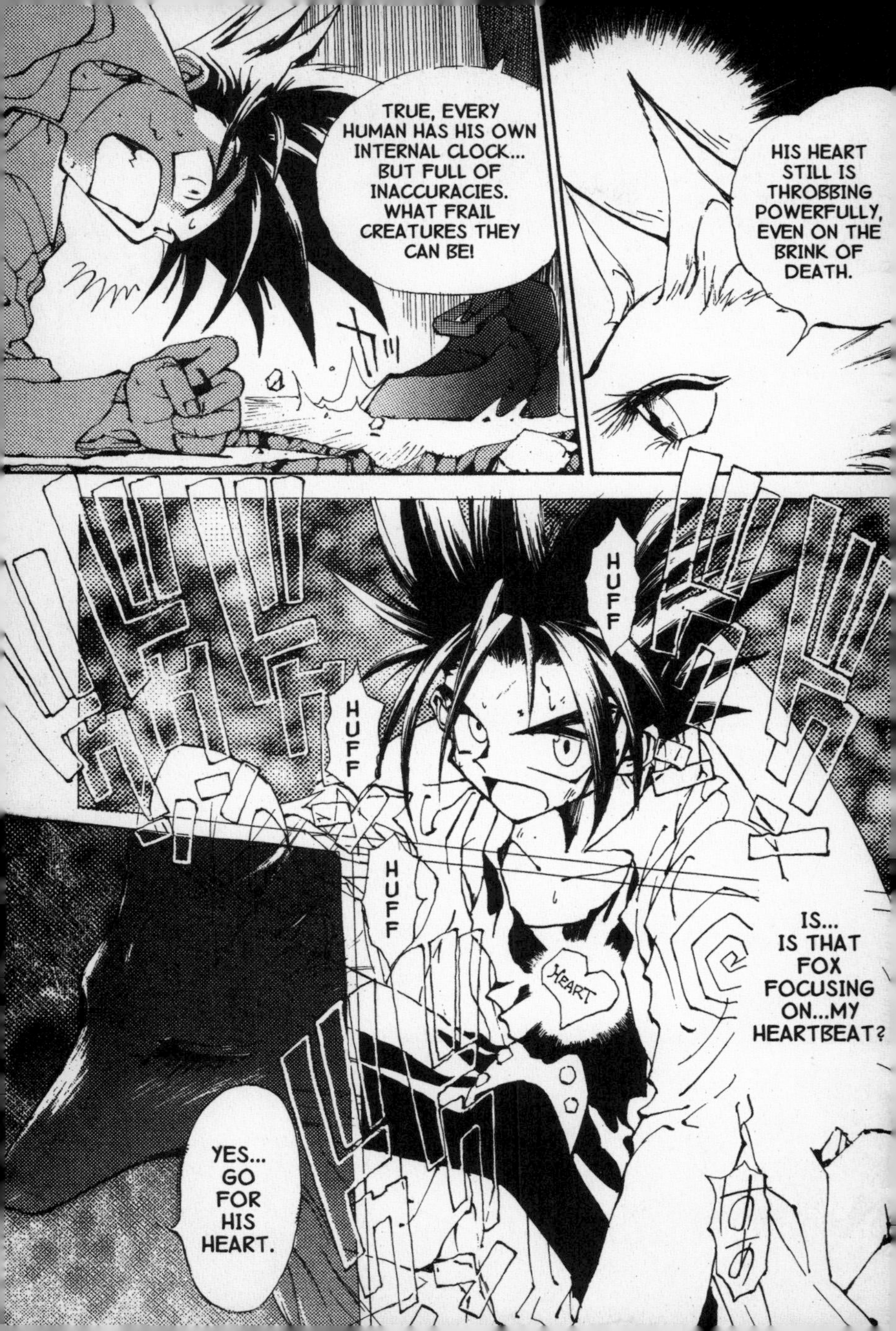
HIS HEART STILL IS THROBBING POWERFULLY, EVEN ON THE BRINK OF DEATH.
TRUE, EVERY HUMAN HAS HIS OWN INTERNAL CLOCK... BUT FULL OF INACCURACIES. WHAT FRAIL CREATURES THEY CAN BE!
HUFF
HUFF
IS... IS THAT FOX FOCUSING ON...MY HEARTBEAT?
HUFF
HEART
YES... GO FOR HIS HEART.

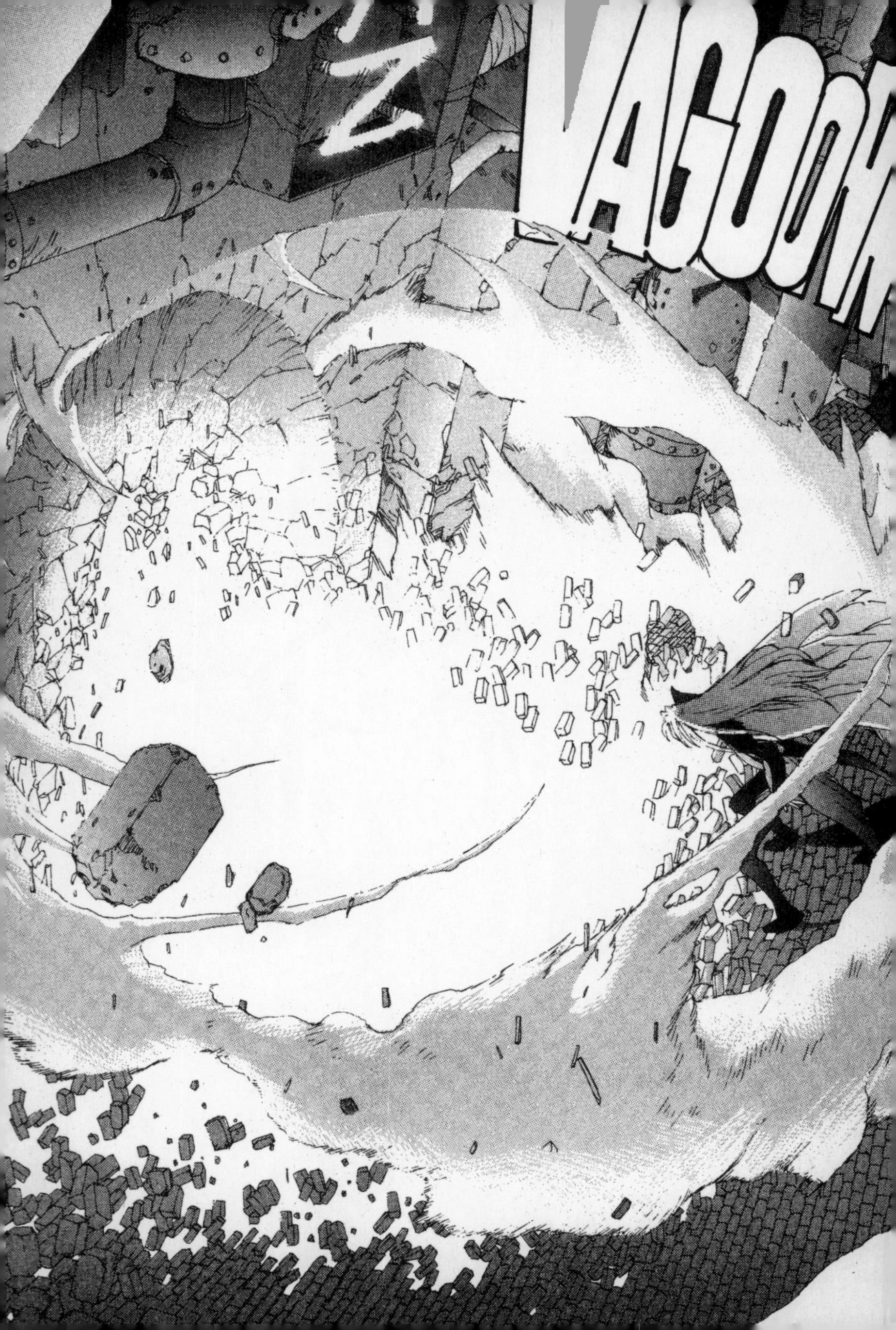
VAGOOM

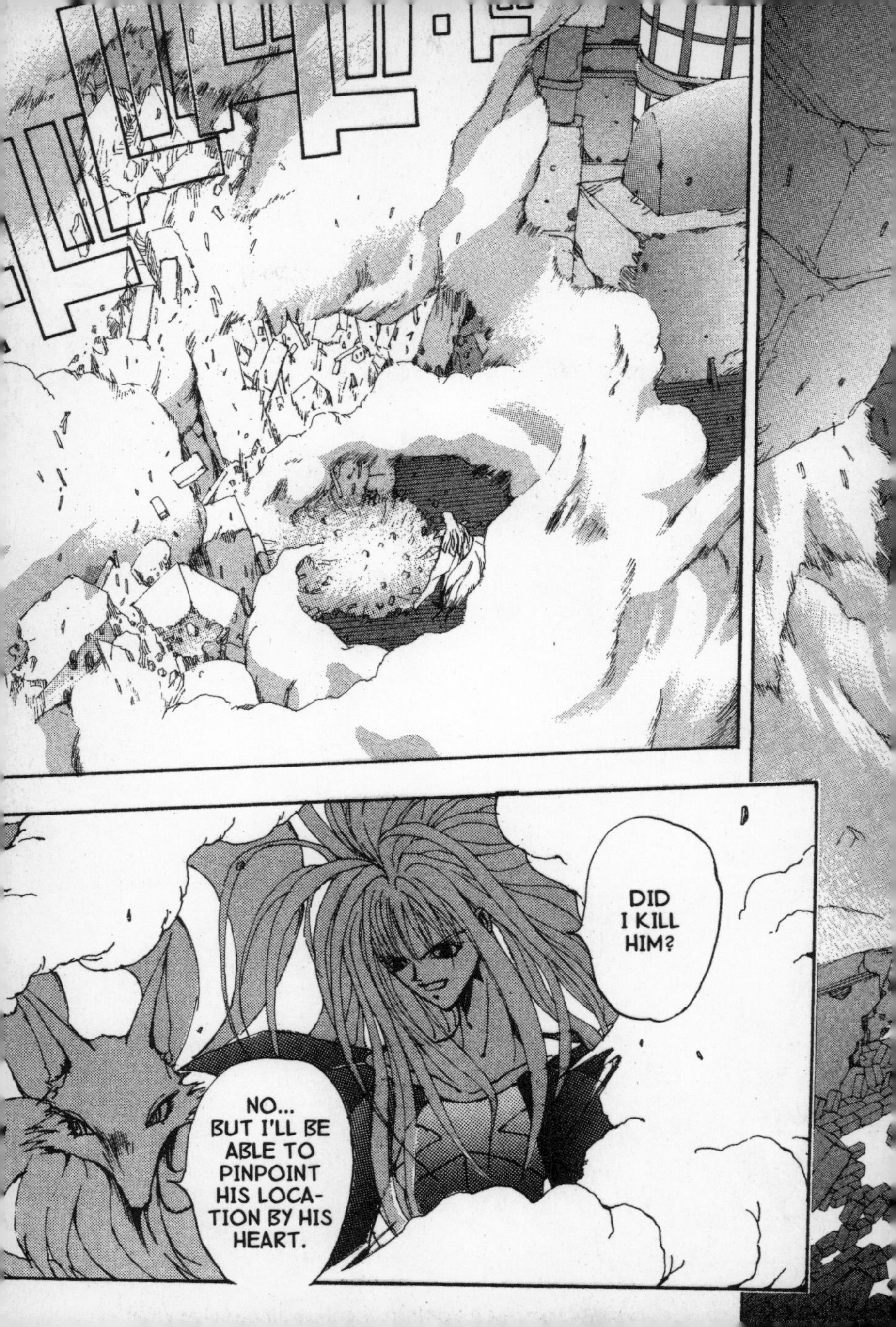
DID I KILL HIM?
NO... BUT I'LL BE ABLE TO PINPOINT HIS LOCA-TION BY HIS HEART.

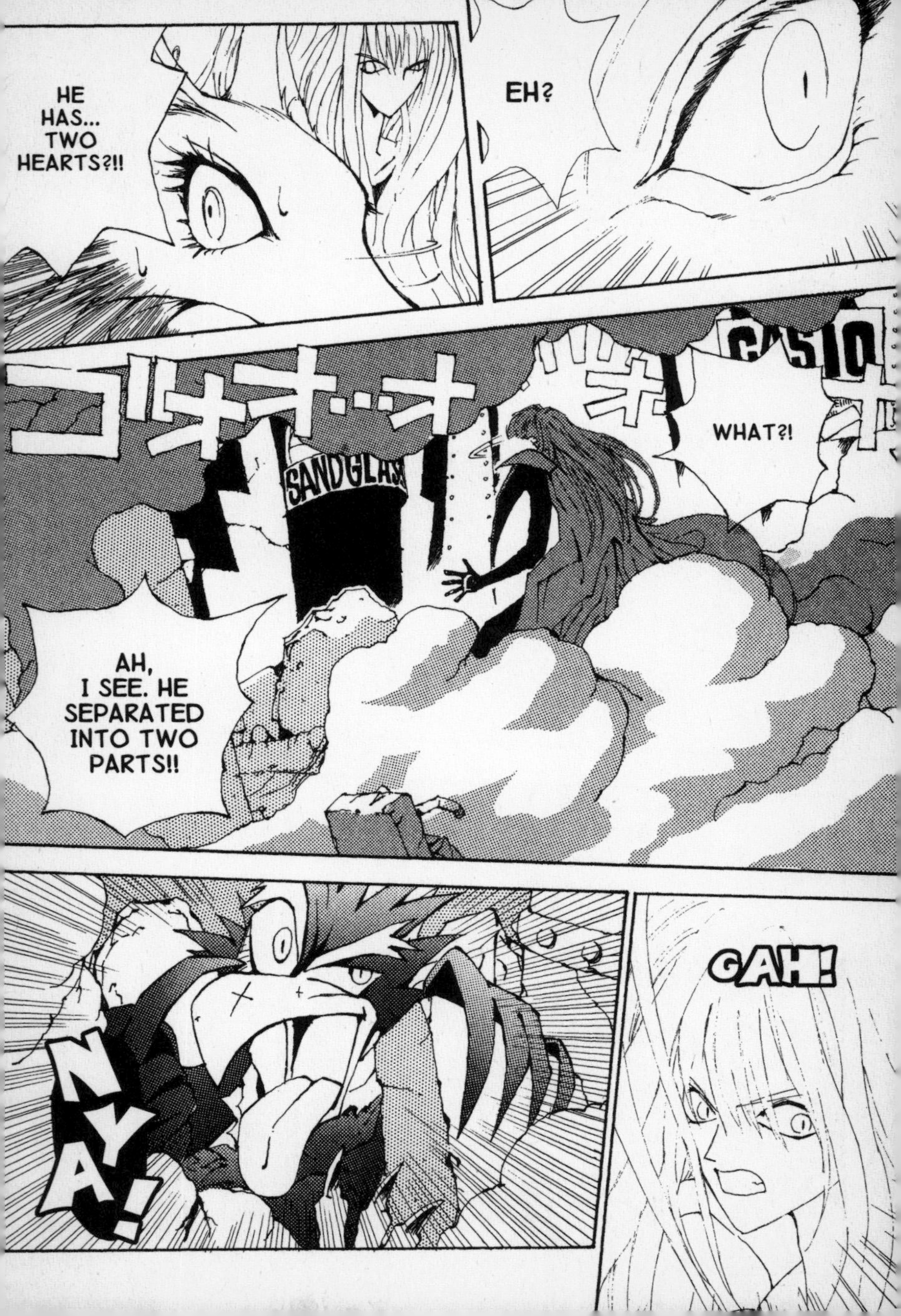
EH?
HE HAS... TWO HEARTS?!!
WHAT?!
AH, I SEE. HE SEPARATED INTO TWO PARTS!!
GAH!
NYA!

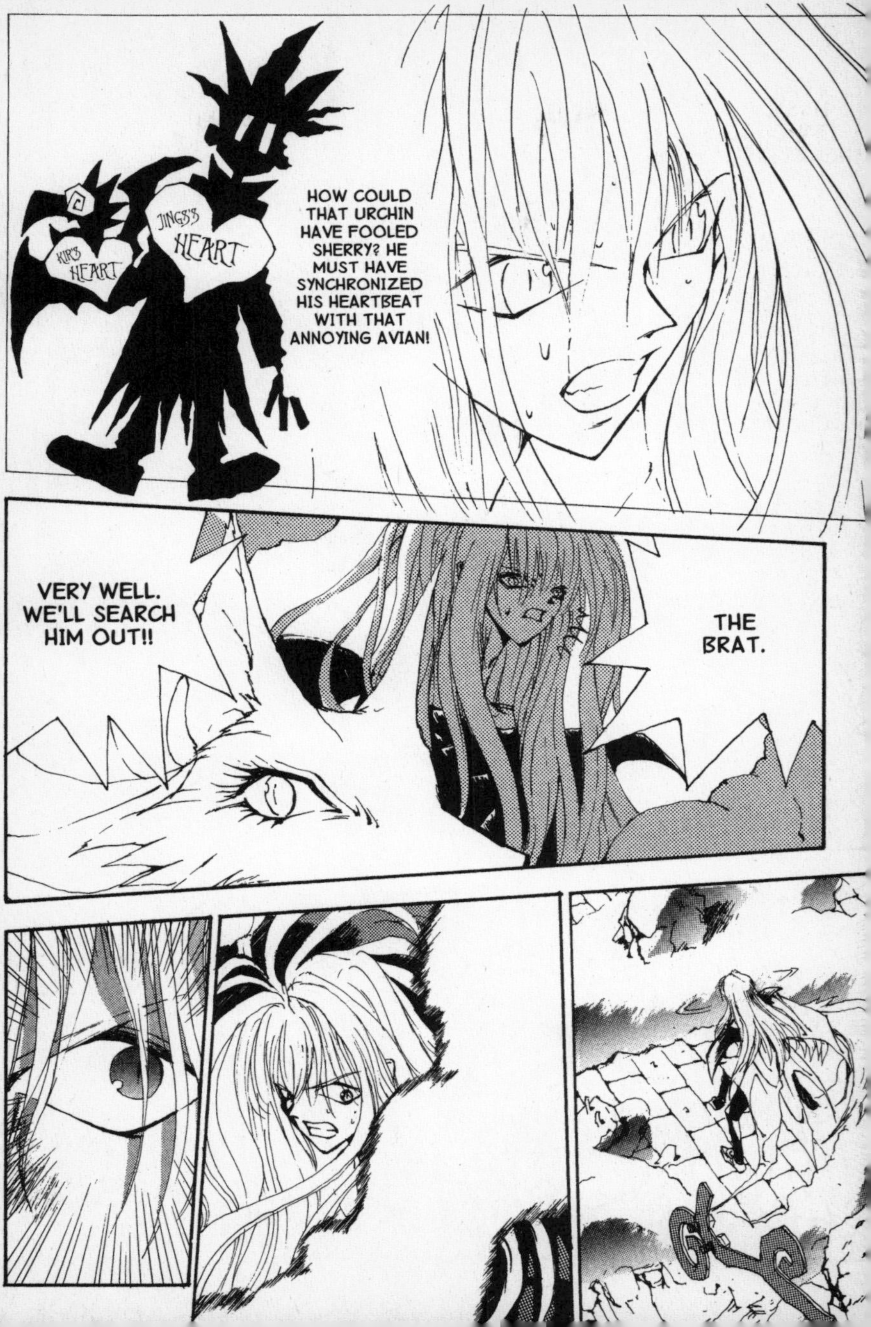
HOW COULD THAT URCHIN HAVE FOOLED SHERRY? HE MUST HAVE SYNCHRONIZED HIS HEARTBEAT WITH THAT ANNOYING AVIAN!
JINGS'S HEART
KIR'S HEART
THE BRAT.
VERY WELL. WE'LL SEARCH HIM OUT!!

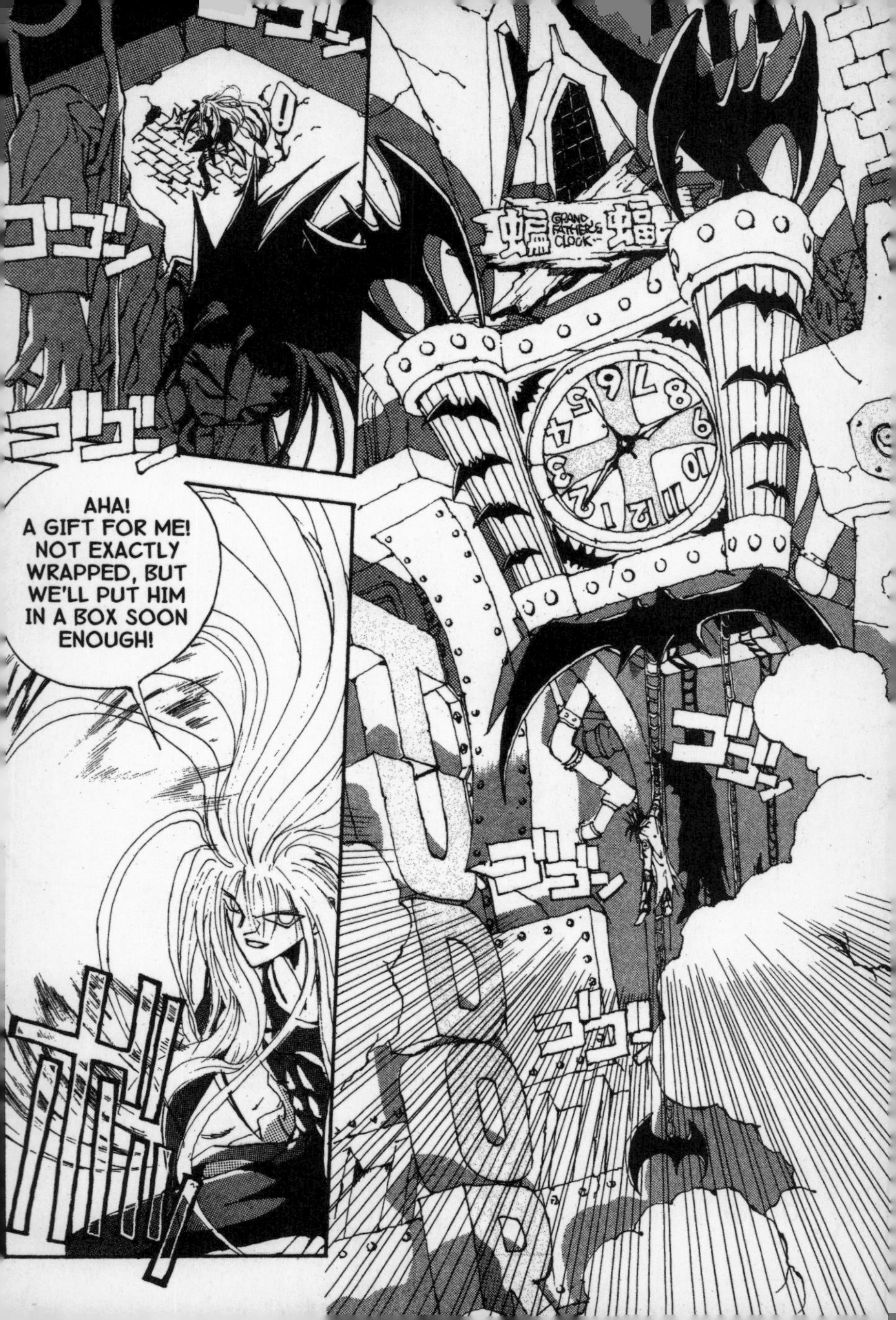
GRAND FATHER'S CLOCK
!
AHA! A GIFT FOR ME! NOT EXACTLY WRAPPED, BUT WE'LL PUT HIM IN A BOX SOON ENOUGH!

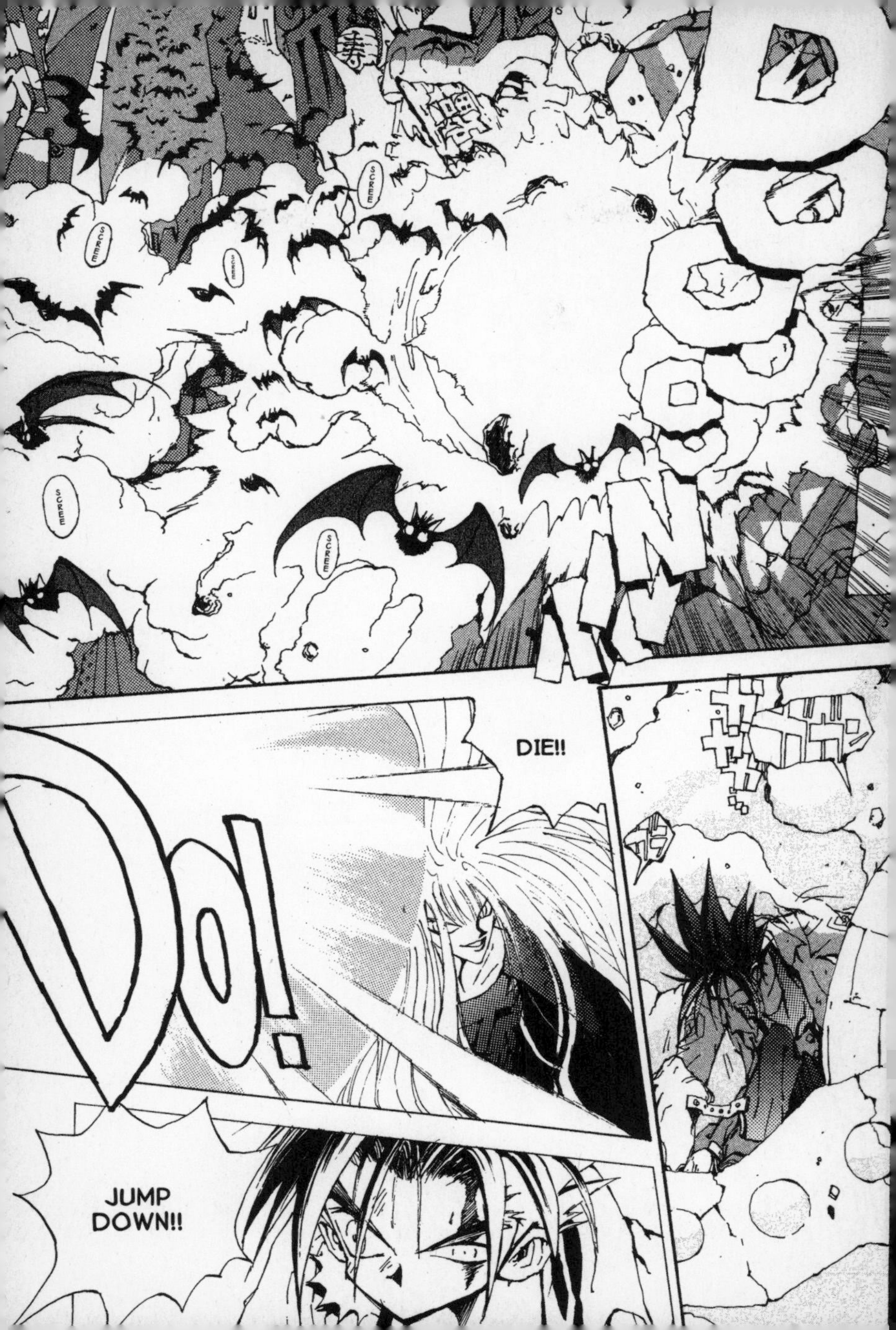
SCREE
SCREE
SCREE
SCREE
SCREE
DOOON
DIE!!
Da!
JUMP DOWN!!

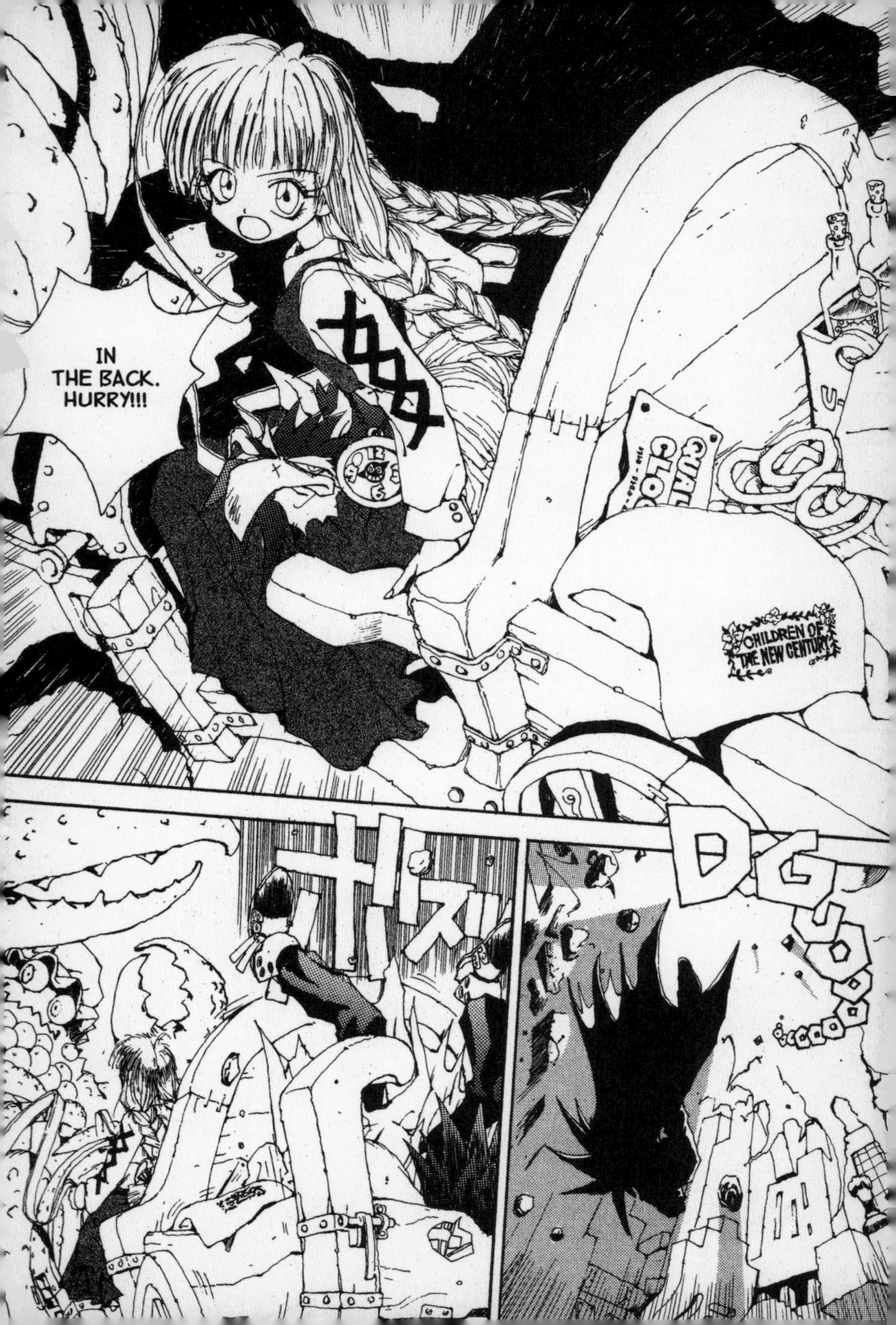
IN THE BACK. HURRY!!!
CHILDREN OF THE NEW CENTURY

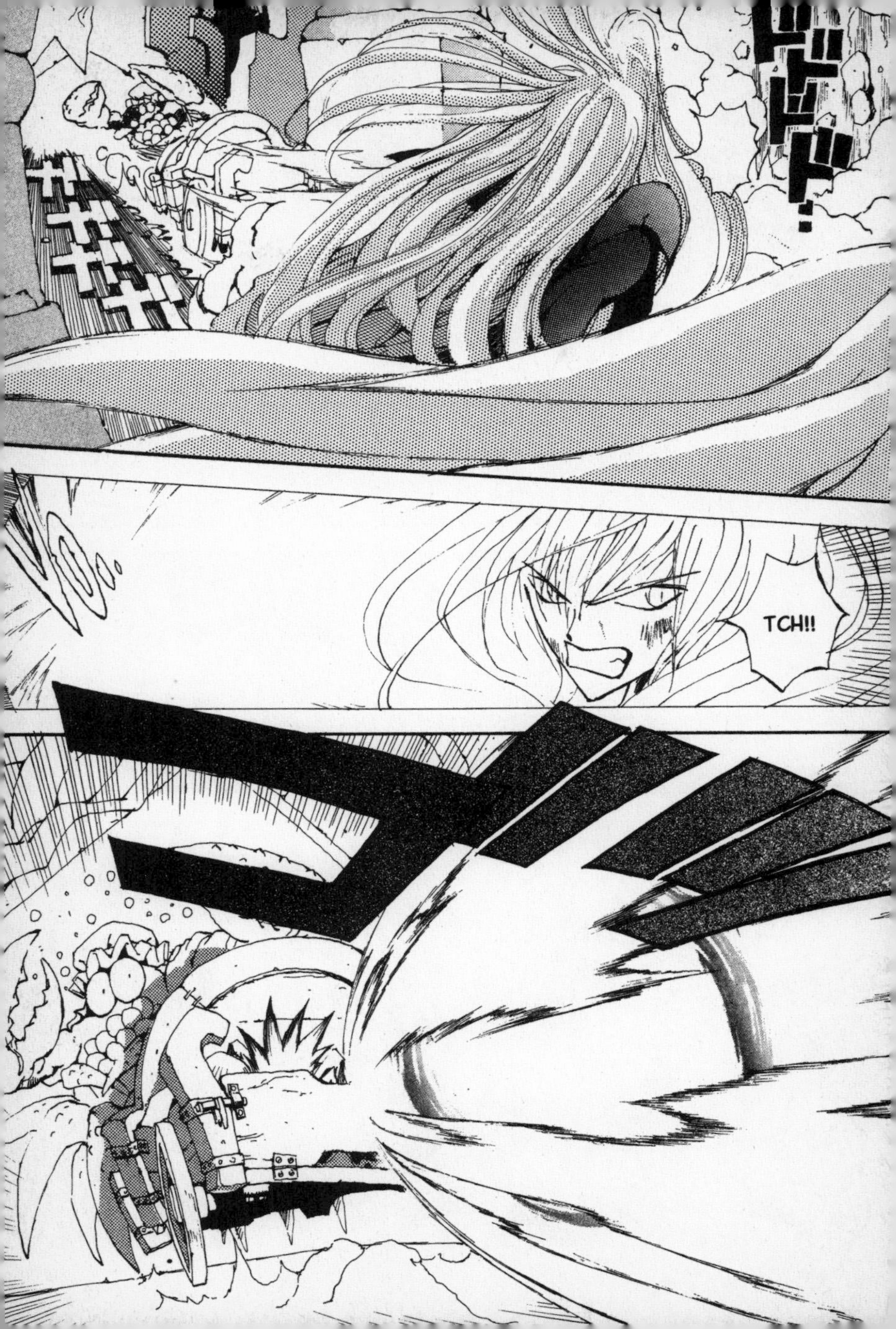
TCH!!

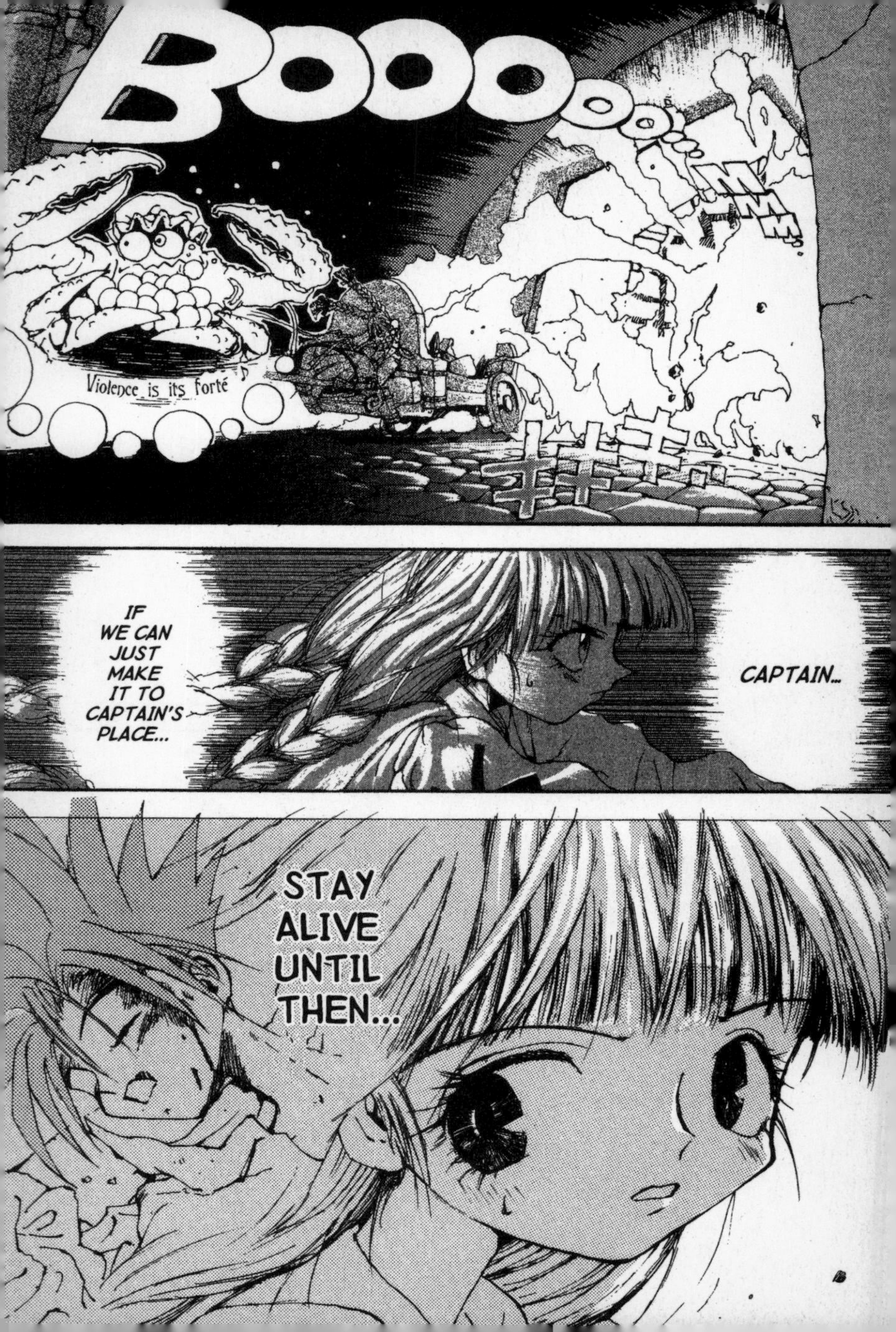
BOOOOOOOOMM
Violence is its forté
CAPTAIN...
IF WE CAN JUST MAKE IT TO CAPTAIN'S PLACE...
STAY ALIVE UNTIL THEN...

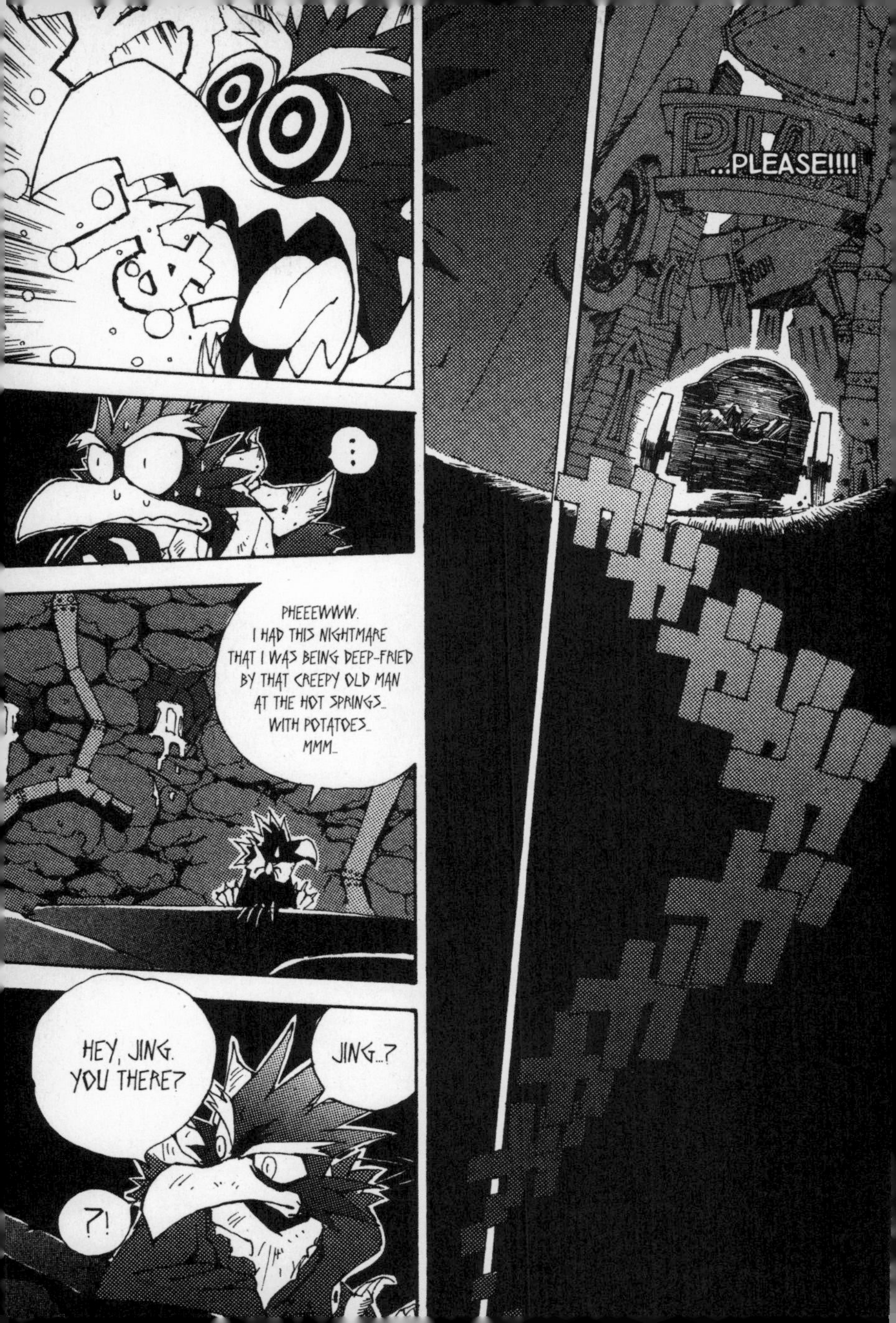
...PLEASE!!!!
...
PHEEEWWW. I HAD THIS NIGHTMARE THAT I WAS BEING DEEP-FRIED BY THAT CREEPY OLD MAN AT THE HOT SPRINGS... WITH POTATOES... MMM...
JING...?
HEY, JING. YOU THERE?
?!

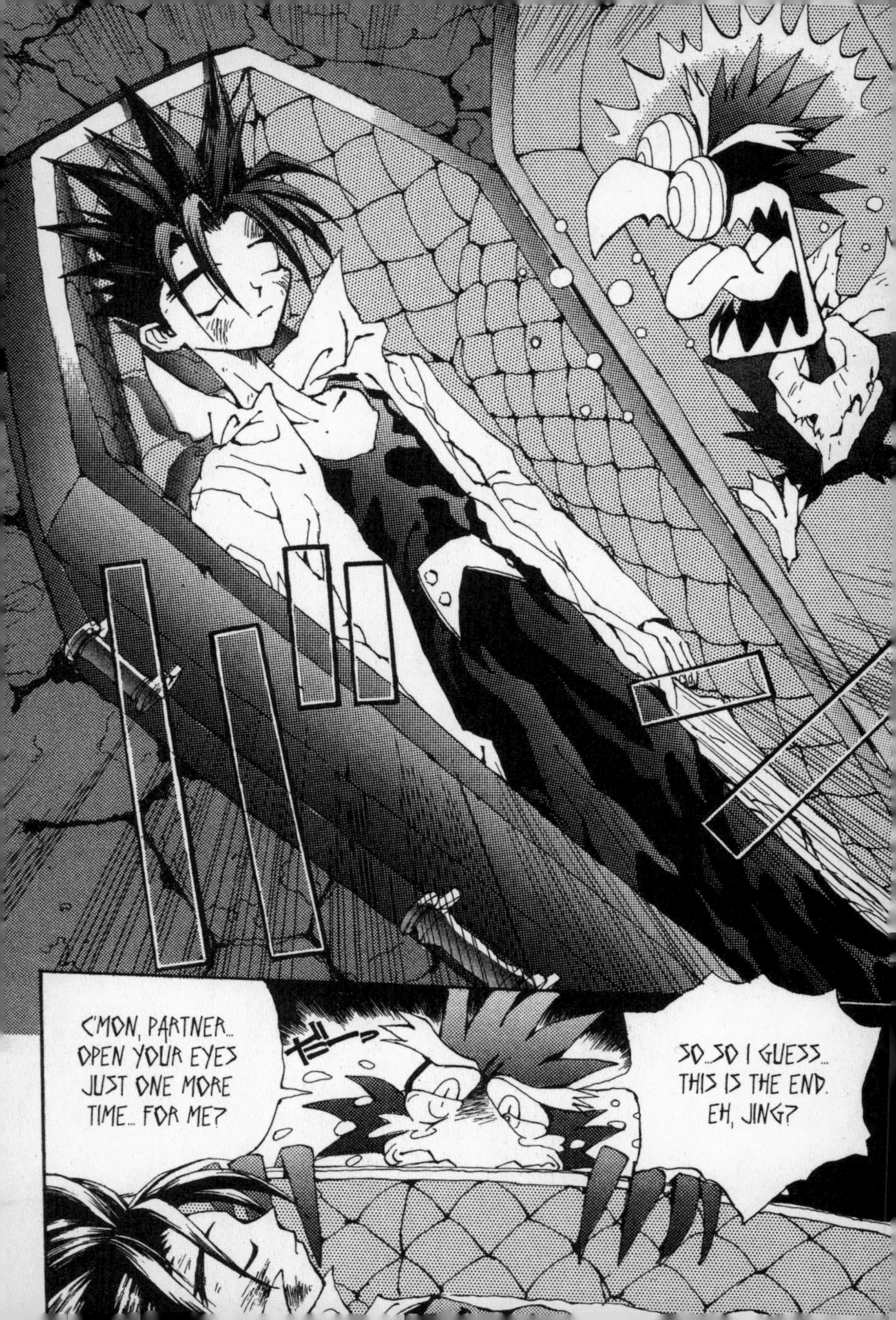
SO...SO I GUESS... THIS IS THE END. EH, JING?
C'MON, PARTNER... OPEN YOUR EYES JUST ONE MORE TIME... FOR ME?

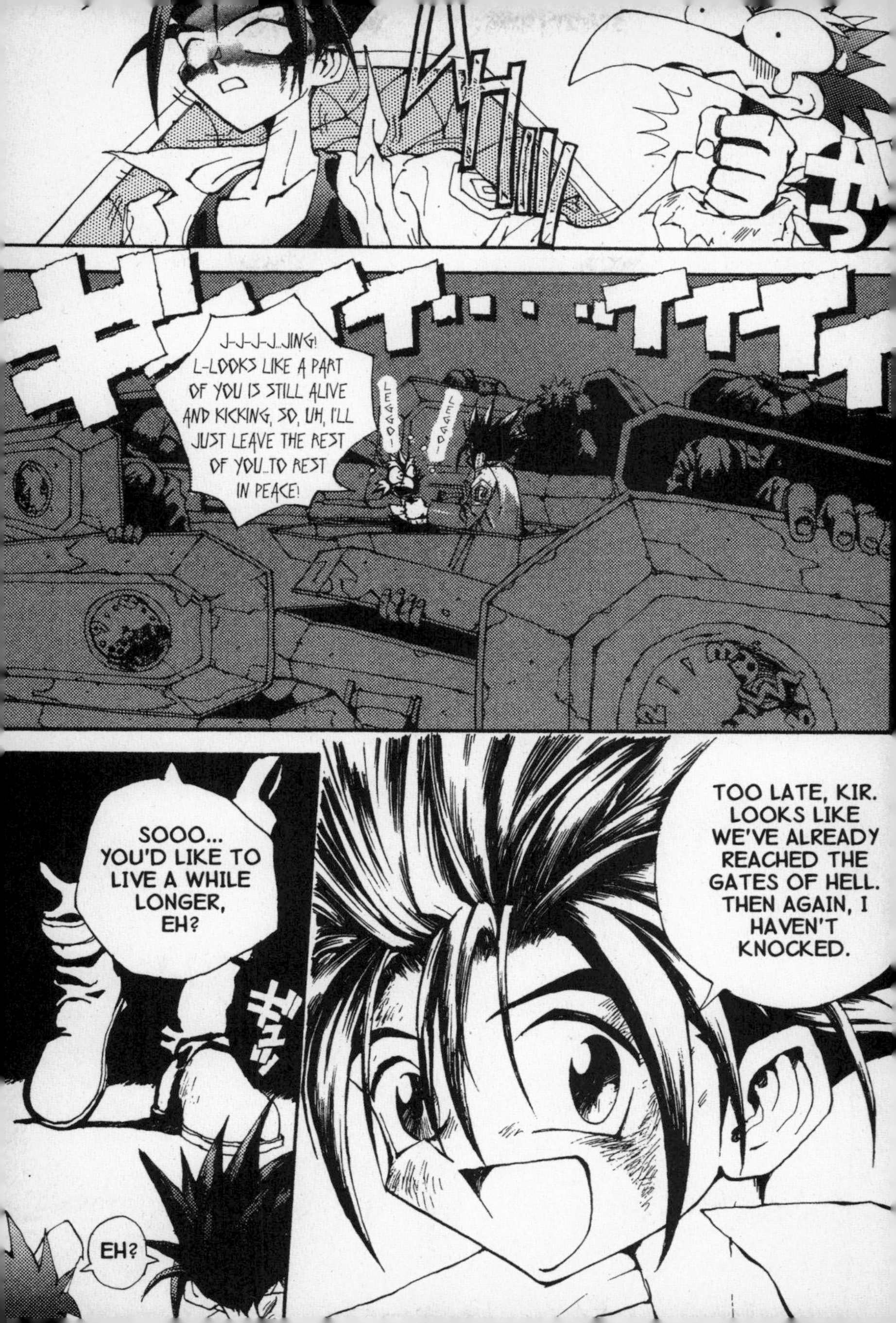
J-J-J-J...JING! L-LOOKS LIKE A PART OF YOU IS STILL ALIVE AND KICKING, SO, UH, I'LL JUST LEAVE THE REST OF YOU...TO REST IN PEACE!
LEGGO!
LEGGO!
TOO LATE, KIR. LOOKS LIKE WE'VE ALREADY REACHED THE GATES OF HELL. THEN AGAIN, I HAVEN'T KNOCKED.
SOOO... YOU'D LIKE TO LIVE A WHILE LONGER, EH?
EH?

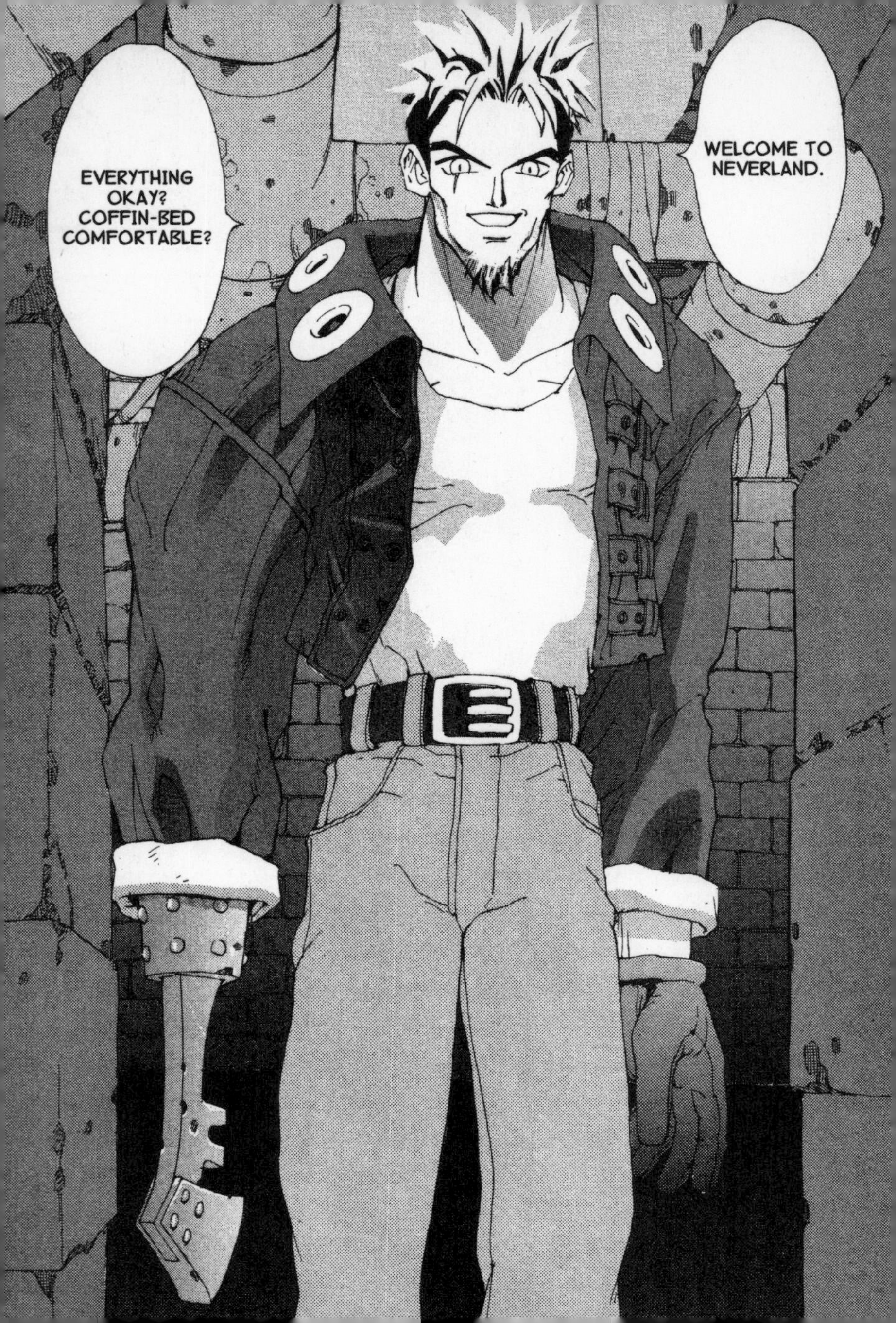
WELCOME TO NEVERLAND.
EVERYTHING OKAY? COFFIN-BED COMFORTABLE?

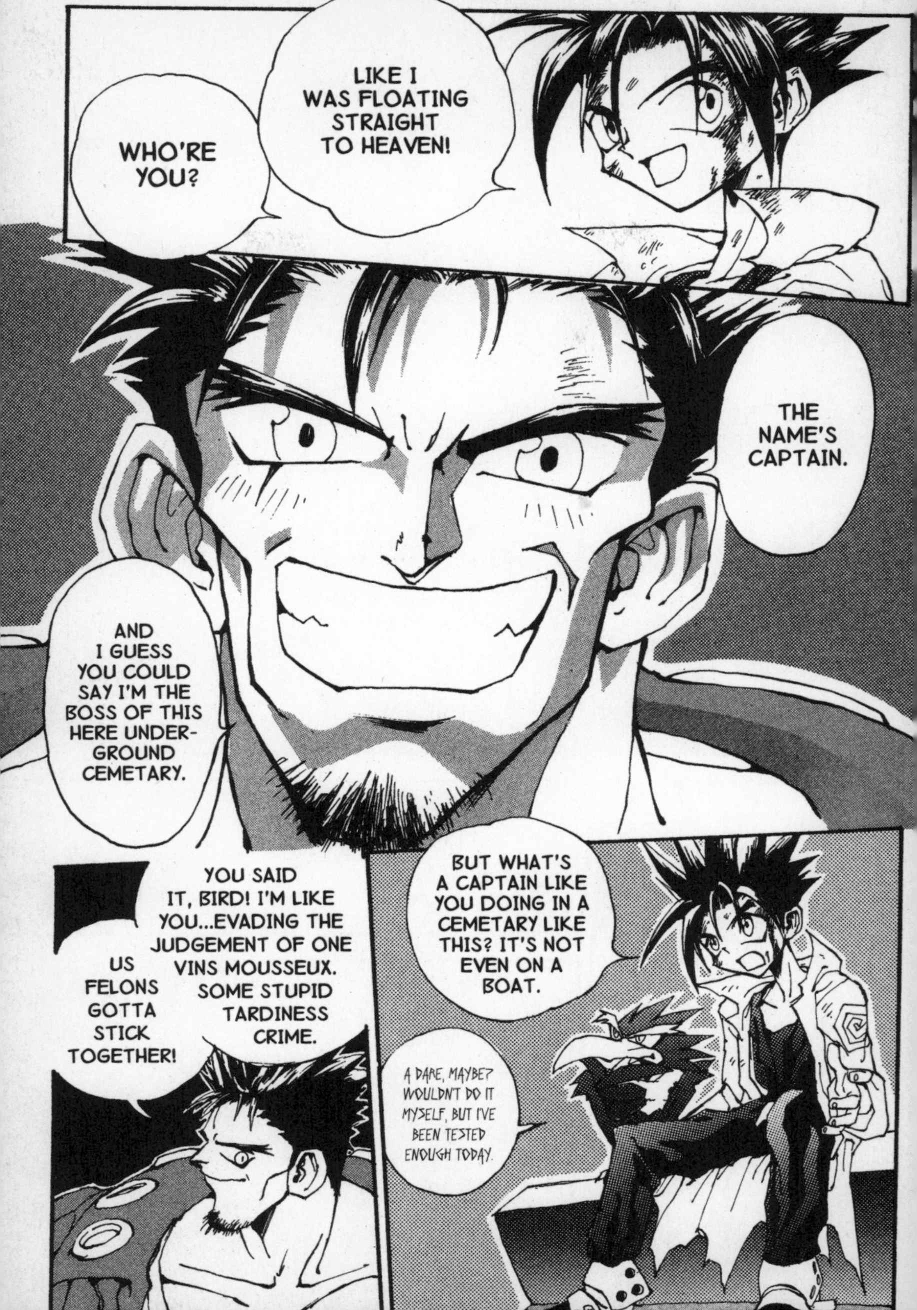
LIKE I WAS FLOATING STRAIGHT TO HEAVEN!
WHO'RE YOU?
THE NAME'S CAPTAIN.
AND I GUESS YOU COULD SAY I'M THE BOSS OF THIS HERE UNDER-GROUND CEMETARY.
BUT WHAT'S A CAPTAIN LIKE YOU DOING IN A CEMETARY LIKE THIS? IT'S NOT EVEN ON A BOAT.
A DARE, MAYBE? WOULDN'T DO IT MYSELF, BUT I'VE BEEN TESTED ENOUGH TODAY.
YOU SAID IT, BIRD! I'M LIKE YOU...EVADING THE JUDGEMENT OF ONE VINS MOUSSEUX. SOME STUPID TARDINESS CRIME.
US FELONS GOTTA STICK TOGETHER!

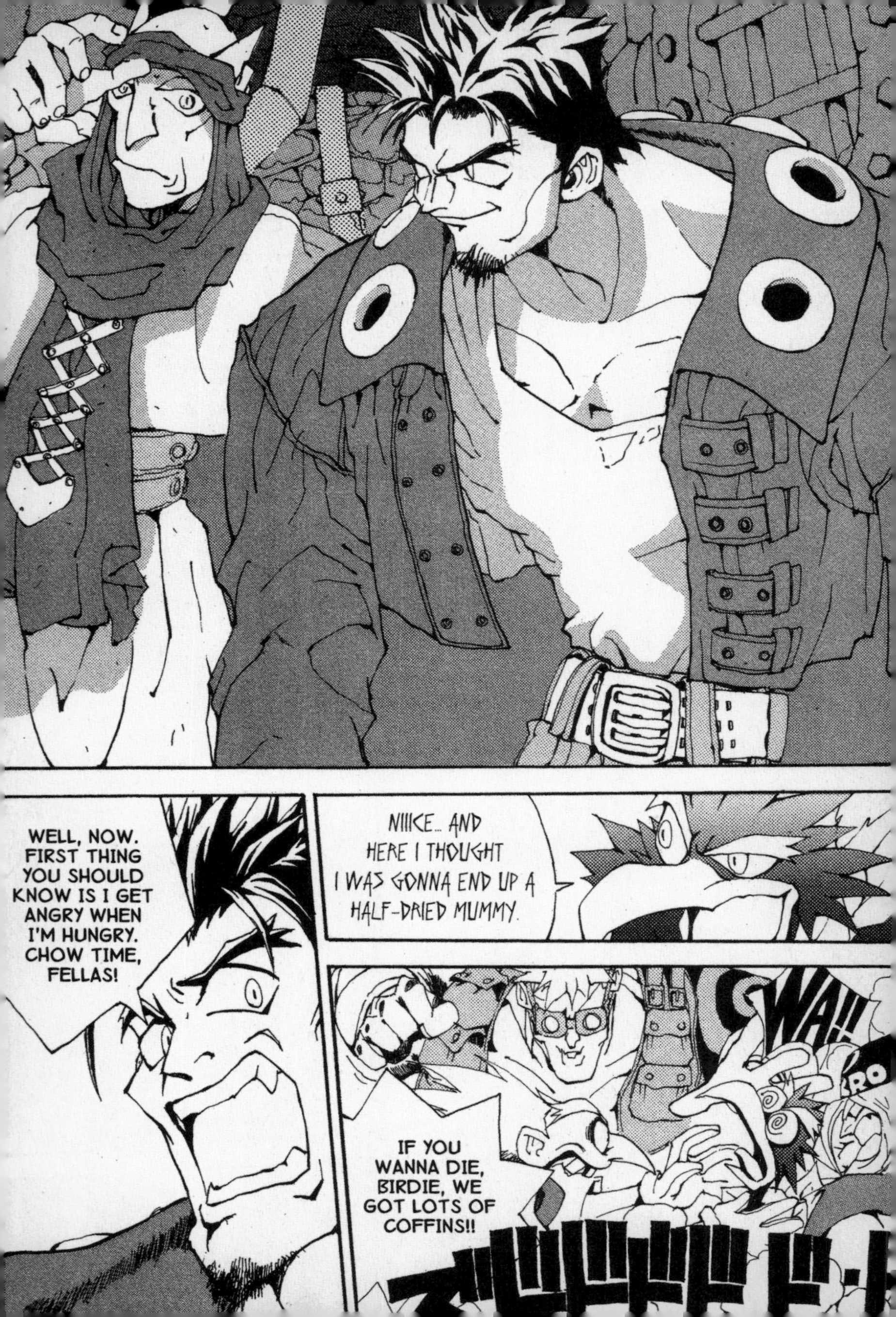
NIIICE... AND HERE I THOUGHT I WAS GONNA END UP A HALF-DRIED MUMMY.
GWA!!
RO
IF YOU WANNA DIE, BIRDIE, WE GOT LOTS OF COFFINS!!
WELL, NOW. FIRST THING YOU SHOULD KNOW IS I GET ANGRY WHEN I'M HUNGRY. CHOW TIME, FELLAS!

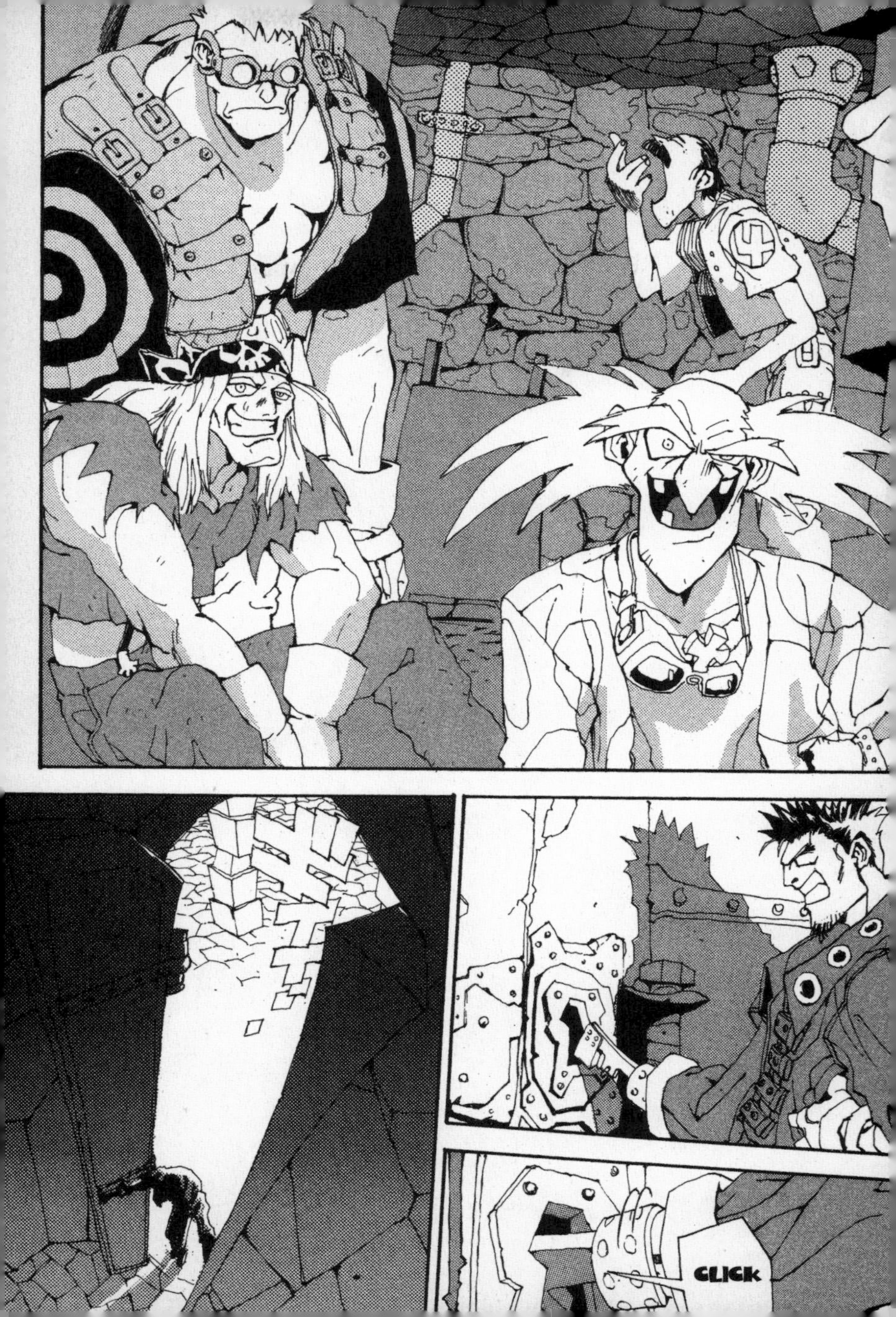
CLICK

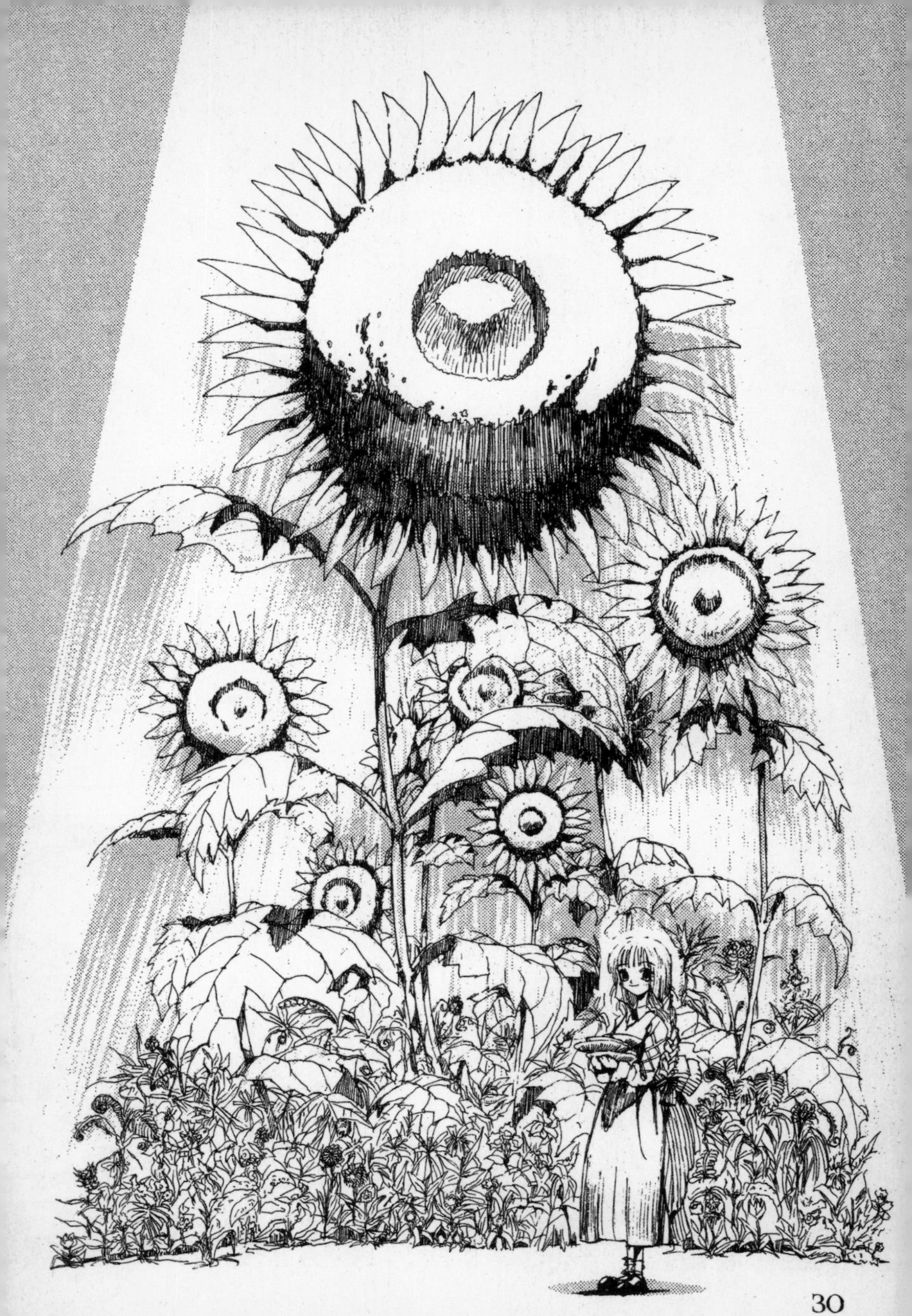

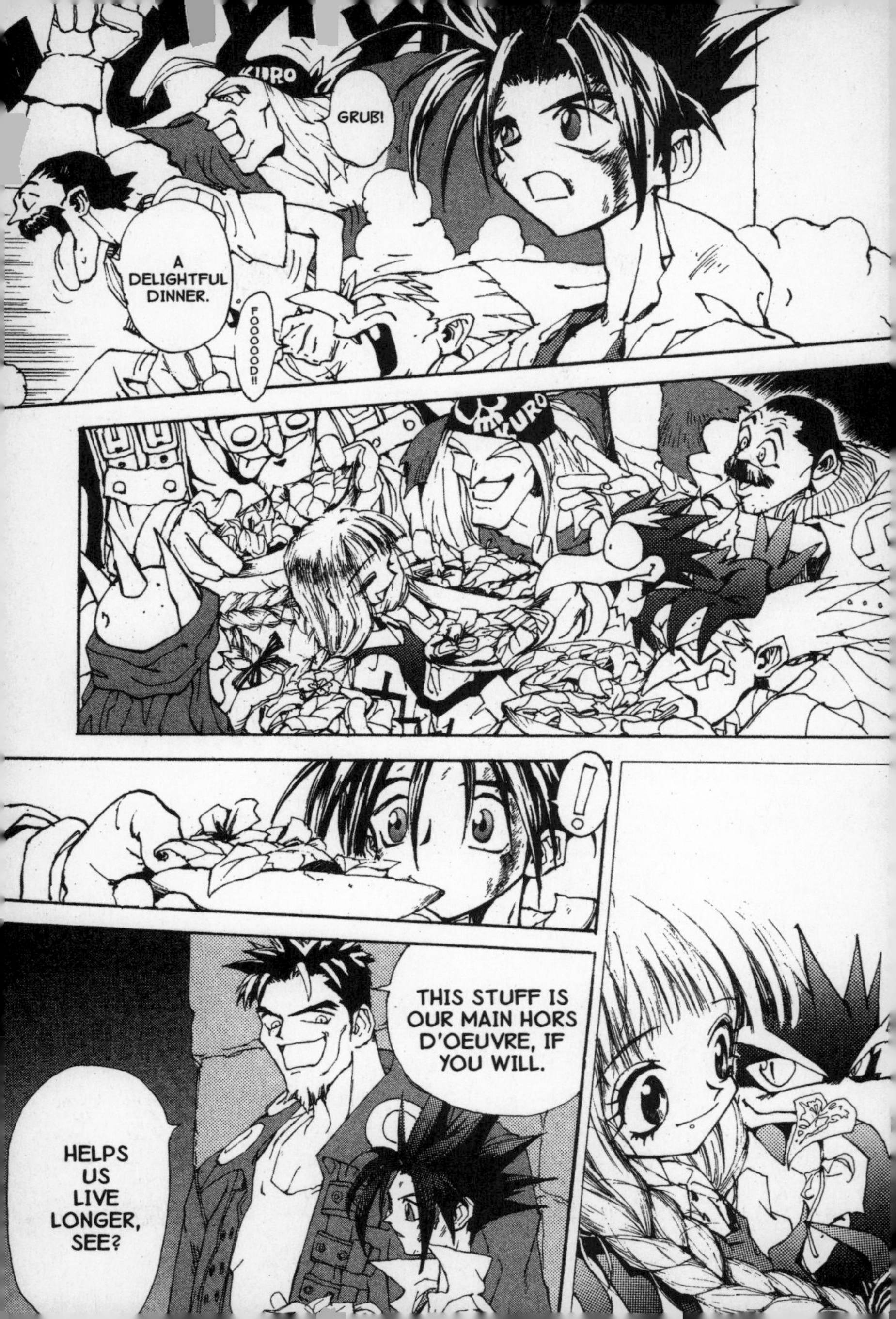
GRUB!
FOOOOOOD!!
A DELIGHTFUL DINNER.
!
THIS STUFF IS OUR MAIN HORS D'OEUVRE, IF YOU WILL.
HELPS US LIVE LONGER, SEE?

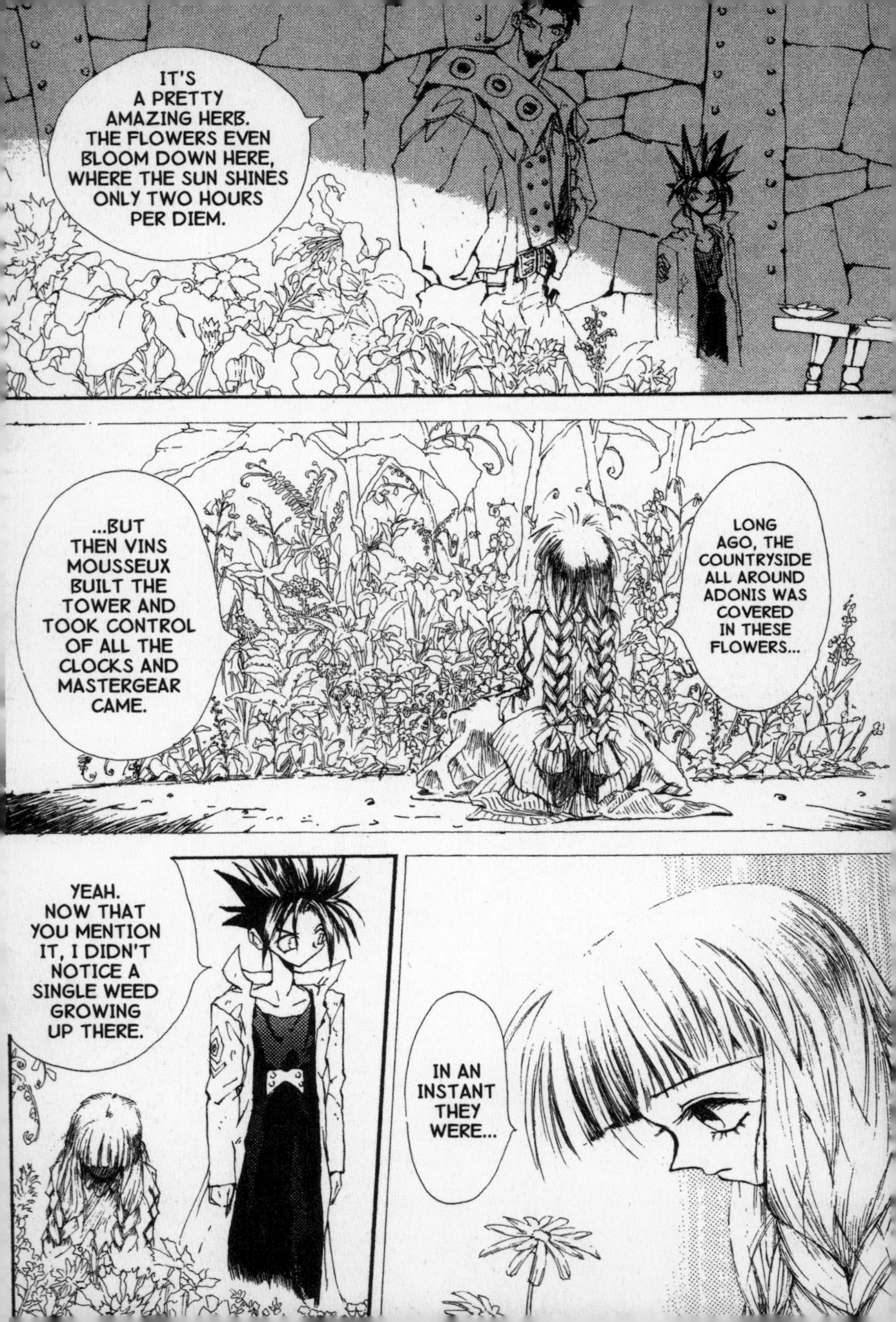
IT'S A PRETTY AMAZING HERB. THE FLOWERS EVEN BLOOM DOWN HERE, WHERE THE SUN SHINES ONLY TWO HOURS PER DIEM.
LONG AGO, THE COUNTRYSIDE ALL AROUND ADONIS WAS COVERED IN THESE FLOWERS...
...BUT THEN VINS MOUSSEUX BUILT THE TOWER AND TOOK CONTROL OF ALL THE CLOCKS AND MASTERGEAR CAME.
IN AN INSTANT THEY WERE...
YEAH. NOW THAT YOU MENTION IT, I DIDN'T NOTICE A SINGLE WEED GROWING UP THERE.

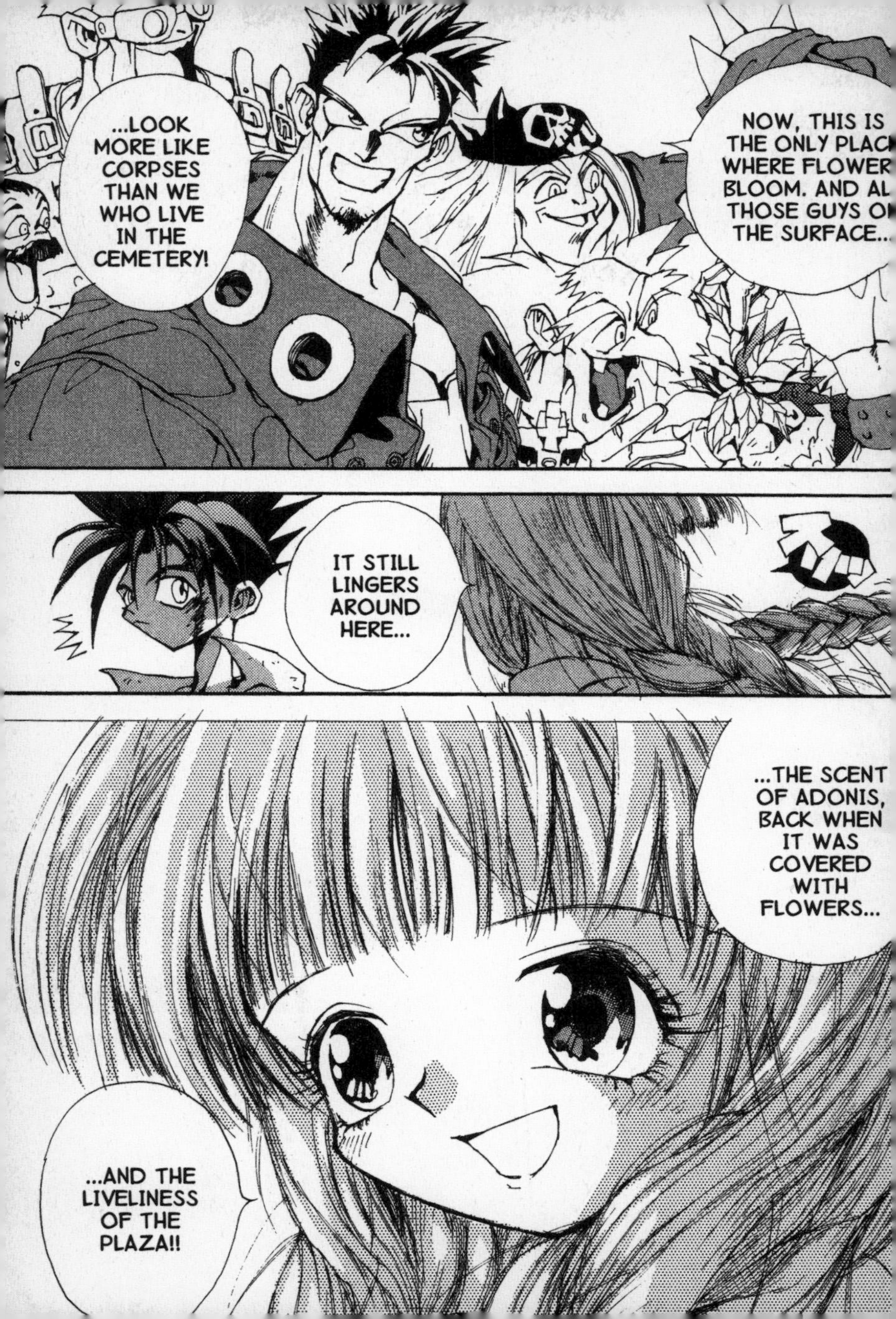
NOW, THIS IS THE ONLY PLAC WHERE FLOWER BLOOM. AND AL THOSE GUYS O THE SURFACE...
...LOOK MORE LIKE CORPSES THAN WE WHO LIVE IN THE CEMETERY!
IT STILL LINGERS AROUND HERE...
...THE SCENT OF ADONIS, BACK WHEN IT WAS COVERED WITH FLOWERS...
...AND THE LIVELINESS OF THE PLAZA!!

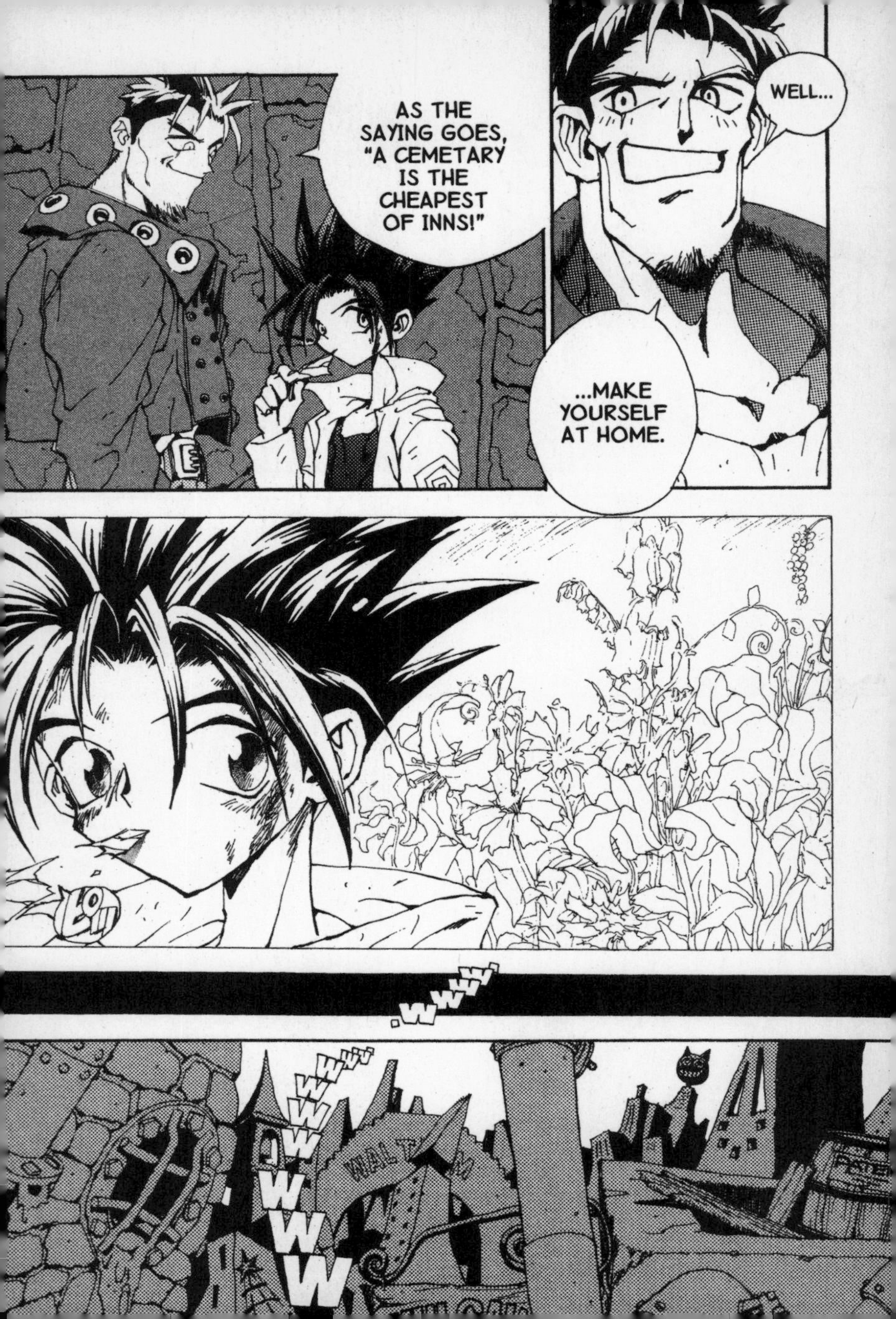
WELL...
...MAKE YOURSELF AT HOME.
AS THE SAYING GOES, "A CEMETARY IS THE CHEAPEST OF INNS!"

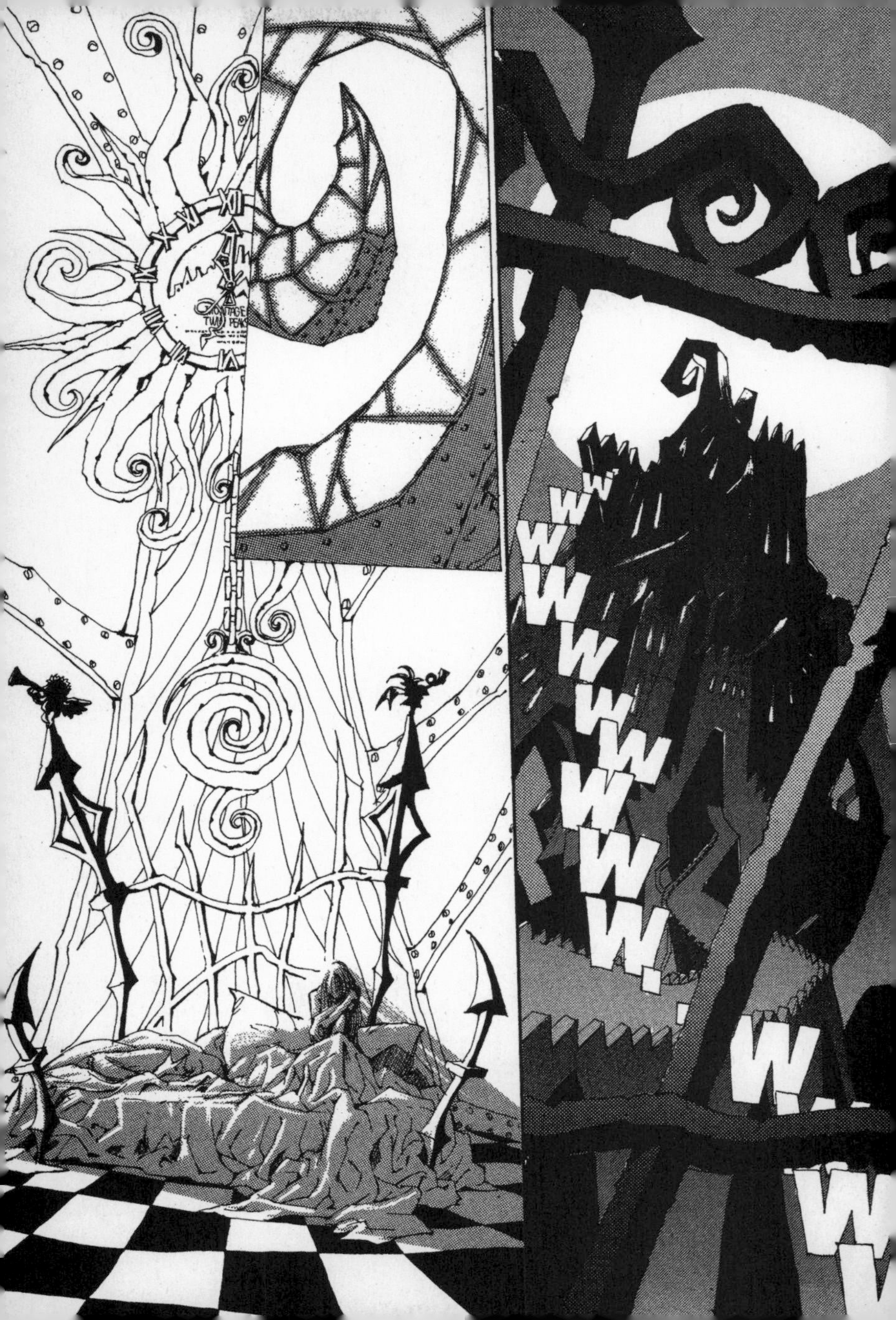
WWWWWWWWWWW.
W.
WW

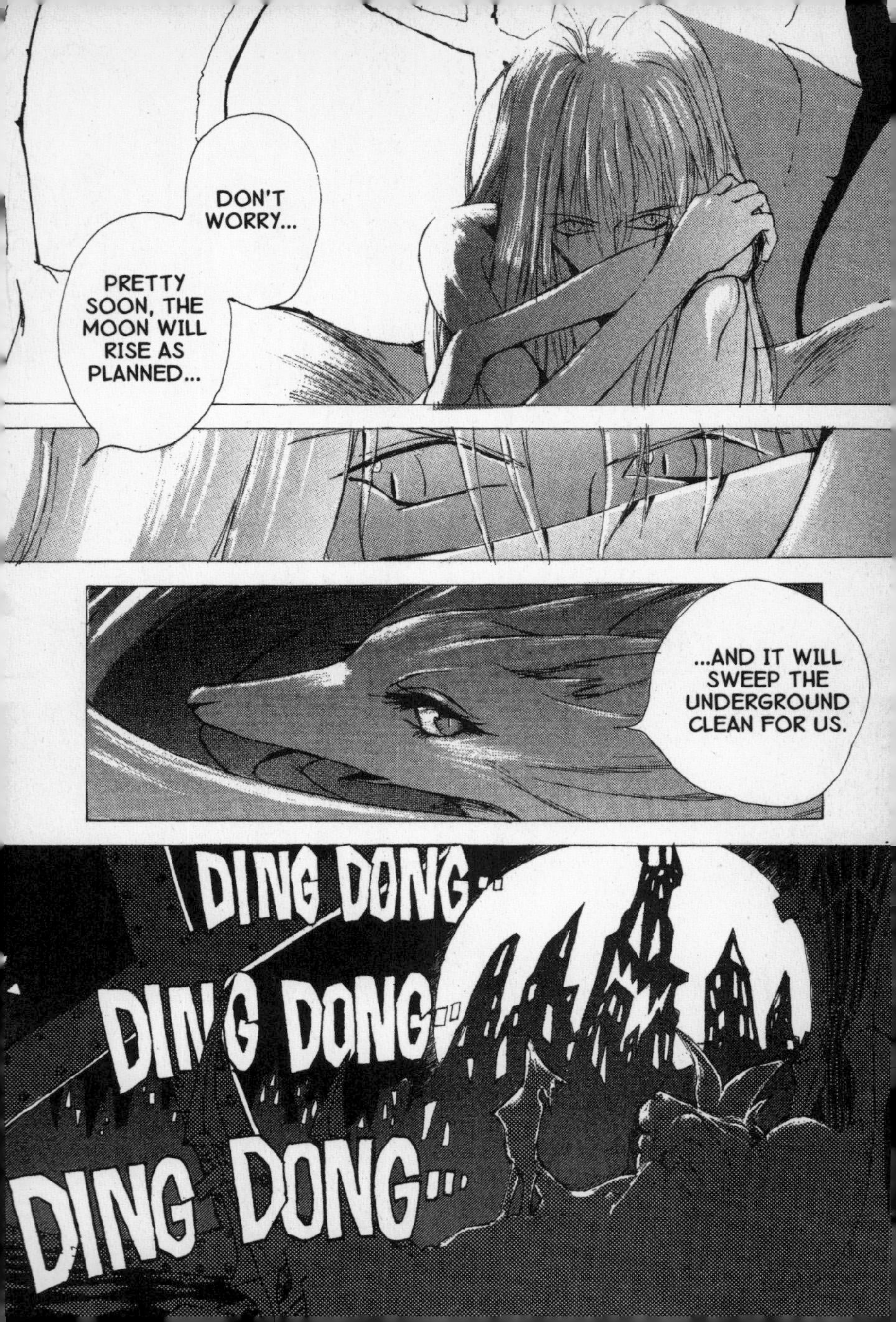
DON'T WORRY...
PRETTY SOON, THE MOON WILL RISE AS PLANNED...
...AND IT WILL SWEEP THE UNDERGROUND CLEAN FOR US.
DING DONG...
DING DONG...
DING DONG...

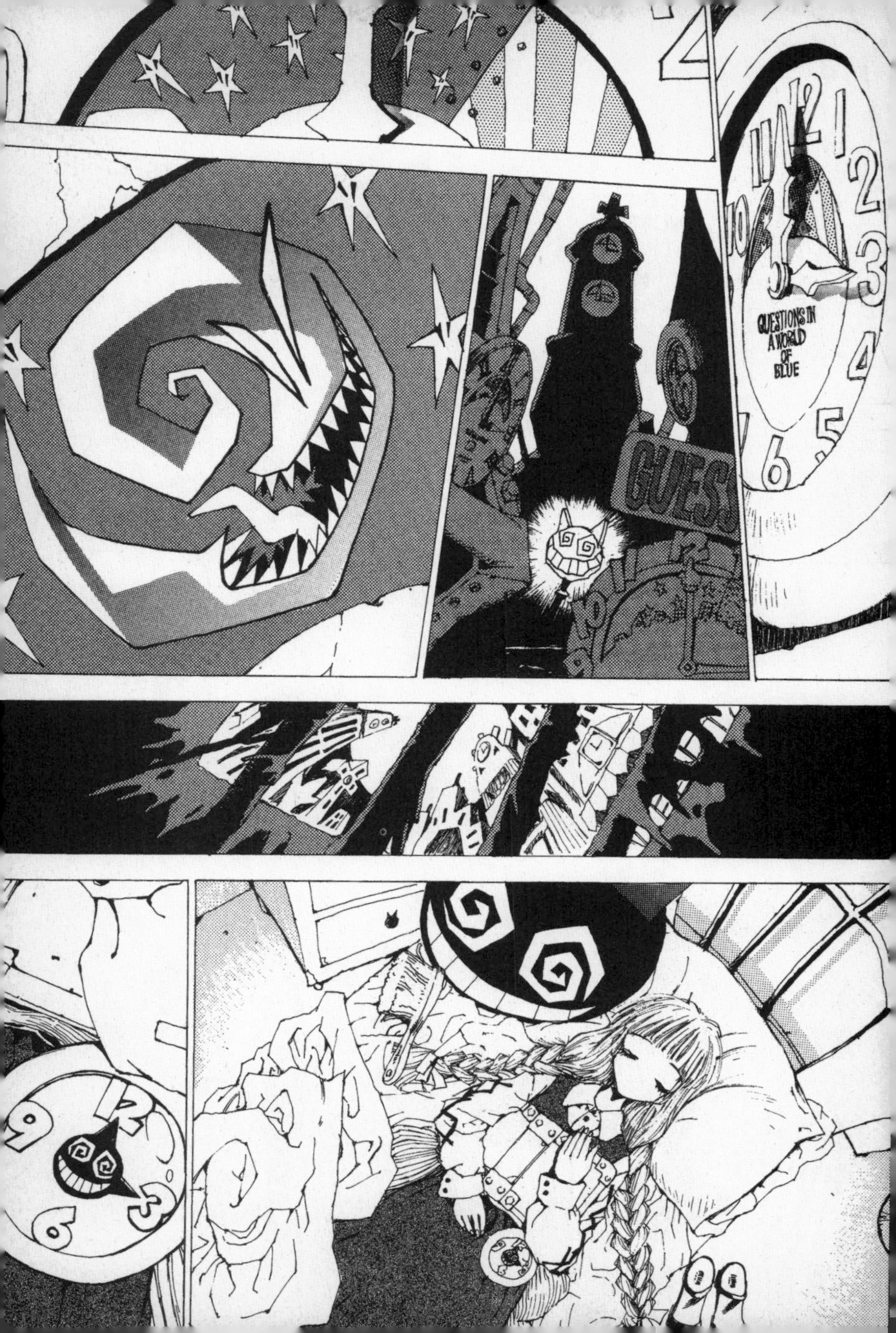
QUESTIONS IN A WORLD OF BLUE
GUESS

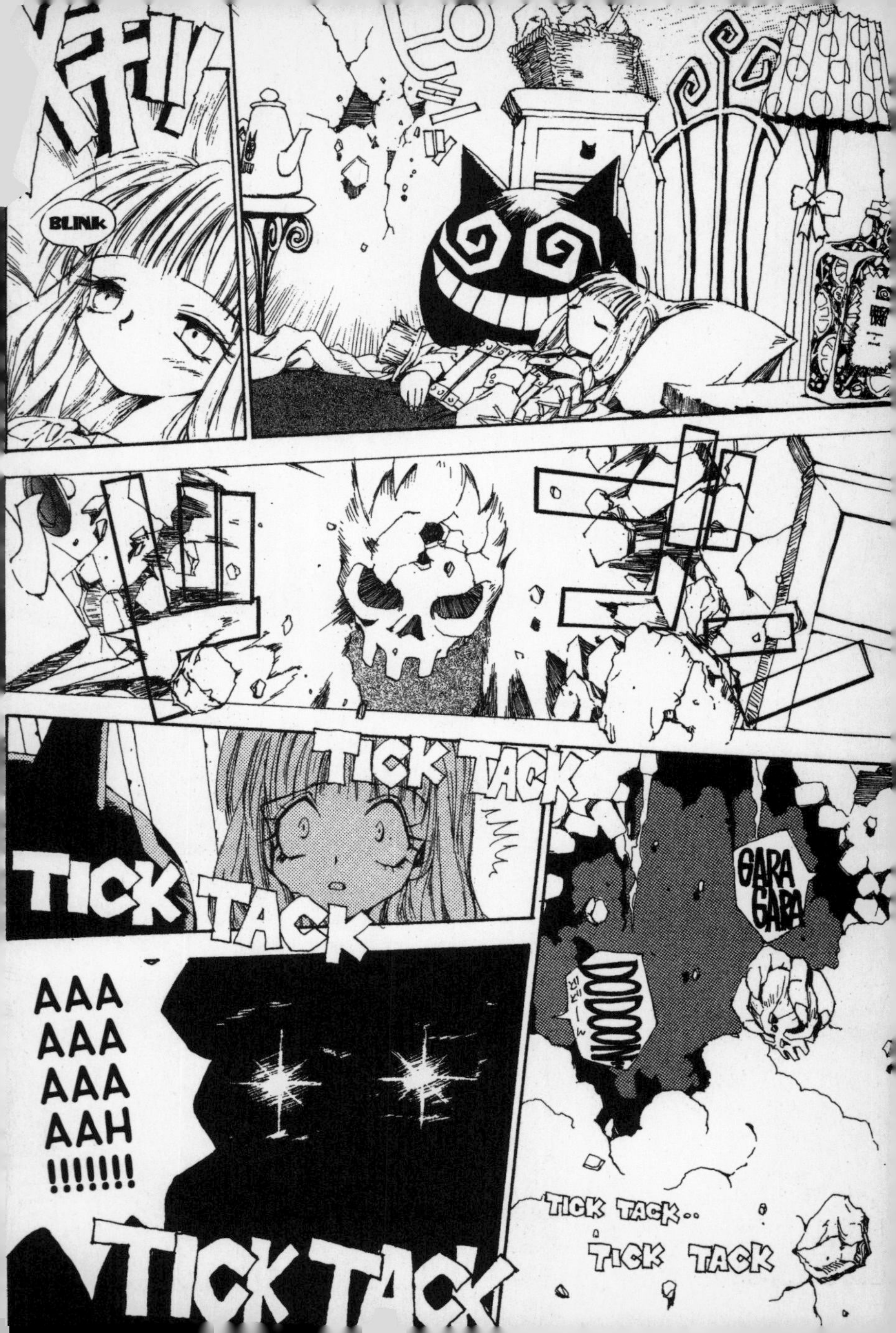
BLINK
GARA GARA
DODOON
TICK TACK..
TICK TACK
TICK TACK
TICK TACK
AAA AAA AAA AAH !!!!!!!
TICK TACK

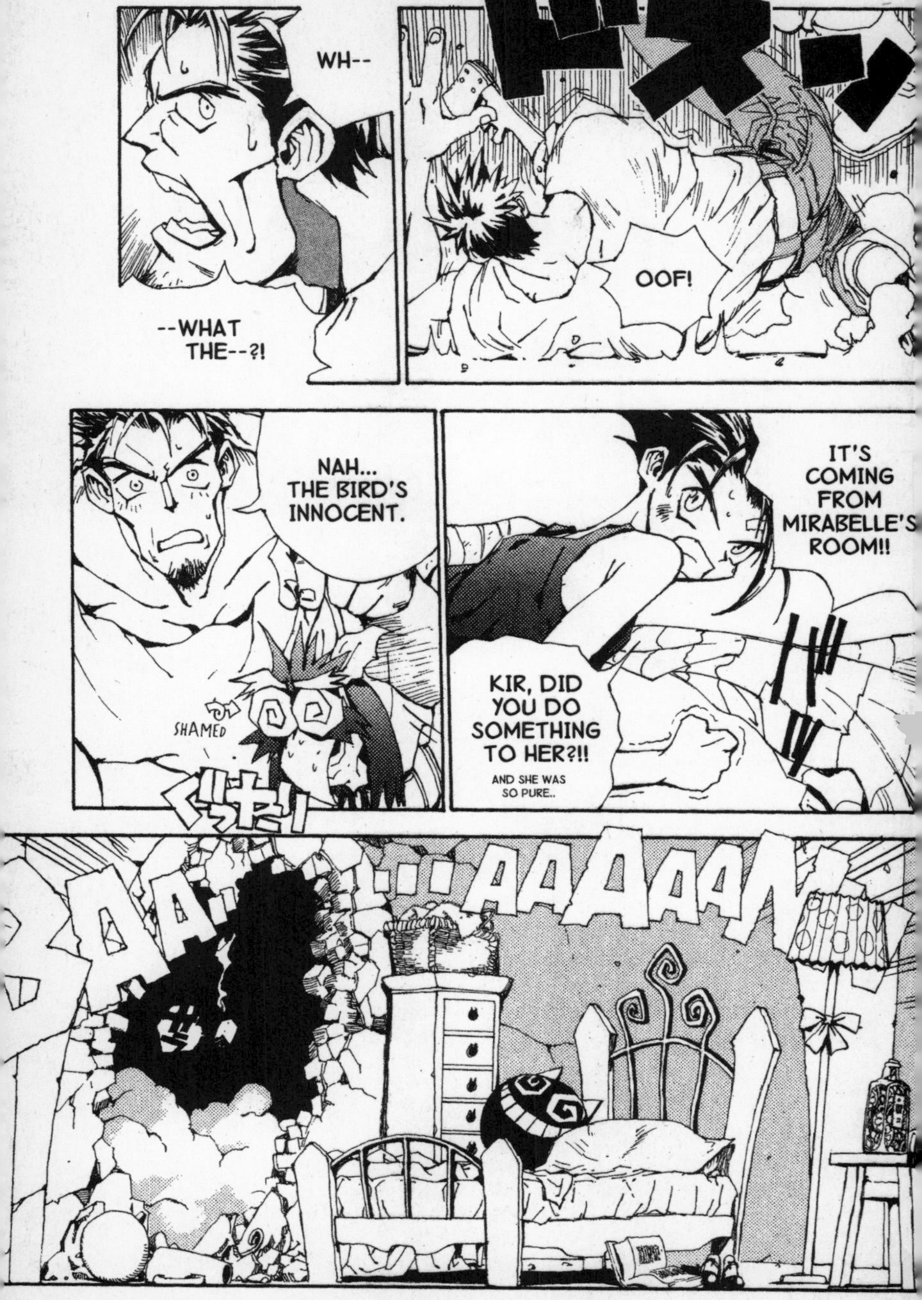
OOF!
WH--
--WHAT THE--?!
IT'S COMING FROM MIRABELLE'S ROOM!!
KIR, DID YOU DO SOMETHING TO HER?!!
AND SHE WAS SO PURE..
NAH... THE BIRD'S INNOCENT.
SHAMED
BAA...AAAAAN

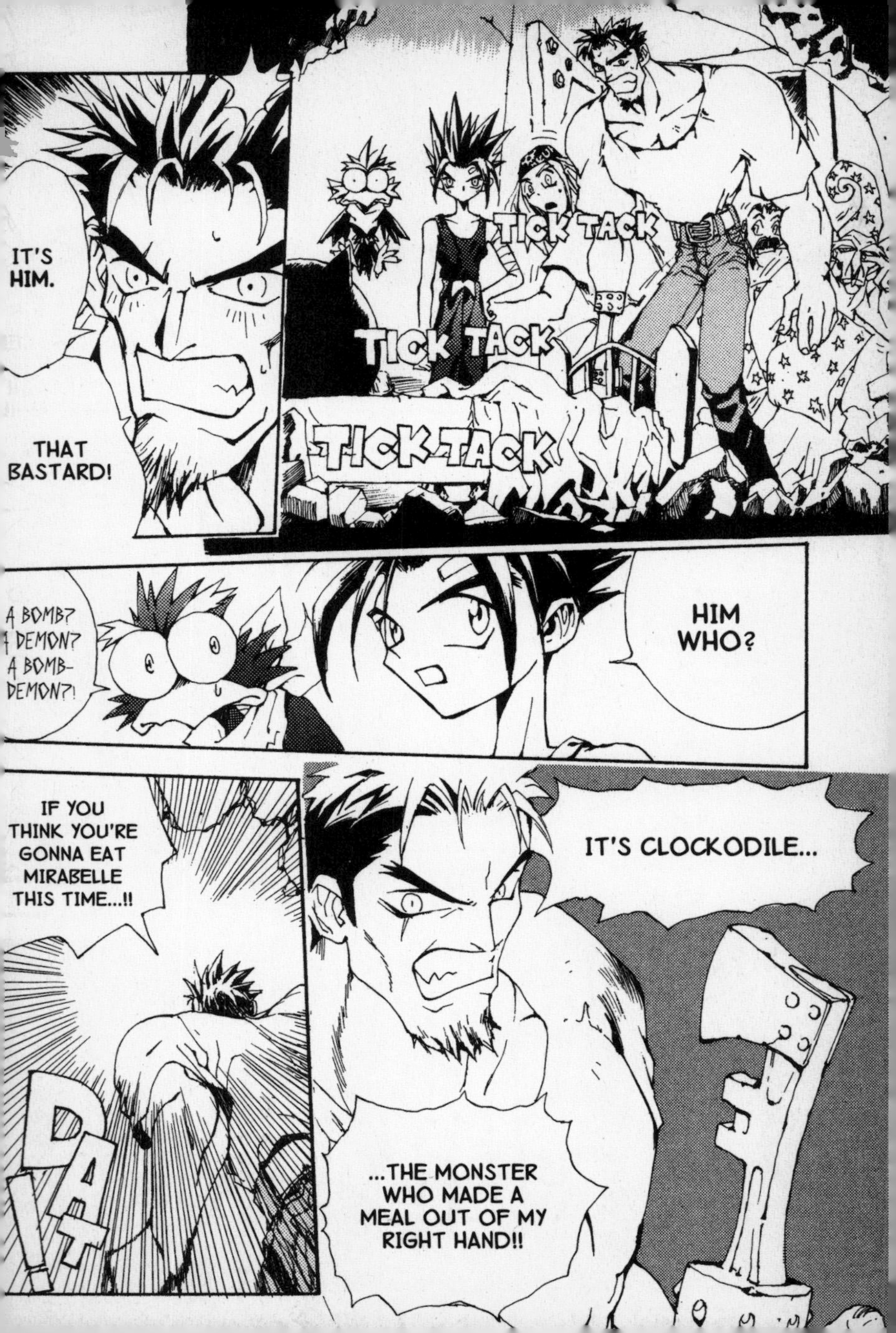
TICK TACK
TICK TACK
TICK TACK
IT'S HIM.
THAT BASTARD!
HIM WHO?
A BOMB? A DEMON? A BOMB-DEMON?!
IT'S CLOCKODILE...
...THE MONSTER WHO MADE A MEAL OUT OF MY RIGHT HAND!!
IF YOU THINK YOU'RE GONNA EAT MIRABELLE THIS TIME...!!
DAT!

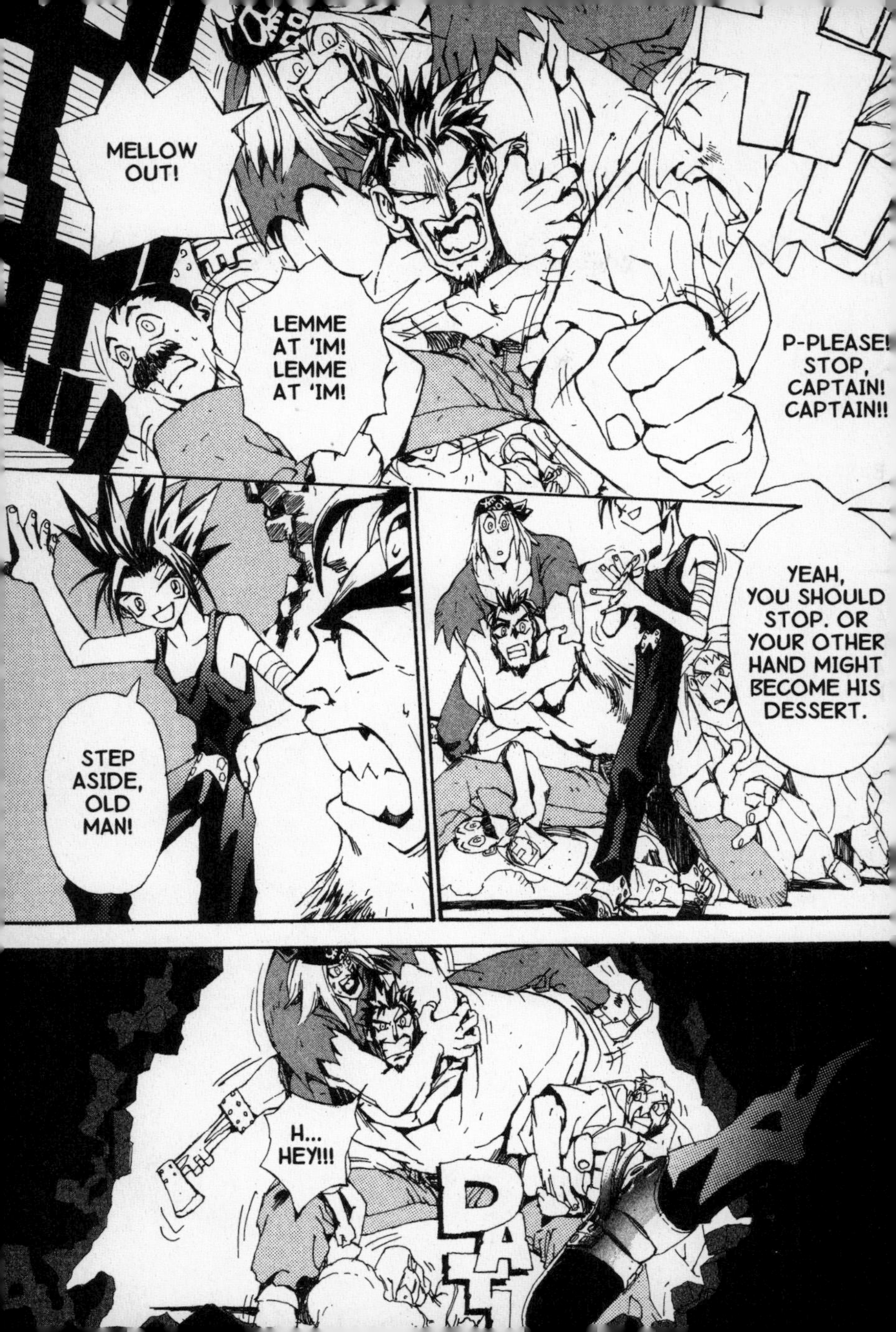
P-PLEASE! STOP, CAPTAIN! CAPTAIN!!
LEMME AT 'IM! LEMME AT 'IM!
MELLOW OUT!
YEAH, YOU SHOULD STOP. OR YOUR OTHER HAND MIGHT BECOME HIS DESSERT.
STEP ASIDE, OLD MAN!
H... HEY!!!
DAT

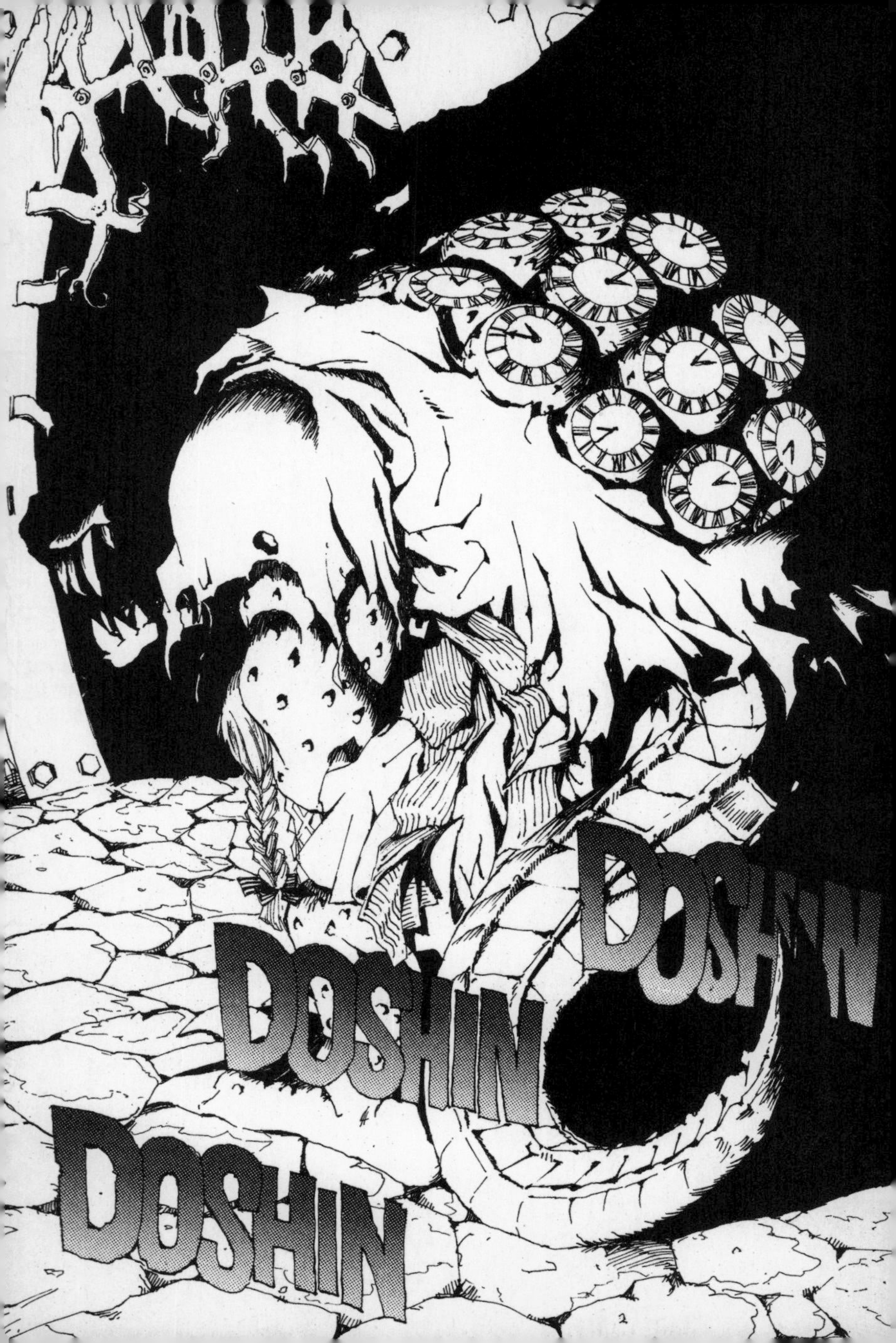
DOSHIN
DOSHIN
DOSHIN

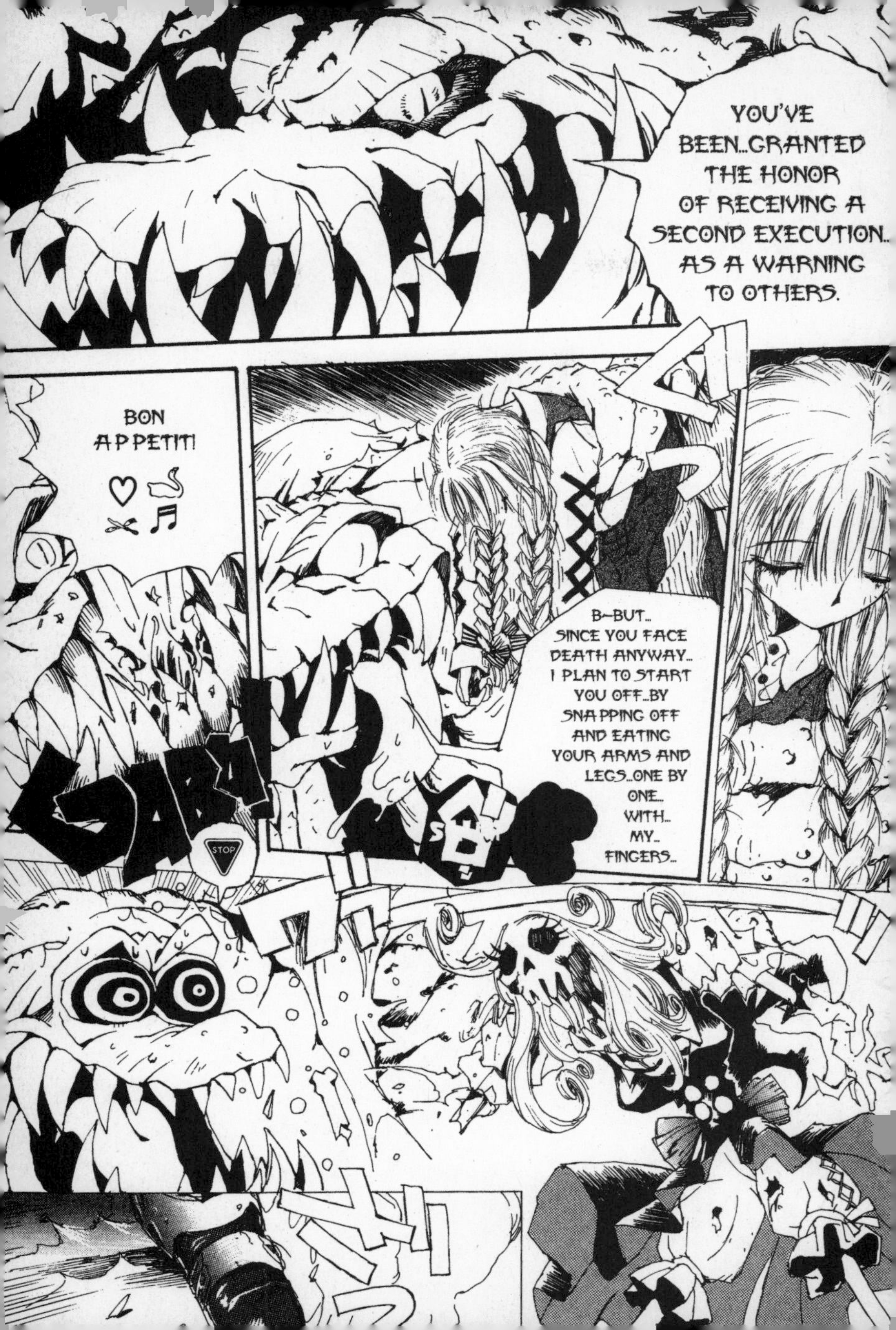
YOU'VE BEEN...GRANTED THE HONOR OF RECEIVING A SECOND EXECUTION... AS A WARNING TO OTHERS.
B-BUT... SINCE YOU FACE DEATH ANYWAY... I PLAN TO START YOU OFF...BY SNAPPING OFF AND EATING YOUR ARMS AND LEGS...ONE BY ONE... WITH... MY... FINGERS...
BON APPETIT!
STOP

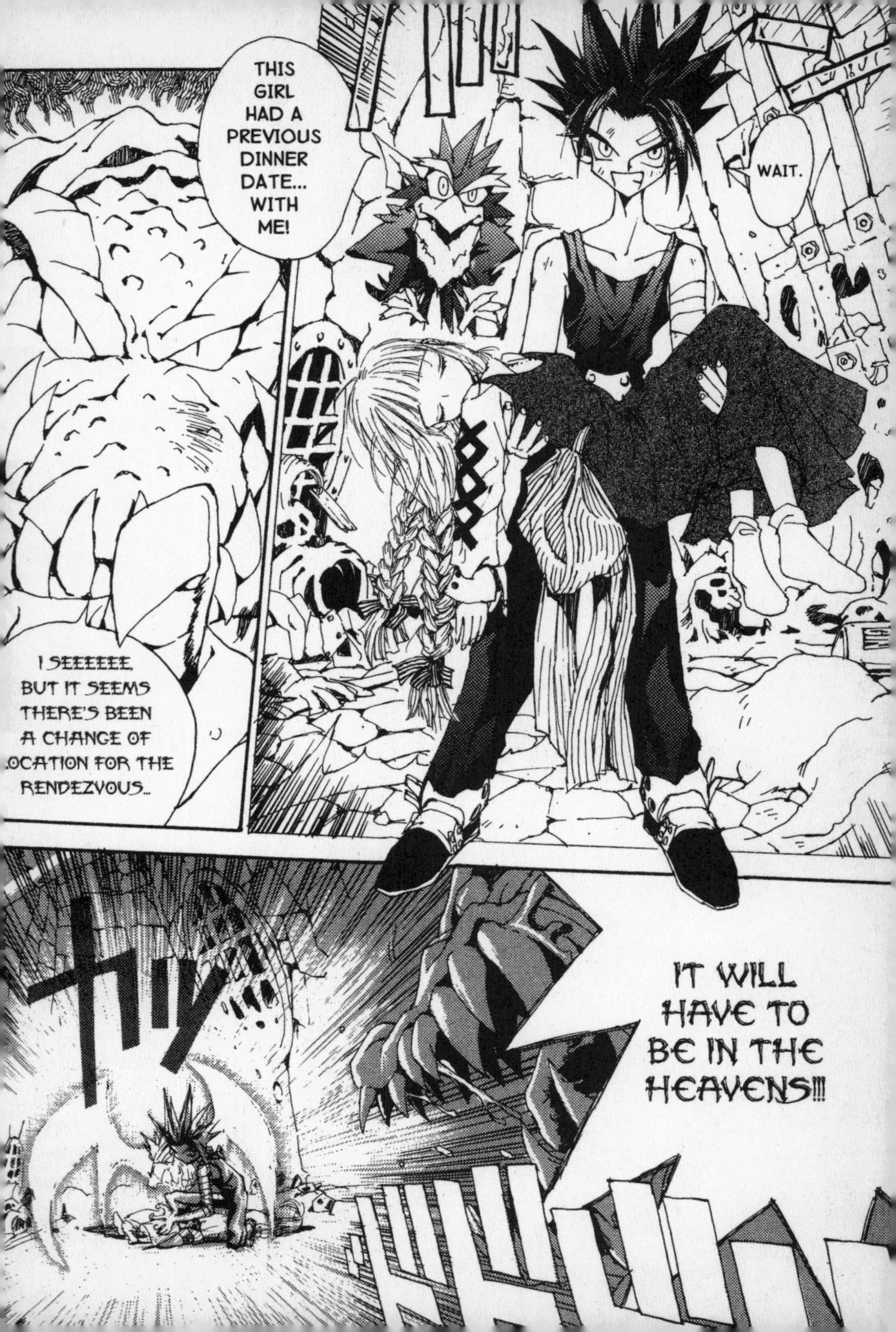
WAIT.
THIS GIRL HAD A PREVIOUS DINNER DATE... WITH ME!
I SEEEEEE, BUT IT SEEMS THERE'S BEEN A CHANGE OF LOCATION FOR THE RENDEZVOUS...
IT WILL HAVE TO BE IN THE HEAVENS!!!

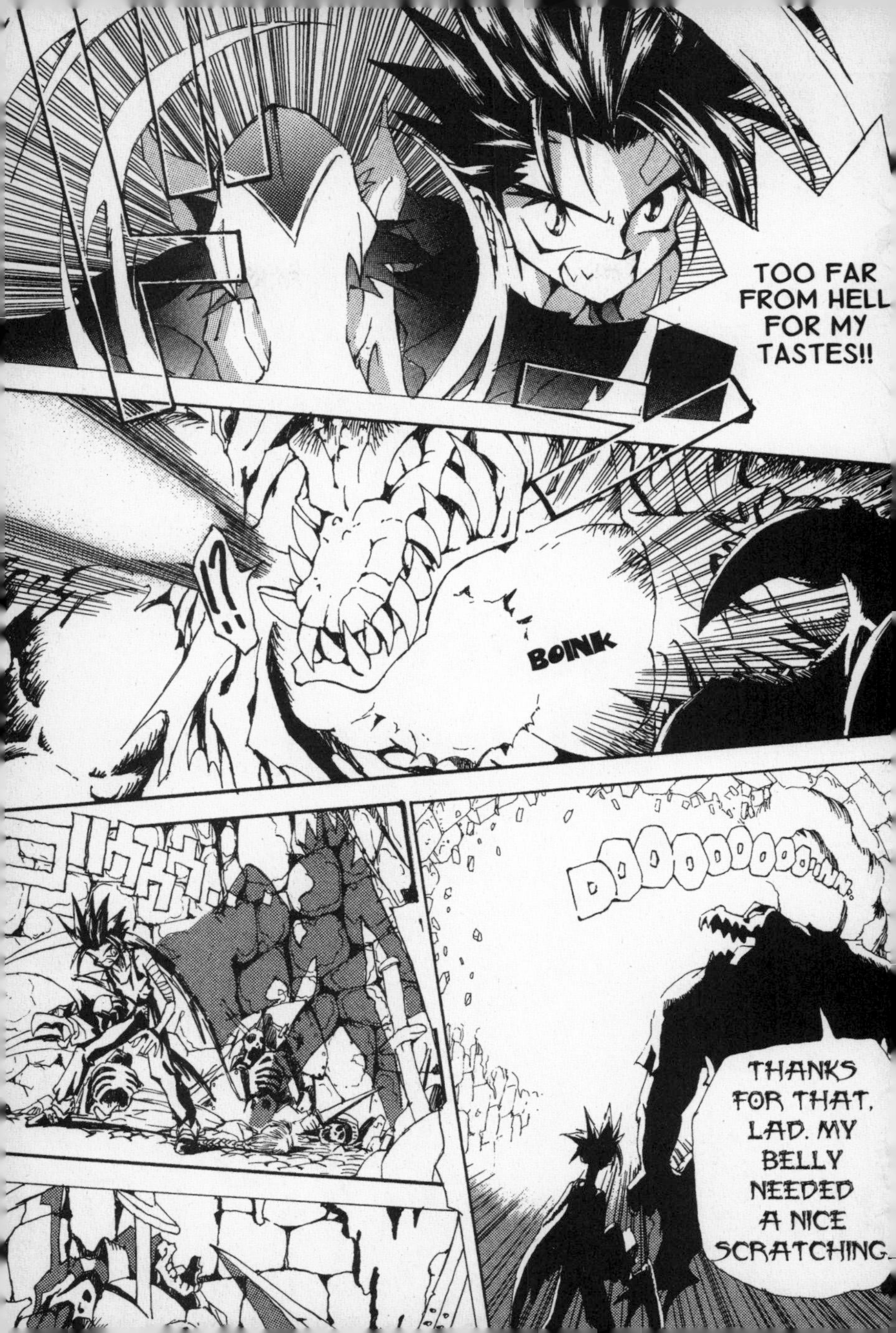
TOO FAR FROM HELL FOR MY TASTES!!
!?
BOINK
DOOOOOOOO...NN.
THANKS FOR THAT, LAD. MY BELLY NEEDED A NICE SCRATCHING.

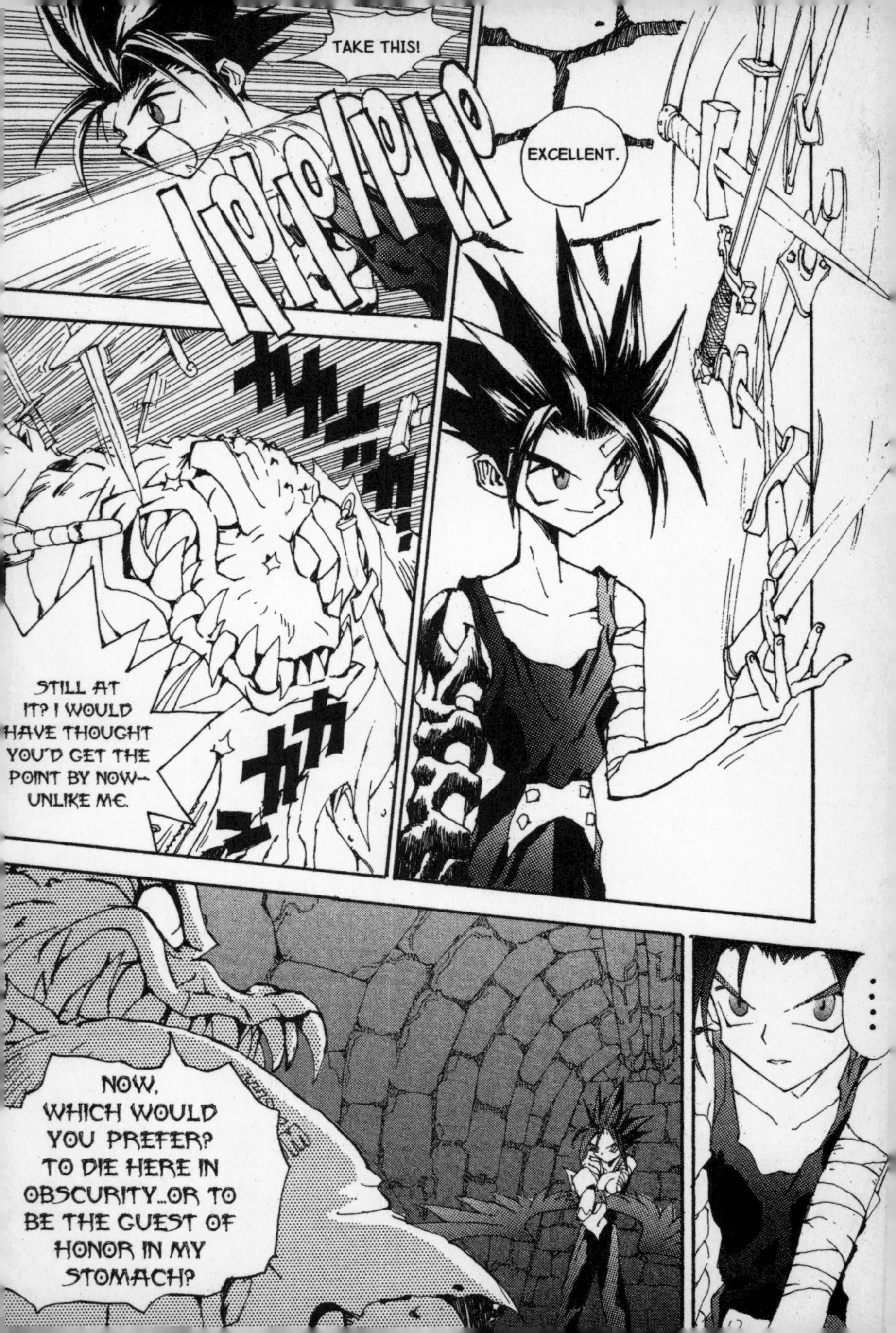
EXCELLENT.
TAKE THIS!
STILL AT IT? I WOULD HAVE THOUGHT YOU'D GET THE POINT BY NOW—UNLIKE ME.
...
NOW, WHICH WOULD YOU PREFER? TO DIE HERE IN OBSCURITY...OR TO BE THE GUEST OF HONOR IN MY STOMACH?

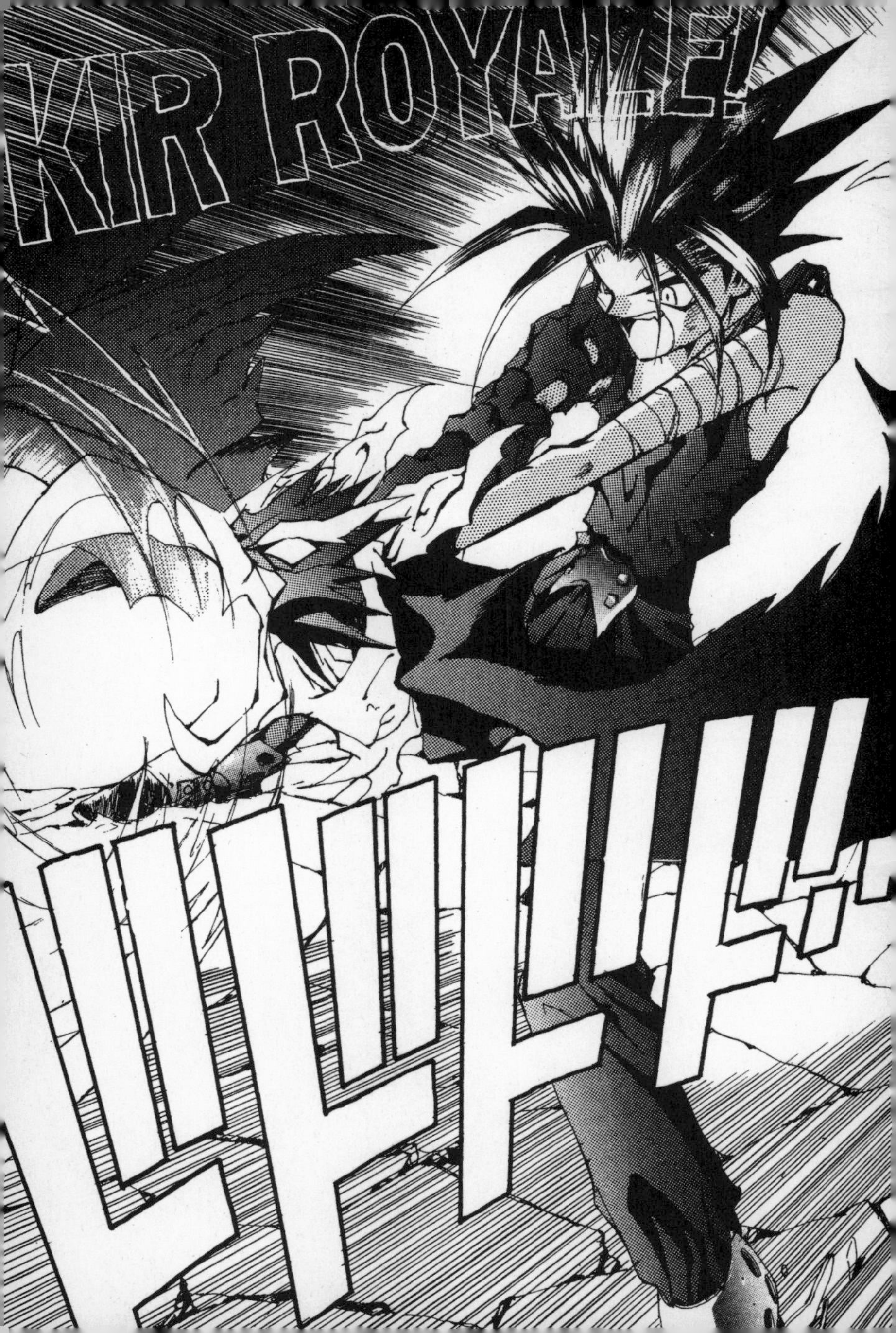
KIR ROYALE!

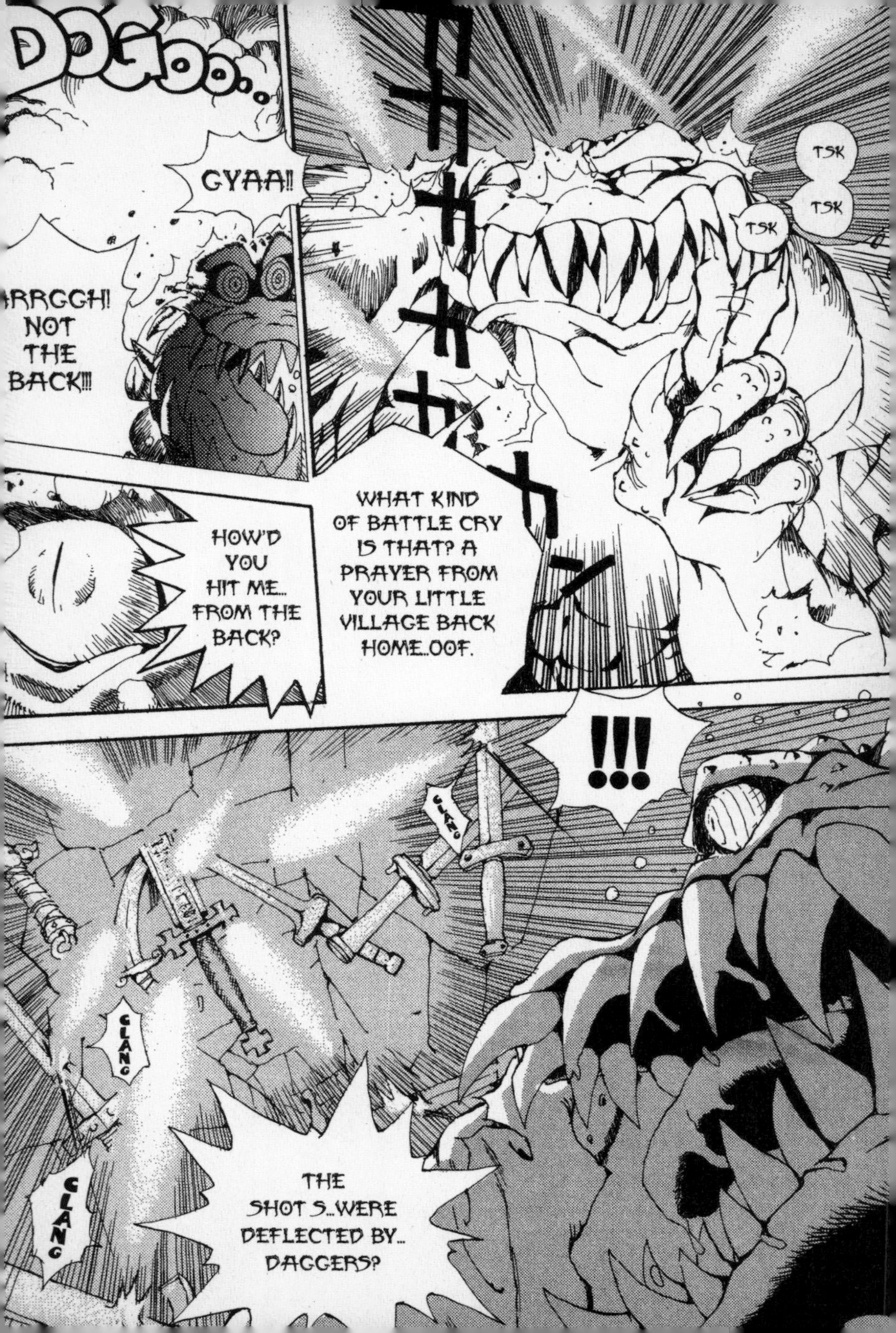
TSK
TSK
TSK
WHAT KIND OF BATTLE CRY IS THAT? A PRAYER FROM YOUR LITTLE VILLAGE BACK HOME...OOF.
DOGOOO...
GYAA!!
ARRGGH! NOT THE BACK!!!
HOW'D YOU HIT ME... FROM THE BACK?
!!!
CLANG
CLANG
CLANG
THE SHOT S...WERE DEFLECTED BY... DAGGERS?

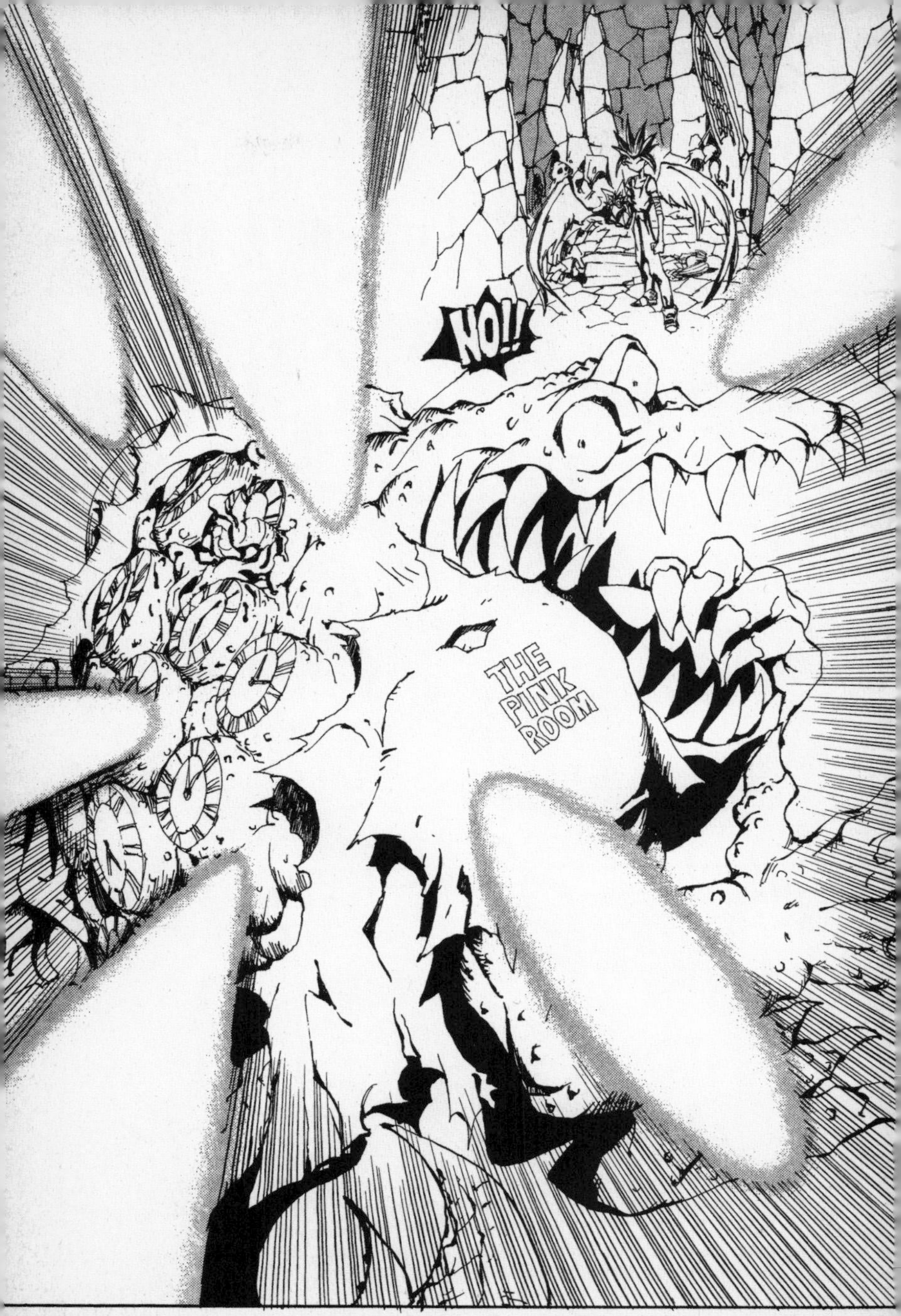
NO!!
THE PINK ROOM

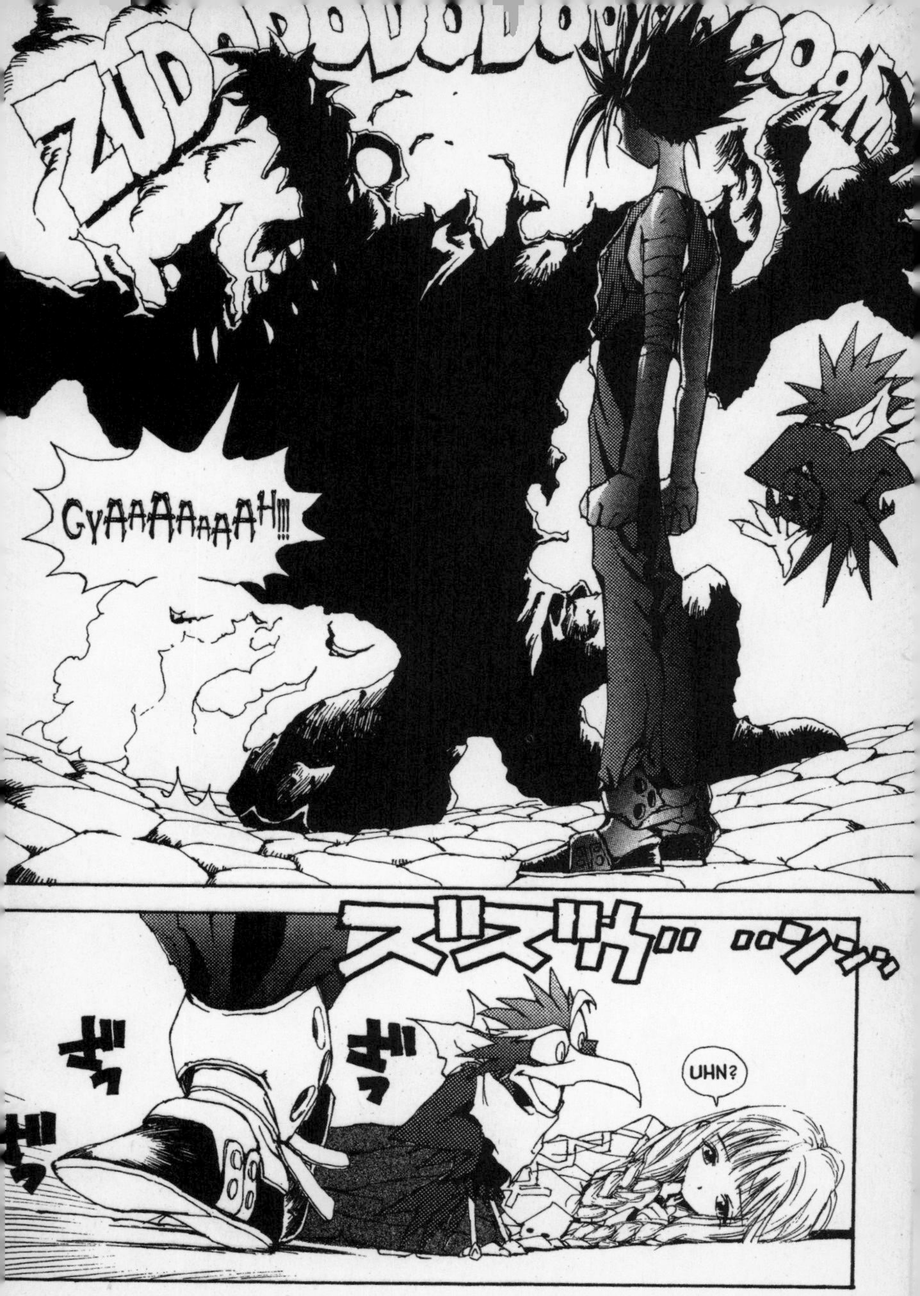
ZUDODODODO
OOM
GYAAAAAAAAH!!!
UHN?

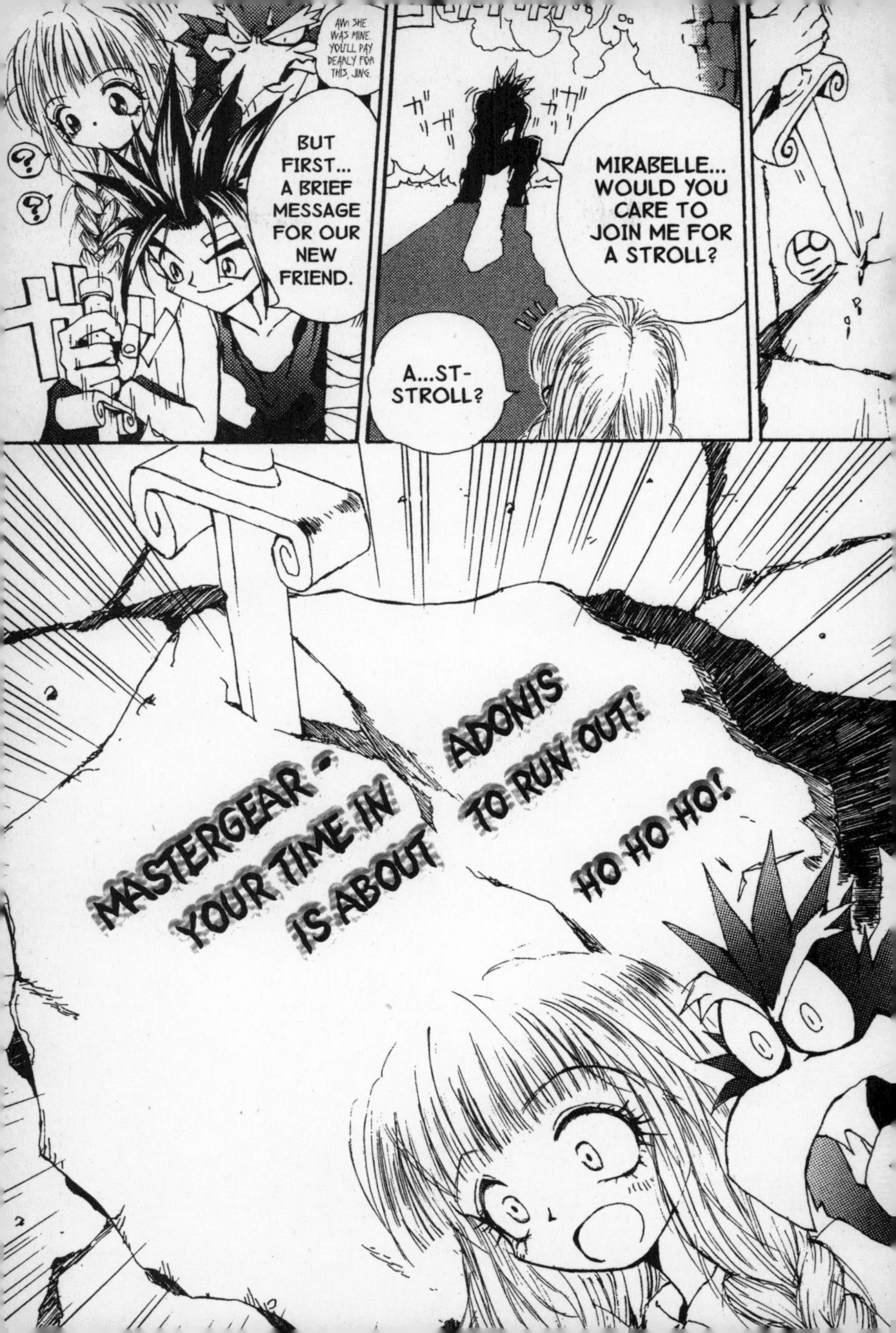
MIRABELLE... WOULD YOU CARE TO JOIN ME FOR A STROLL?
A...ST-STROLL?
AW, SHE WAS MINE. YOU'LL PAY DEARLY FOR THIS, JING.
BUT FIRST... A BRIEF MESSAGE FOR OUR NEW FRIEND.
MASTERGEAR - YOUR TIME IN ADONIS IS ABOUT TO RUN OUT!
HO HO HO!

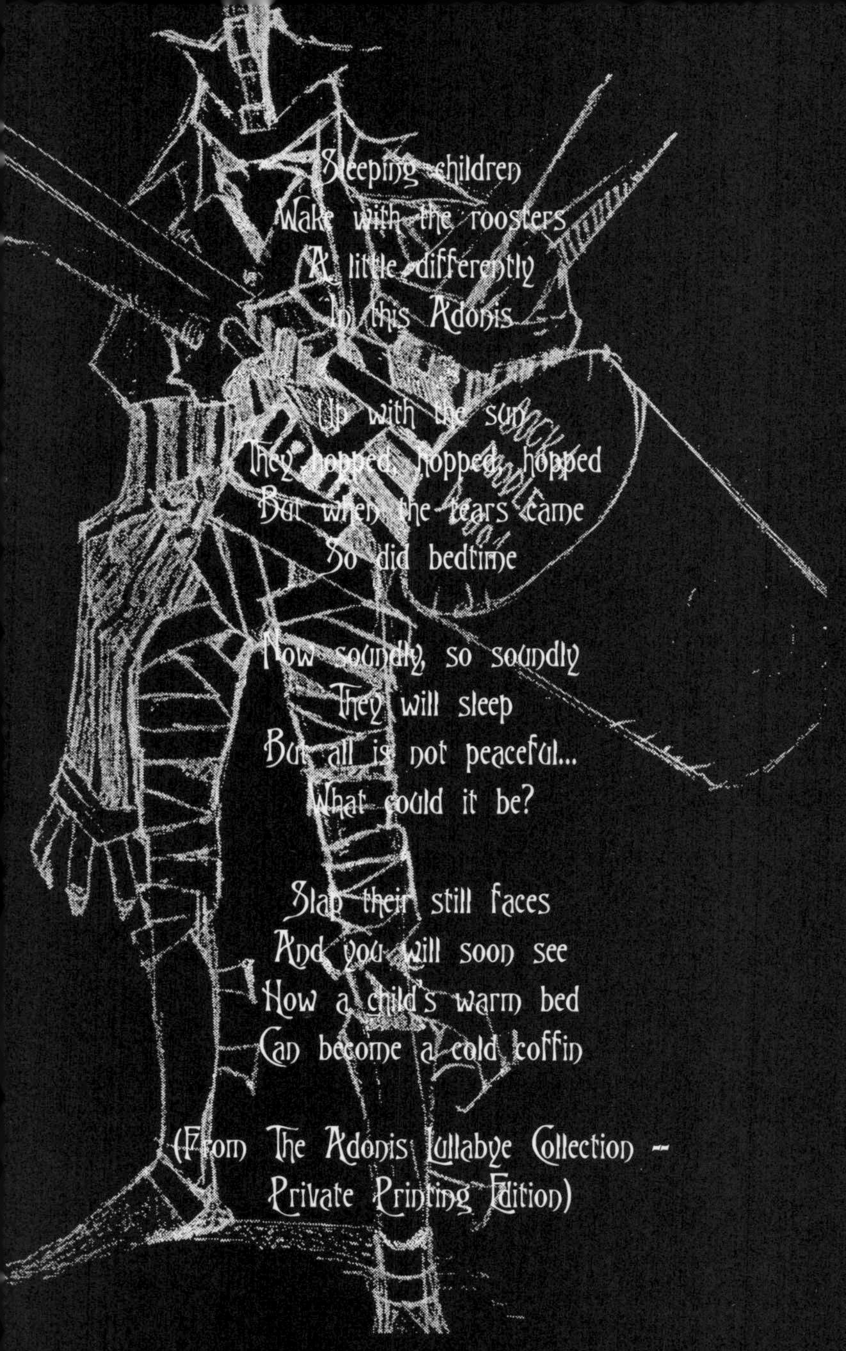

Sleeping children
Wake with the roosters
A little differently
In this Adonis

Up with the sun
They hopped, hopped, hopped
But when the tears came
So did bedtime

Now soundly, so soundly
They will sleep
But all is not peaceful...
What could it be?

Slap their still faces
And you will soon see
How a child's warm bed
Can become a cold coffin

(From The Adonis Lullabye Collection --
Private Printing Edition)

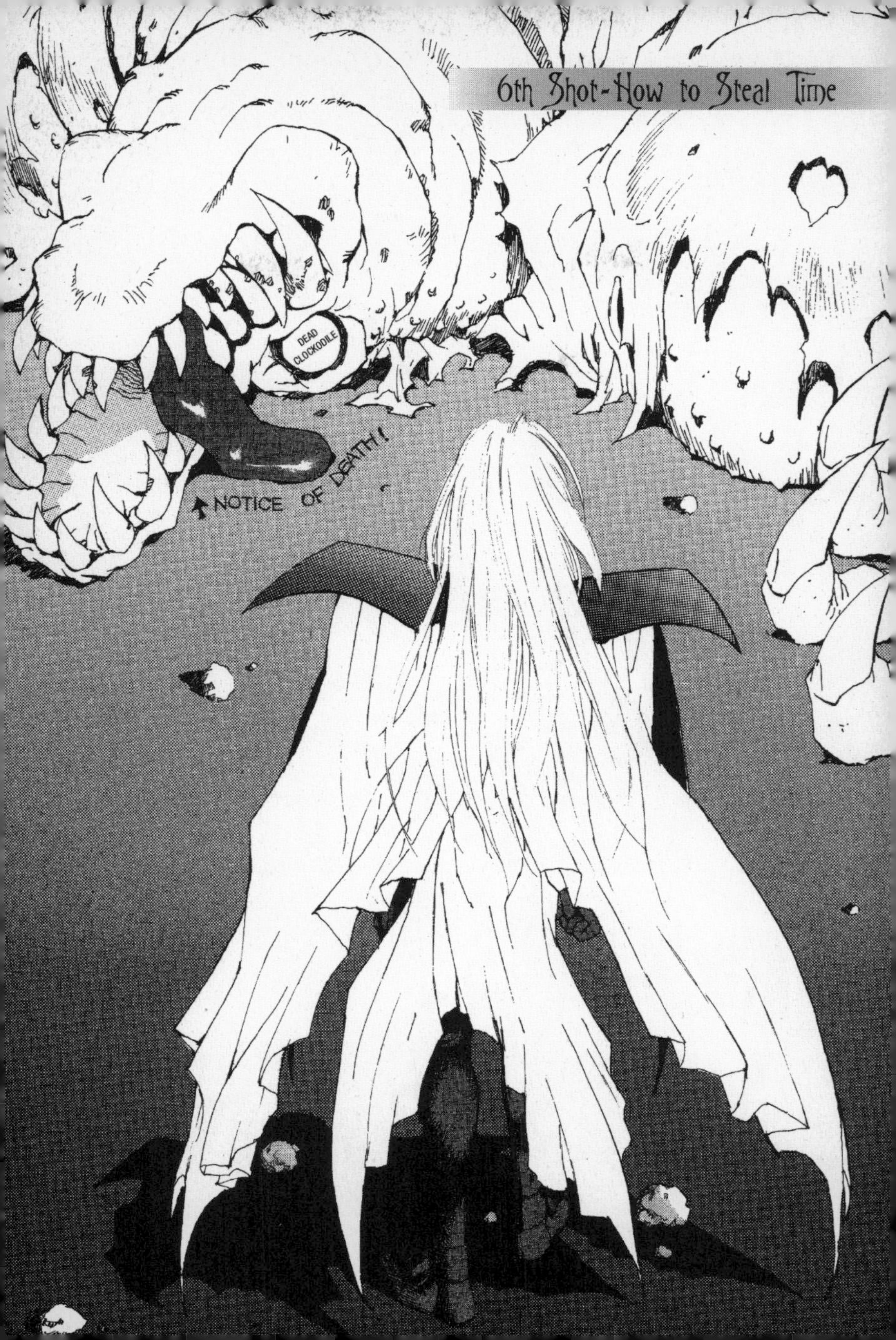
6th Shot-How to Steal Time
DEAD CLOCKODILE
NOTICE OF DEATH!

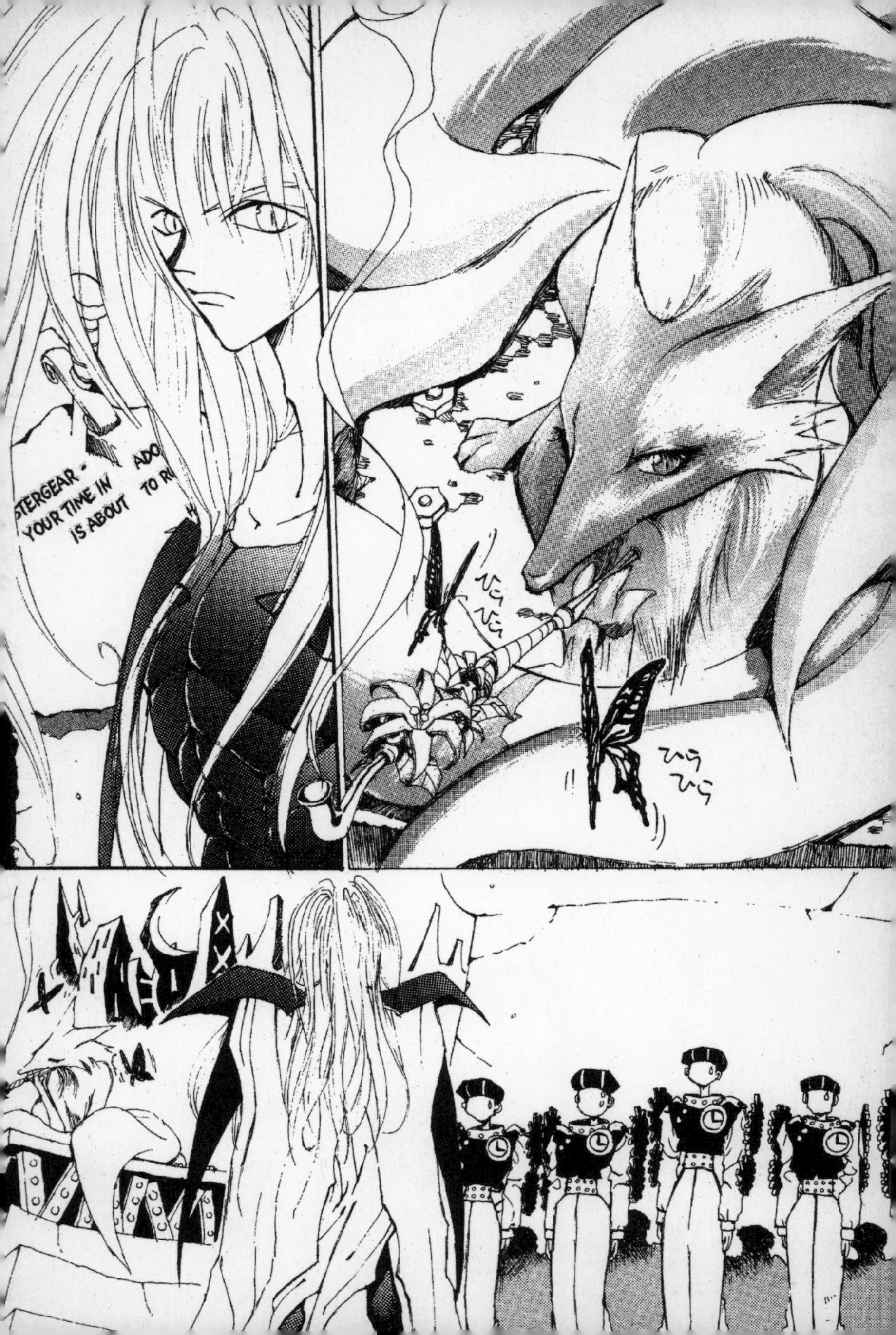

ひら ひら
ひら ひら
STERGEAR - YOUR TIME IN IS ABOUT
ADO TO R

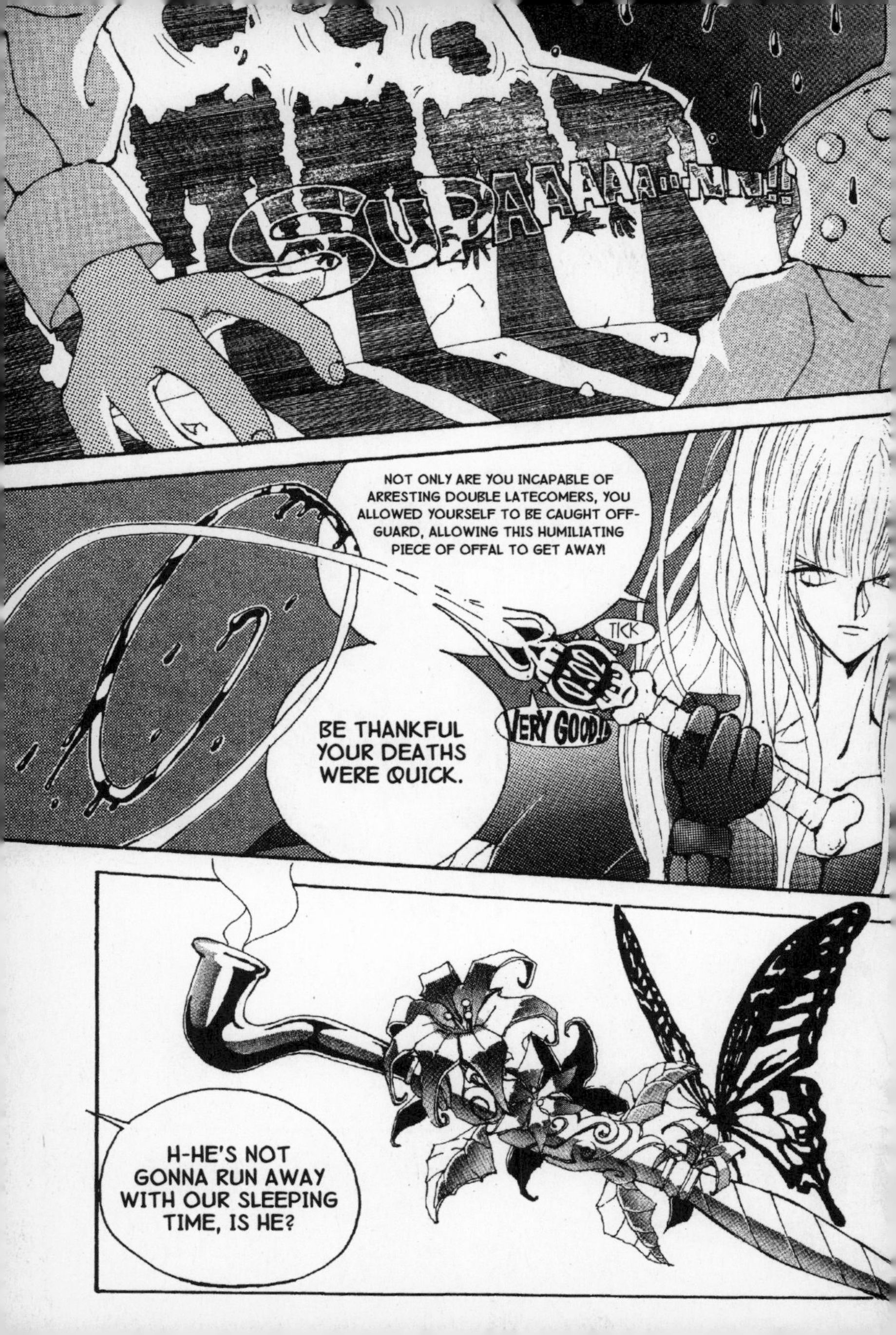
SUPAAAA..NN!!
NOT ONLY ARE YOU INCAPABLE OF ARRESTING DOUBLE LATECOMERS, YOU ALLOWED YOURSELF TO BE CAUGHT OFF-GUARD, ALLOWING THIS HUMILIATING PIECE OF OFFAL TO GET AWAY!
TICK
VERY GOOD!!
BE THANKFUL YOUR DEATHS WERE QUICK.
H-HE'S NOT GONNA RUN AWAY WITH OUR SLEEPING TIME, IS HE?

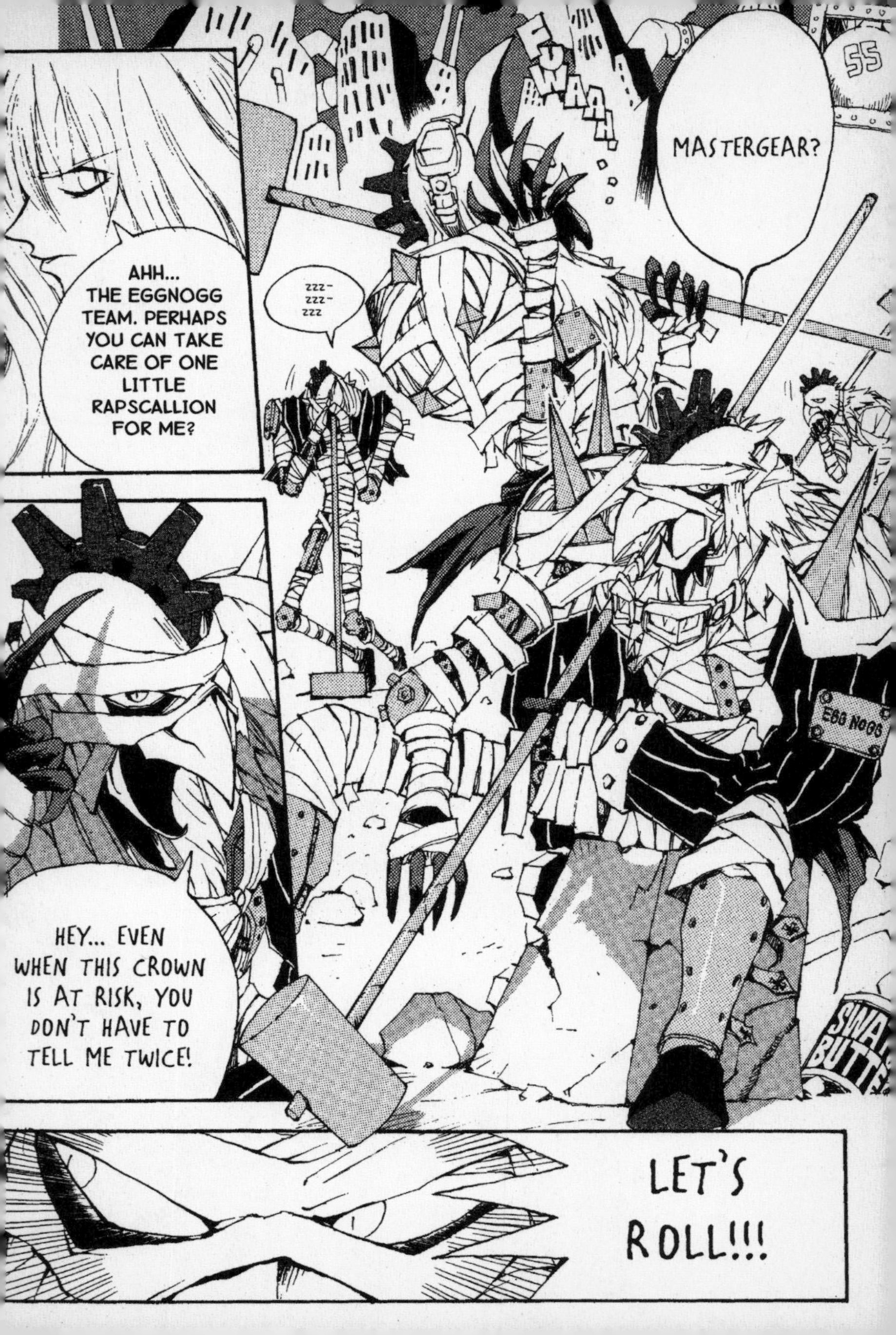
55
MASTERGEAR?
FUWAAAH
ZZZ- ZZZ- ZZZ
EGG NOGG
AHH... THE EGGNOGG TEAM. PERHAPS YOU CAN TAKE CARE OF ONE LITTLE RAPSCALLION FOR ME?
HEY... EVEN WHEN THIS CROWN IS AT RISK, YOU DON'T HAVE TO TELL ME TWICE!
LET'S ROLL!!!

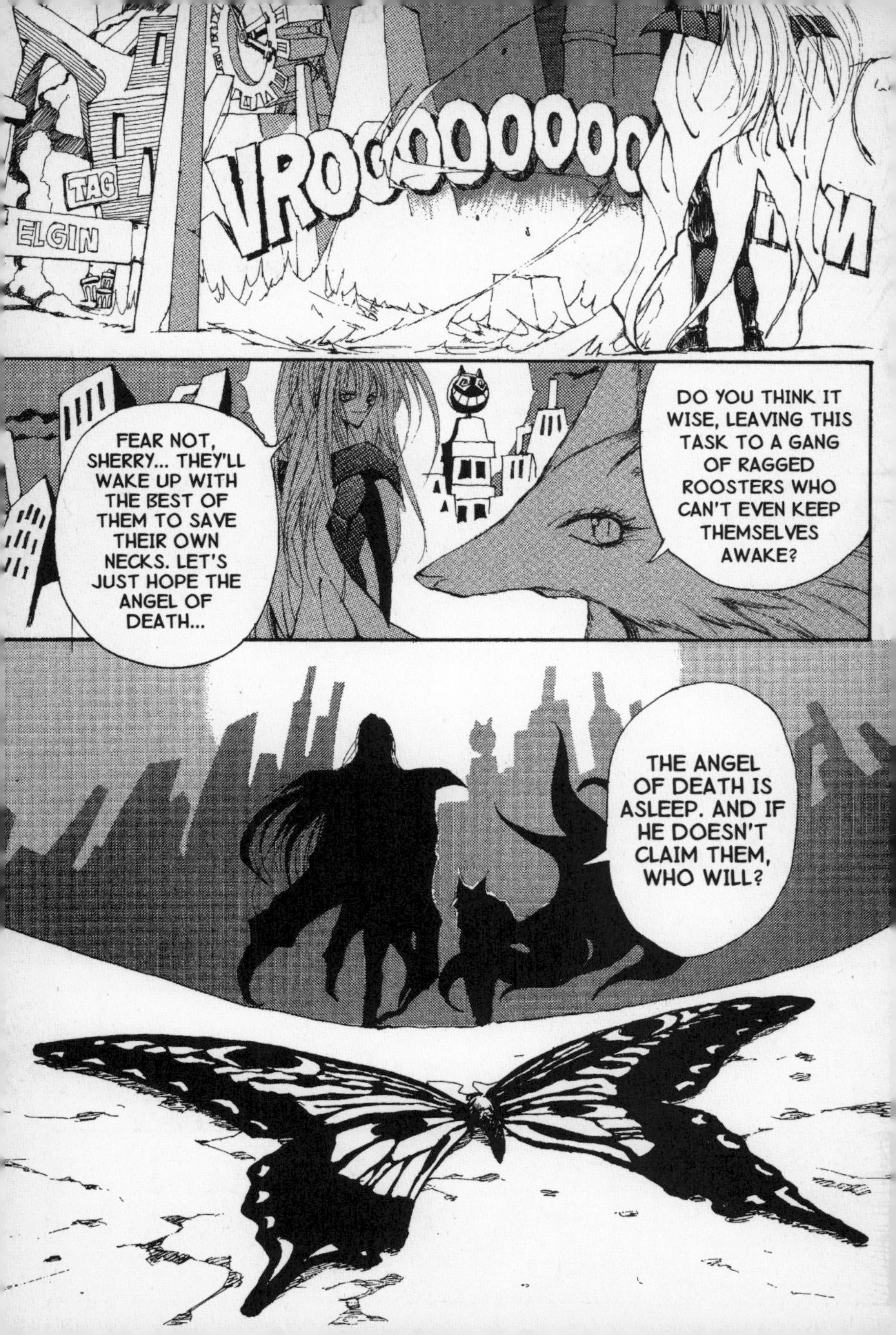
VROOOOOOOOM
TAG
ELGIN
DO YOU THINK IT WISE, LEAVING THIS TASK TO A GANG OF RAGGED ROOSTERS WHO CAN'T EVEN KEEP THEMSELVES AWAKE?
FEAR NOT, SHERRY... THEY'LL WAKE UP WITH THE BEST OF THEM TO SAVE THEIR OWN NECKS. LET'S JUST HOPE THE ANGEL OF DEATH...
THE ANGEL OF DEATH IS ASLEEP. AND IF HE DOESN'T CLAIM THEM, WHO WILL?

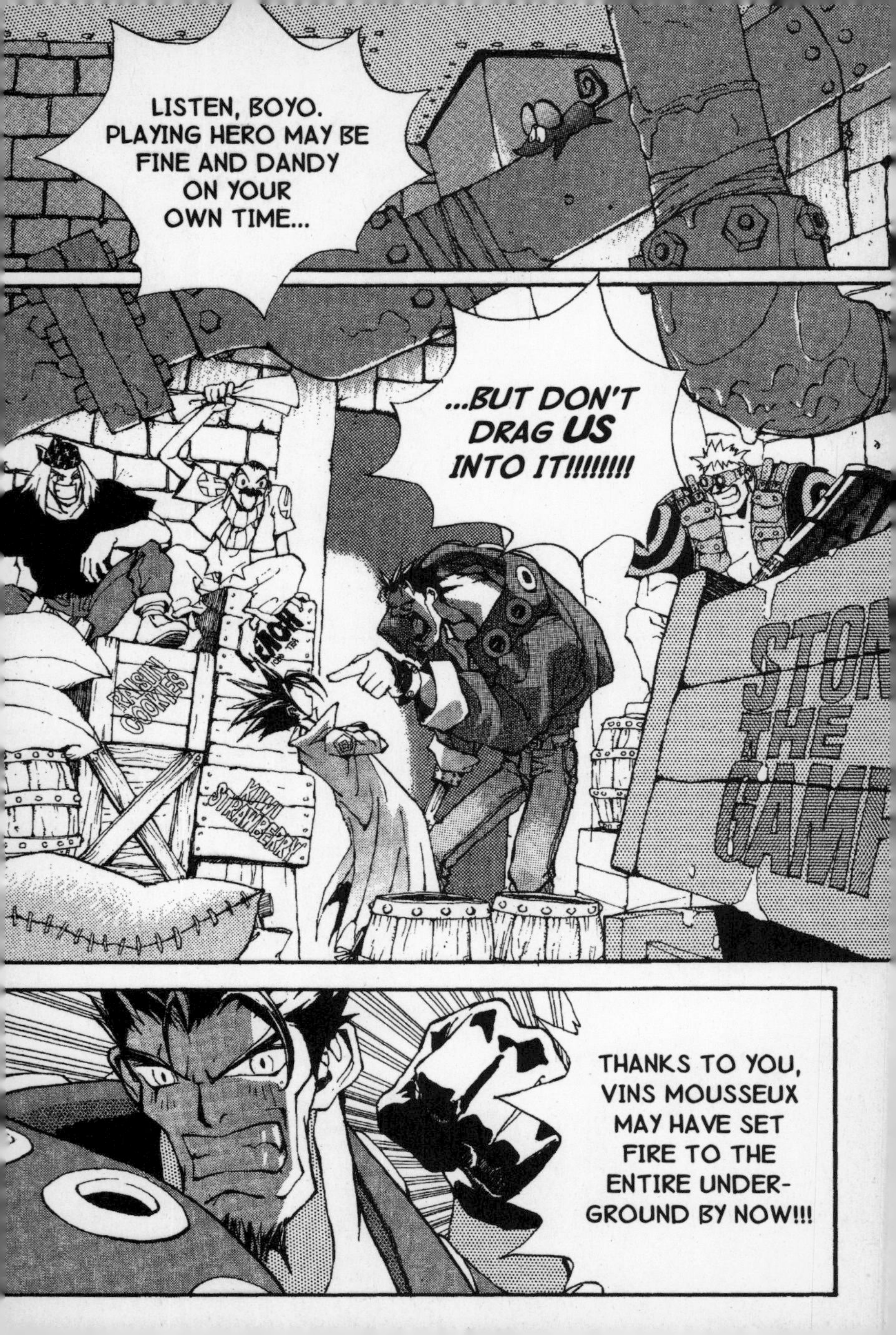
LISTEN, BOYO. PLAYING HERO MAY BE FINE AND DANDY ON YOUR OWN TIME...
...BUT DON'T DRAG US INTO IT!!!!!!!!
RAISIN COOKIES
KIWI STRAWBERRY
THANKS TO YOU, VINS MOUSSEUX MAY HAVE SET FIRE TO THE ENTIRE UNDER-GROUND BY NOW!!!

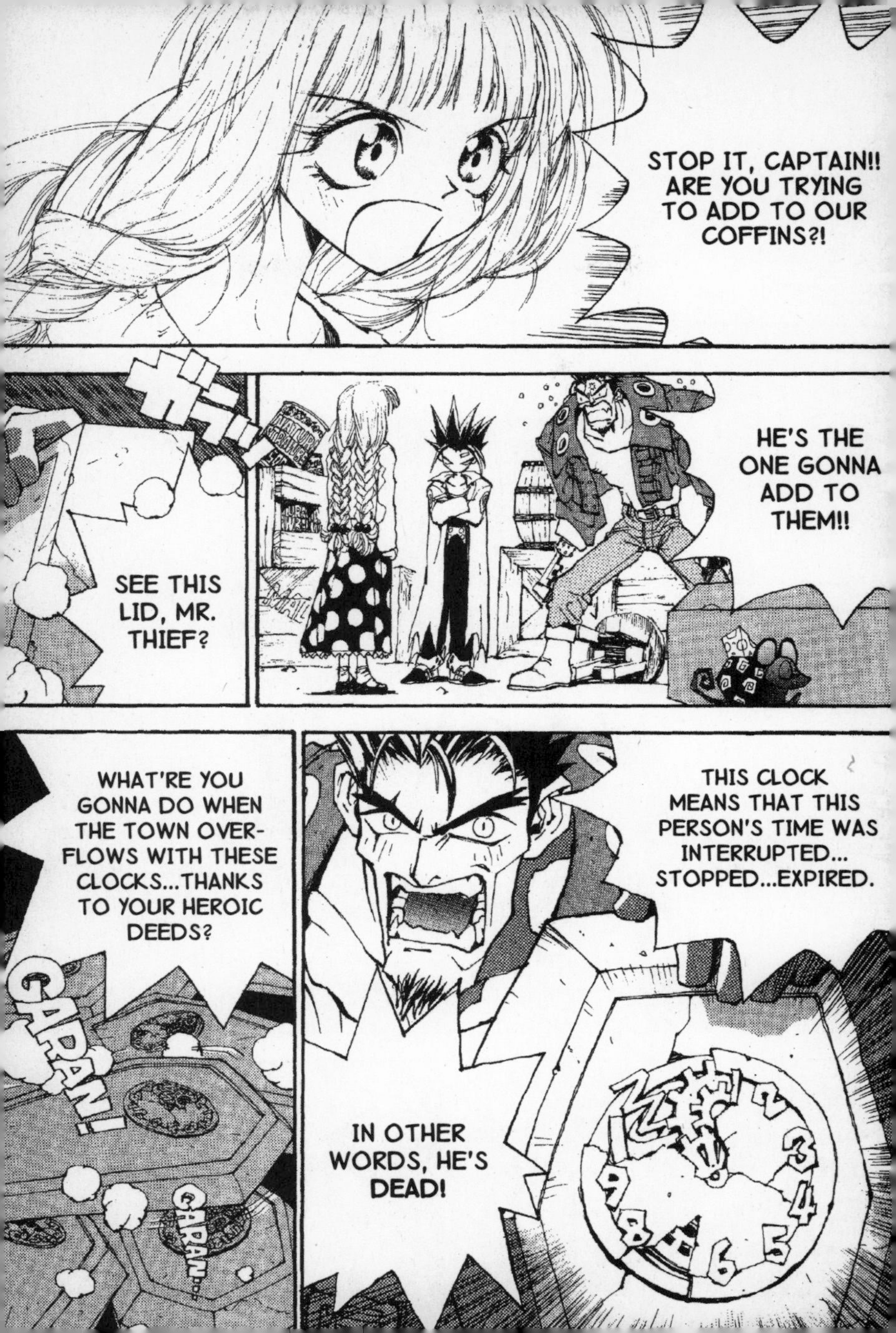
STOP IT, CAPTAIN!! ARE YOU TRYING TO ADD TO OUR COFFINS?!
HE'S THE ONE GONNA ADD TO THEM!!
SEE THIS LID, MR. THIEF?
THIS CLOCK MEANS THAT THIS PERSON'S TIME WAS INTERRUPTED... STOPPED...EXPIRED.
IN OTHER WORDS, HE'S DEAD!
WHAT'RE YOU GONNA DO WHEN THE TOWN OVER-FLOWS WITH THESE CLOCKS...THANKS TO YOUR HEROIC DEEDS?
GARAN!
GARAN...

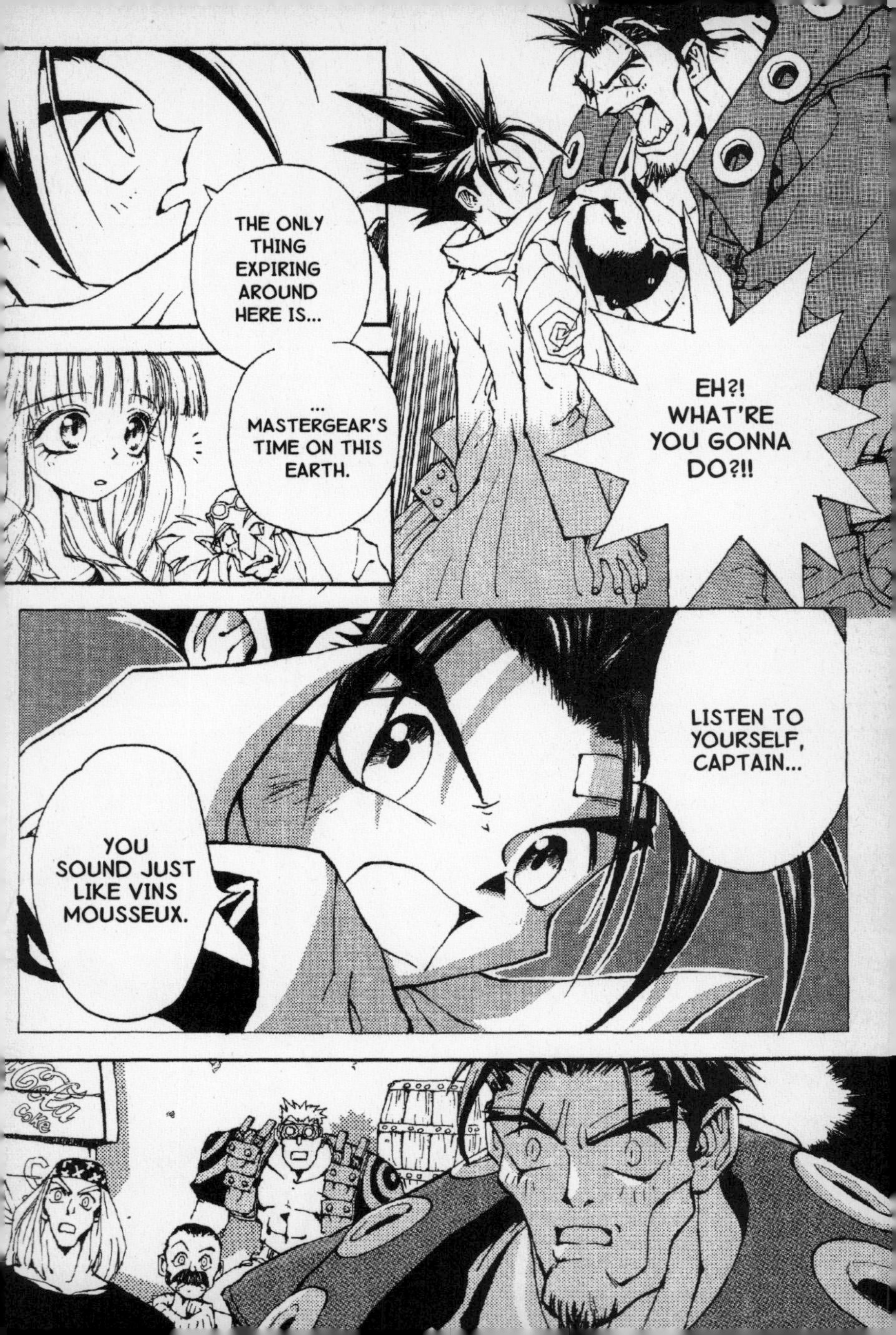
EH?! WHAT'RE YOU GONNA DO?!!
THE ONLY THING EXPIRING AROUND HERE IS...
... MASTERGEAR'S TIME ON THIS EARTH.
LISTEN TO YOURSELF, CAPTAIN...
YOU SOUND JUST LIKE VINS MOUSSEUX.

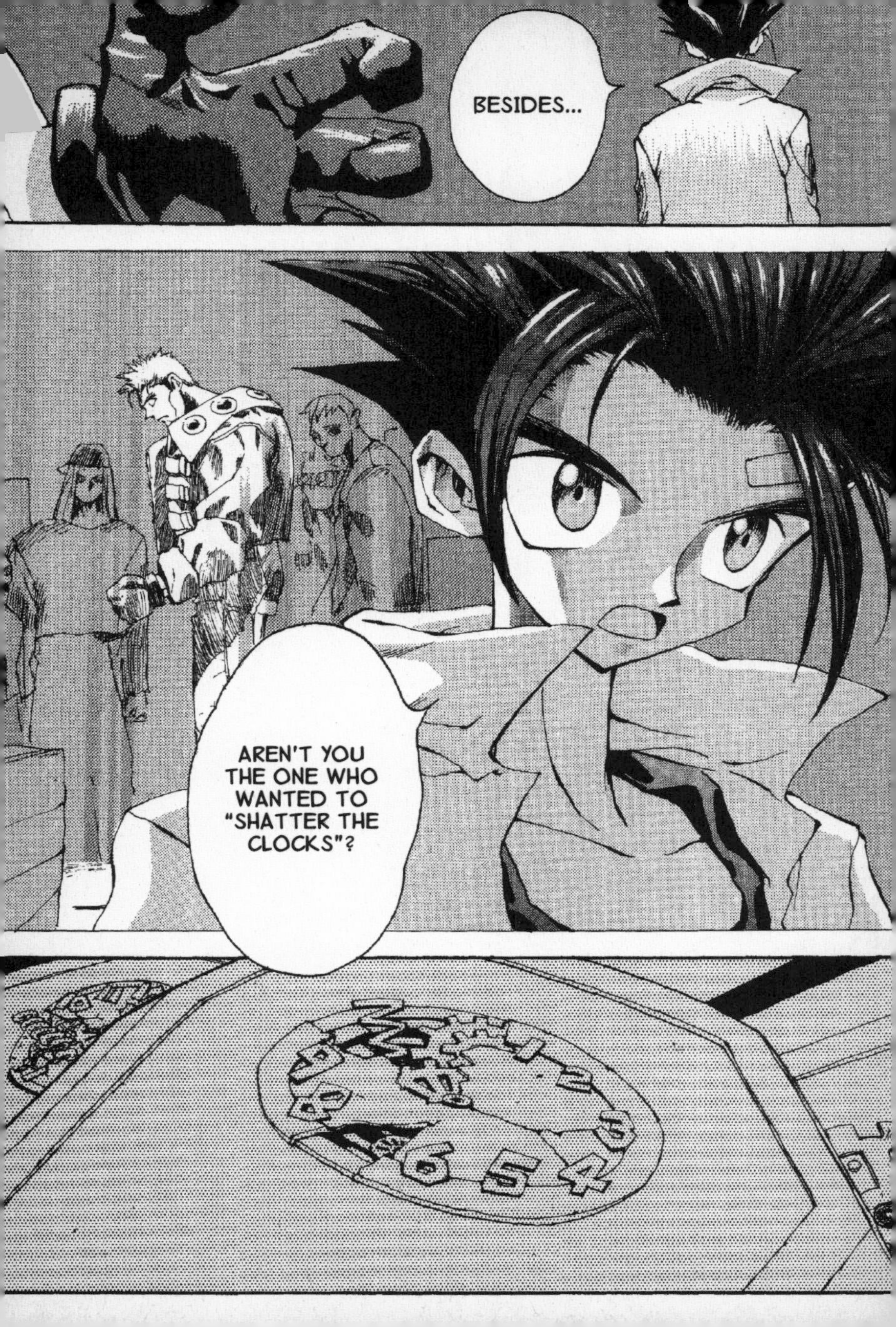
BESIDES...
AREN'T YOU THE ONE WHO WANTED TO "SHATTER THE CLOCKS"?

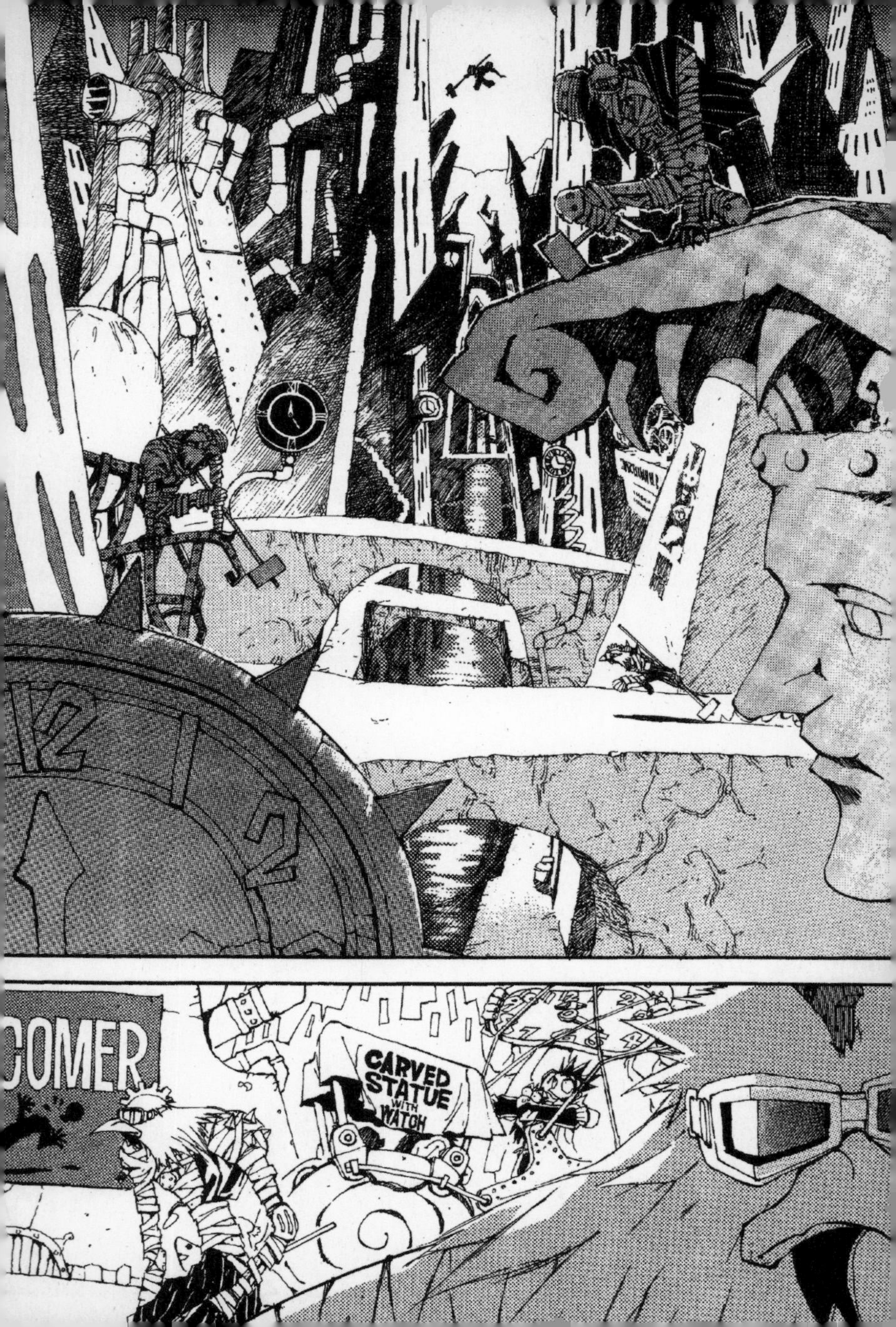
CARVED STATUE WITH WATCH
COMER

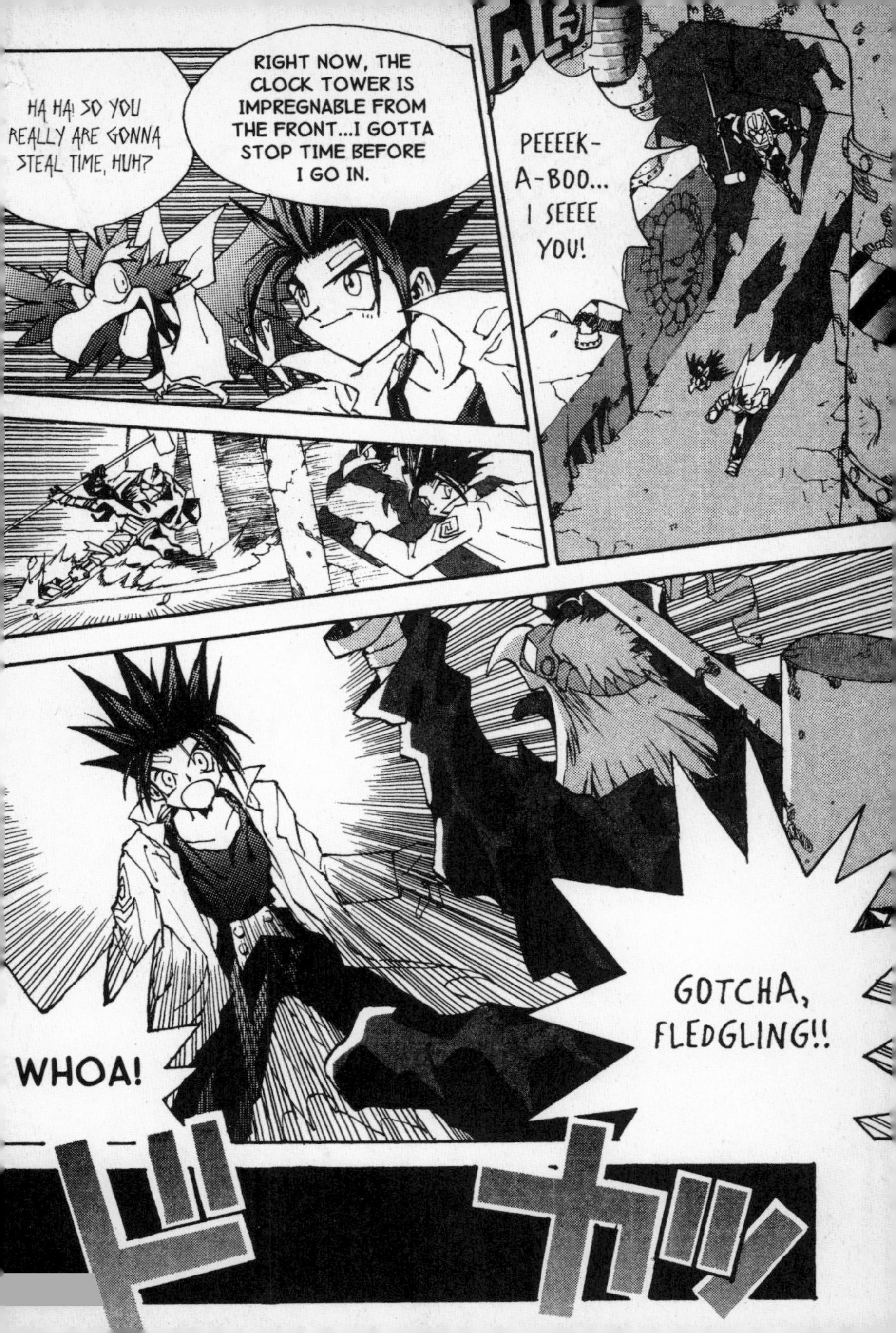
PEEEEK-A-BOO... I SEEEE YOU!
RIGHT NOW, THE CLOCK TOWER IS IMPREGNABLE FROM THE FRONT...I GOTTA STOP TIME BEFORE I GO IN.
HA HA! SO YOU REALLY ARE GONNA STEAL TIME, HUH?
GOTCHA, FLEDGLING!!
WHOA!
ドガッ

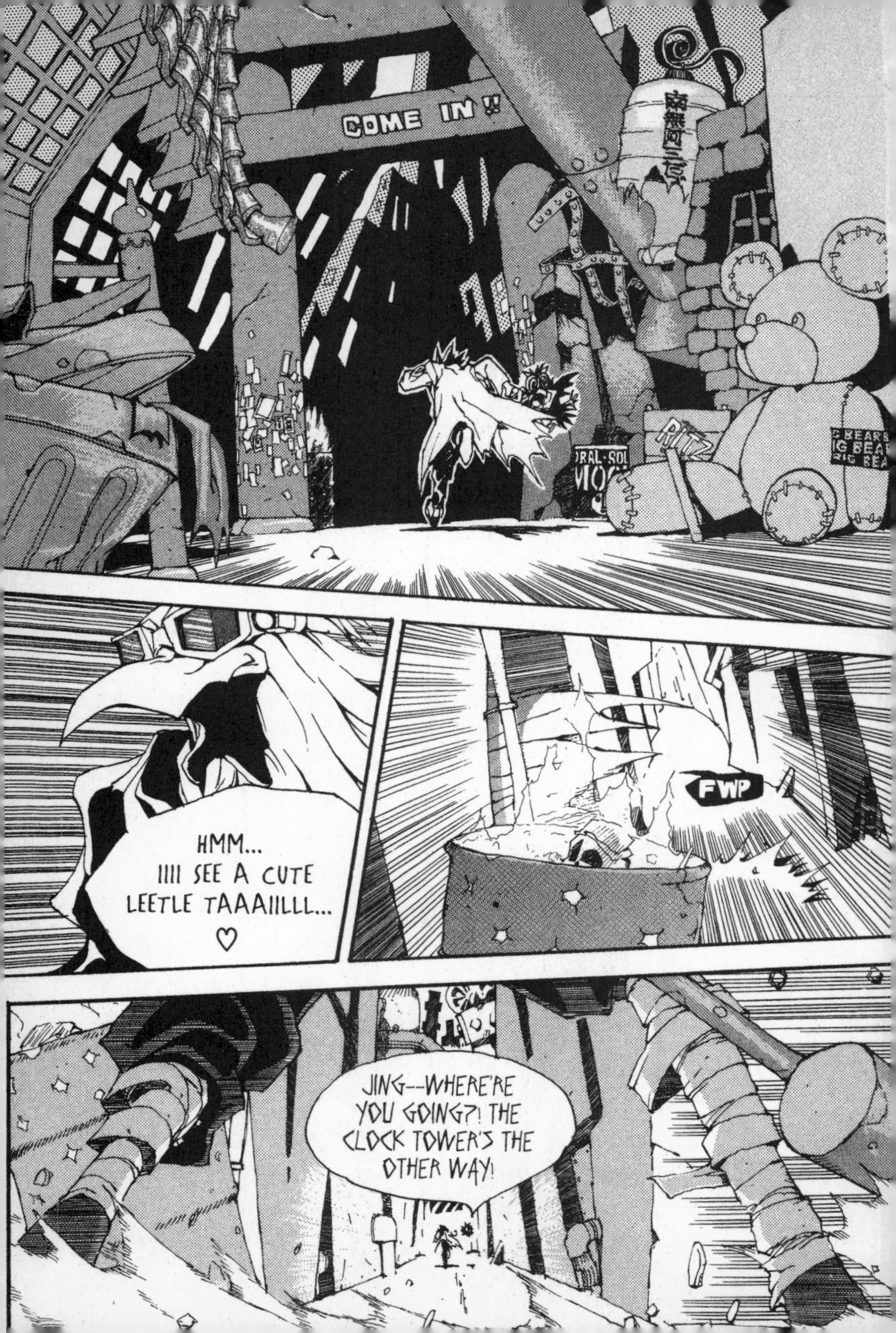
COME IN !!
FWP
HMM... IIII SEE A CUTE LEETLE TAAAIILLL... ♡
JING--WHERE'RE YOU GOING?! THE CLOCK TOWER'S THE OTHER WAY!

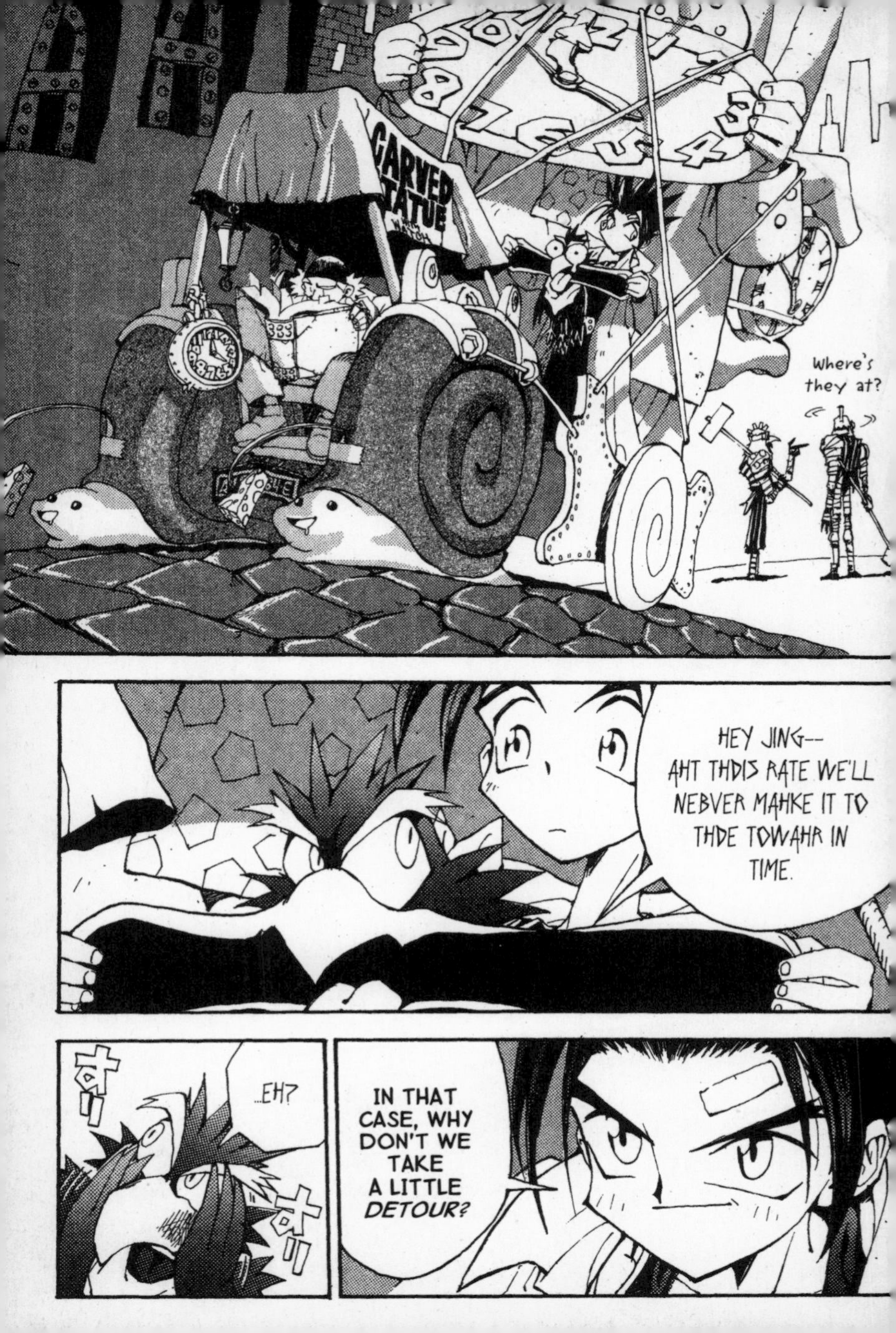
Where's they at?
CARVED STATUE
HEY JING--
AHT THDIS RATE WE'LL NEBVER MAHKE IT TO THDE TOWAHR IN TIME.
IN THAT CASE, WHY DON'T WE TAKE A LITTLE *DETOUR?*
...EH?

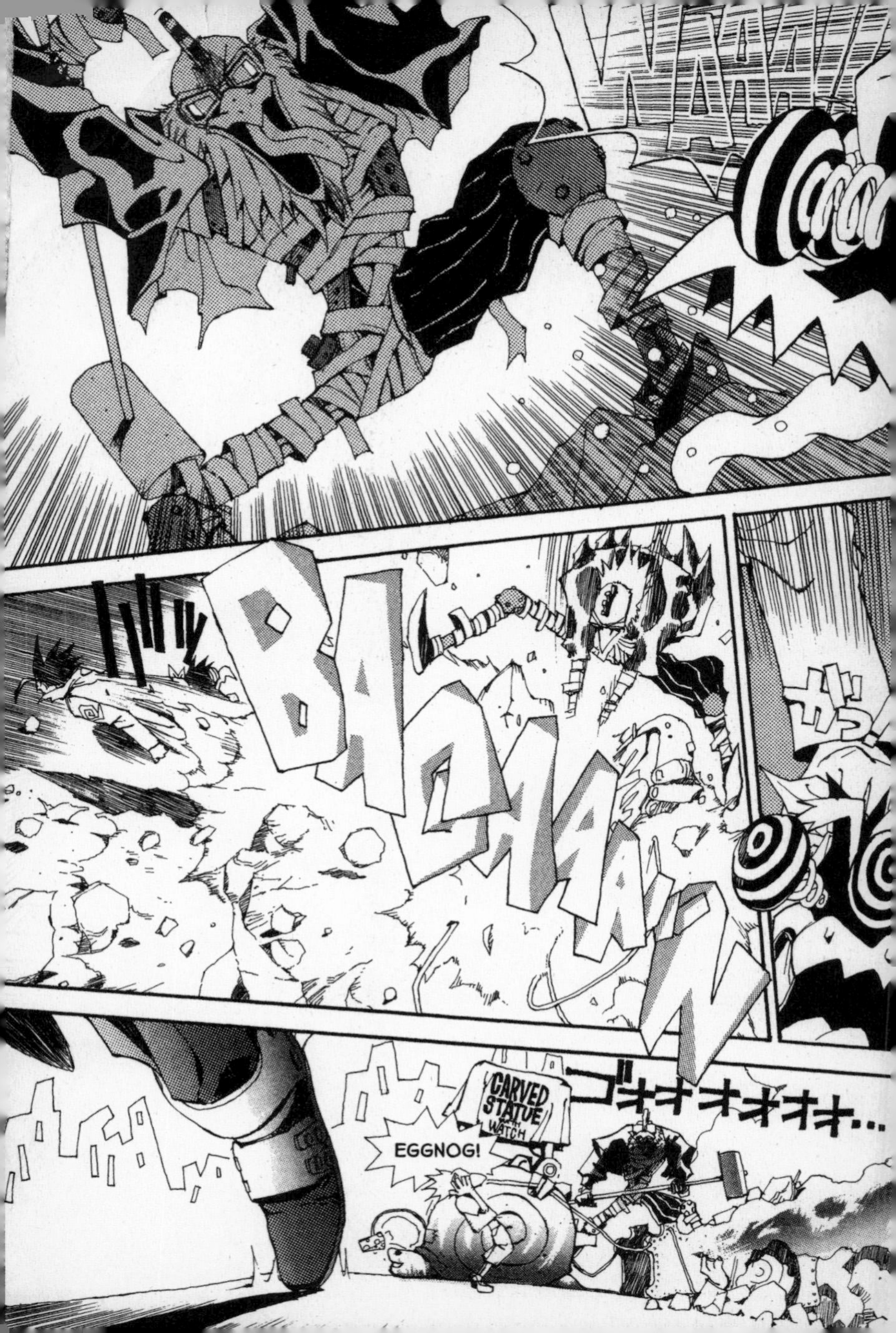
WAAAH!!
がっ!
BADAAAN
CARVED STATUE WITH WATCH
ゴオオオオオオ…
EGGNOG!

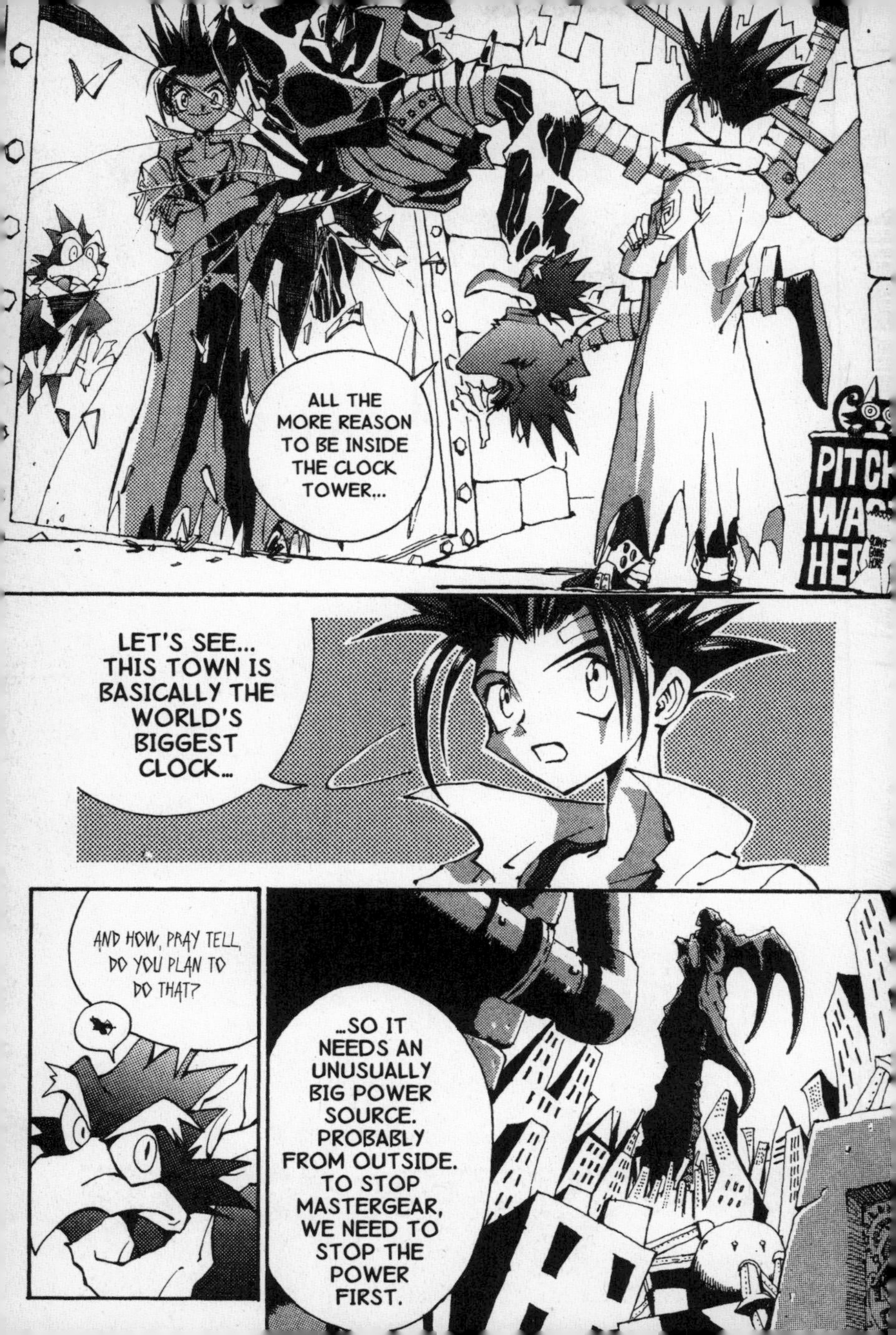
ALL THE MORE REASON TO BE INSIDE THE CLOCK TOWER...
PITCH
LET'S SEE... THIS TOWN IS BASICALLY THE WORLD'S BIGGEST CLOCK...
...SO IT NEEDS AN UNUSUALLY BIG POWER SOURCE. PROBABLY FROM OUTSIDE. TO STOP MASTERGEAR, WE NEED TO STOP THE POWER FIRST.
AND HOW, PRAY TELL, DO YOU PLAN TO DO THAT?

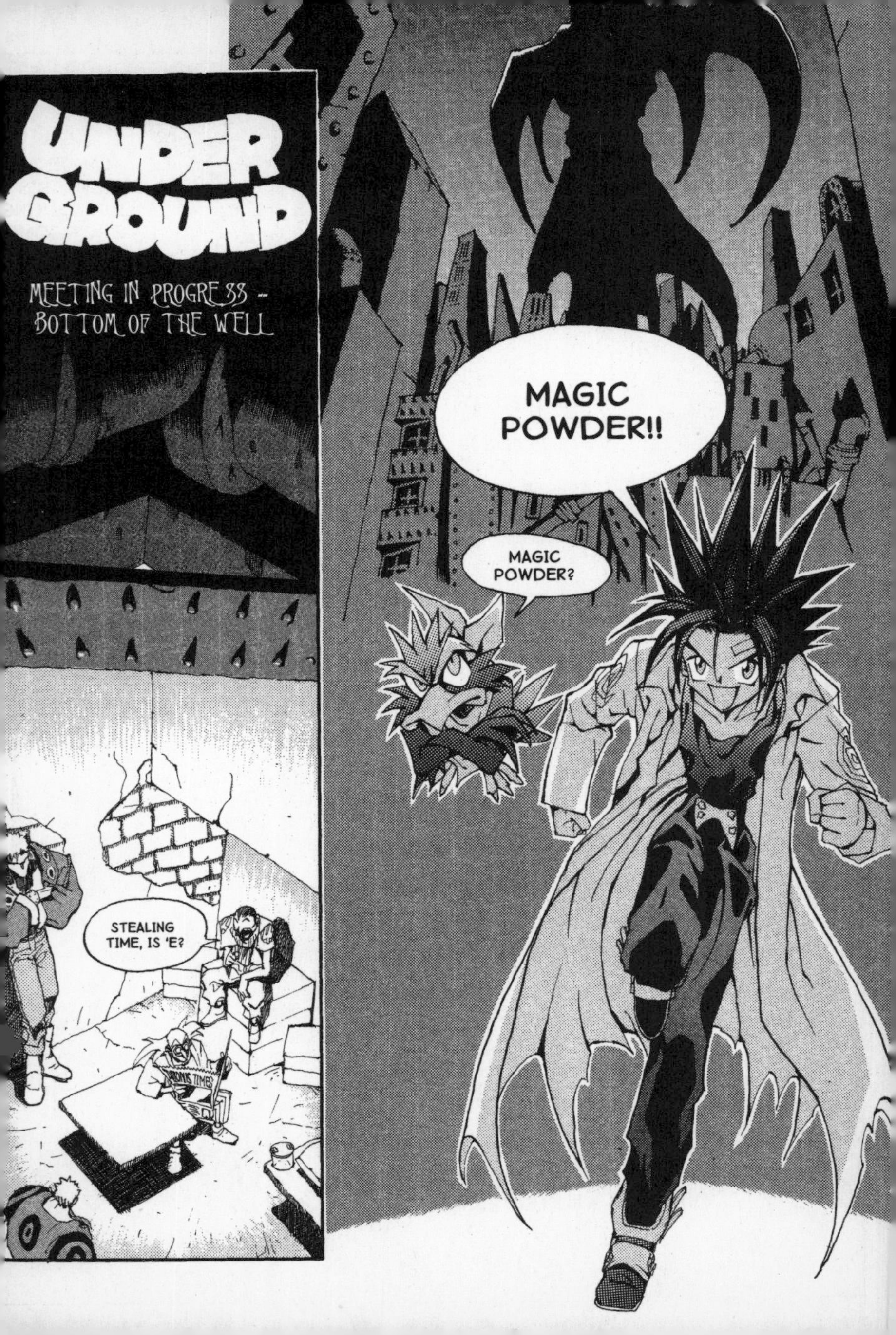
MAGIC POWDER!!
MAGIC POWDER?
UNDER GROUND
MEETING IN PROGRESS --
BOTTOM OF THE WELL
STEALING TIME, IS 'E?

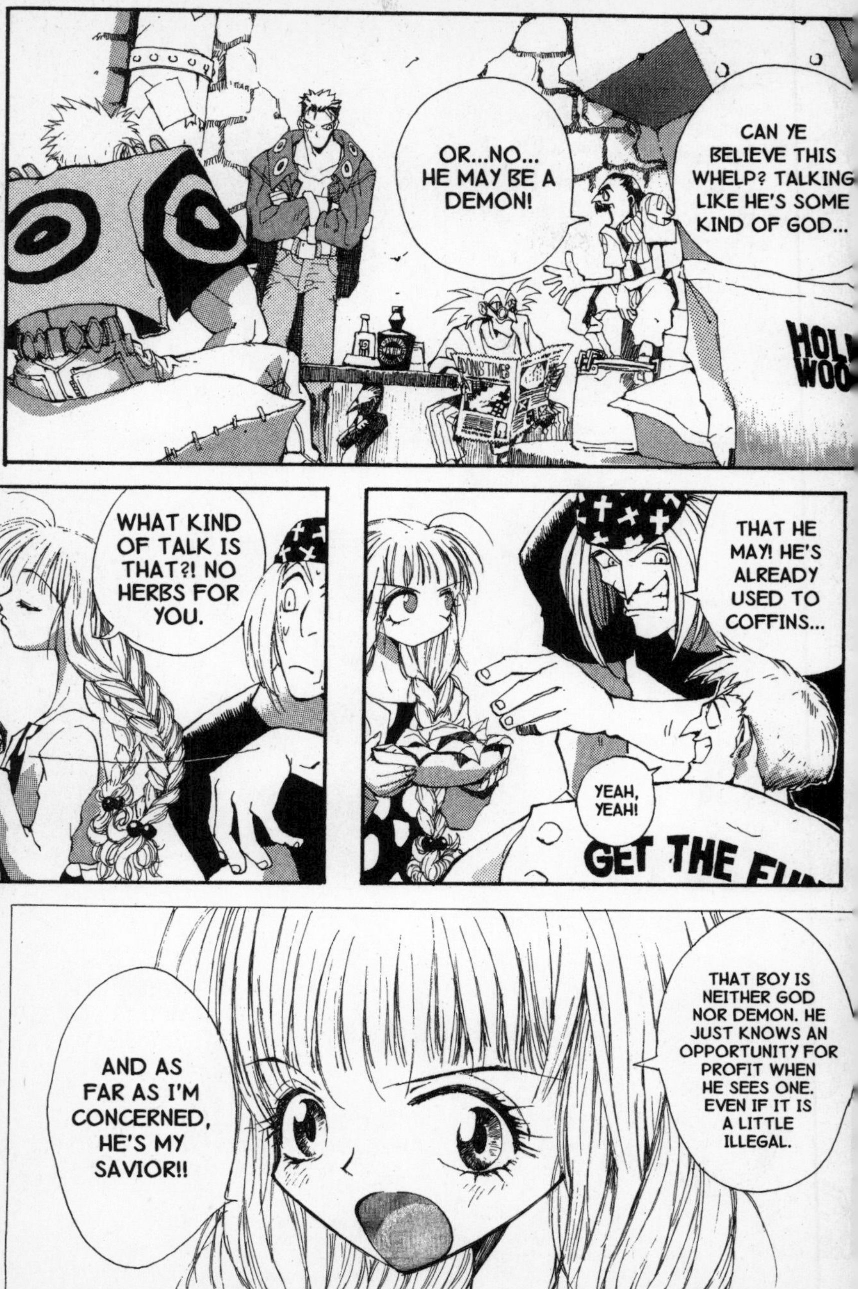
CAN YE BELIEVE THIS WHELP? TALKING LIKE HE'S SOME KIND OF GOD...
OR...NO... HE MAY BE A DEMON!
THAT HE MAY! HE'S ALREADY USED TO COFFINS...
YEAH, YEAH!
WHAT KIND OF TALK IS THAT?! NO HERBS FOR YOU.
THAT BOY IS NEITHER GOD NOR DEMON. HE JUST KNOWS AN OPPORTUNITY FOR PROFIT WHEN HE SEES ONE. EVEN IF IT IS A LITTLE ILLEGAL.
AND AS FAR AS I'M CONCERNED, HE'S MY SAVIOR!!

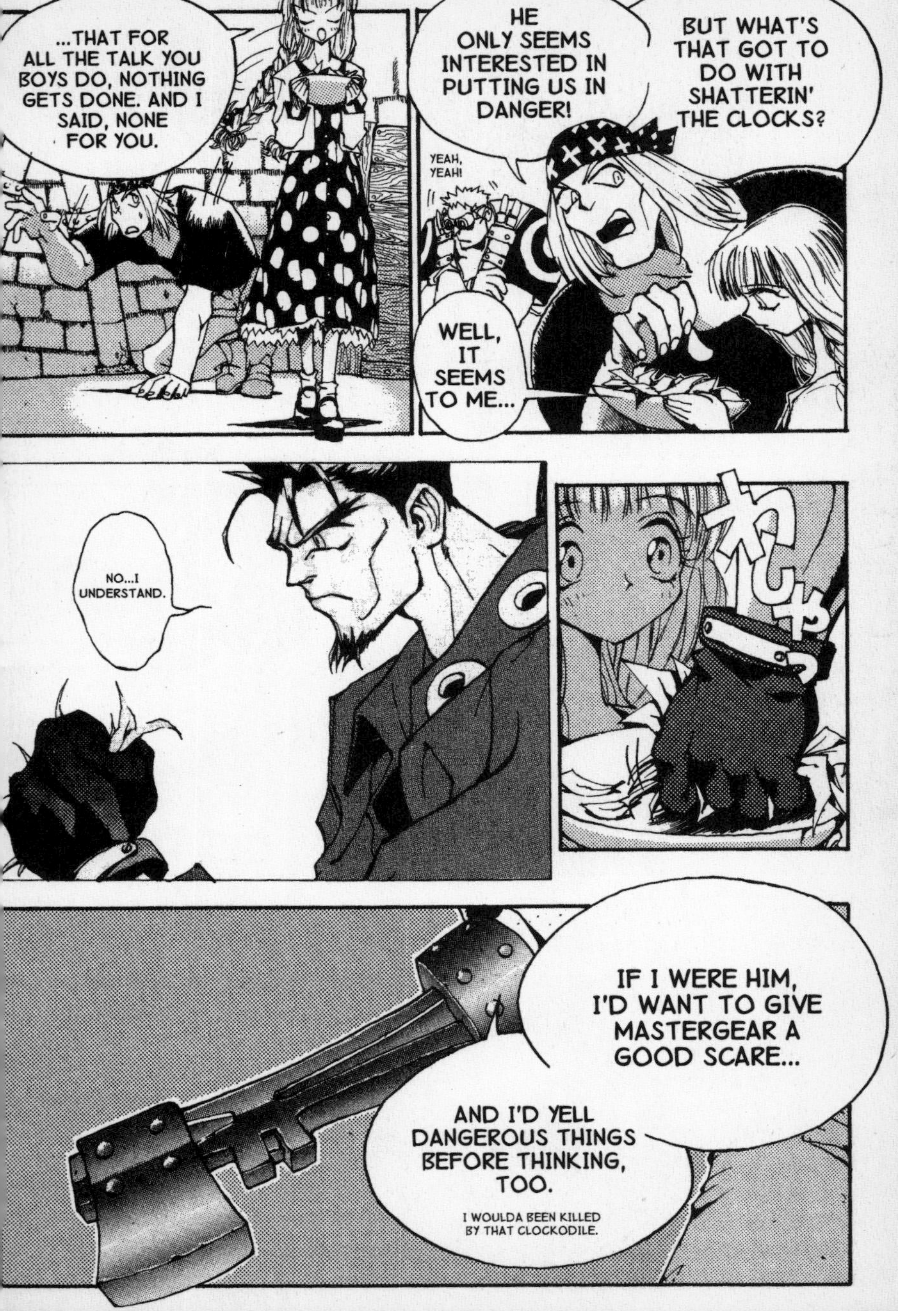
BUT WHAT'S THAT GOT TO DO WITH SHATTERIN' THE CLOCKS?
HE ONLY SEEMS INTERESTED IN PUTTING US IN DANGER!
YEAH, YEAH!
WELL, IT SEEMS TO ME...
...THAT FOR ALL THE TALK YOU BOYS DO, NOTHING GETS DONE. AND I SAID, NONE FOR YOU.
NO...I UNDERSTAND.
IF I WERE HIM, I'D WANT TO GIVE MASTERGEAR A GOOD SCARE...
AND I'D YELL DANGEROUS THINGS BEFORE THINKING, TOO.
I WOULDA BEEN KILLED BY THAT CLOCKODILE.

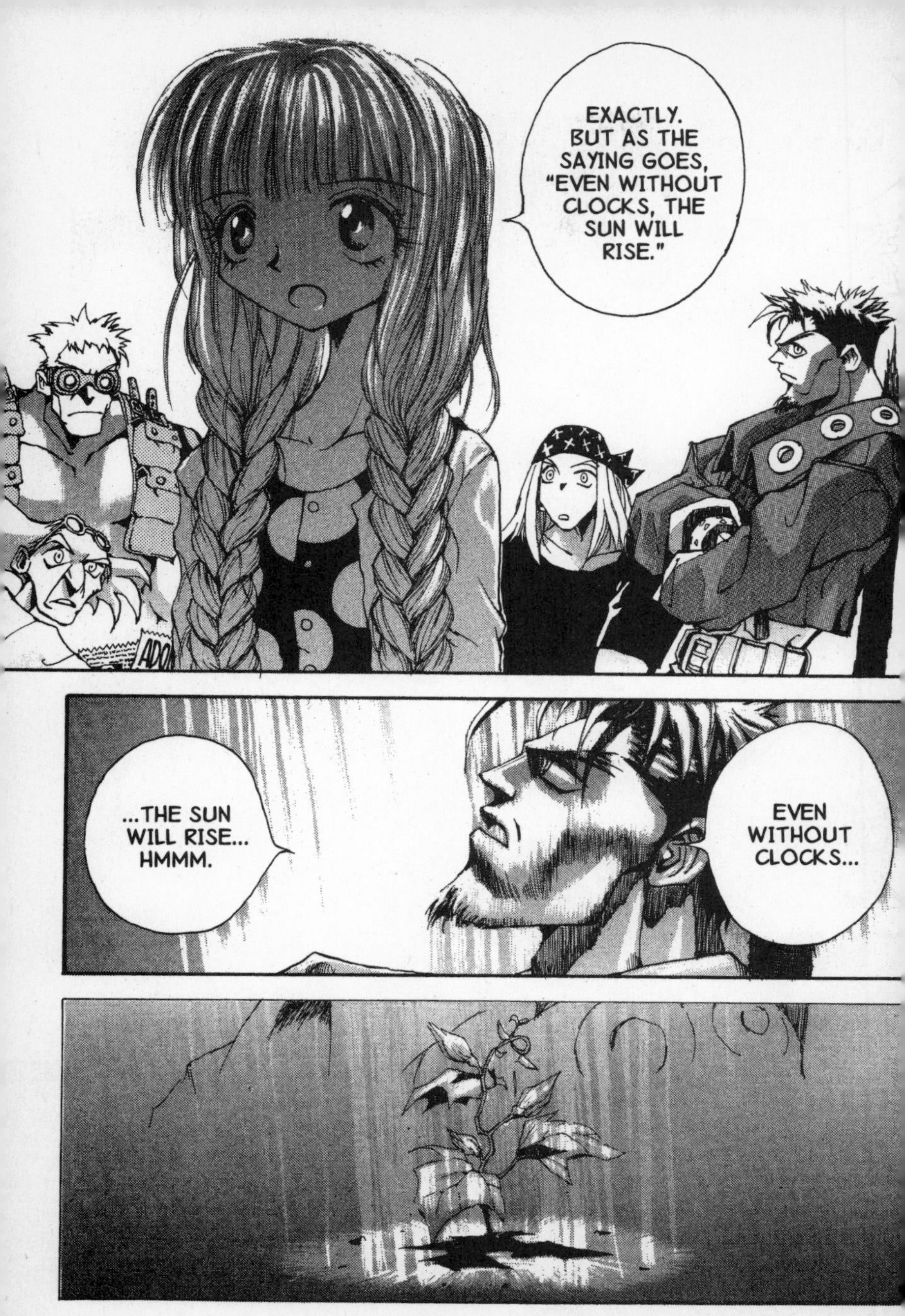
EXACTLY. BUT AS THE SAYING GOES, "EVEN WITHOUT CLOCKS, THE SUN WILL RISE."
EVEN WITHOUT CLOCKS...
...THE SUN WILL RISE... HMMM.

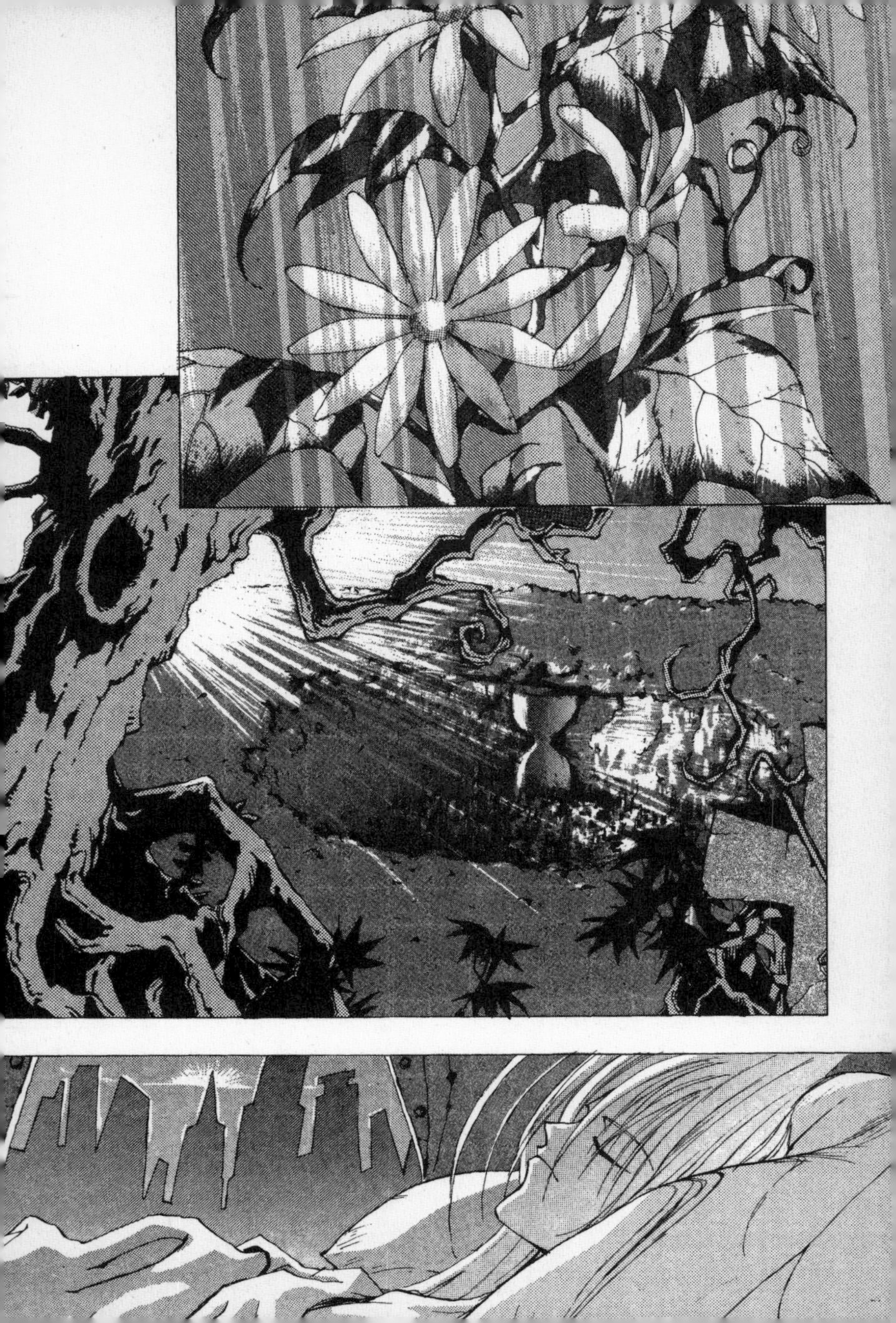

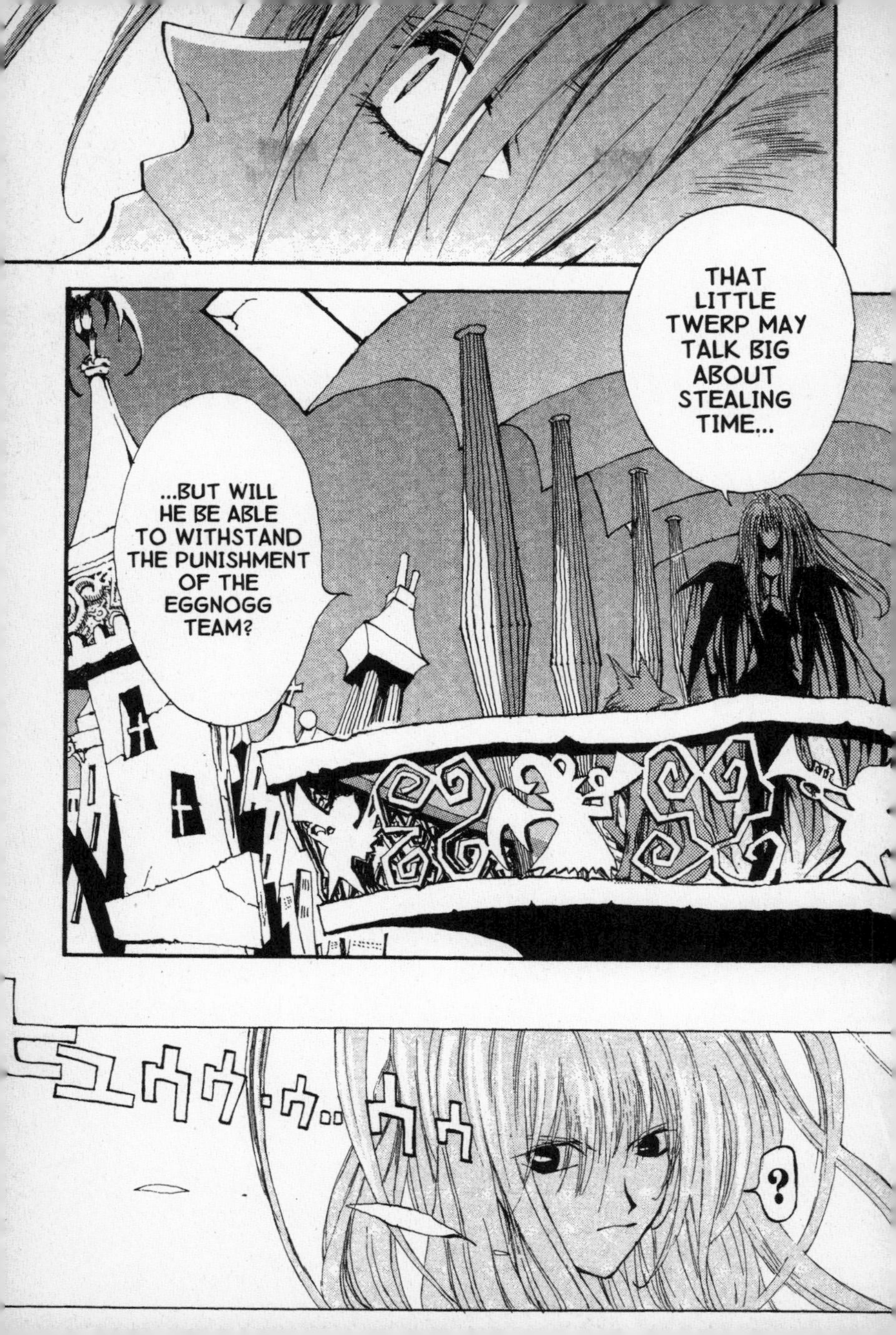
THAT LITTLE TWERP MAY TALK BIG ABOUT STEALING TIME...
...BUT WILL HE BE ABLE TO WITHSTAND THE PUNISHMENT OF THE EGGNOGG TEAM?
ニュウウ・ウ‥ウウ
?

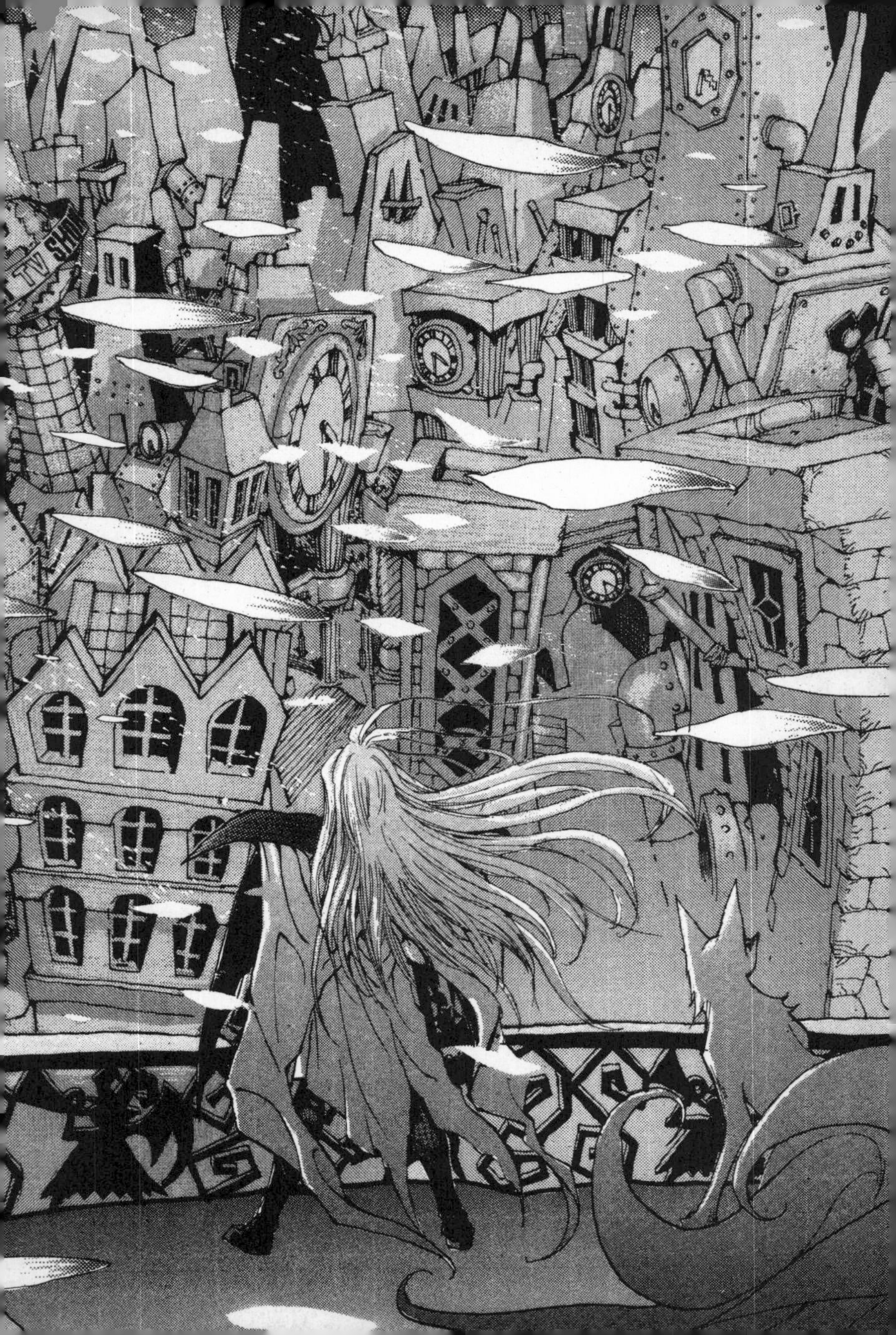
TV SH

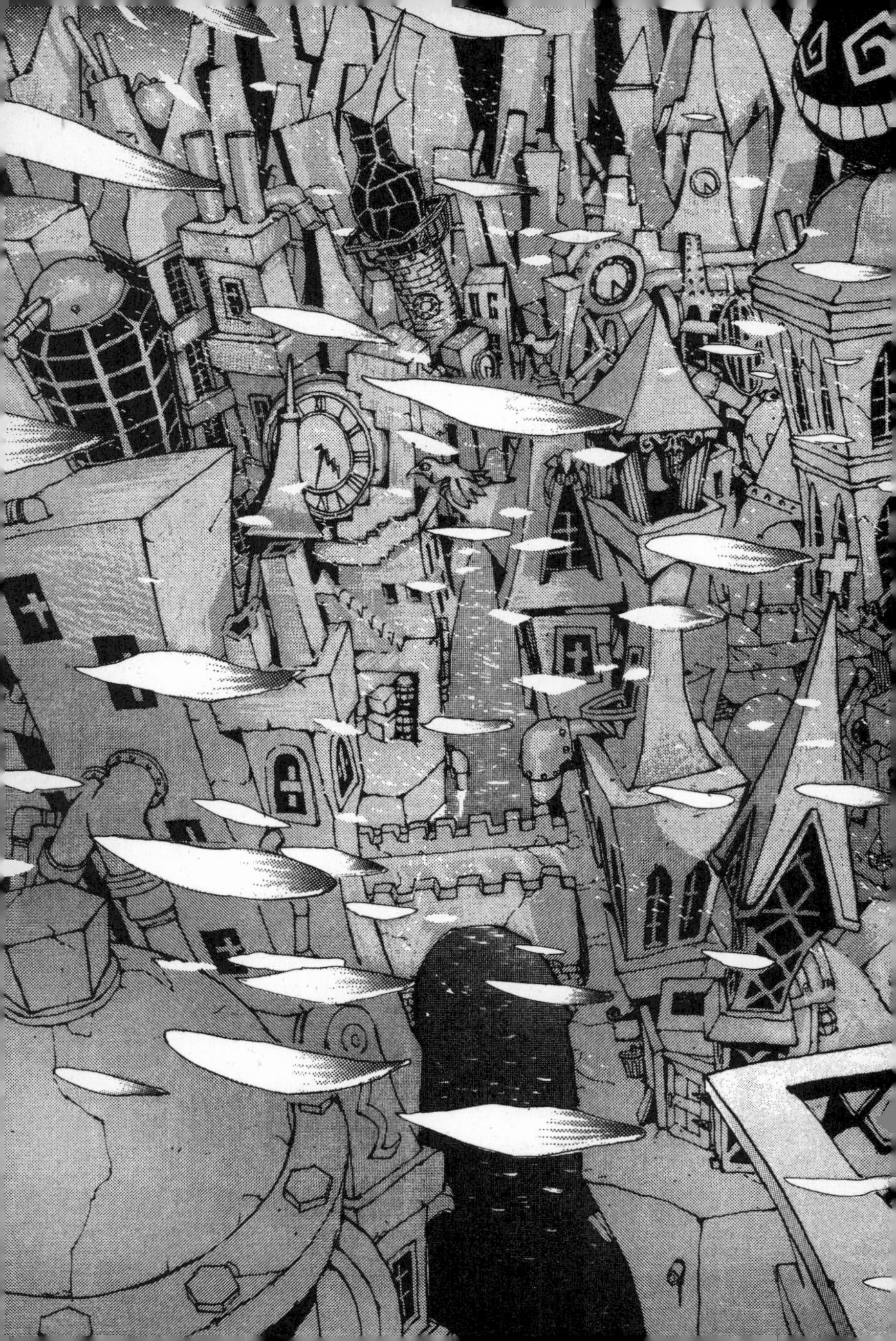

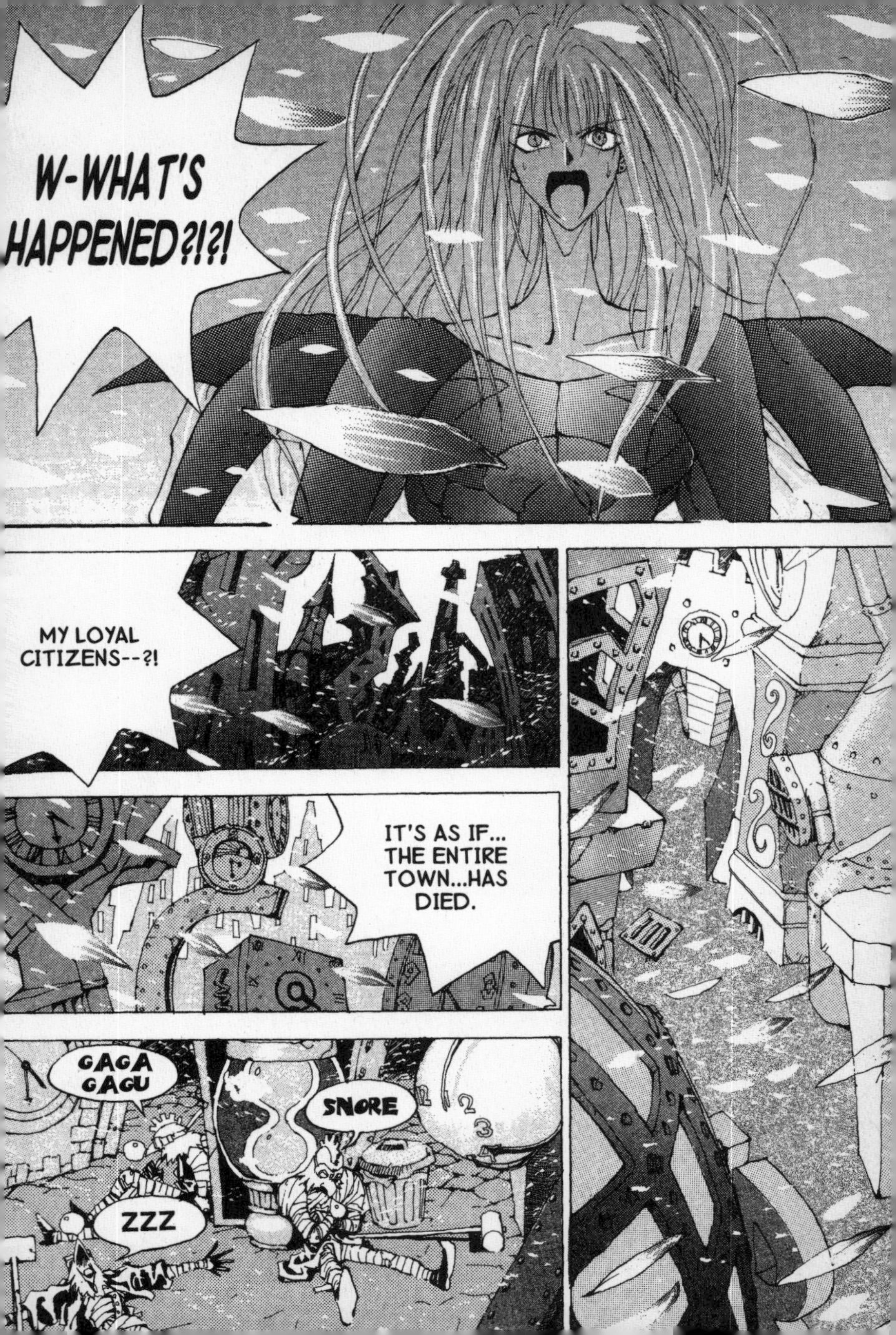
W-WHAT'S HAPPENED?!?!
MY LOYAL CITIZENS--?!
IT'S AS IF... THE ENTIRE TOWN...HAS DIED.
SNORE
GAGA GAGU
ZZZ

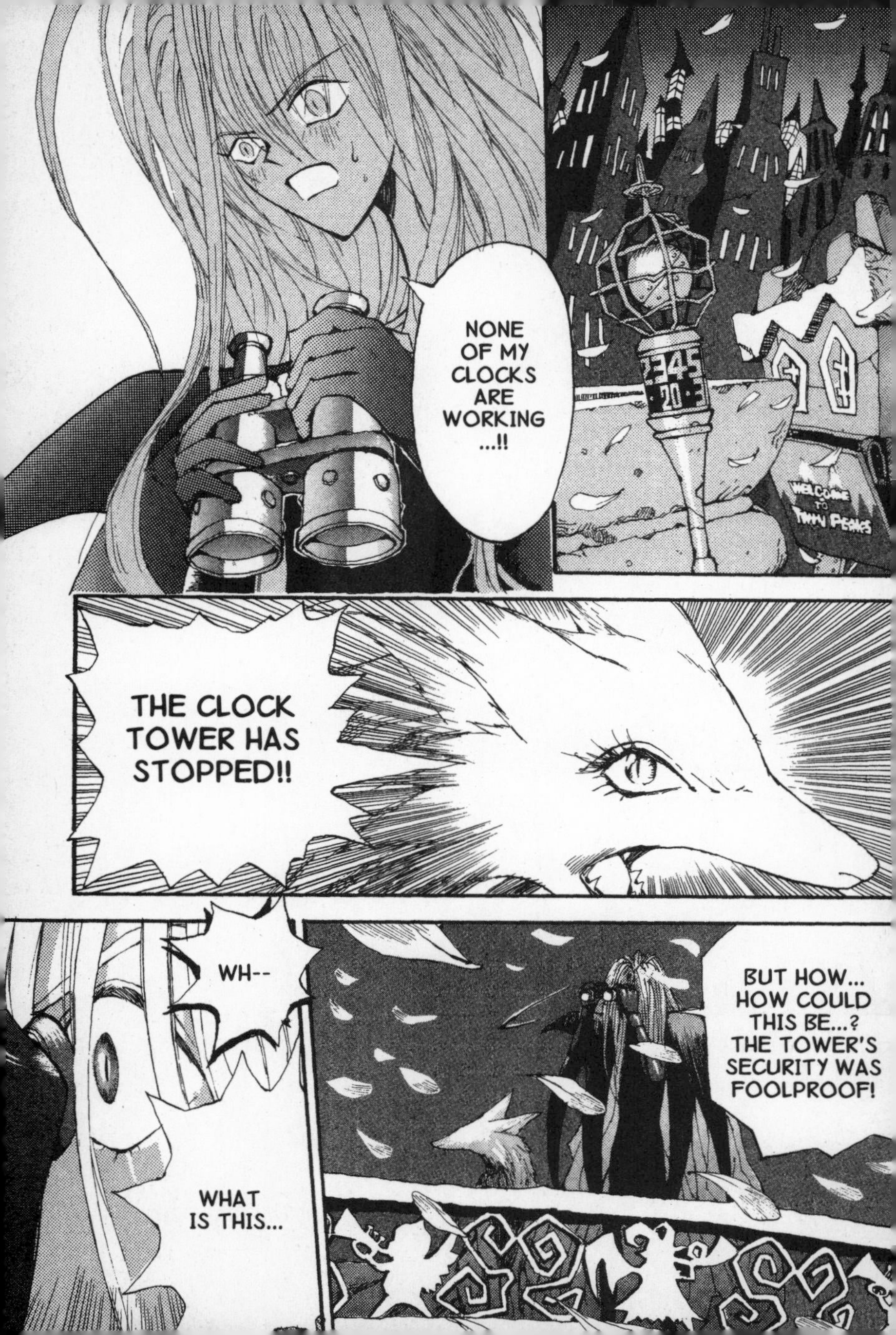
WELCOME TO TWIN PEAKS
NONE OF MY CLOCKS ARE WORKING ...!!
THE CLOCK TOWER HAS STOPPED!!
BUT HOW... HOW COULD THIS BE...? THE TOWER'S SECURITY WAS FOOLPROOF!
WH--
WHAT IS THIS...

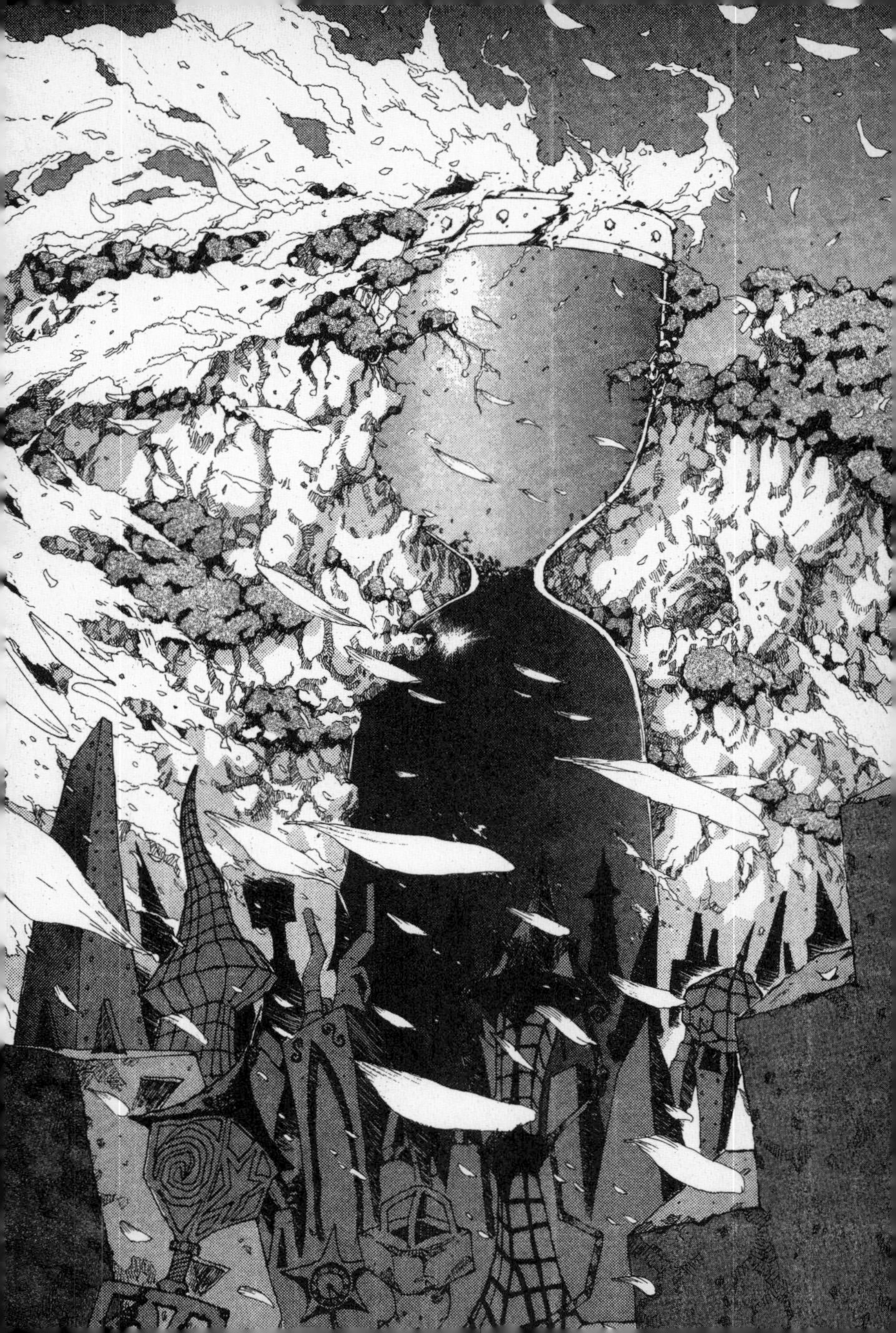

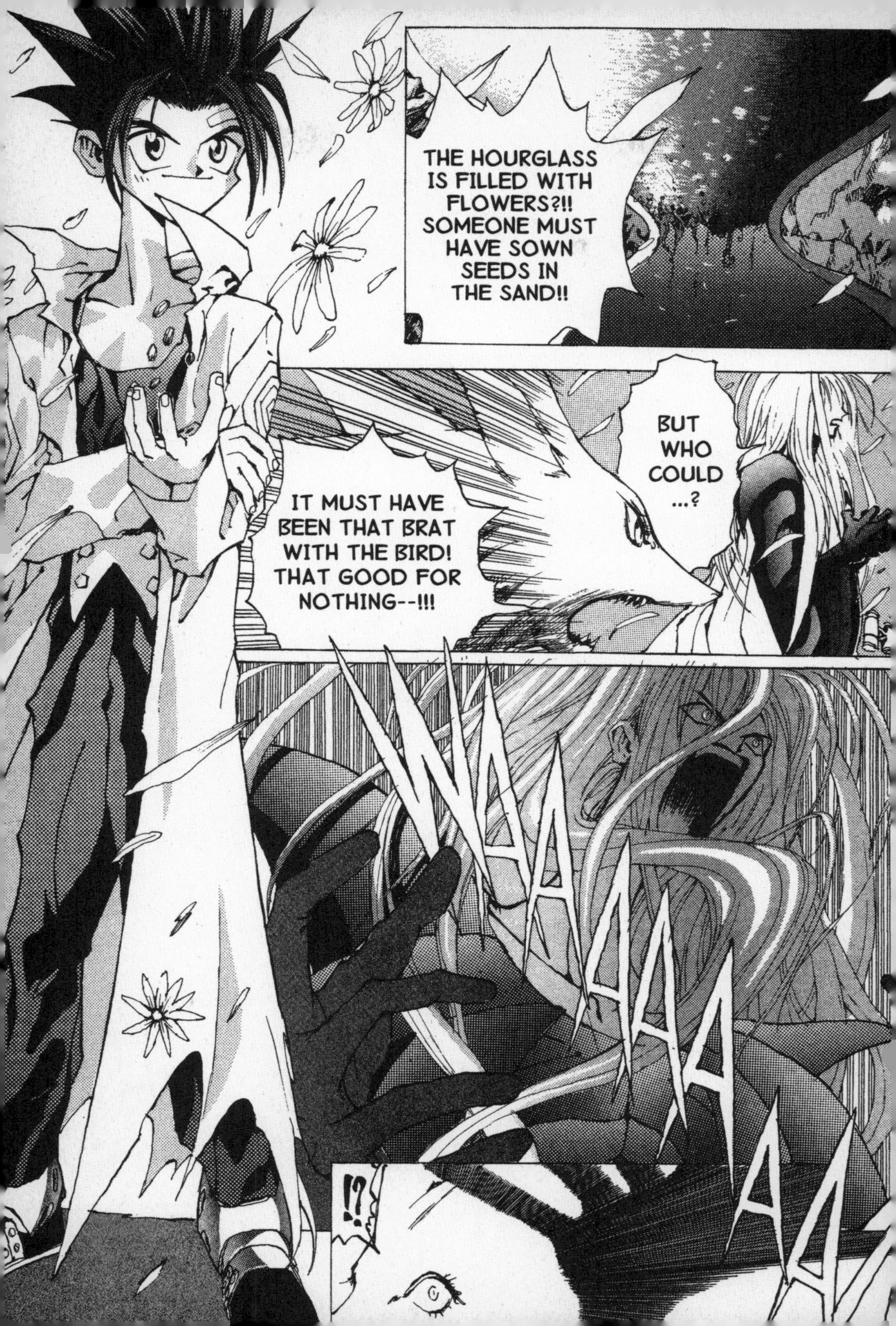
THE HOURGLASS IS FILLED WITH FLOWERS?!! SOMEONE MUST HAVE SOWN SEEDS IN THE SAND!!
BUT WHO COULD ...?
IT MUST HAVE BEEN THAT BRAT WITH THE BIRD! THAT GOOD FOR NOTHING--!!!
WAAAAAAAAA
!?

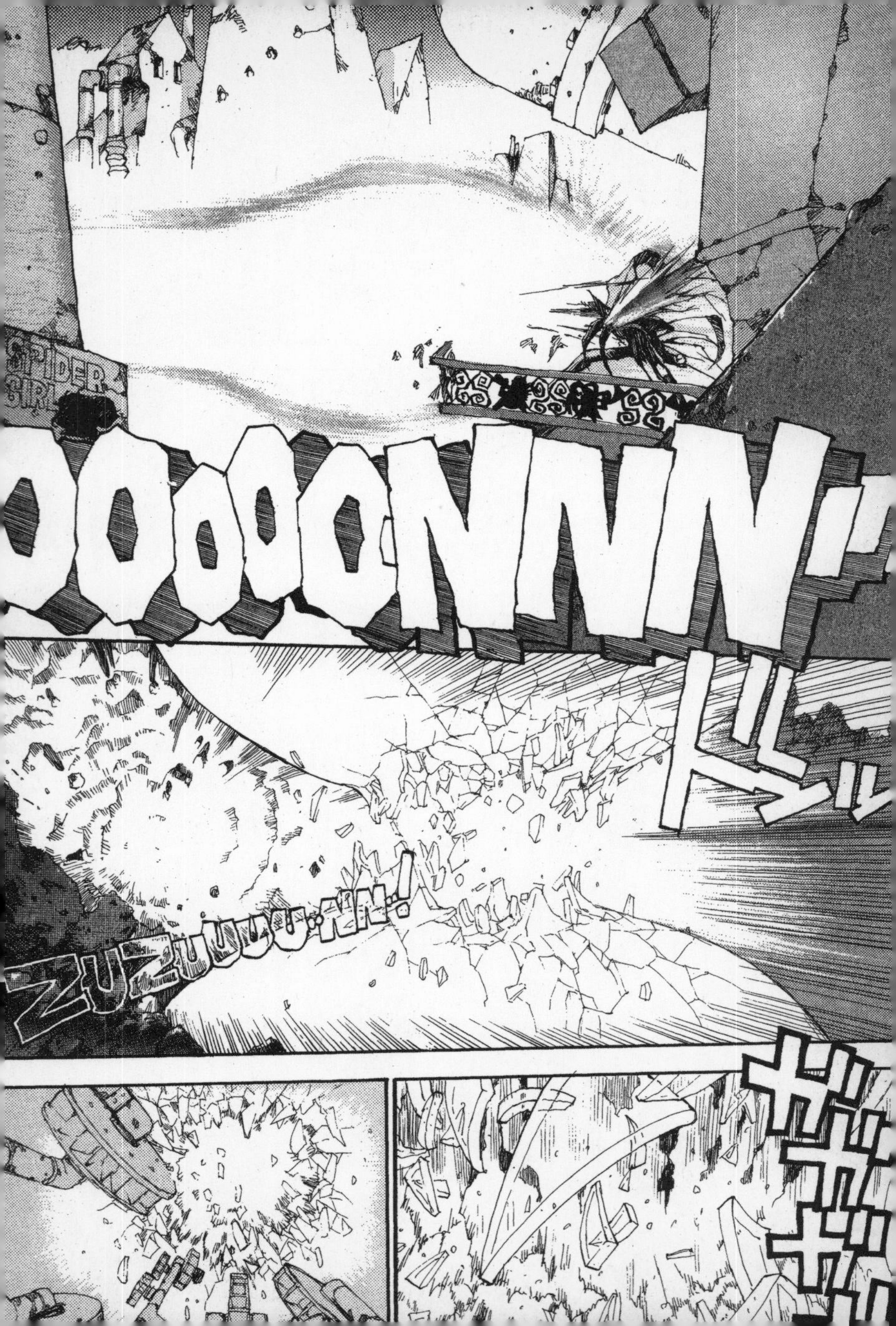
SPIDER GIRL
OOOOO-NNN!!
ドッ
ZUZUUUU-NN!
ガガガガ

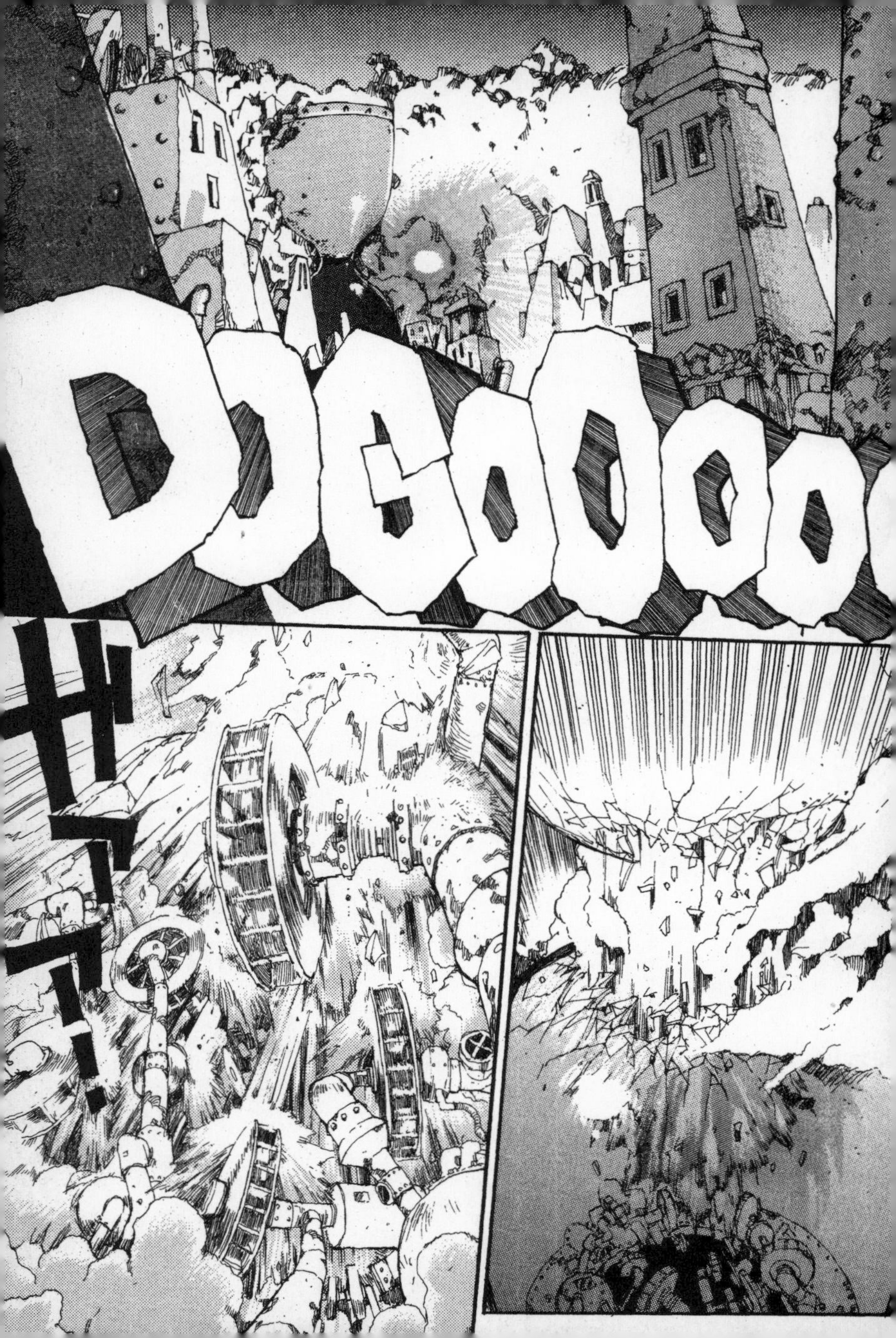
DOGOOOOO

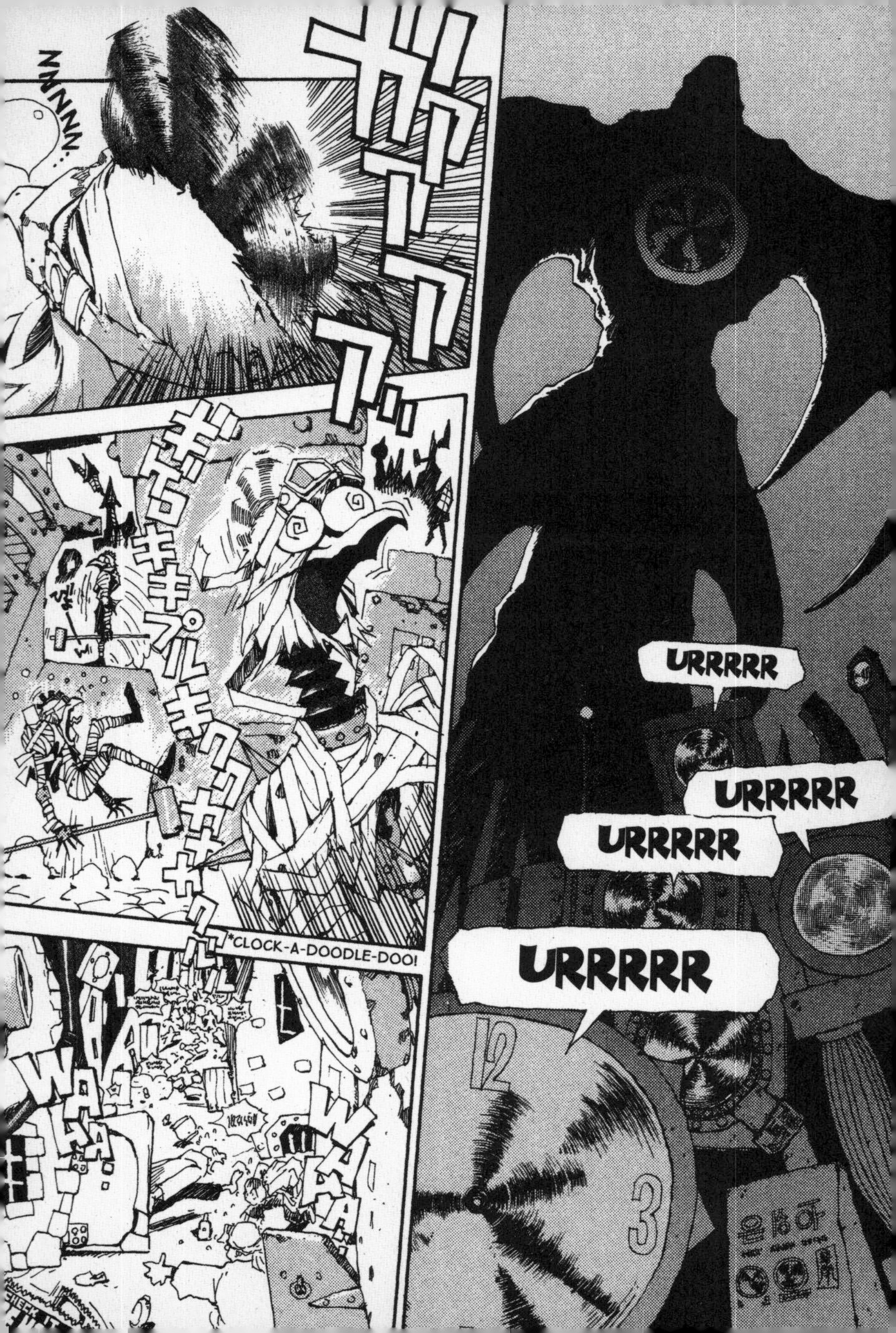
URRRRR
URRRRR
URRRRR
URRRRR
*CLOCK-A-DOODLE-DOO!

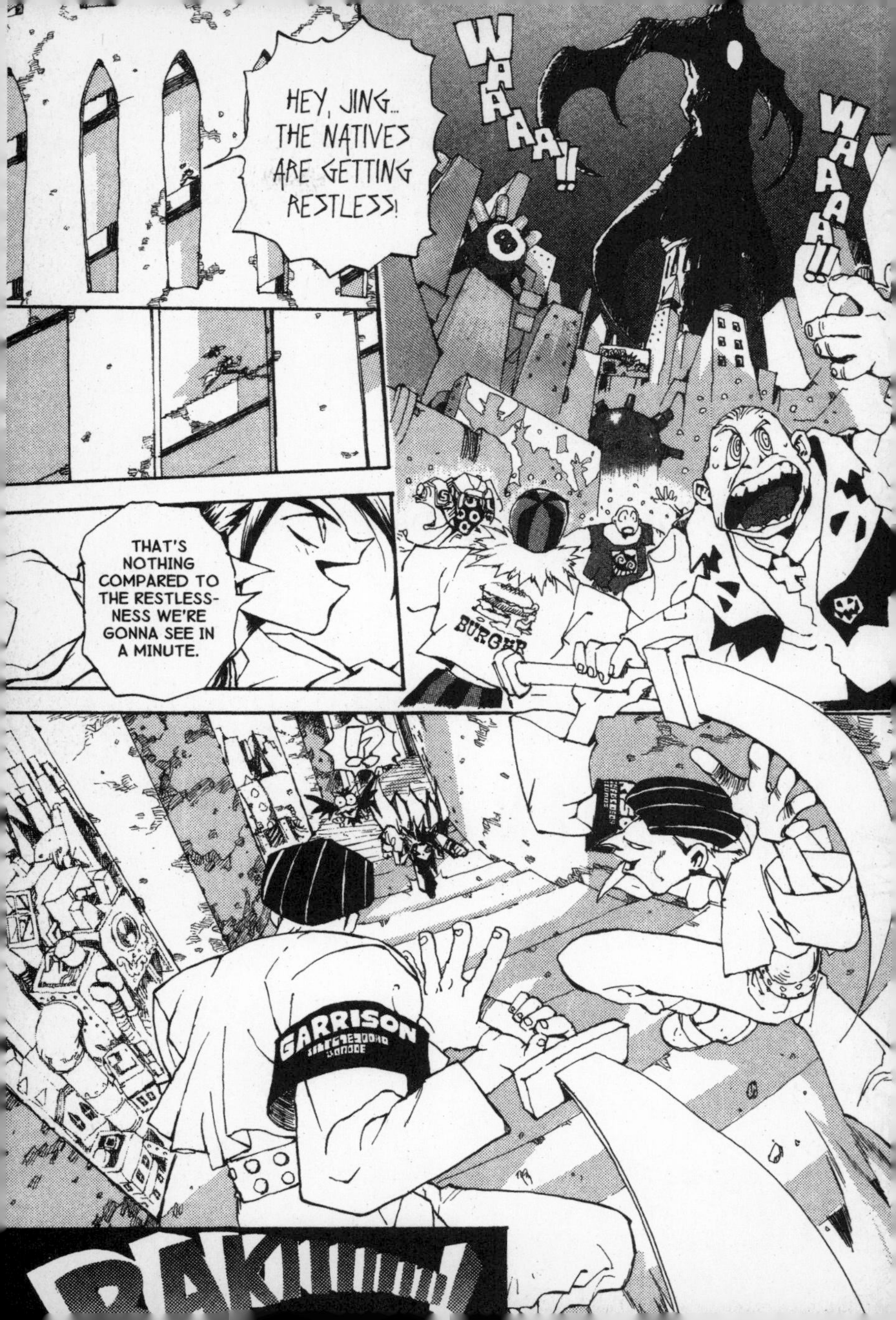
WAAAA!!
WAAAA!!
HEY, JING... THE NATIVES ARE GETTING RESTLESS!
THAT'S NOTHING COMPARED TO THE RESTLESSNESS WE'RE GONNA SEE IN A MINUTE.
BURGER
GARRISON
BAK!!!!!!!

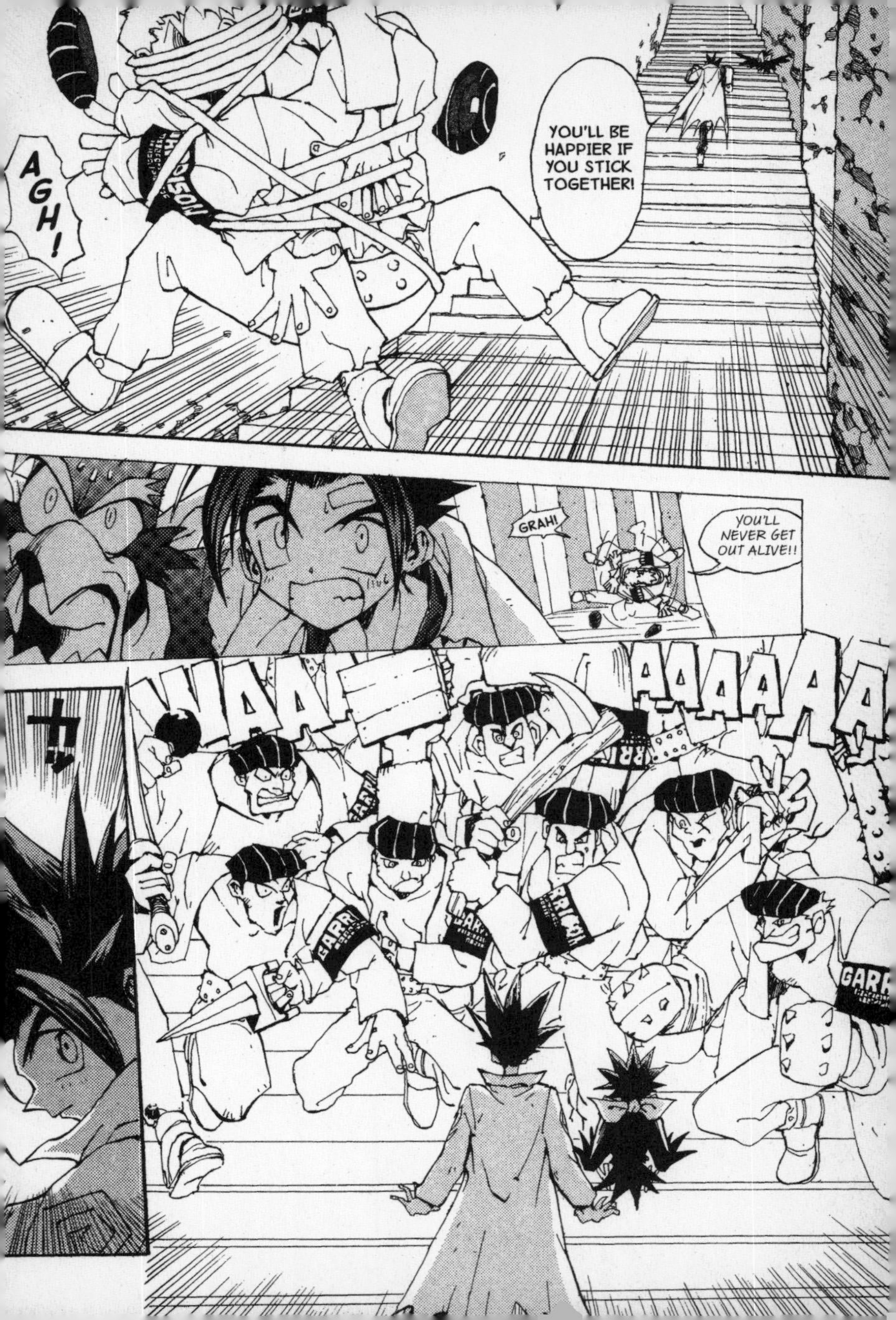
YOU'LL BE HAPPIER IF YOU STICK TOGETHER!
AGH!
YOU'LL NEVER GET OUT ALIVE!!
GRAH!
WAA—AAAAAA

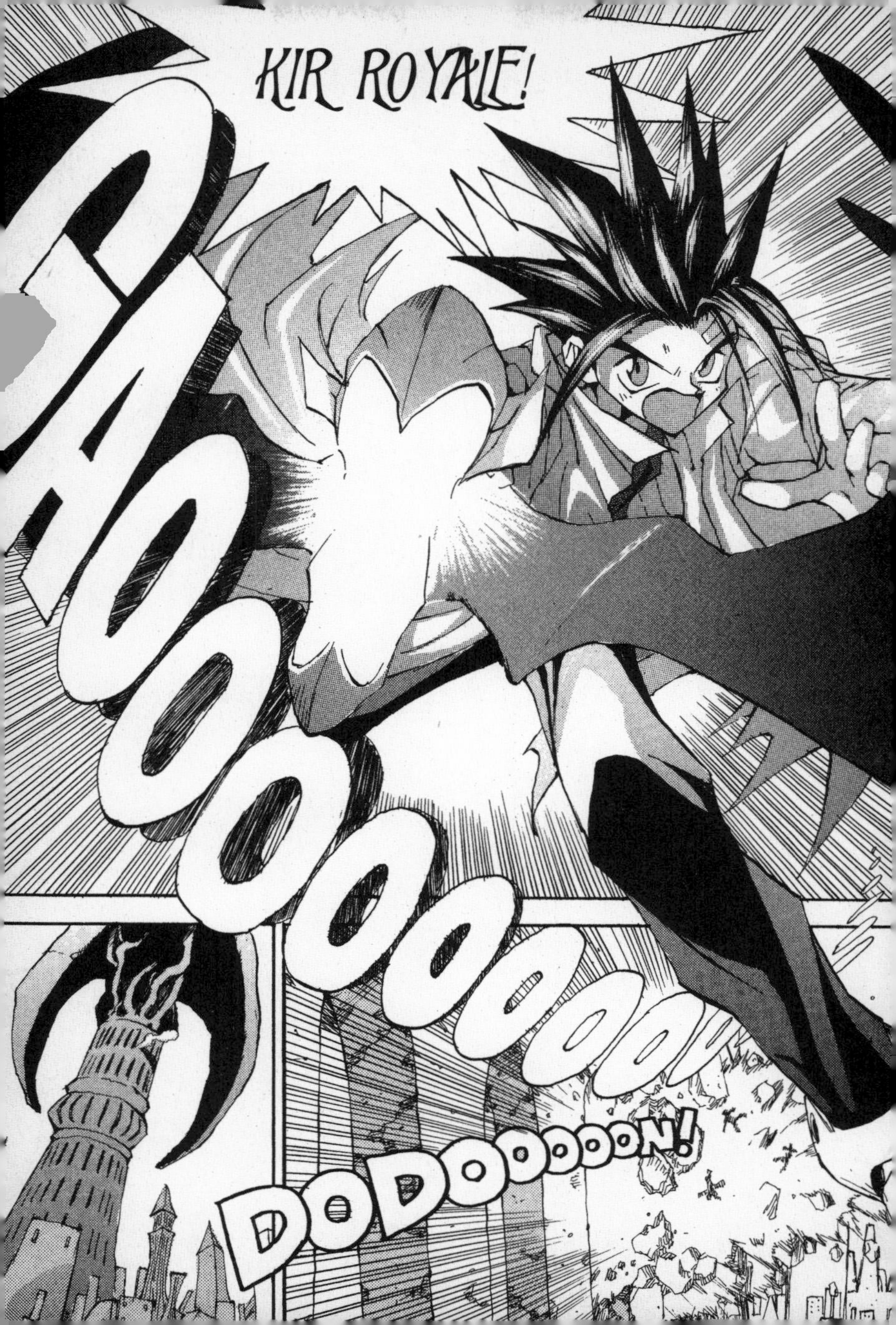
KIR ROYALE!
GOOOOOOOO!
DODOOOOOON!

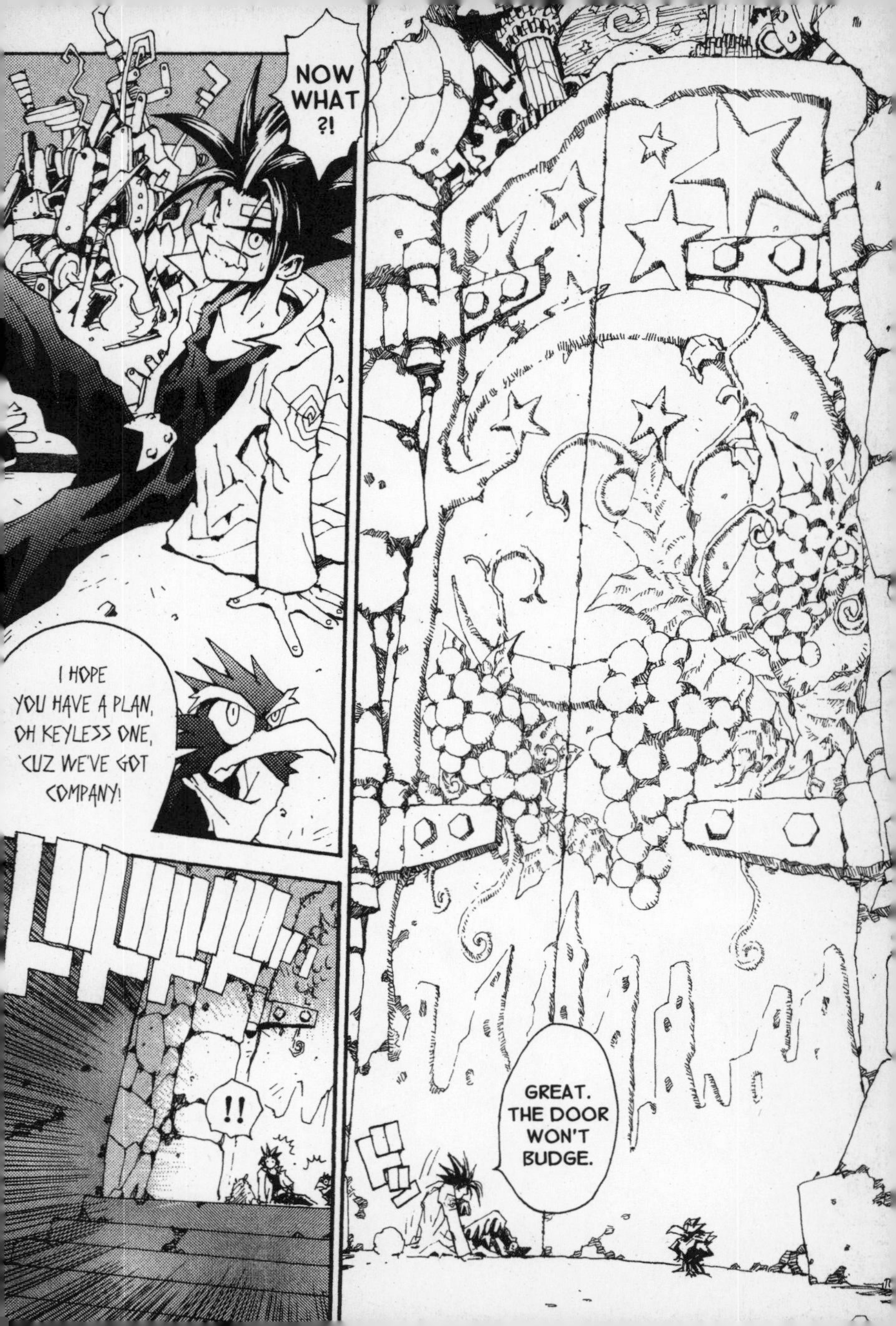
GREAT. THE DOOR WON'T BUDGE.
NOW WHAT ?!
I HOPE YOU HAVE A PLAN, OH KEYLESS ONE, 'CUZ WE'VE GOT COMPANY!
!!

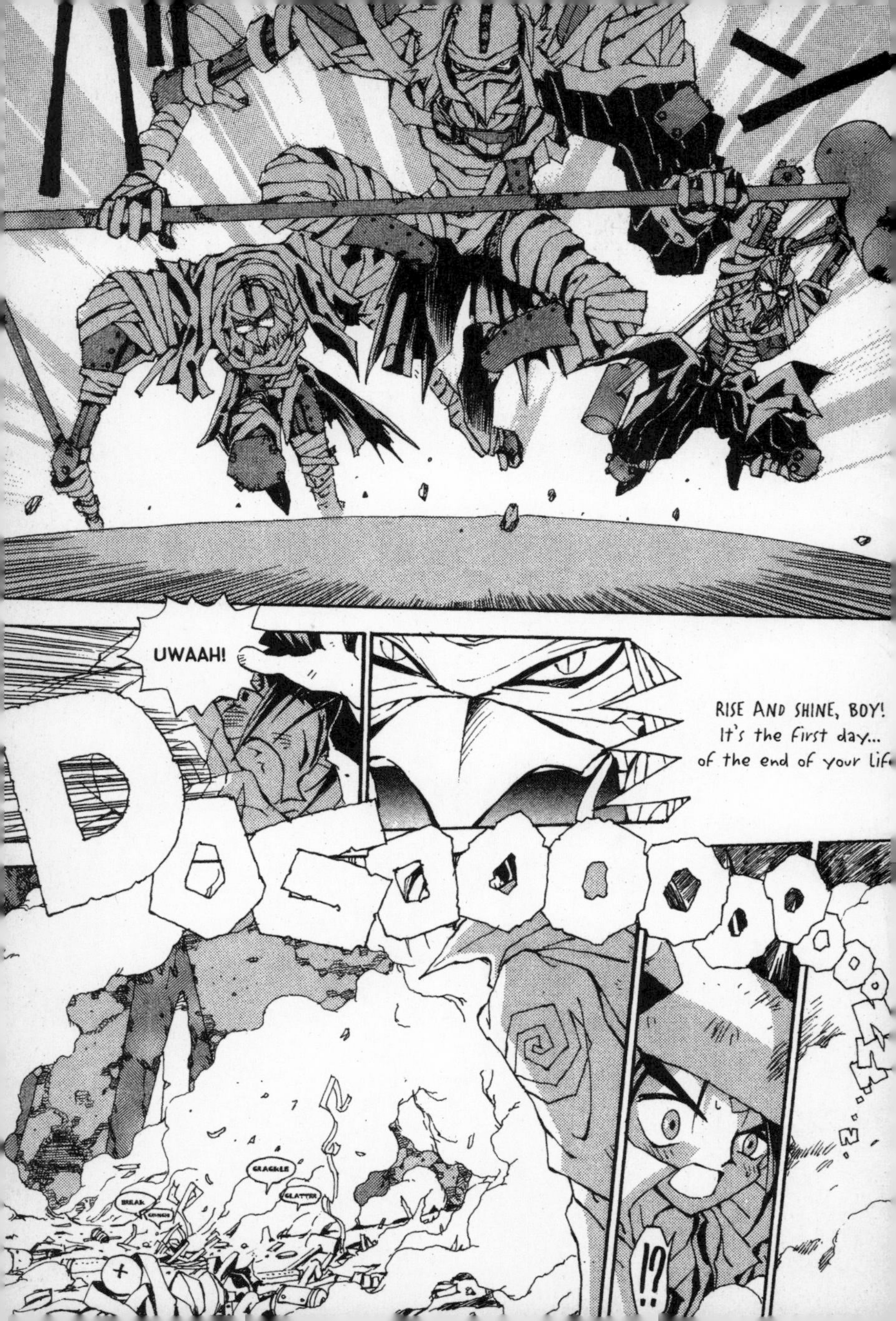
RISE AND SHINE, BOY! It's the first day... of the end of your lif
UWAAH!
DO-OOOOOOOOOOOOOMN
CRACKLE
CLATTER
BREAK
CRUNCH
!?

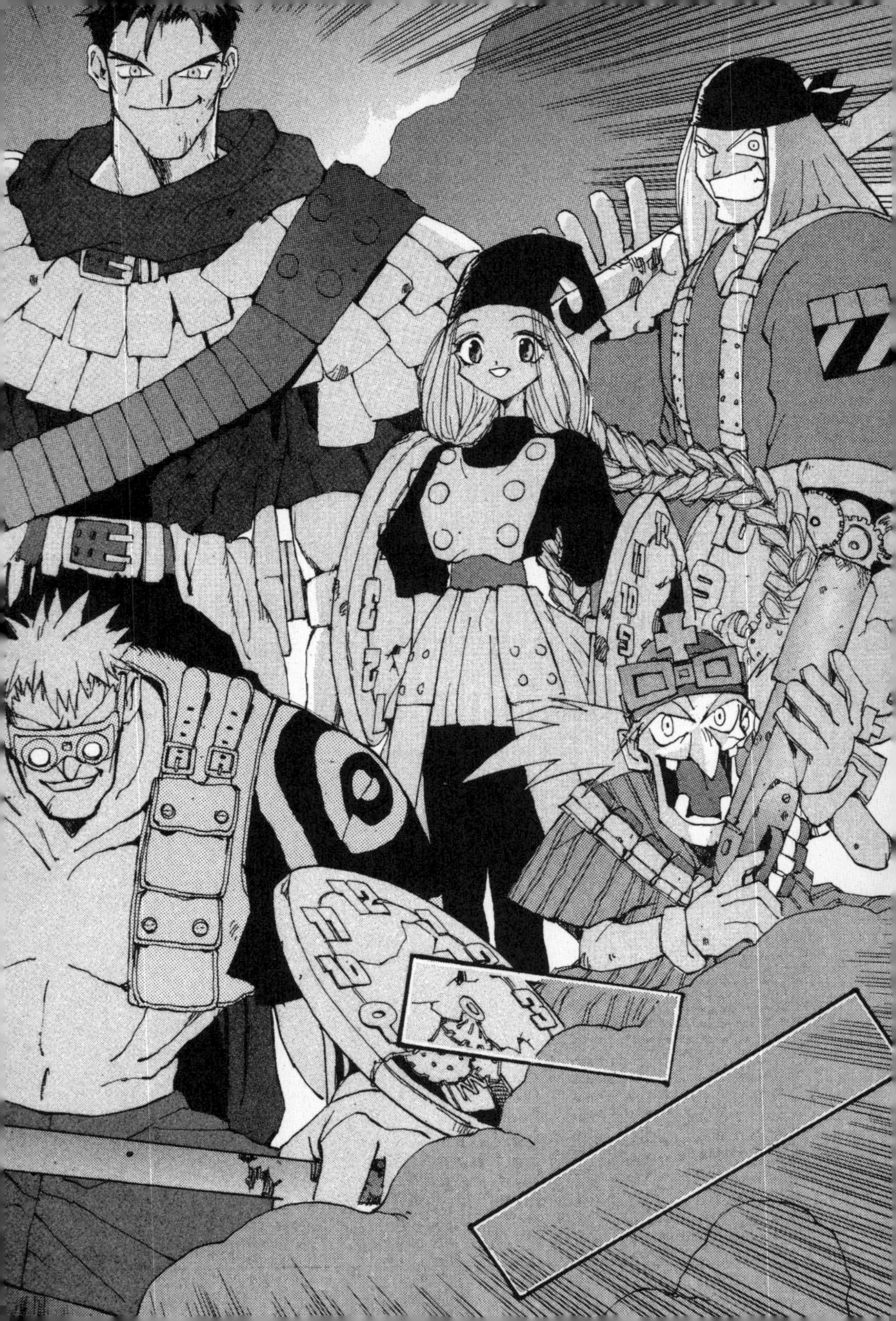

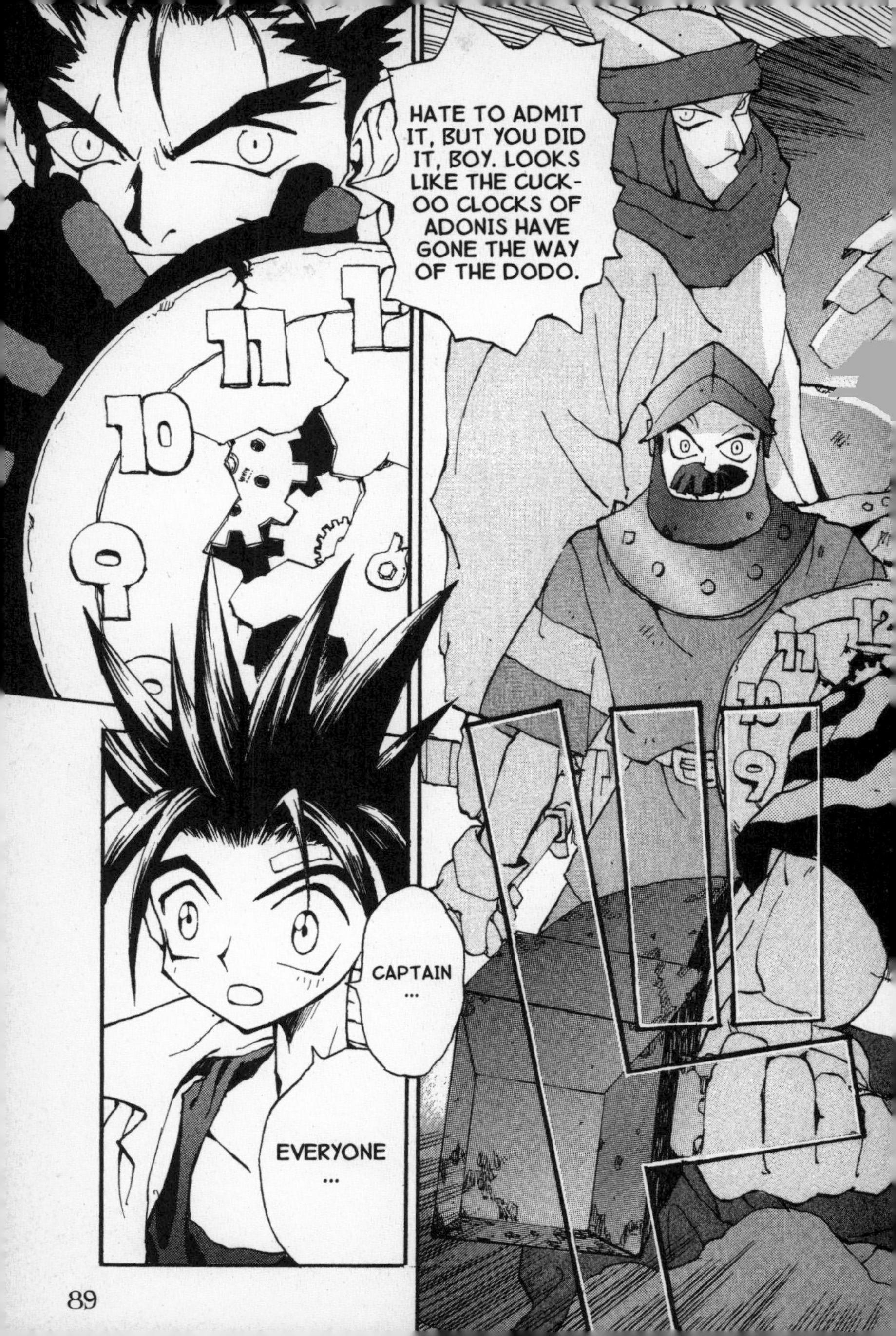
HATE TO ADMIT IT, BUT YOU DID IT, BOY. LOOKS LIKE THE CUCK-OO CLOCKS OF ADONIS HAVE GONE THE WAY OF THE DODO.
CAPTAIN ...
EVERYONE ...

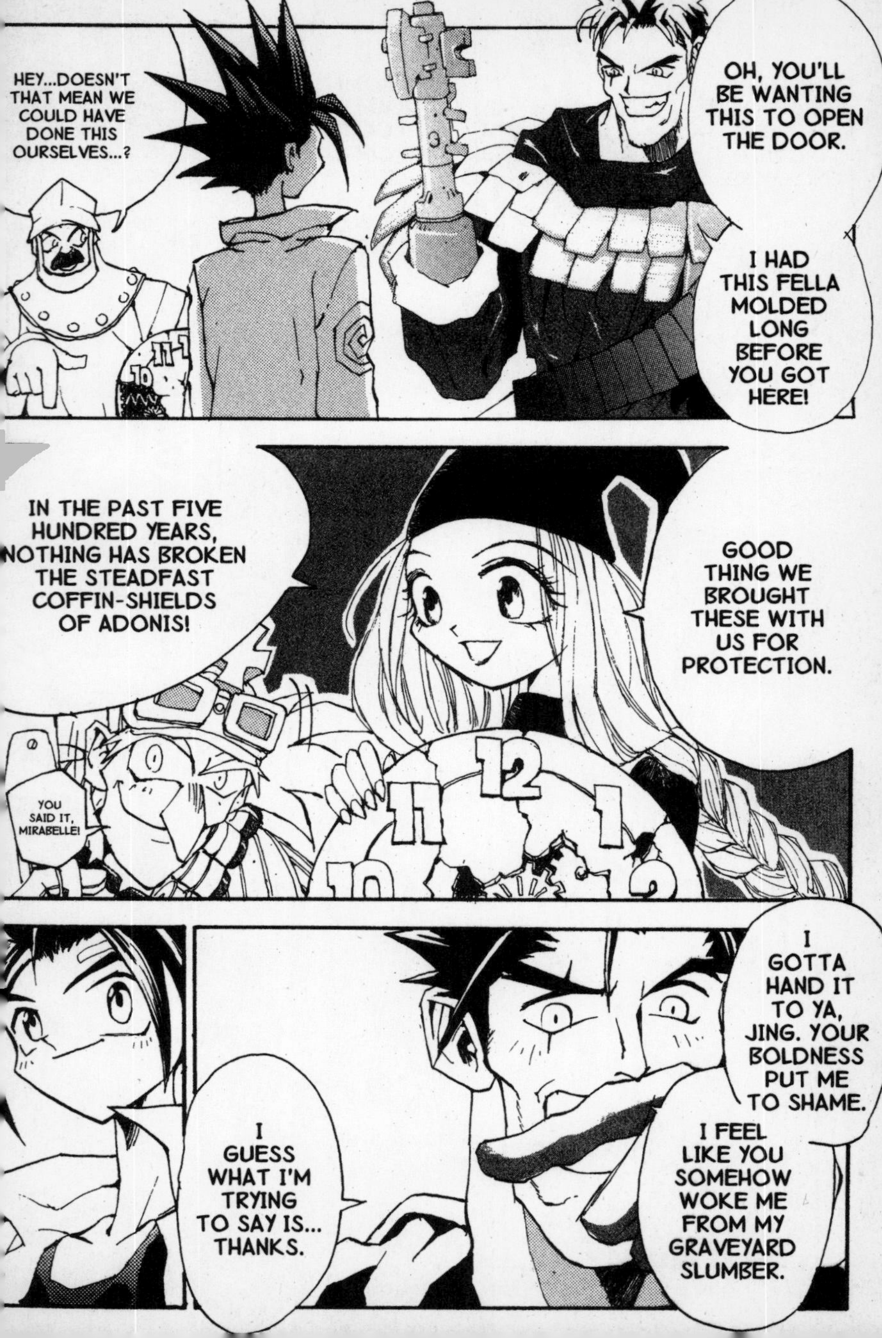
OH, YOU'LL BE WANTING THIS TO OPEN THE DOOR.
I HAD THIS FELLA MOLDED LONG BEFORE YOU GOT HERE!
HEY...DOESN'T THAT MEAN WE COULD HAVE DONE THIS OURSELVES...?
GOOD THING WE BROUGHT THESE WITH US FOR PROTECTION.
IN THE PAST FIVE HUNDRED YEARS, NOTHING HAS BROKEN THE STEADFAST COFFIN-SHIELDS OF ADONIS!
YOU SAID IT, MIRABELLE!
I GOTTA HAND IT TO YA, JING. YOUR BOLDNESS PUT ME TO SHAME.
I FEEL LIKE YOU SOMEHOW WOKE ME FROM MY GRAVEYARD SLUMBER.
I GUESS WHAT I'M TRYING TO SAY IS... THANKS.

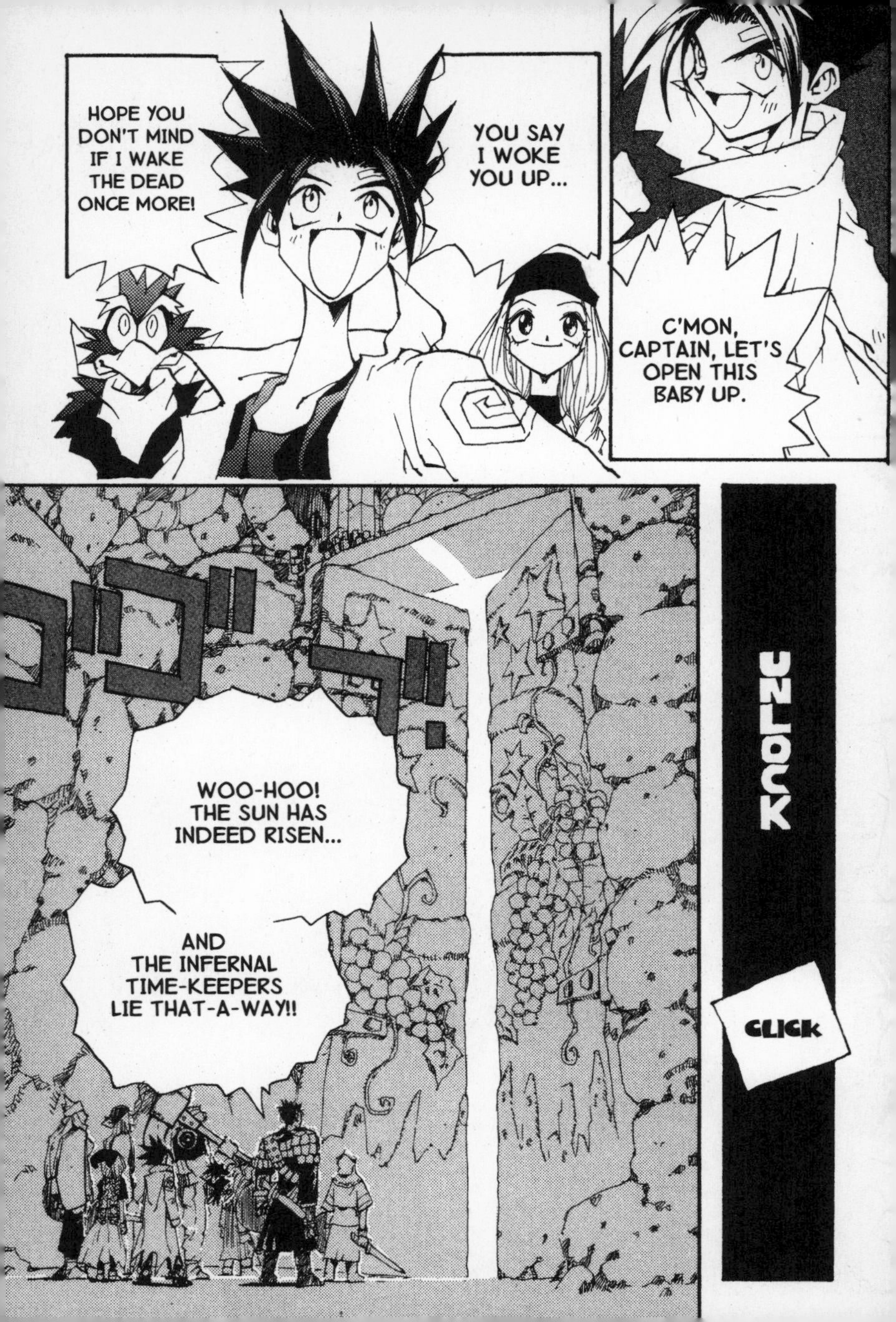
C'MON, CAPTAIN, LET'S OPEN THIS BABY UP.
YOU SAY I WOKE YOU UP...
HOPE YOU DON'T MIND IF I WAKE THE DEAD ONCE MORE!
UNLOCK
CLICK
WOO-HOO! THE SUN HAS INDEED RISEN...
AND THE INFERNAL TIME-KEEPERS LIE THAT-A-WAY!!

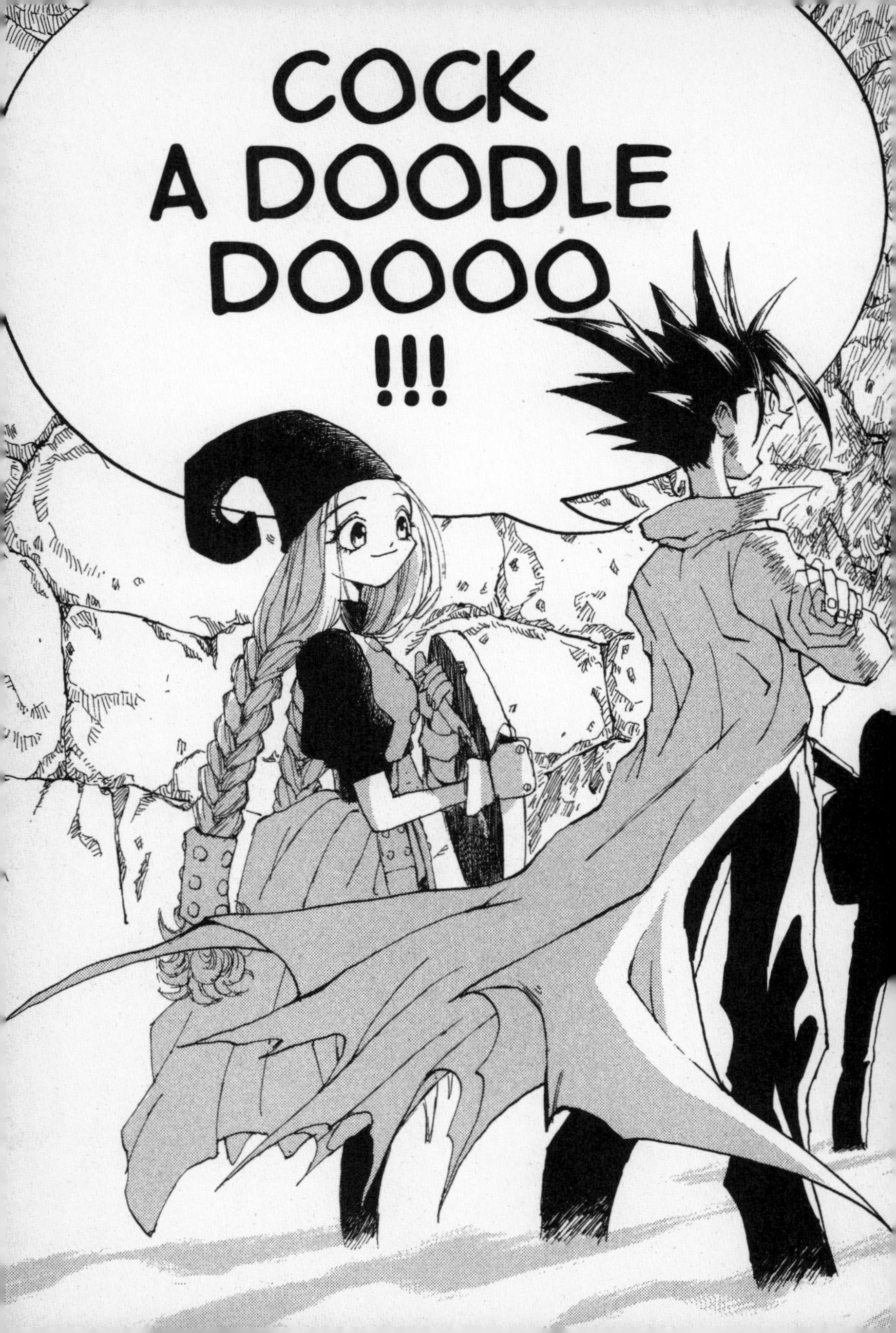
COCK A DOODLE DOOOOO !!!

GRAPE STEPPING SONG

Hey, step! C'mon, step!!
It's time to pluck some clockwork grapes
And wake this town of timely slaves

Do it, step! Do that step!!
No time to be carefree or sleep
Check the barrel—up time creeps

Hey, step! C'mon, step!!
Go round-n-round-n-round like gears
Wind up your courage, lose your fears

Do it, step! Do that step!!
Morning's coming, sure as tides
Without the clocks, the sun will rise!!!

(From the oral tradition
of the Imps of Adonis)

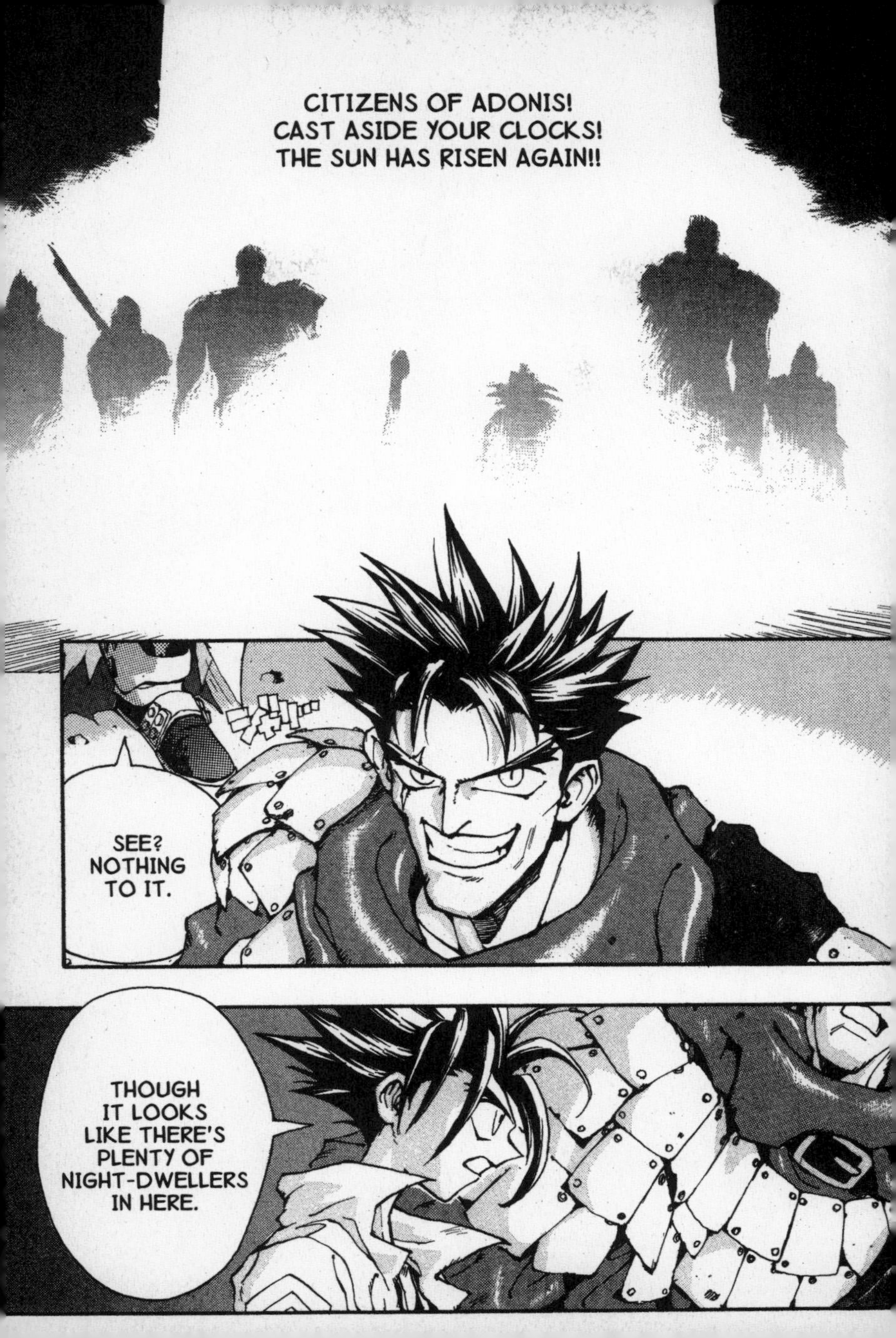
CITIZENS OF ADONIS! CAST ASIDE YOUR CLOCKS! THE SUN HAS RISEN AGAIN!!
SEE? NOTHING TO IT.
THOUGH IT LOOKS LIKE THERE'S PLENTY OF NIGHT-DWELLERS IN HERE.

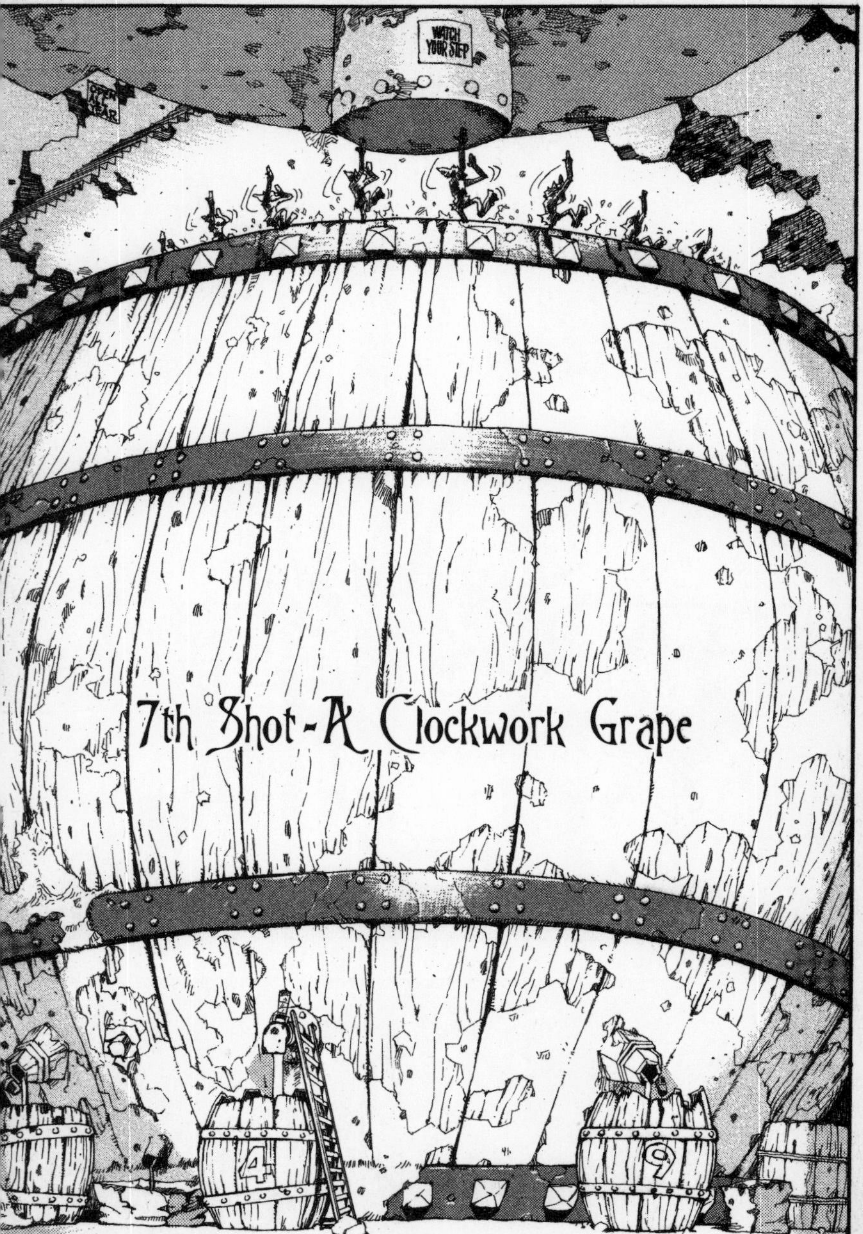
WATCH YOUR STEP
OPEN ALL YEAR
7th Shot - A Clockwork Grape
4
9

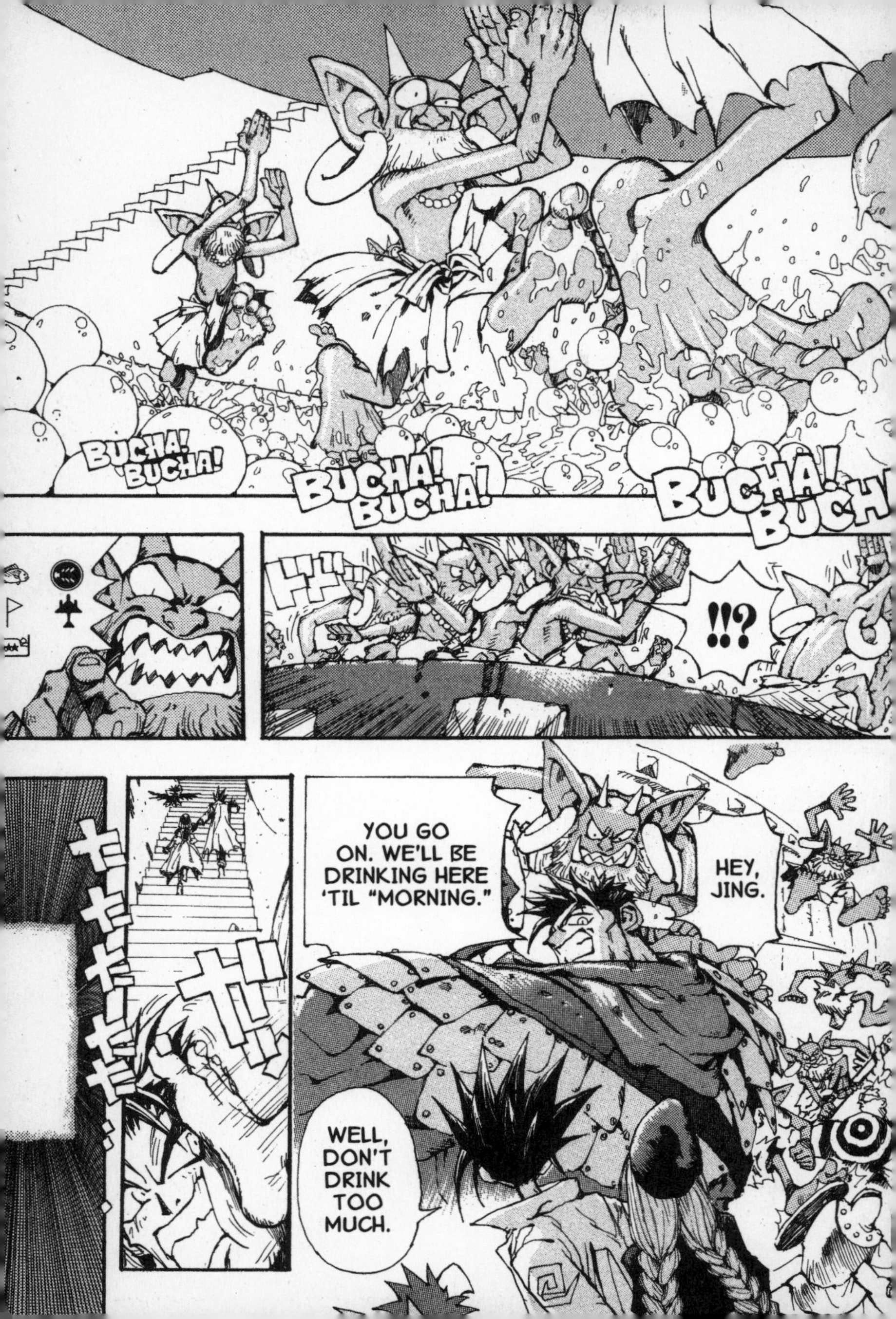
BUCHA! BUCH
BUCHA! BUCHA!
BUCHA! BUCHA!
!!?
HEY, JING.
YOU GO ON. WE'LL BE DRINKING HERE 'TIL "MORNING."
WELL, DON'T DRINK TOO MUCH.

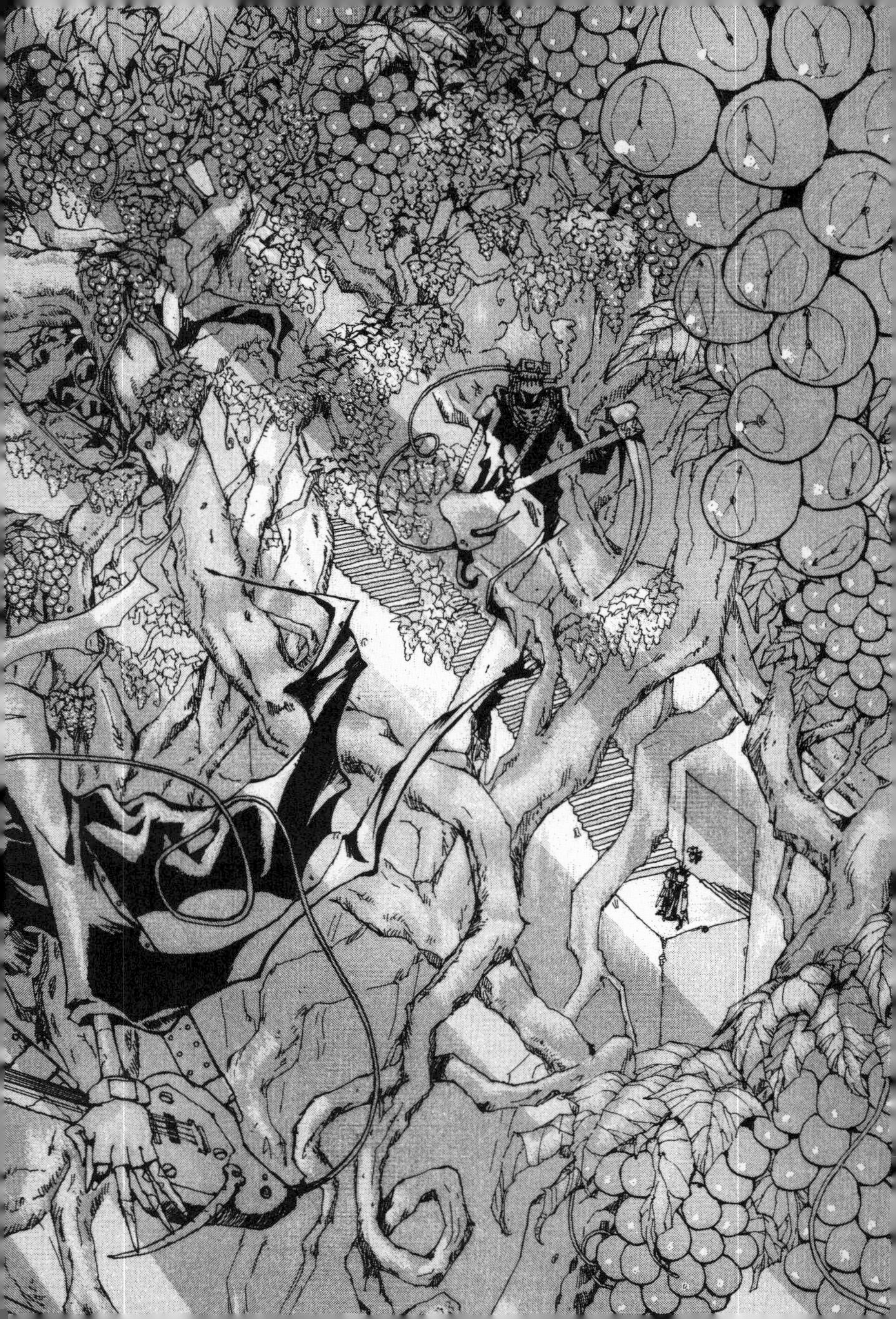

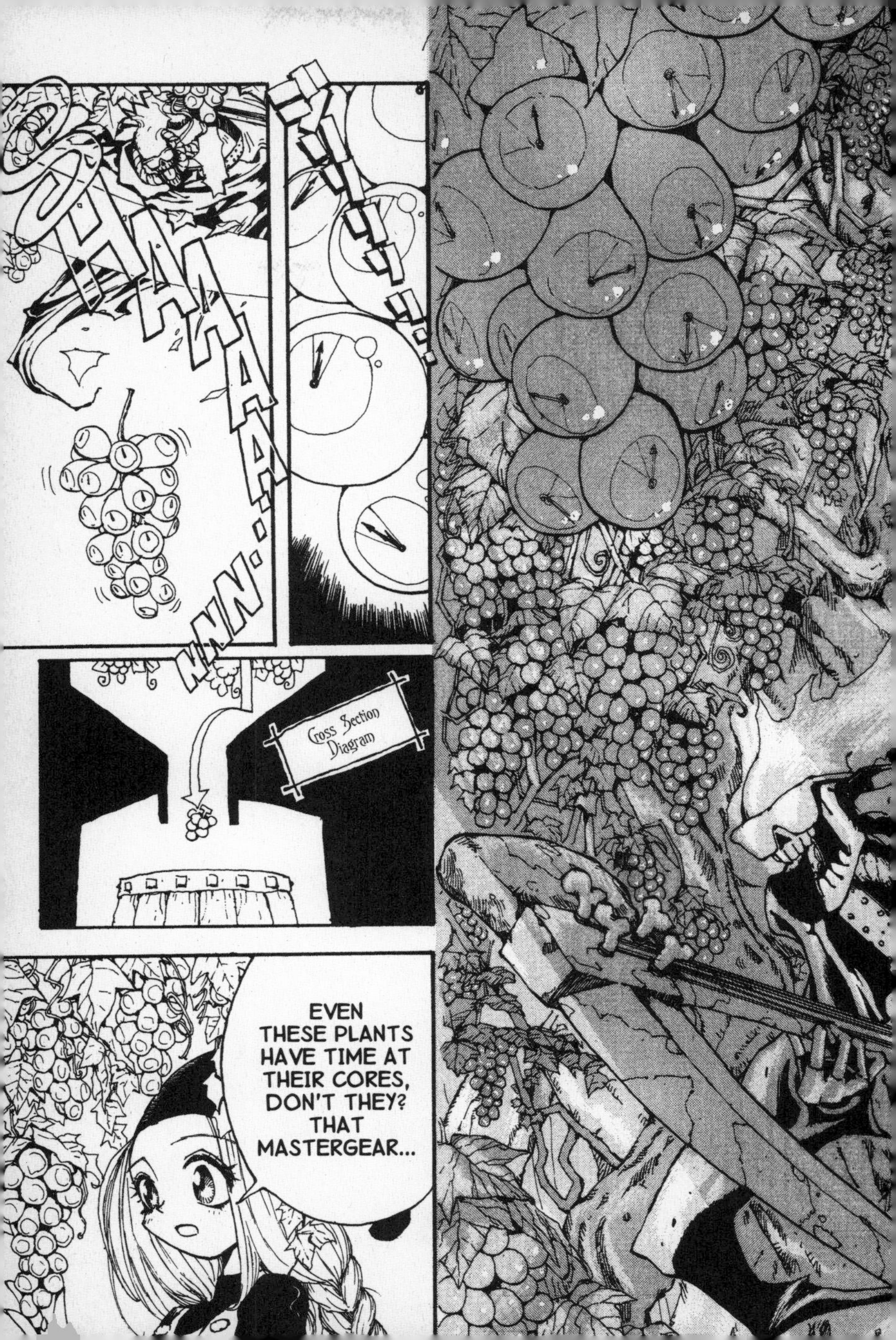
SHAAAA...NNN
Cross Section Diagram
EVEN THESE PLANTS HAVE TIME AT THEIR CORES, DON'T THEY? THAT MASTERGEAR...

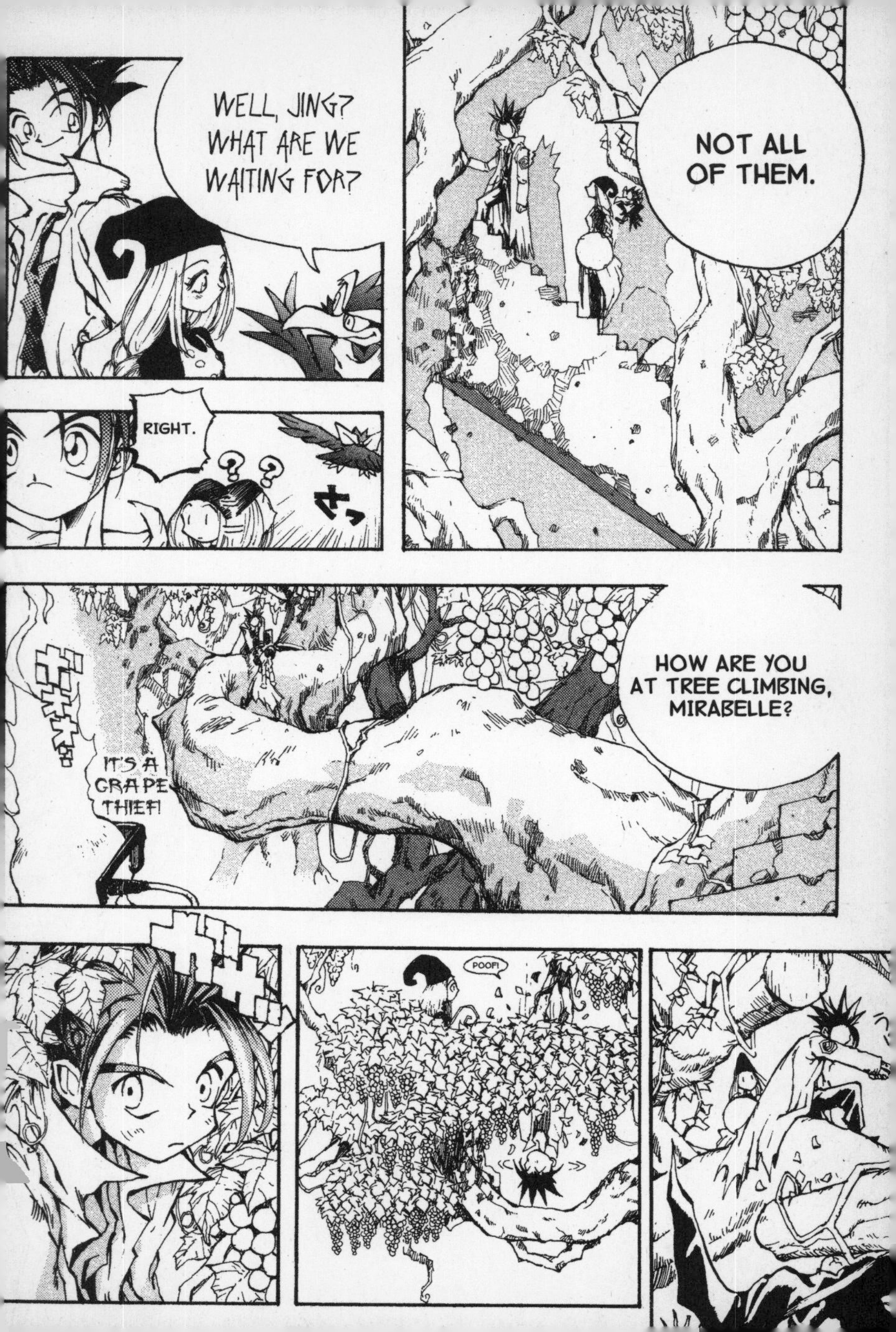
NOT ALL OF THEM.
WELL, JING? WHAT ARE WE WAITING FOR?
RIGHT.
さっ
HOW ARE YOU AT TREE CLIMBING, MIRABELLE?
IT'S A GRAPE THIEF!
POOF!

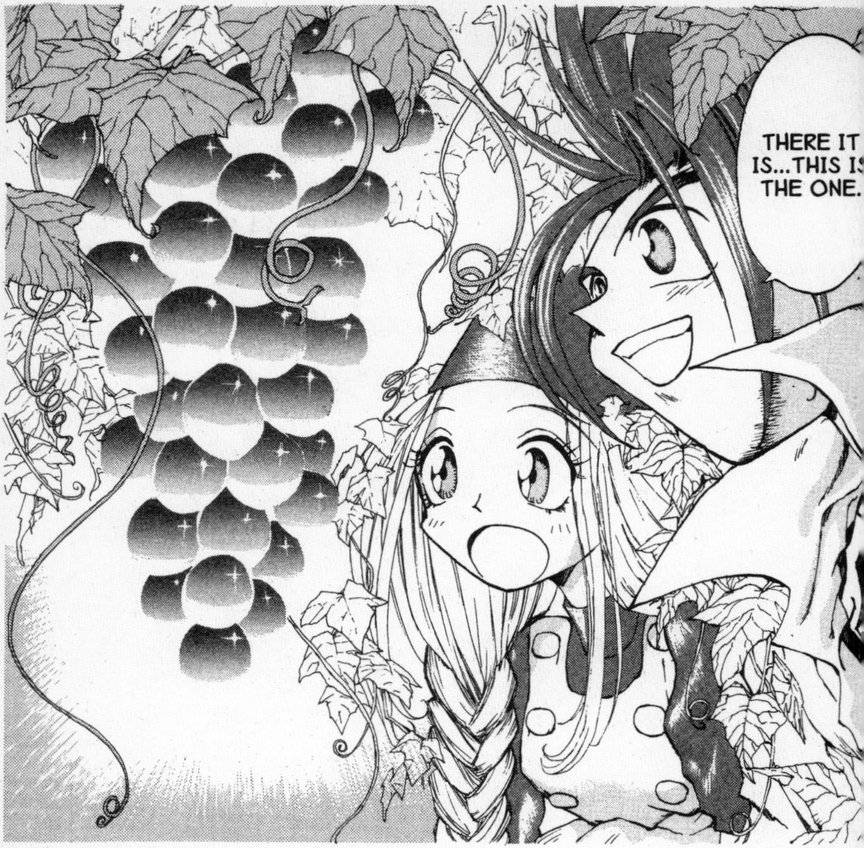
THERE IT IS...THIS IS THE ONE.

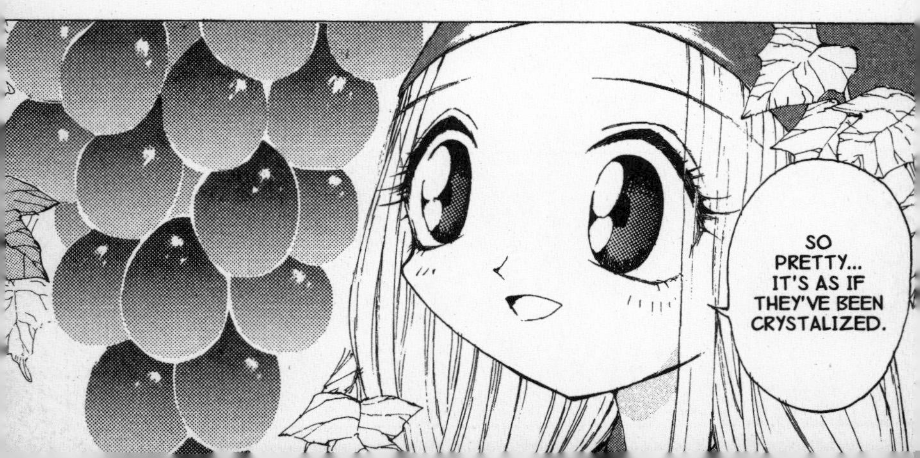
SO PRETTY... IT'S AS IF THEY'VE BEEN CRYSTALIZED.

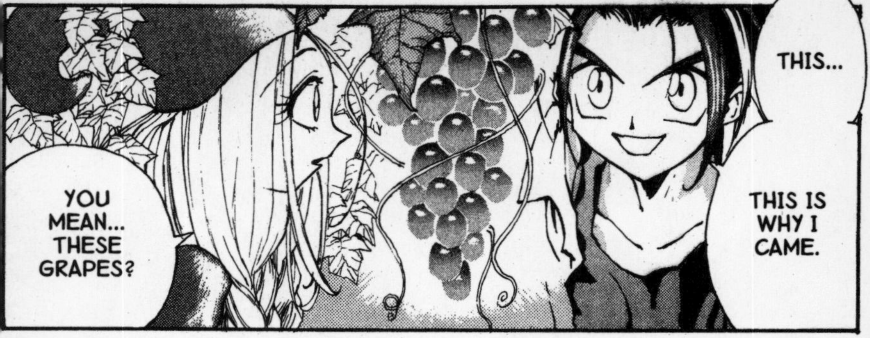
THIS...
THIS IS WHY I CAME.
YOU MEAN... THESE GRAPES?

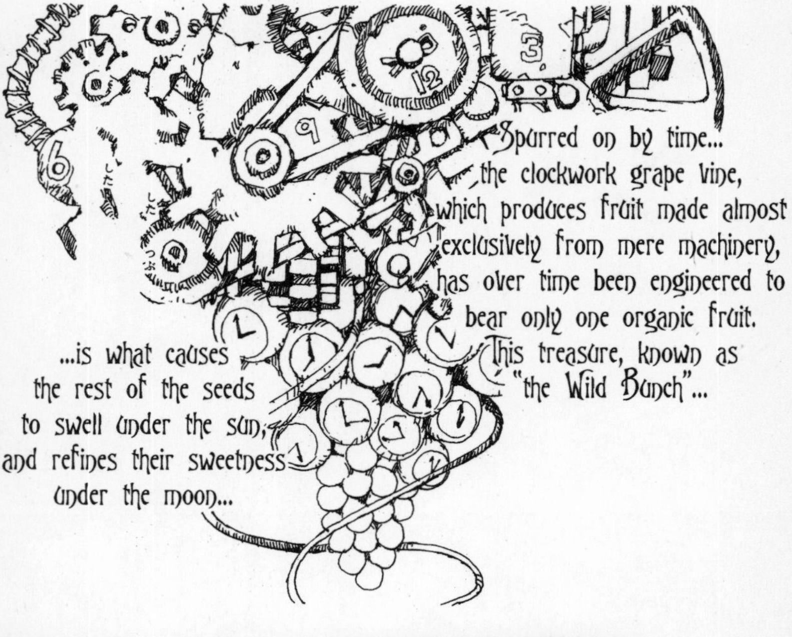
Spurred on by time... the clockwork grape vine, which produces fruit made almost exclusively from mere machinery, has over time been engineered to bear only one organic fruit. This treasure, known as "the Wild Bunch"...
...is what causes the rest of the seeds to swell under the sun, and refines their sweetness under the moon...

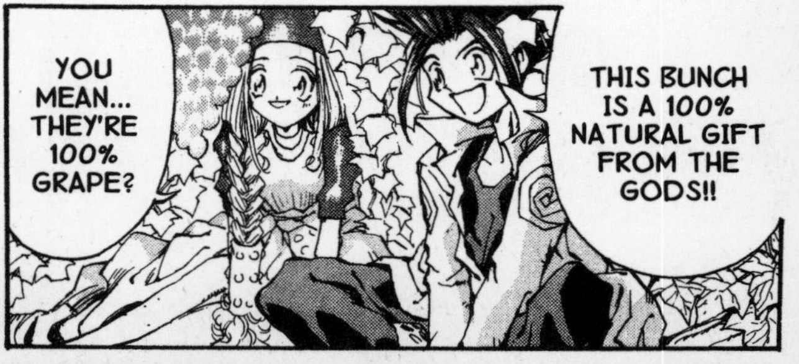
THIS BUNCH IS A 100% NATURAL GIFT FROM THE GODS!!
YOU MEAN... THEY'RE 100% GRAPE?

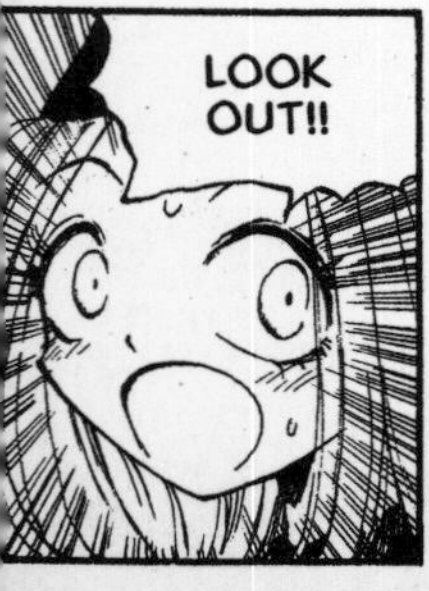
LOOK OUT!!

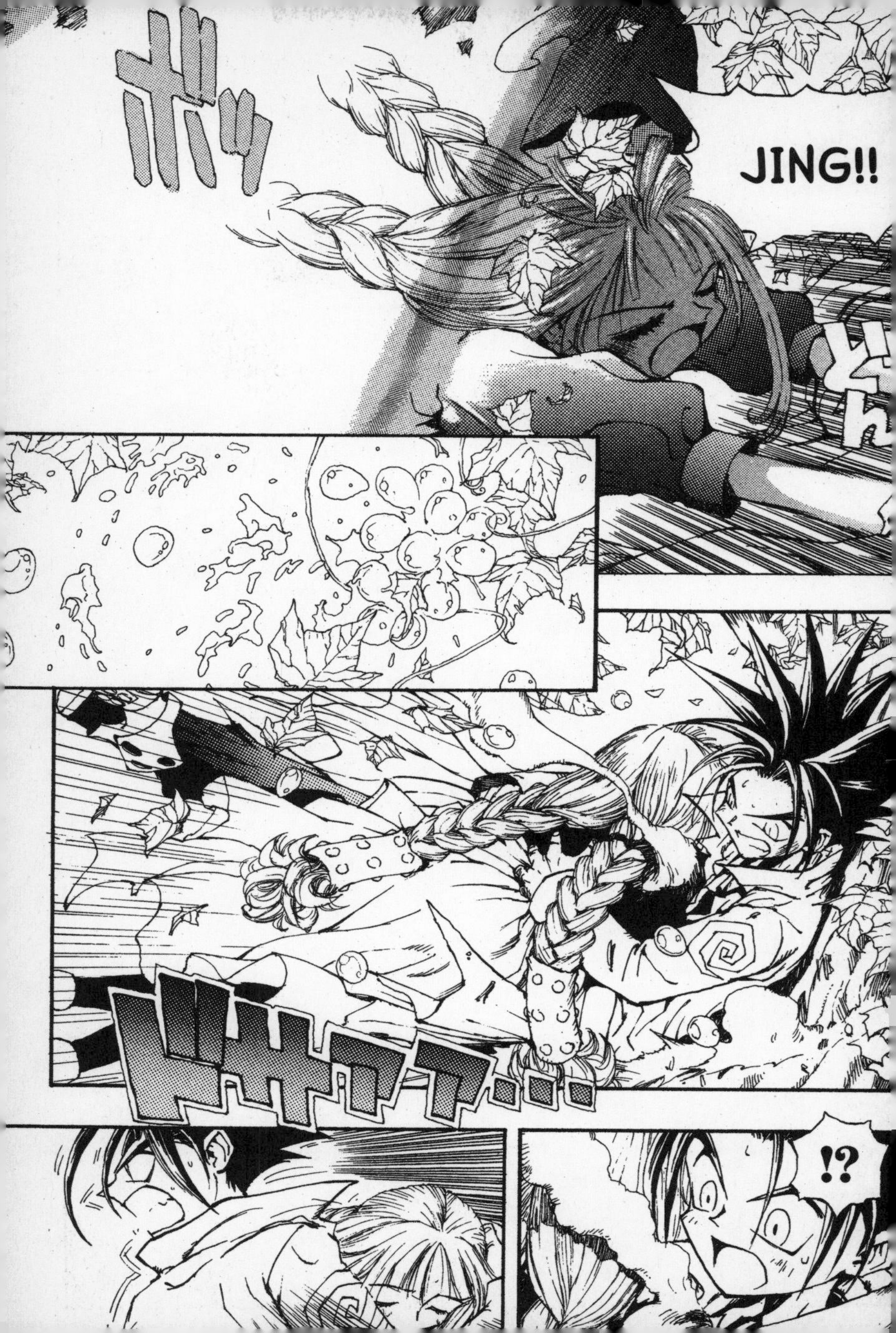
JING!!
!?

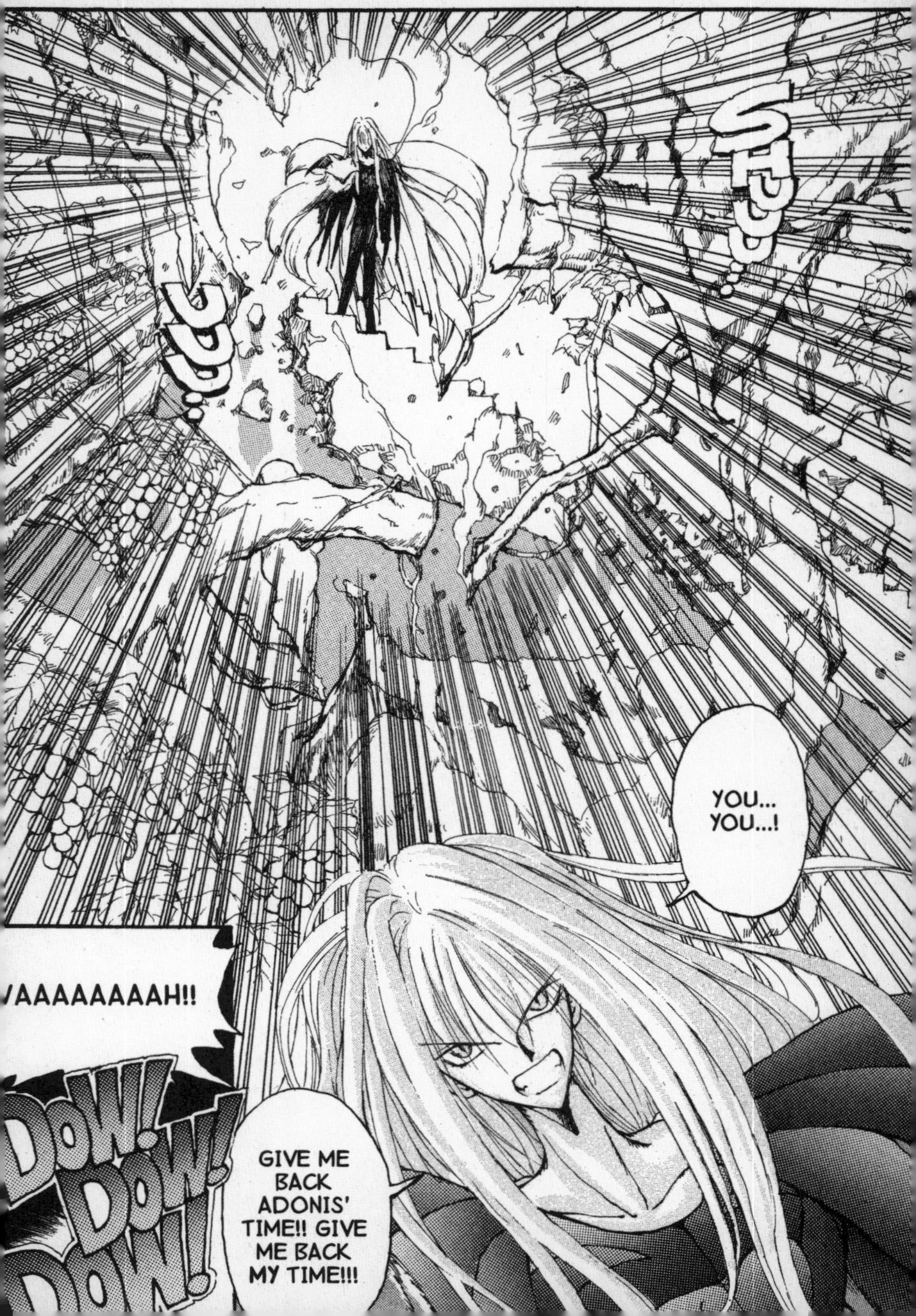
SHUUU
UUU
YOU... YOU...!
AAAAAAAAH!!
GIVE ME BACK ADONIS' TIME!! GIVE ME BACK MY TIME!!!
DOW! DOW! DOW! DOW!!

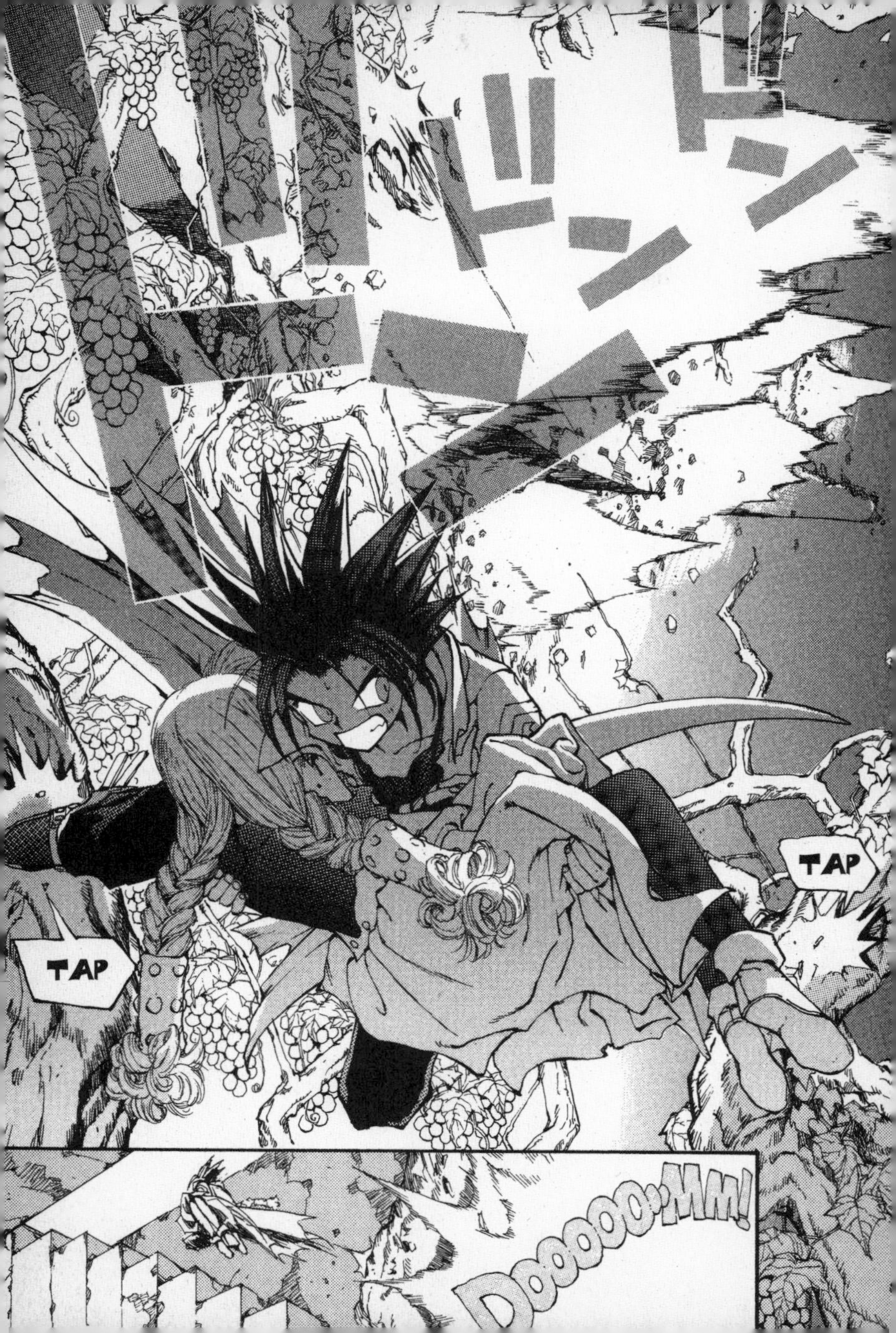
TAP
TAP
DOOOOO-MM!

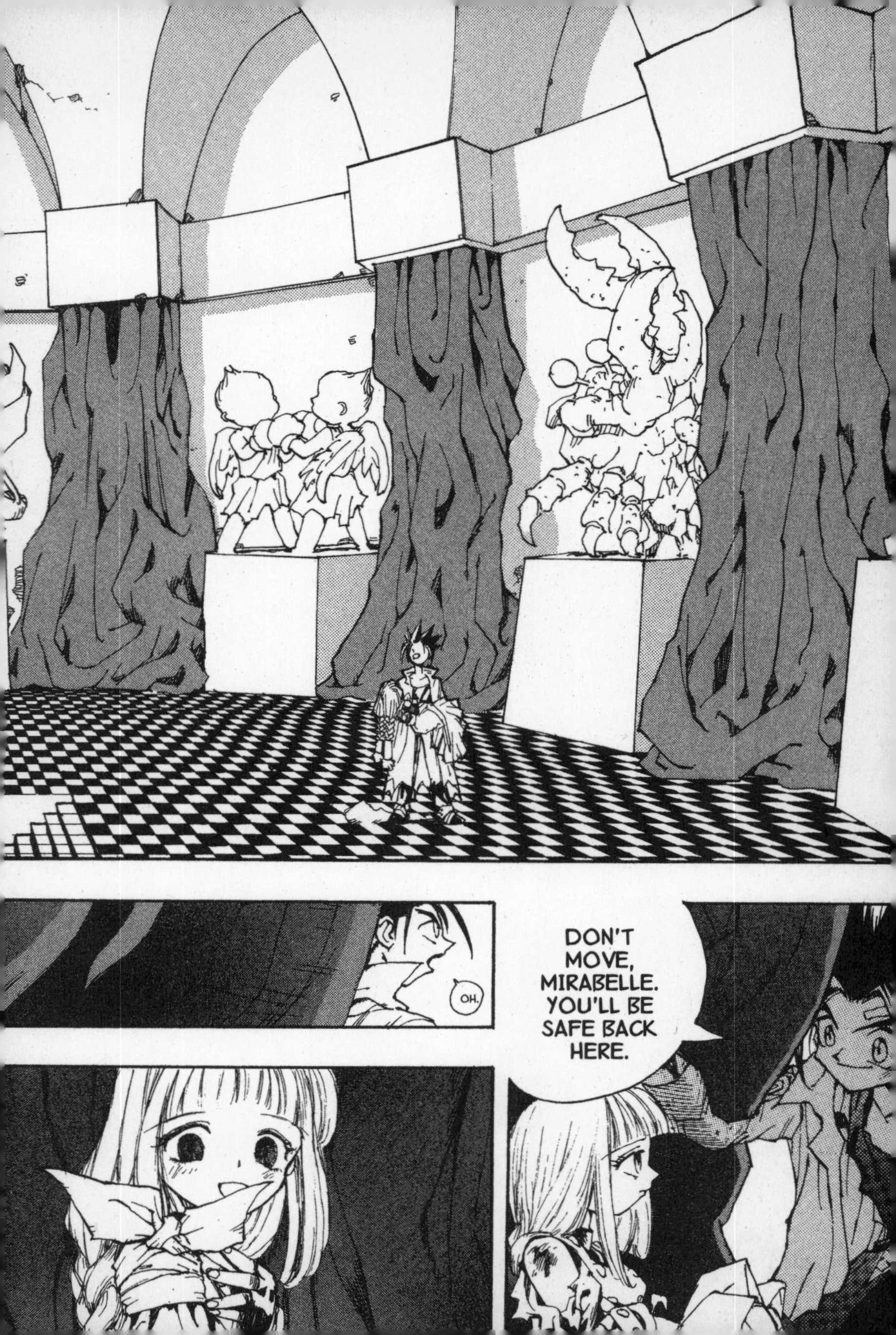
OH.
DON'T MOVE, MIRABELLE. YOU'LL BE SAFE BACK HERE.

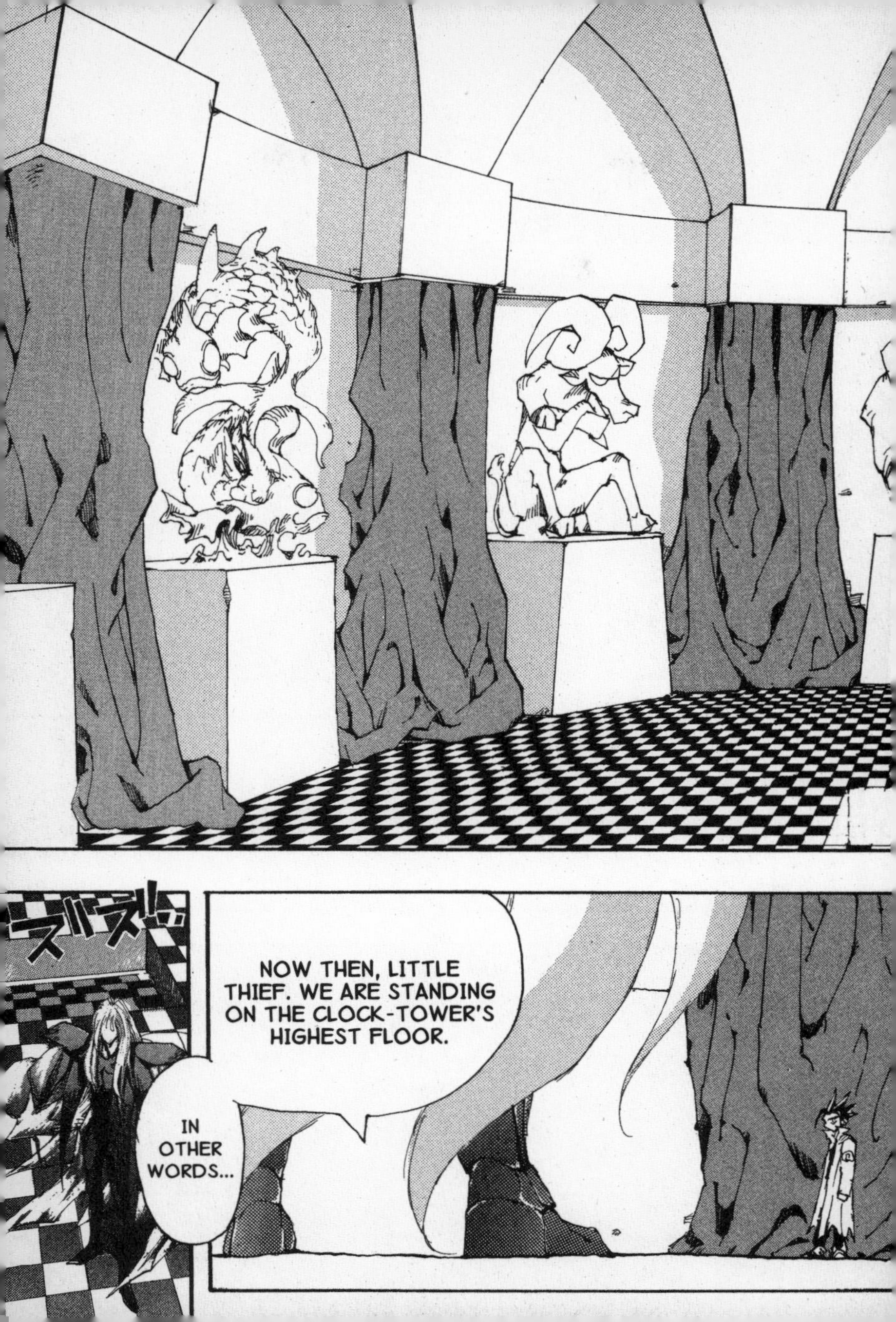
NOW THEN, LITTLE THIEF. WE ARE STANDING ON THE CLOCK-TOWER'S HIGHEST FLOOR.
IN OTHER WORDS...

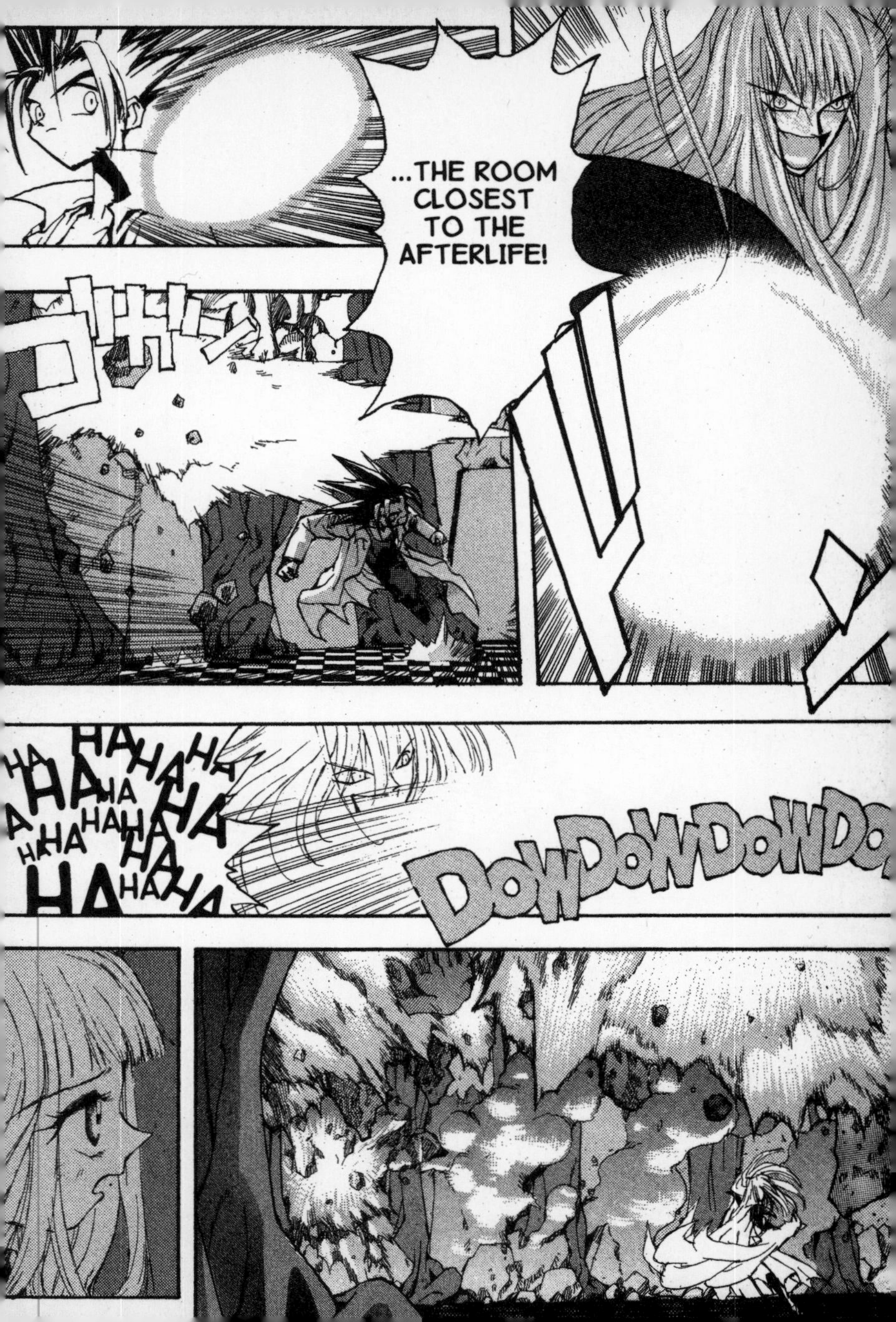
...THE ROOM CLOSEST TO THE AFTERLIFE!
HA HA HA HA HA HA HA HA HA HA HA HA HA HA HA HA HA
DOWDOWDOWDO

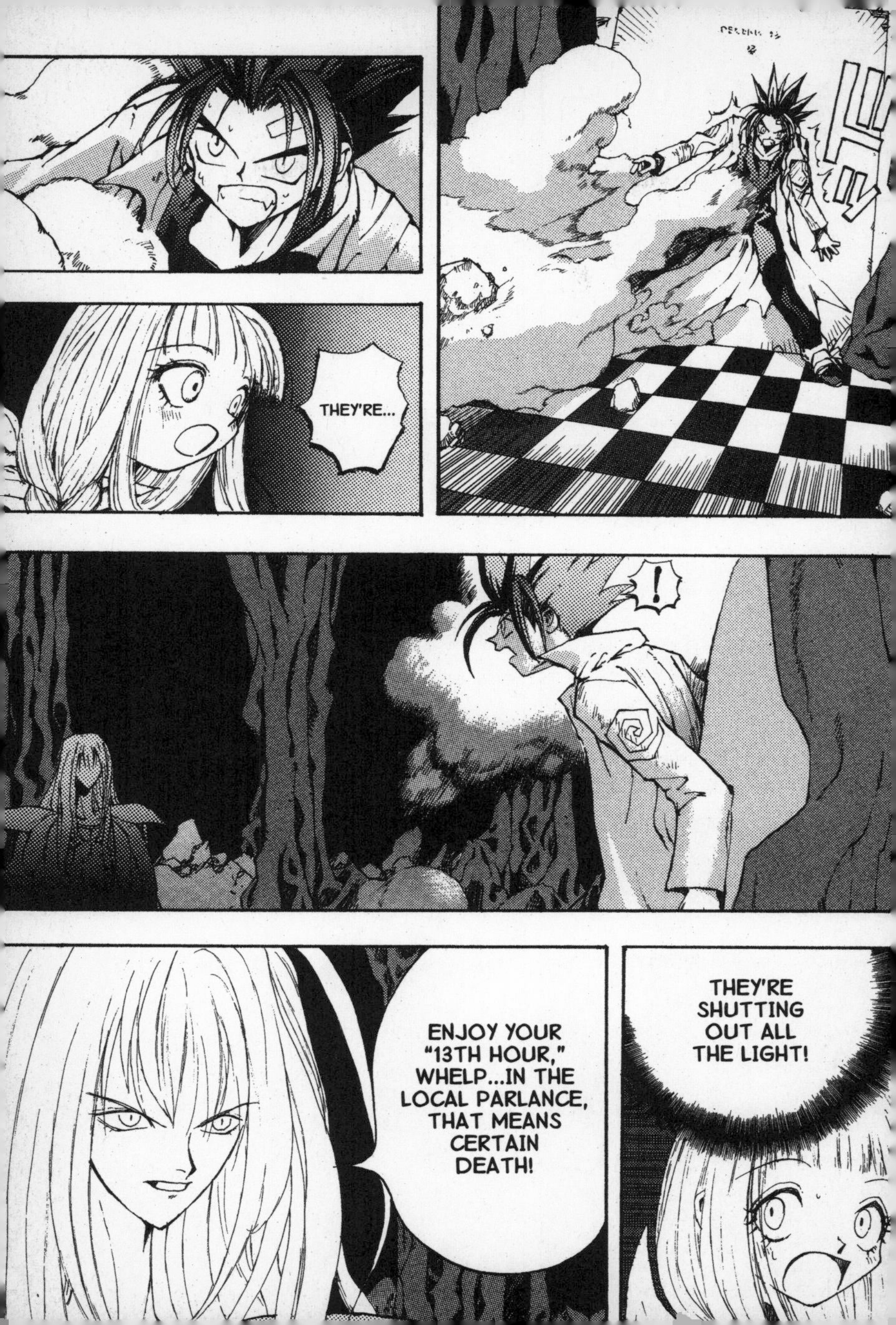
THEY'RE...
!
THEY'RE SHUTTING OUT ALL THE LIGHT!
ENJOY YOUR "13TH HOUR," WHELP...IN THE LOCAL PARLANCE, THAT MEANS CERTAIN DEATH!

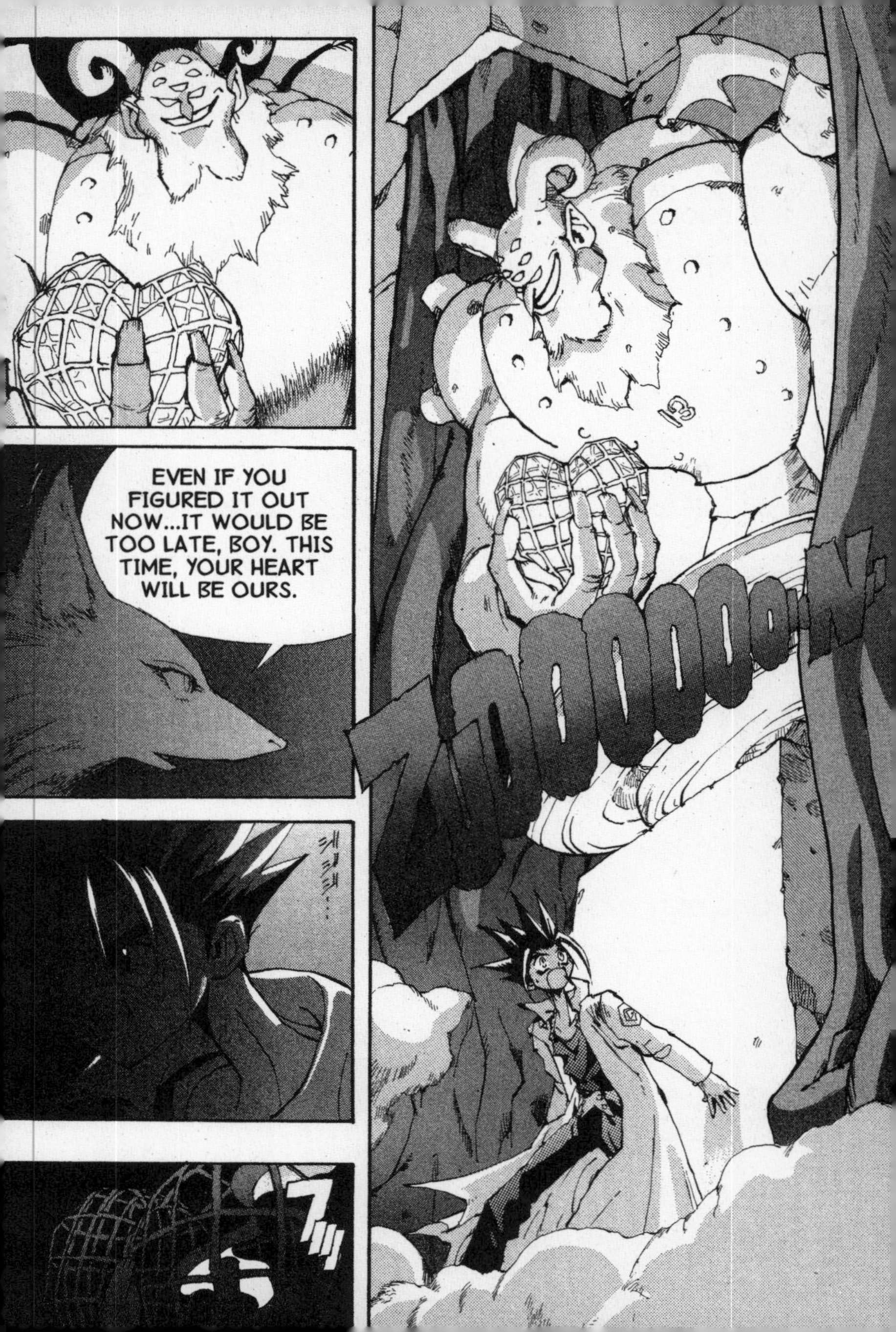
ZOOOOOOOOOON
EVEN IF YOU FIGURED IT OUT NOW...IT WOULD BE TOO LATE, BOY. THIS TIME, YOUR HEART WILL BE OURS.

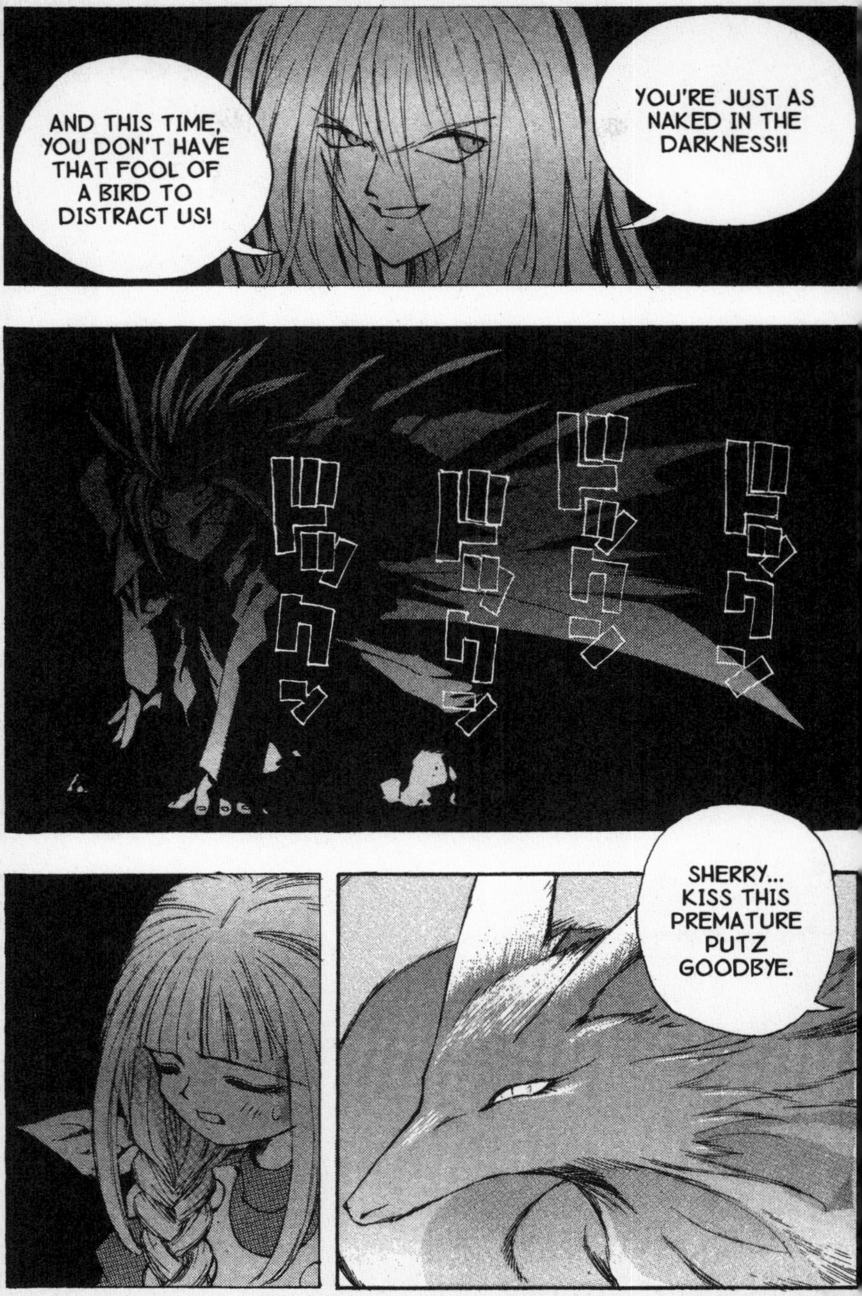
YOU'RE JUST AS NAKED IN THE DARKNESS!!
AND THIS TIME, YOU DON'T HAVE THAT FOOL OF A BIRD TO DISTRACT US!
ドクンッ
ドクンッ
ドクンッ
ドクンッ
SHERRY... KISS THIS PREMATURE PUTZ GOODBYE.

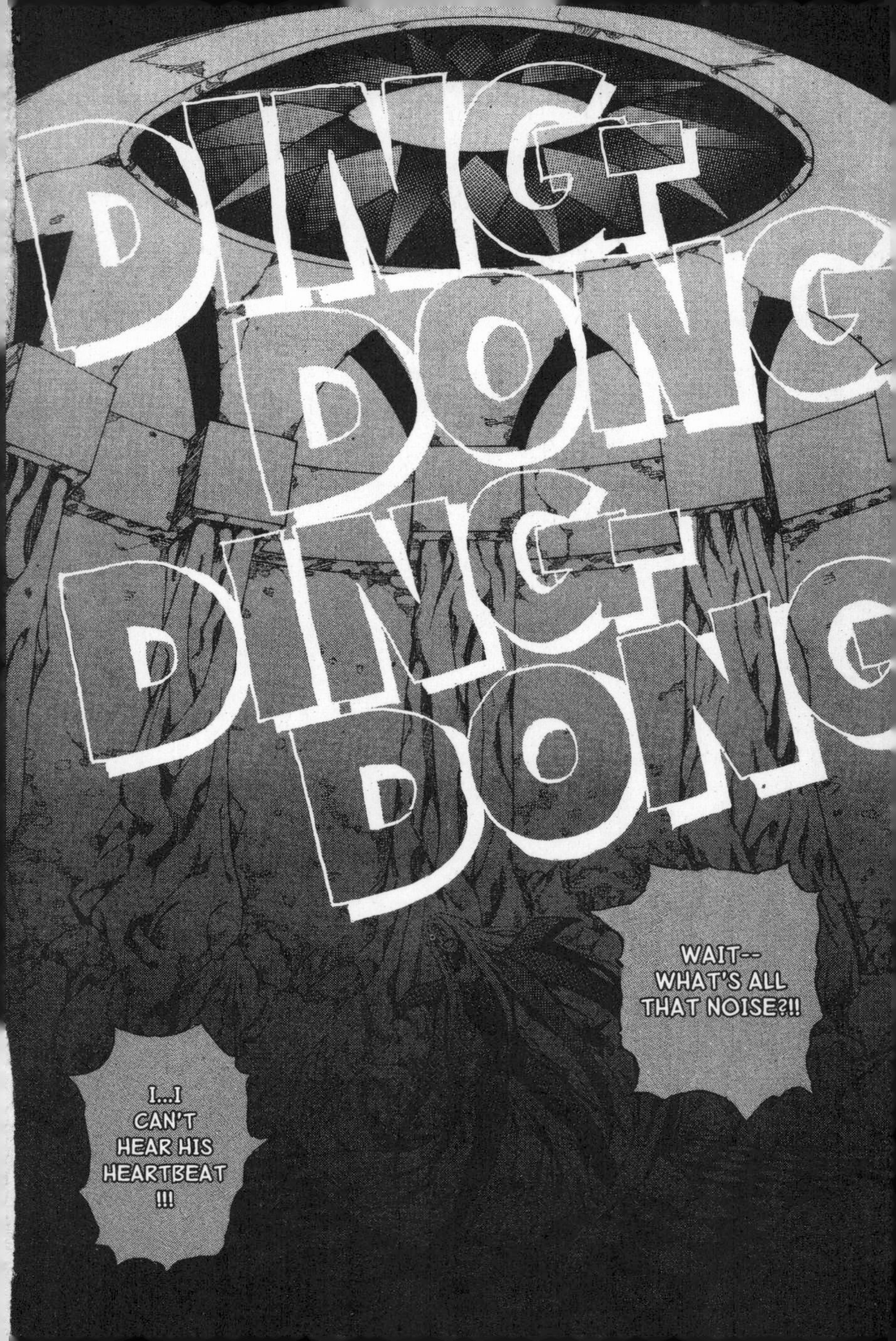
DING DONG DING DONG
WAIT-- WHAT'S ALL THAT NOISE?!!
I...I CAN'T HEAR HIS HEARTBEAT !!!

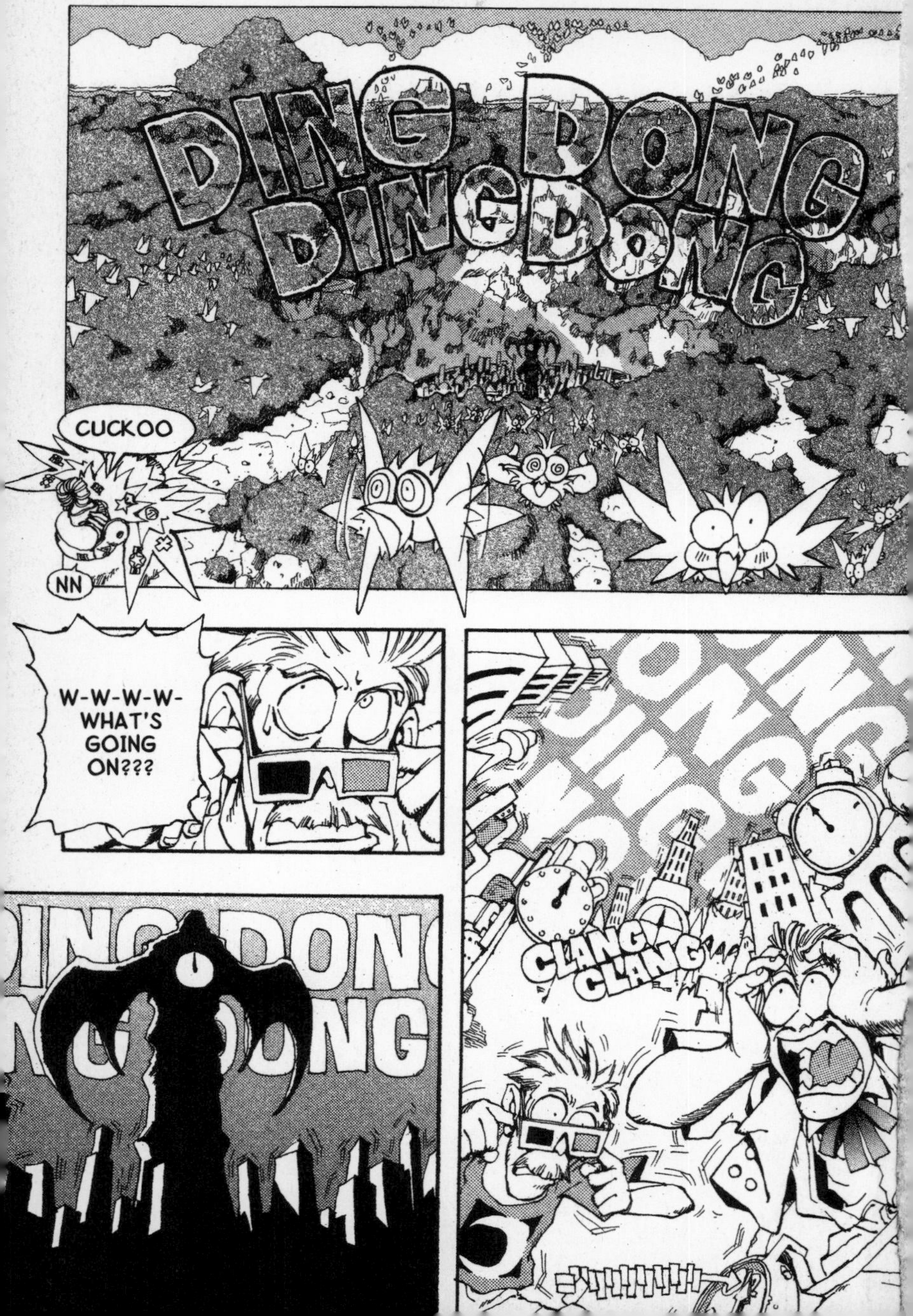
DING DONG
DING DONG
CUCKOO
NN
CLANG
CLANG
W-W-W-W-WHAT'S GOING ON???

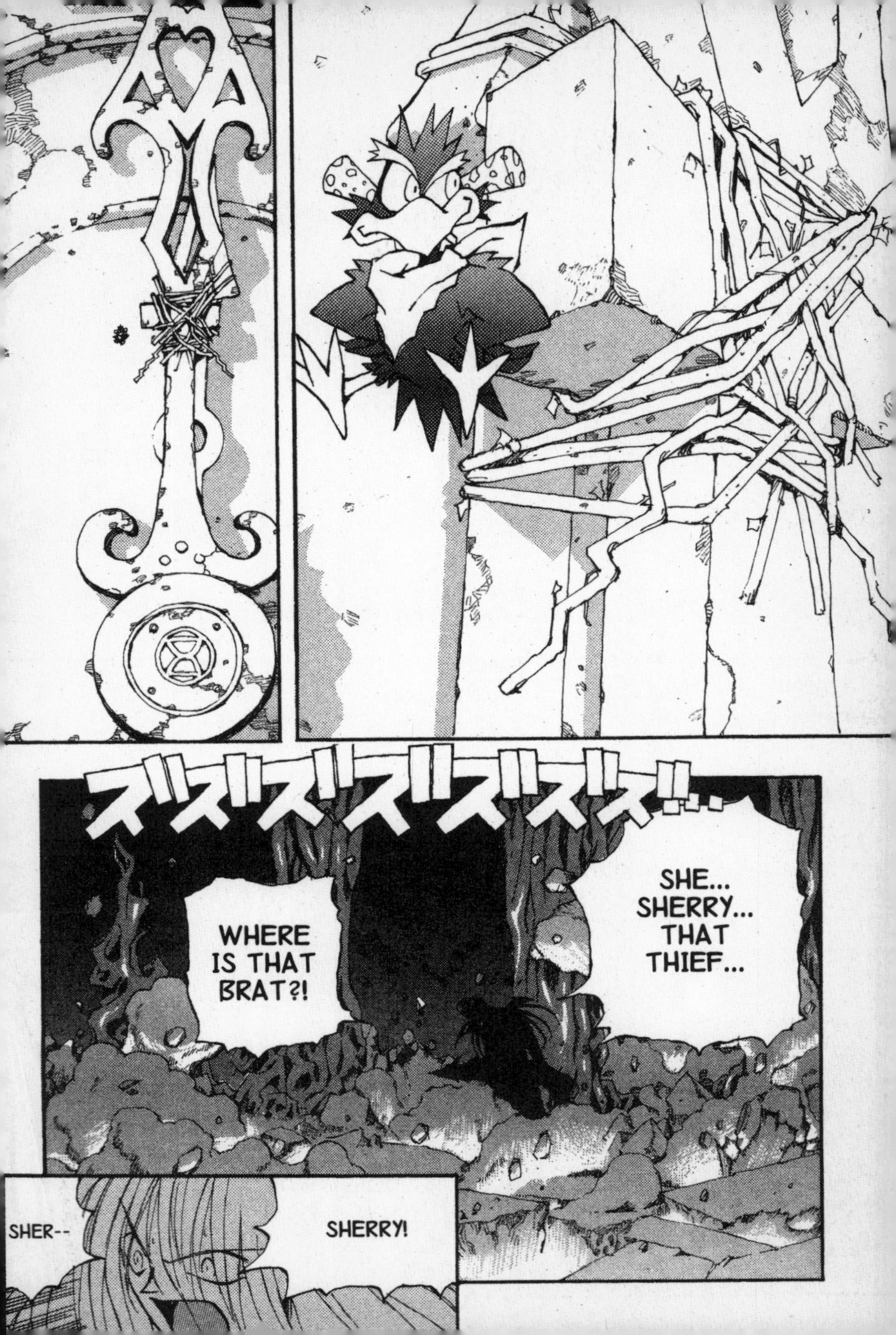
ズズズズズズ!!..
SHE... SHERRY... THAT THIEF...
WHERE IS THAT BRAT?!
SHERRY!
SHER--

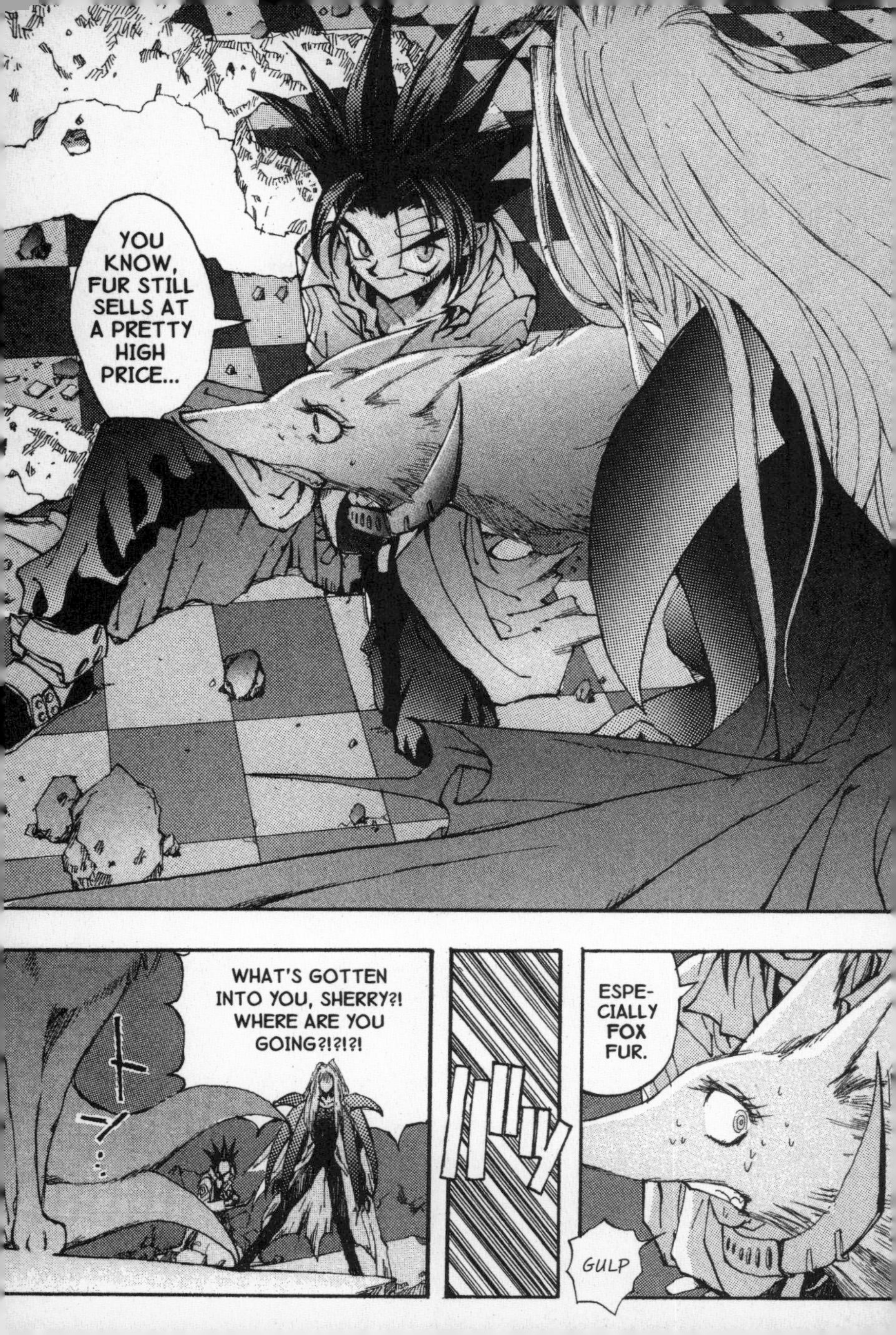
YOU KNOW, FUR STILL SELLS AT A PRETTY HIGH PRICE...
ESPE-CIALLY FOX FUR.
GULP
WHAT'S GOTTEN INTO YOU, SHERRY?! WHERE ARE YOU GOING?!?!?!

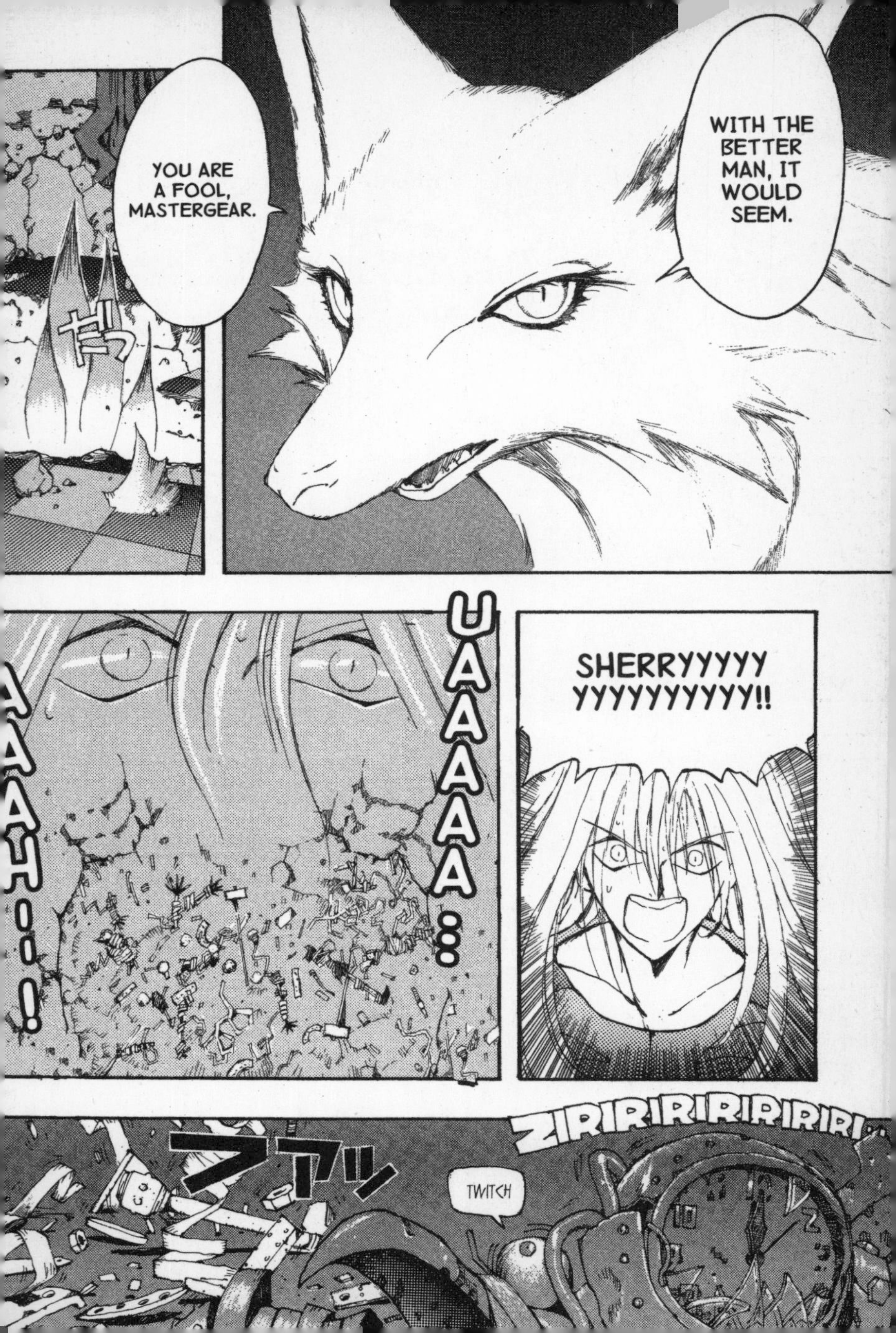
WITH THE BETTER MAN, IT WOULD SEEM.
YOU ARE A FOOL, MASTERGEAR.
SHERRYYYYY YYYYYYYYYY!!
UAAAAAA..
AAAAH..!
ZIRIRIRIRIRIRIRI..
TWITCH

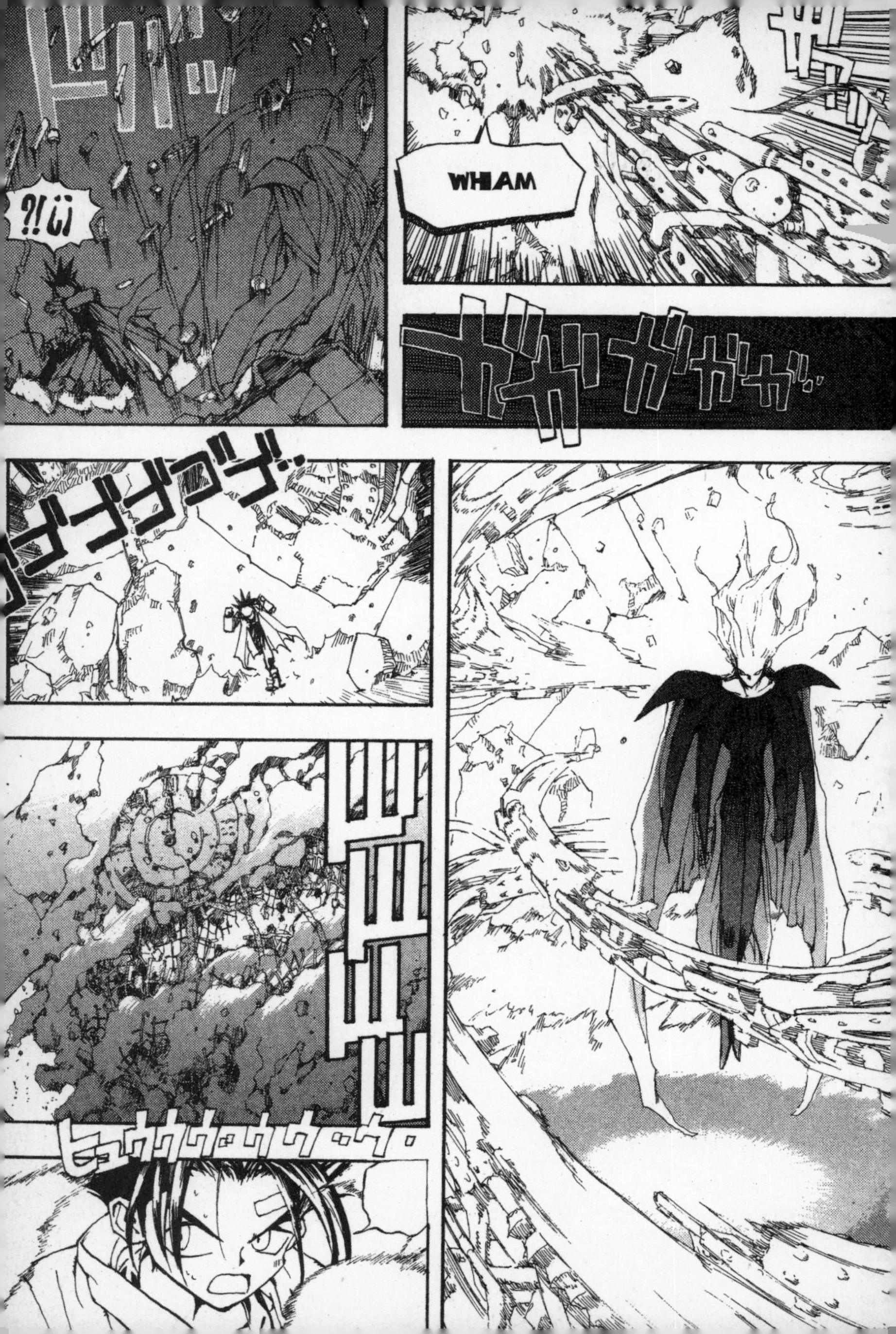
WHAM
?!!

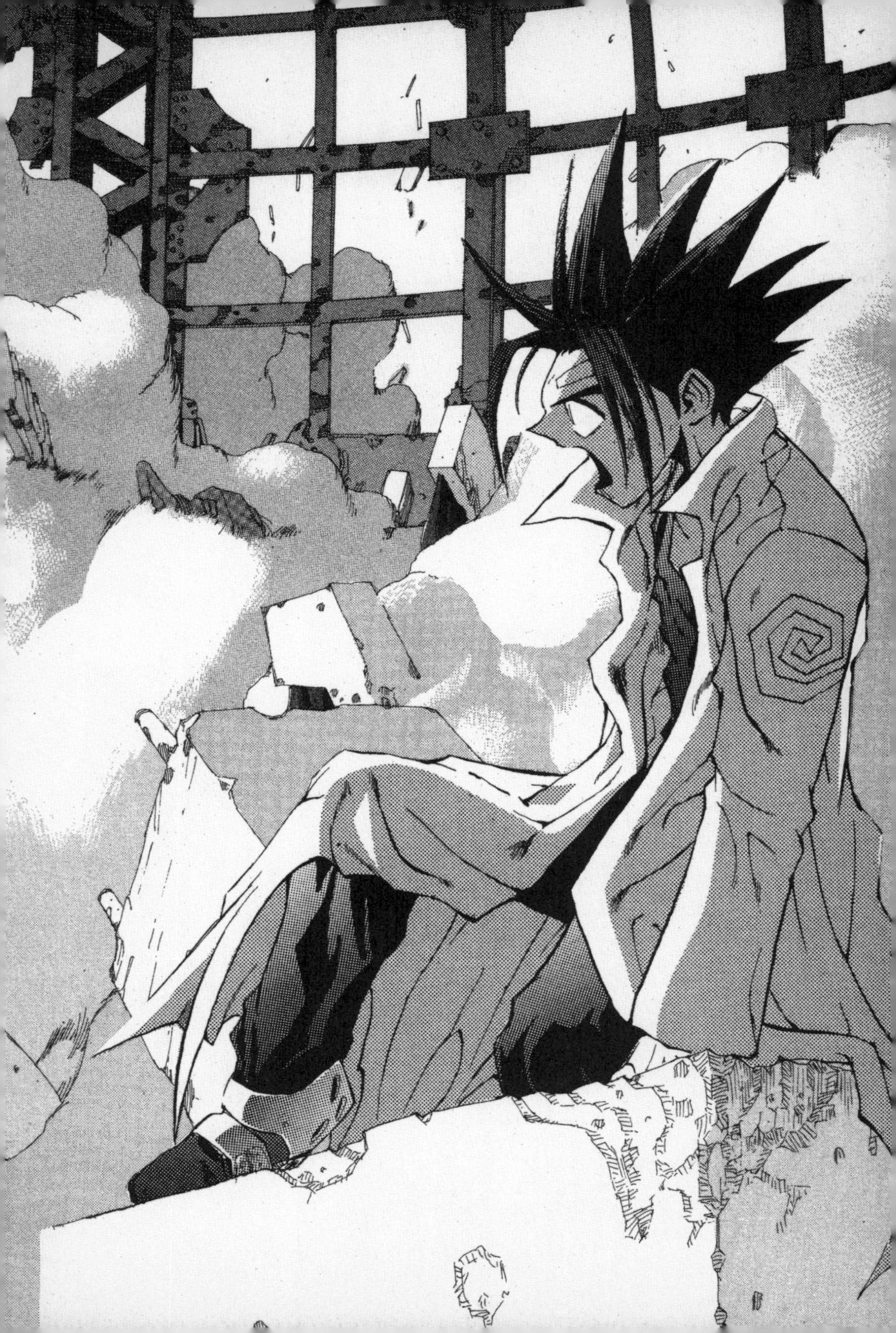

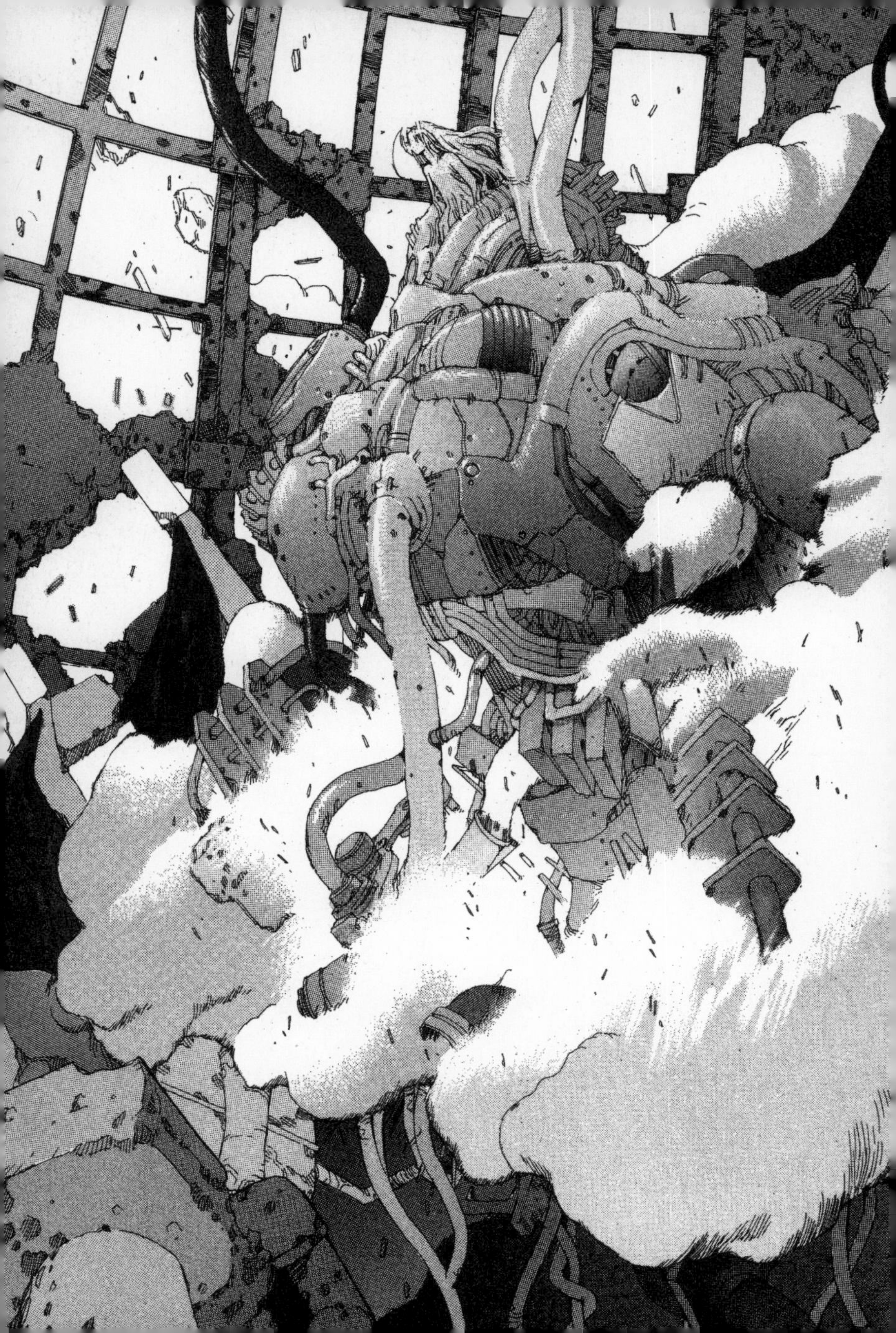

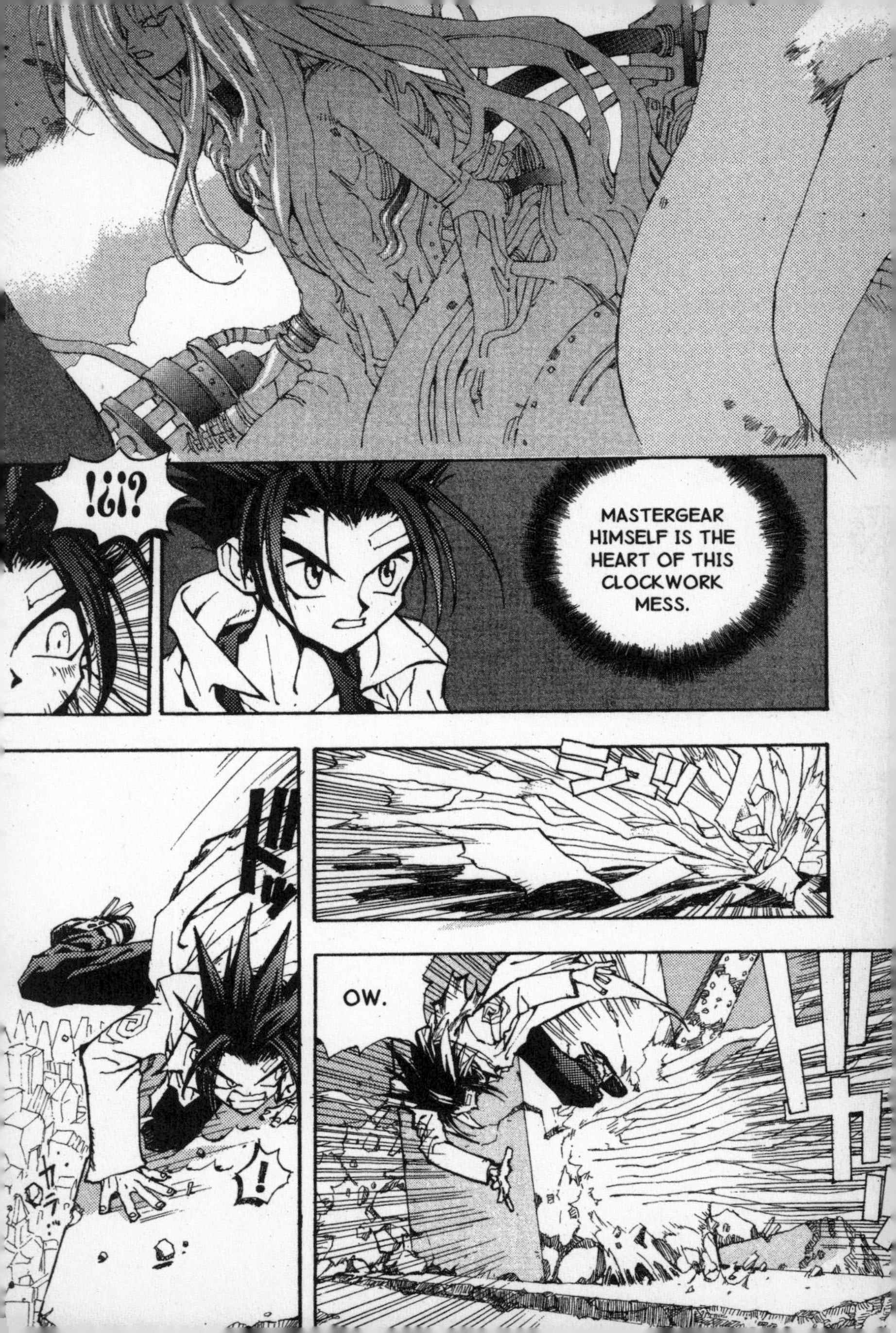
MASTERGEAR HIMSELF IS THE HEART OF THIS CLOCKWORK MESS.
!¿¡?
OW.
!

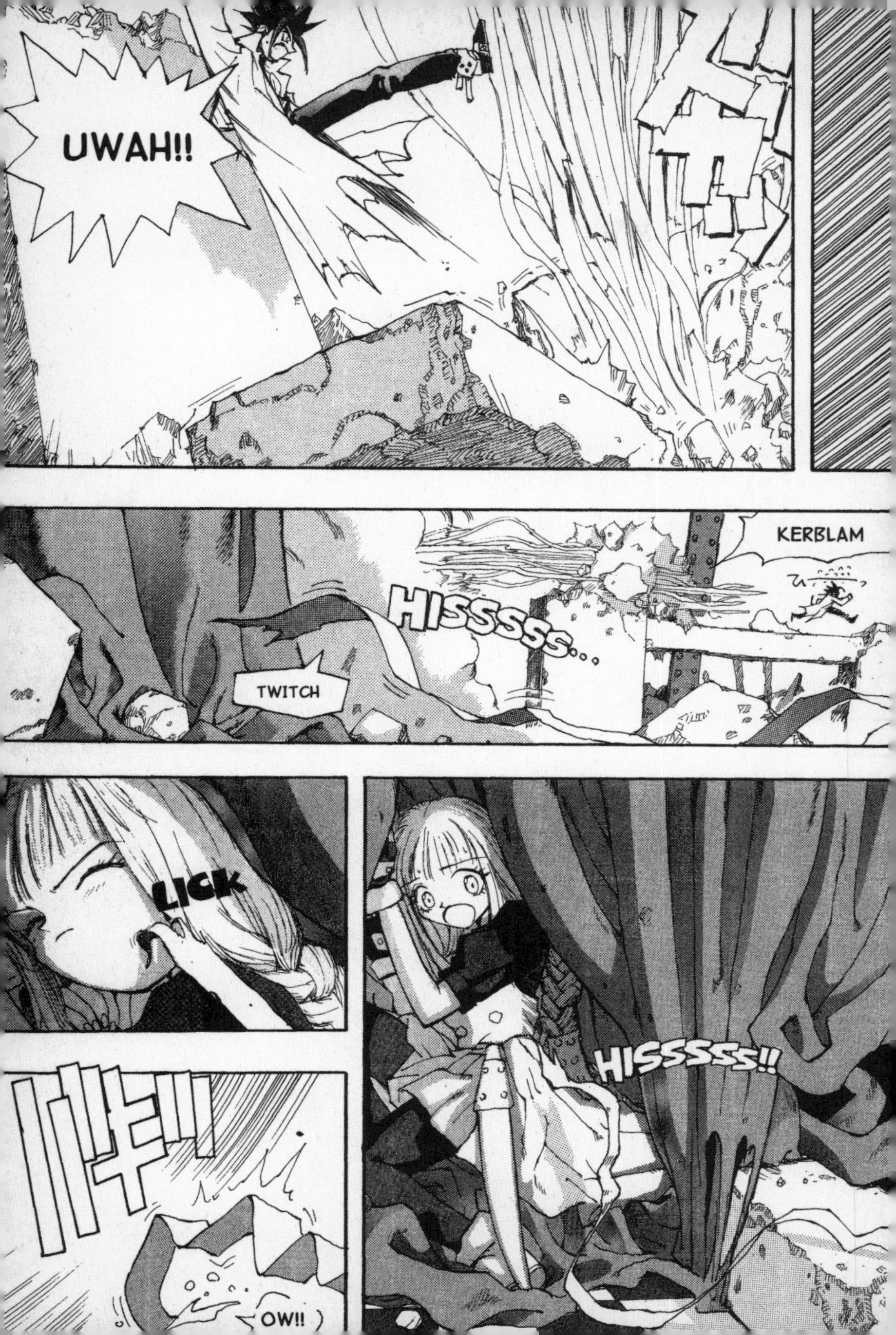
UWAH!!
KERBLAM
HISSSSS...
TWITCH
HISSSSS!!
LICK
OW!!

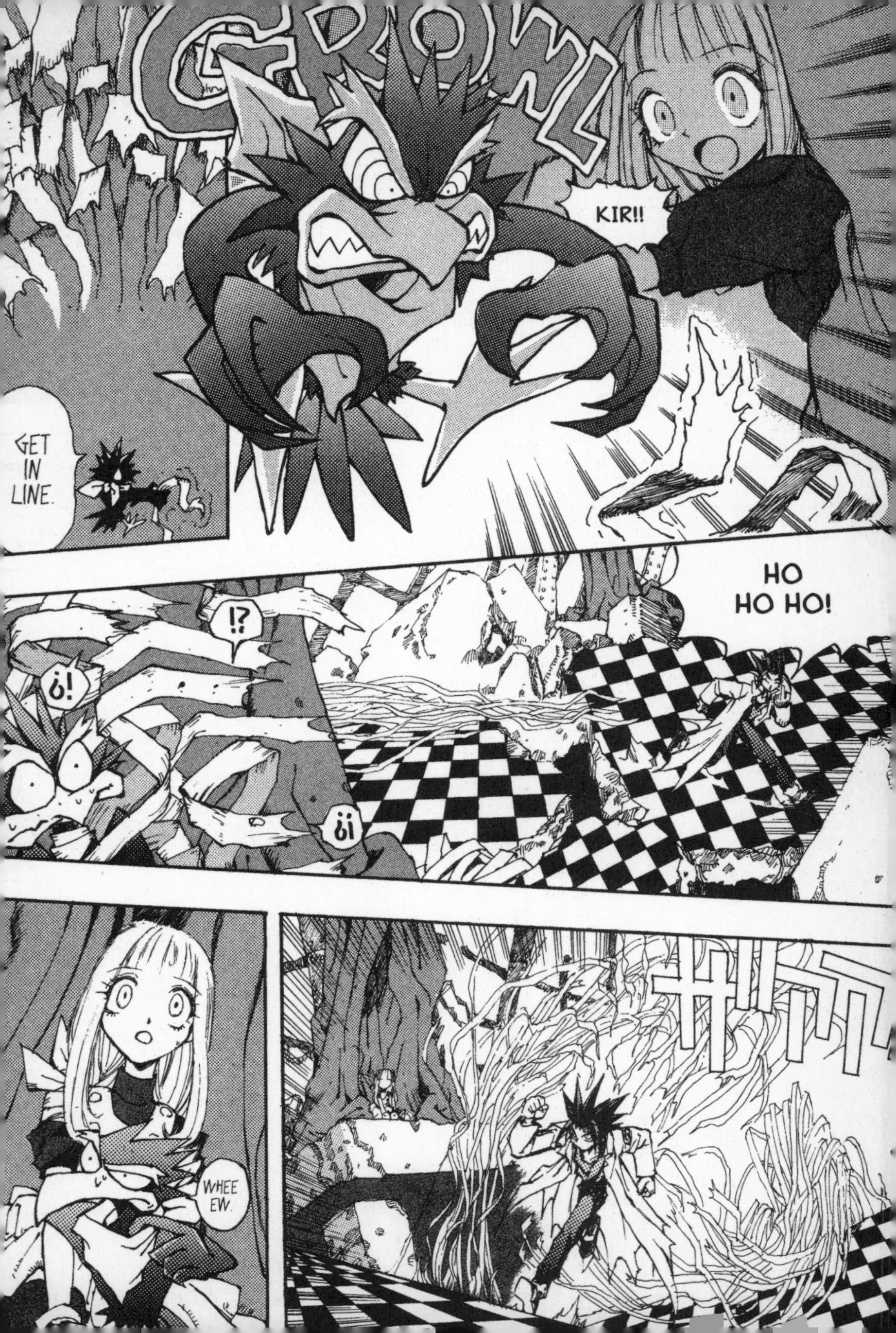
GROWL
KIR!!
GET IN LINE.
HO HO HO!
!?
¿!
¡¿
WHEE EW.

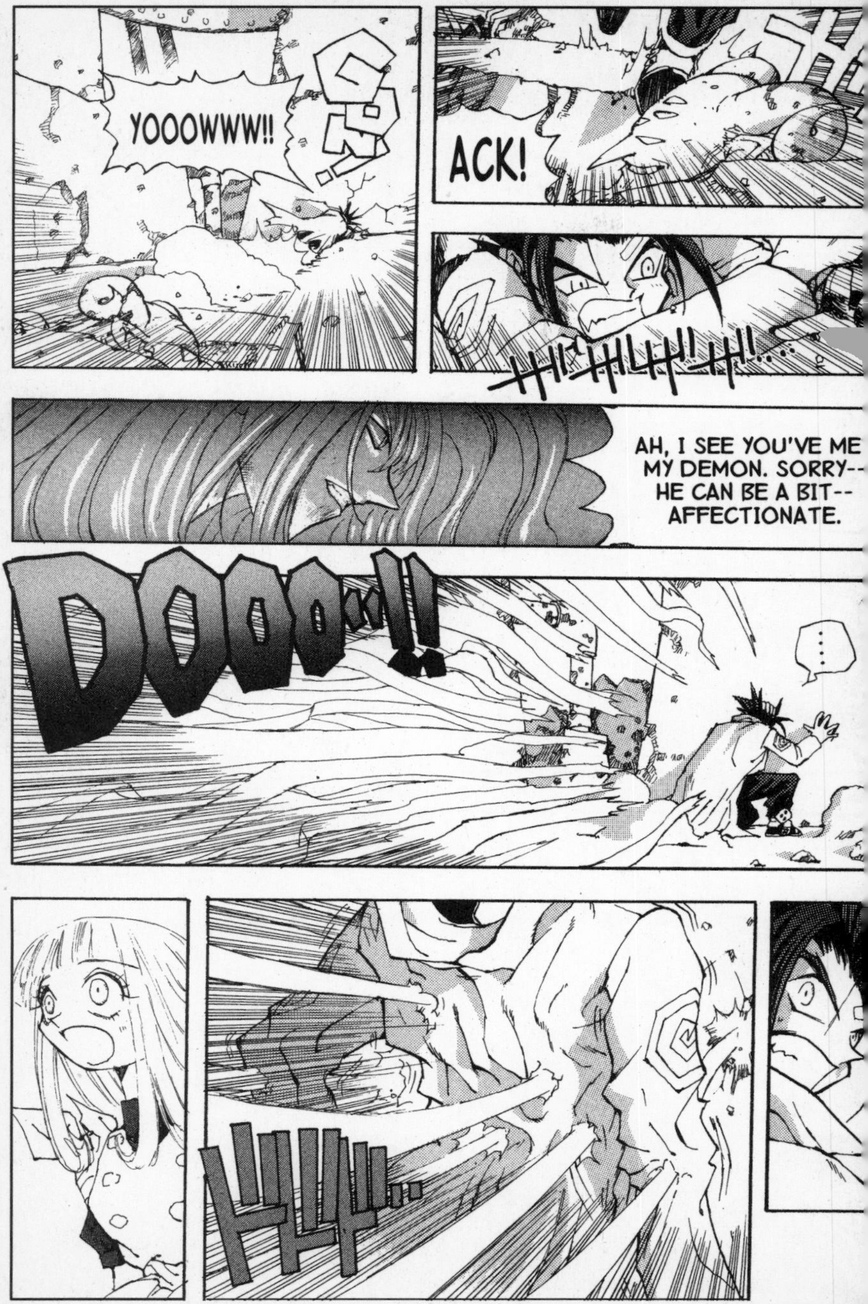
ACK!
YOOOWWW!!
AH, I SEE YOU'VE ME MY DEMON. SORRY-- HE CAN BE A BIT-- AFFECTIONATE.
....

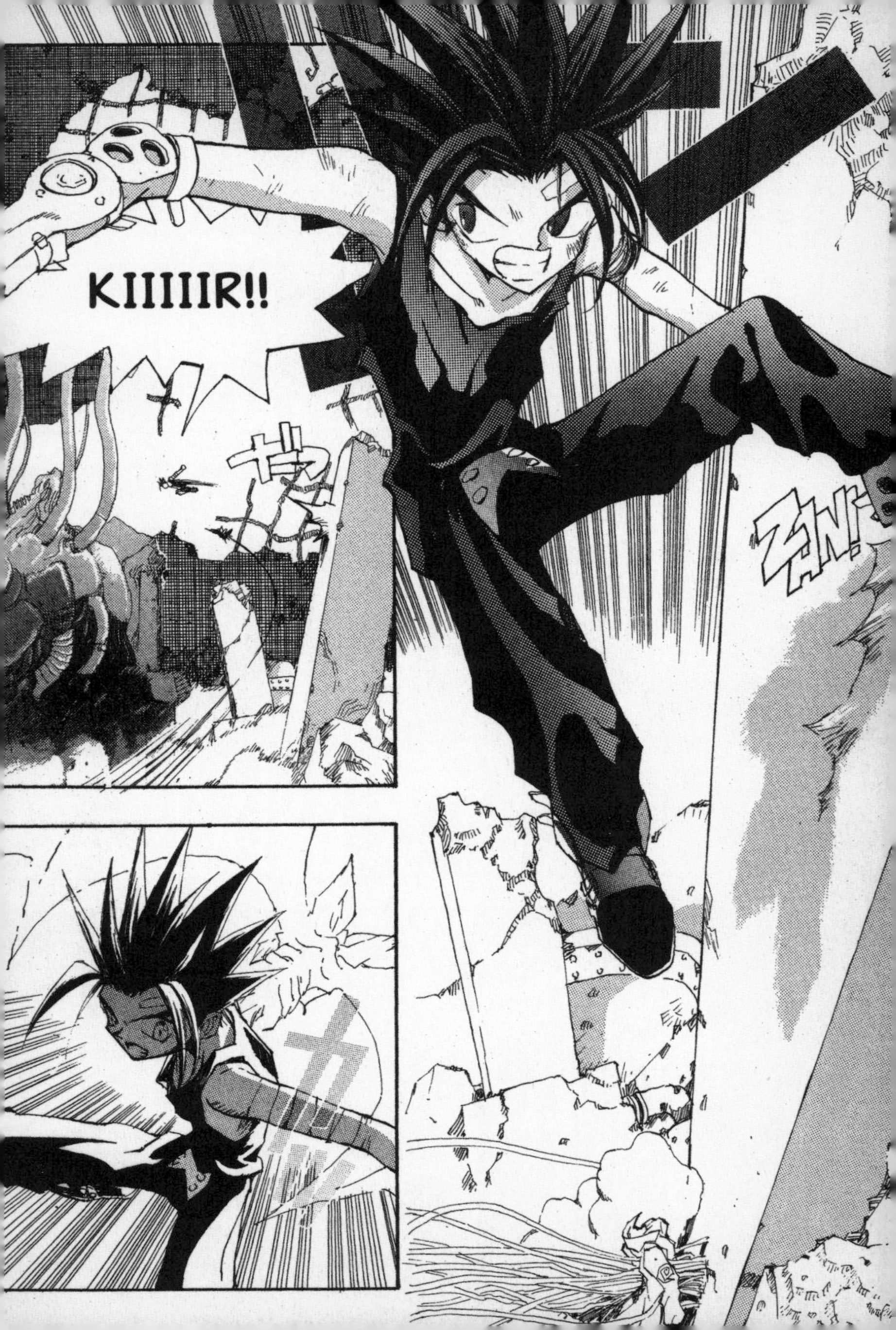
ZAN!
KIIIIIR!!

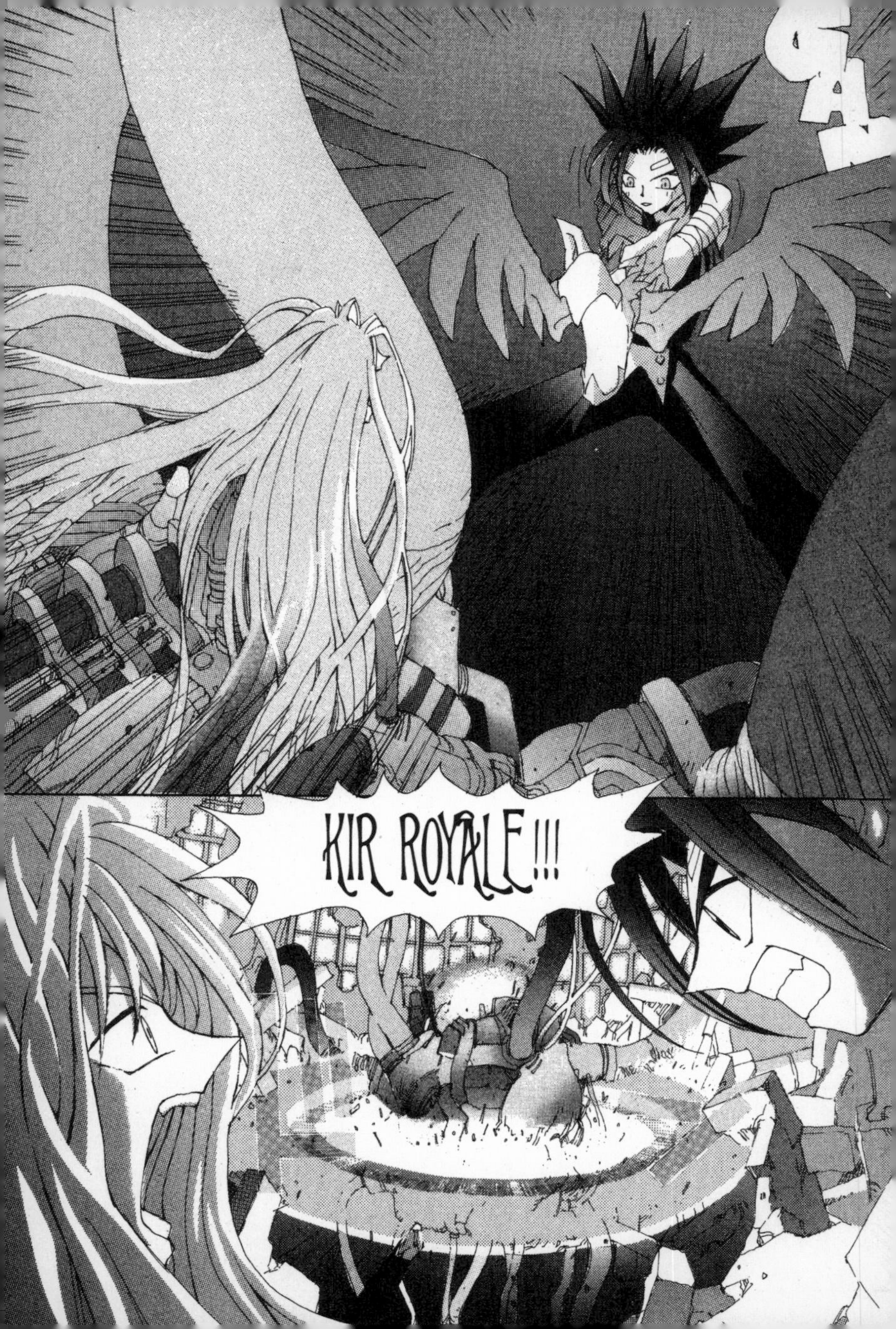
GA
KIR ROYALE!!!

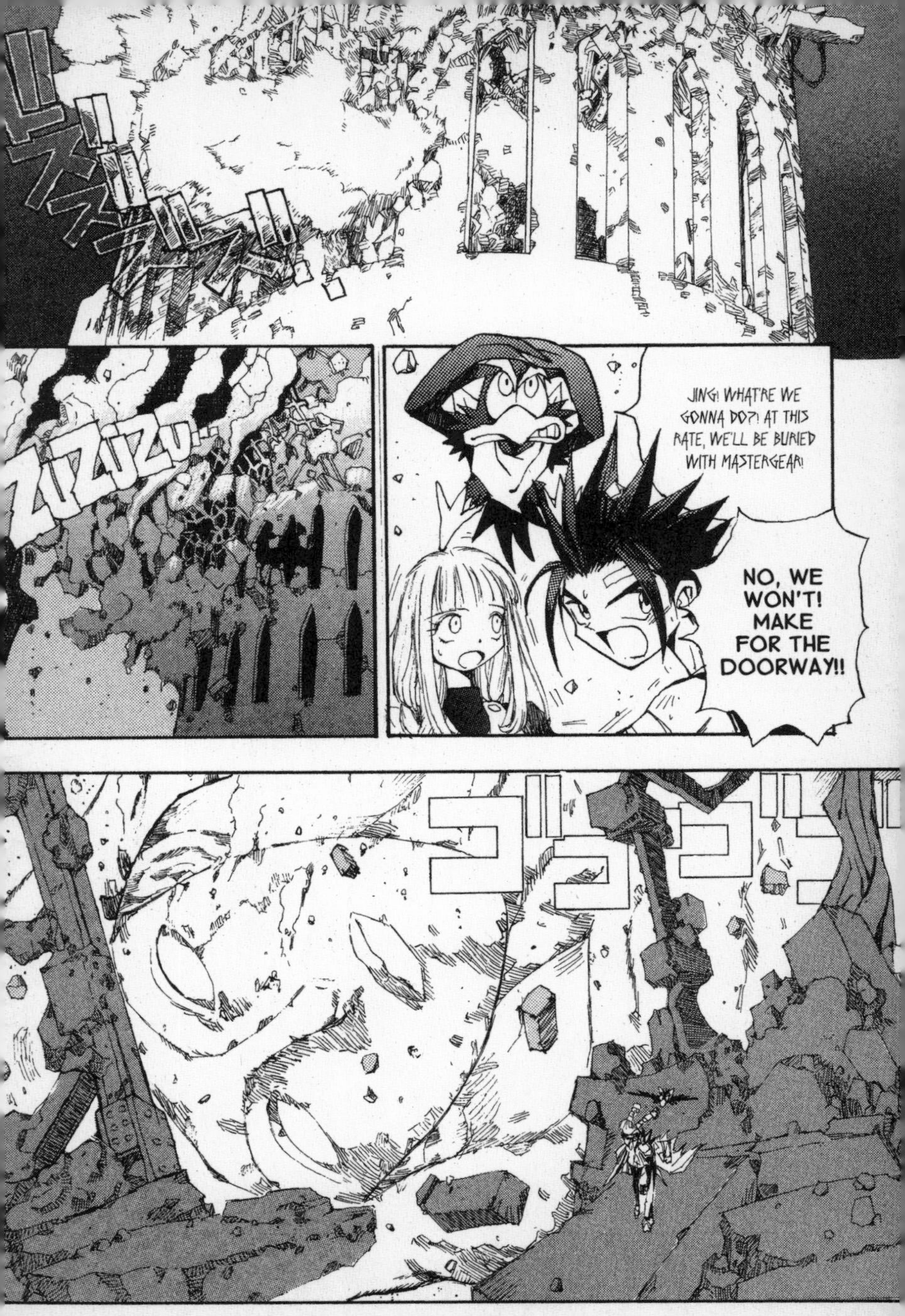
JING! WHAT'RE WE GONNA DO?! AT THIS RATE, WE'LL BE BURIED WITH MASTERGEAR!
NO, WE WON'T! MAKE FOR THE DOORWAY!!
ZUZUZUZU...

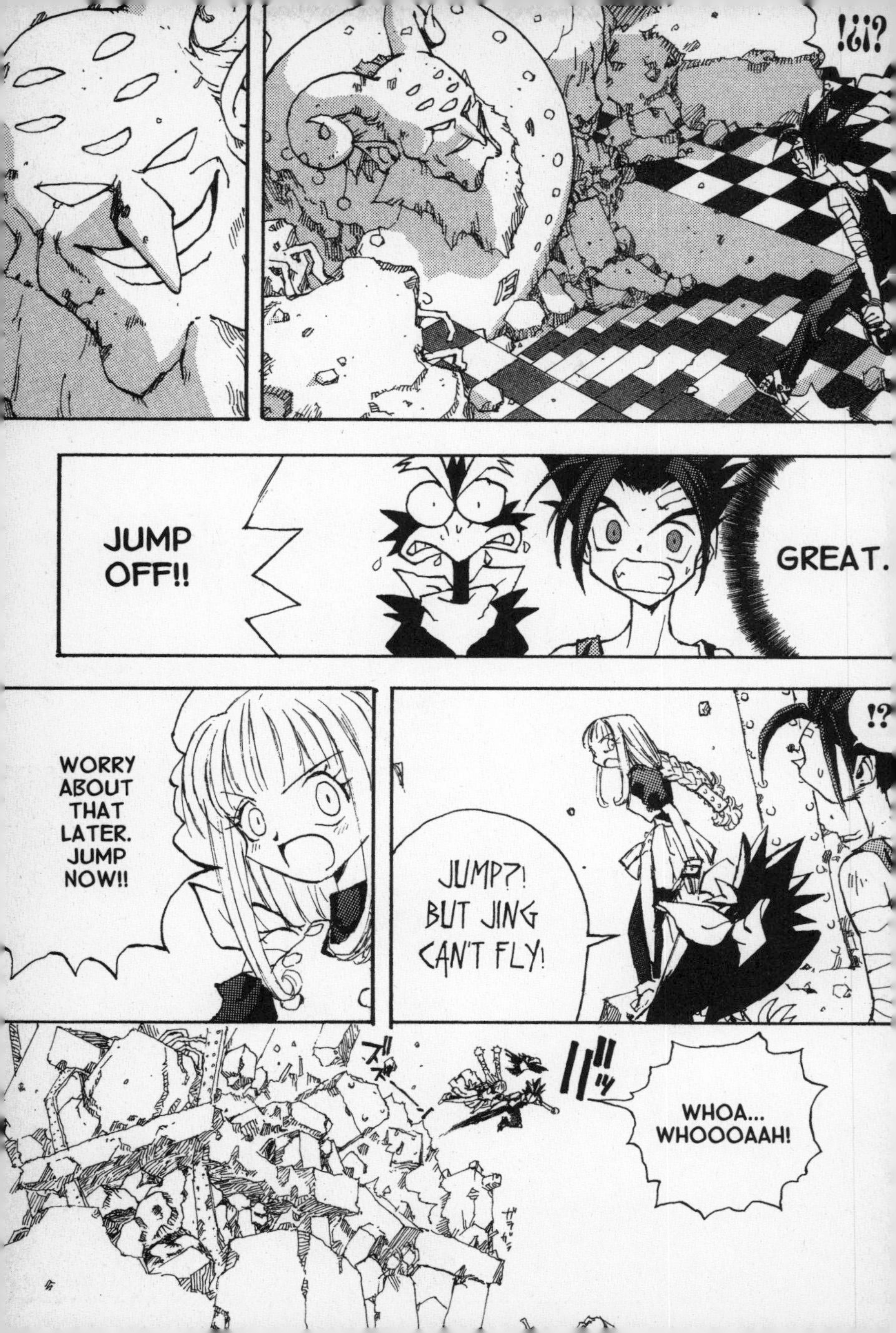
!¿?
GREAT.
JUMP OFF!!
!?
JUMP?! BUT JING CAN'T FLY!
WORRY ABOUT THAT LATER. JUMP NOW!!
WHOA... WHOOOAAH!

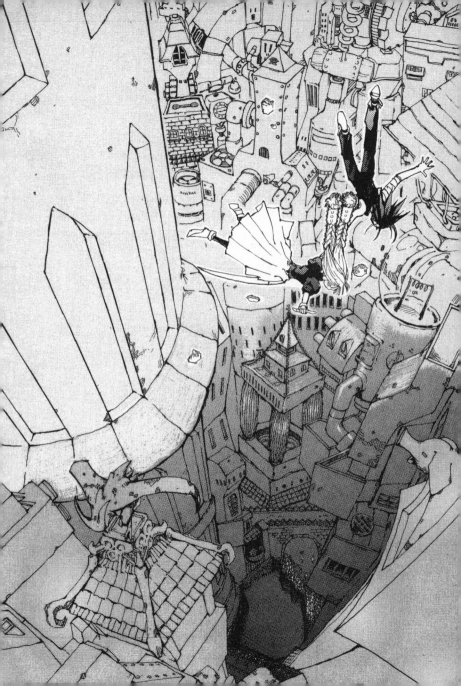

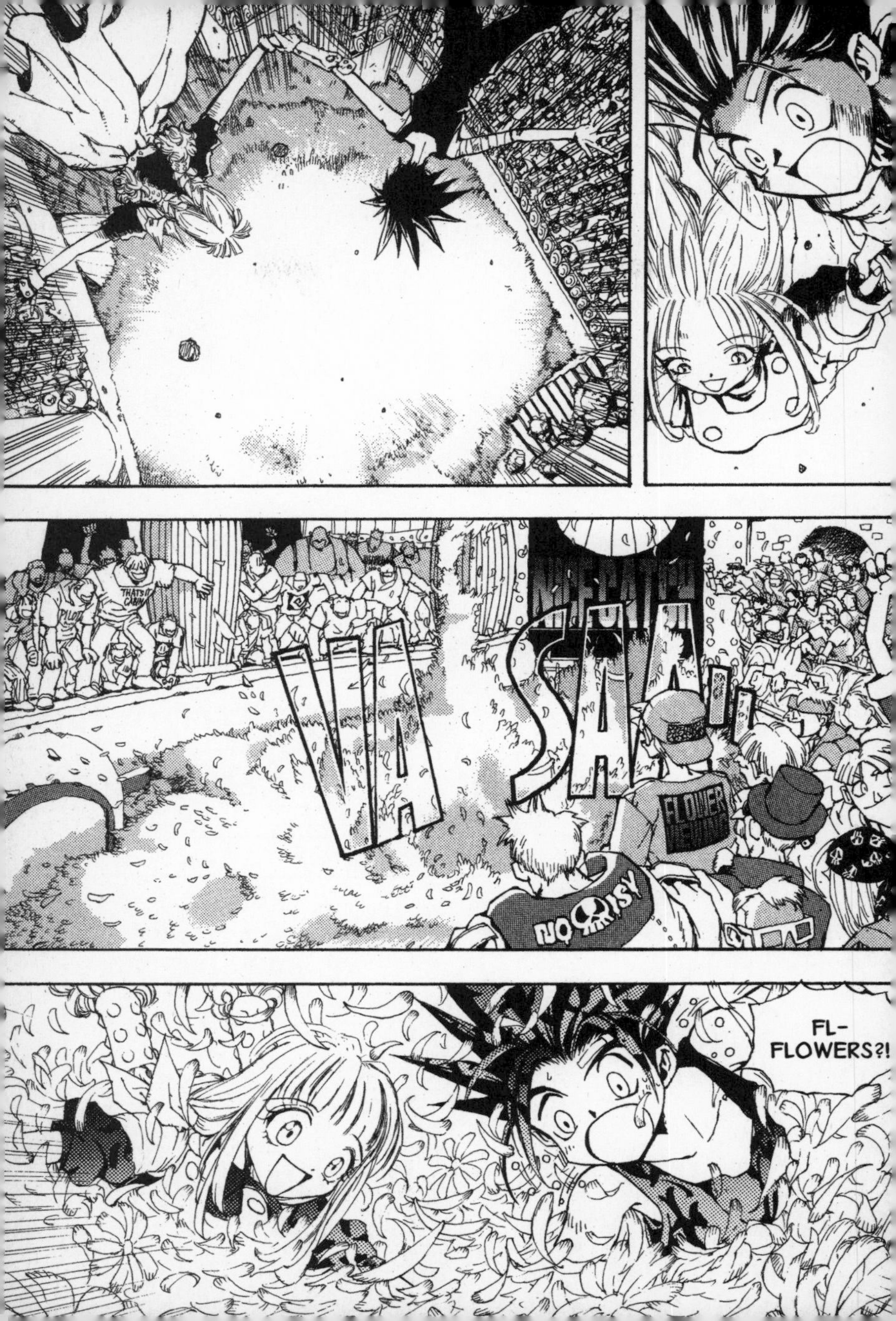
VASA..
FL- FLOWERS?!

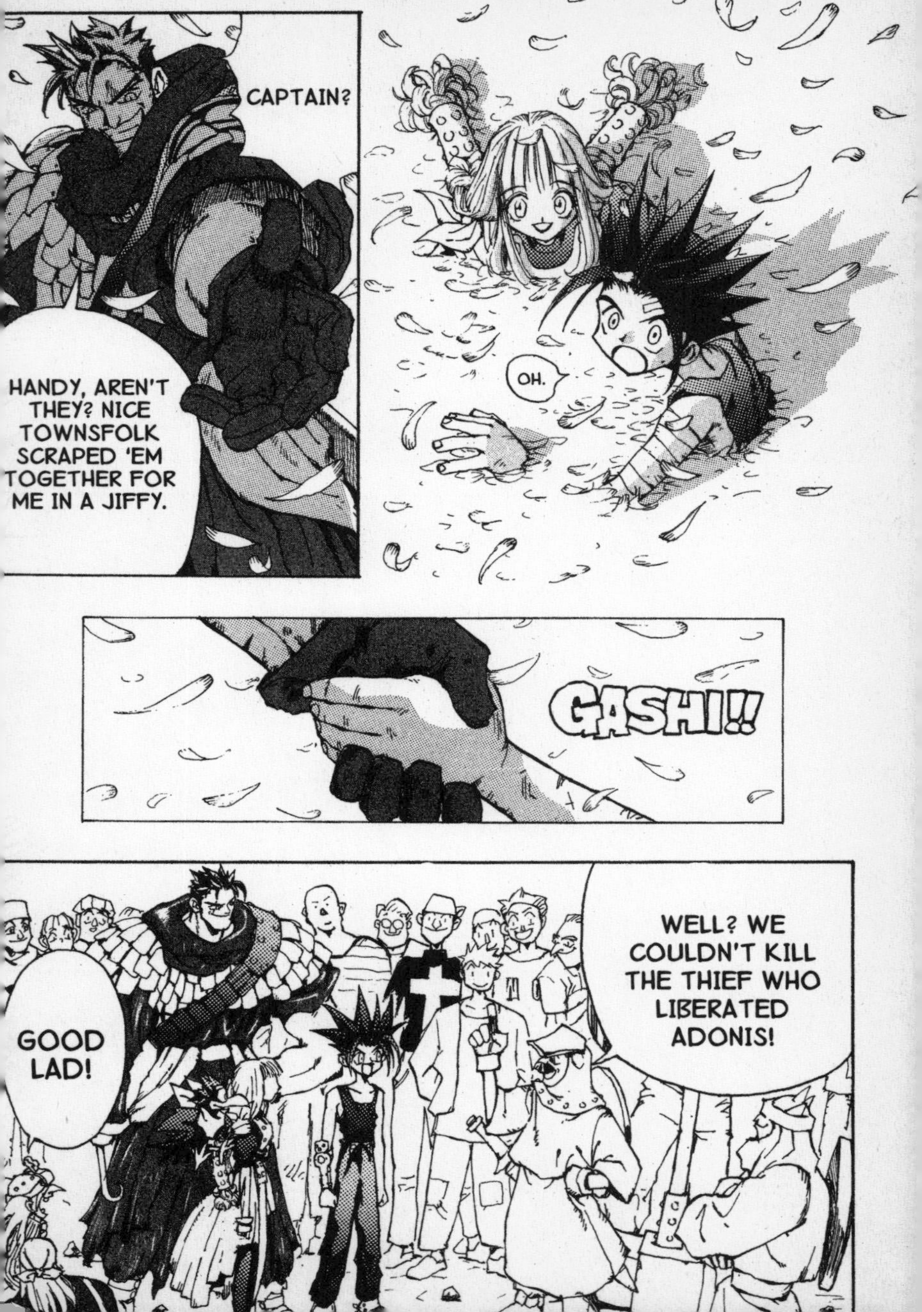
OH.
CAPTAIN?
HANDY, AREN'T THEY? NICE TOWNSFOLK SCRAPED 'EM TOGETHER FOR ME IN A JIFFY.
GASHI!!
WELL? WE COULDN'T KILL THE THIEF WHO LIBERATED ADONIS!
GOOD LAD!

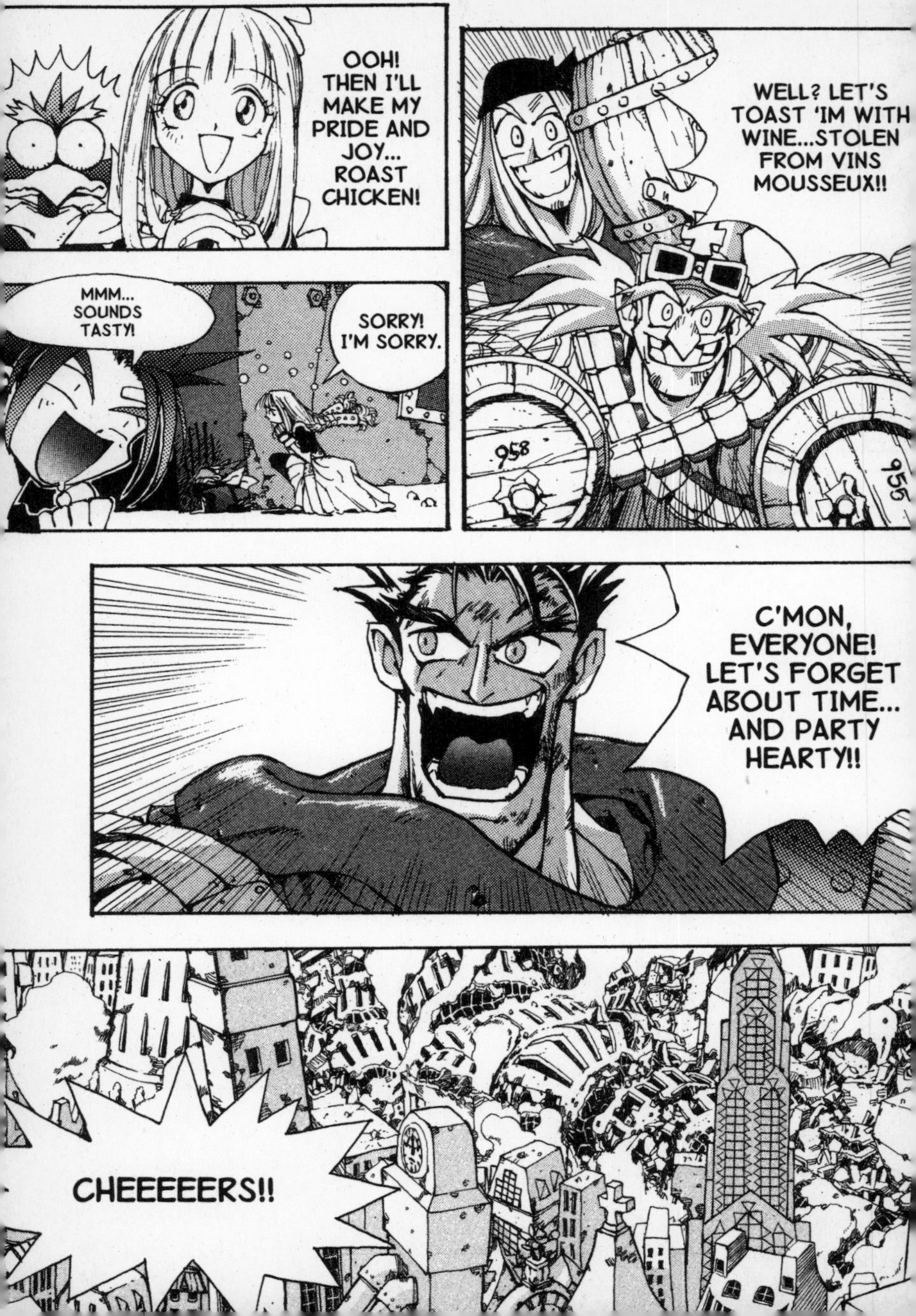
WELL? LET'S TOAST 'IM WITH WINE...STOLEN FROM VINS MOUSSEUX!!
958
955
OOH! THEN I'LL MAKE MY PRIDE AND JOY... ROAST CHICKEN!
SORRY! I'M SORRY.
MMM... SOUNDS TASTY!
C'MON, EVERYONE! LET'S FORGET ABOUT TIME... AND PARTY HEARTY!!
CHEEEEERS!!

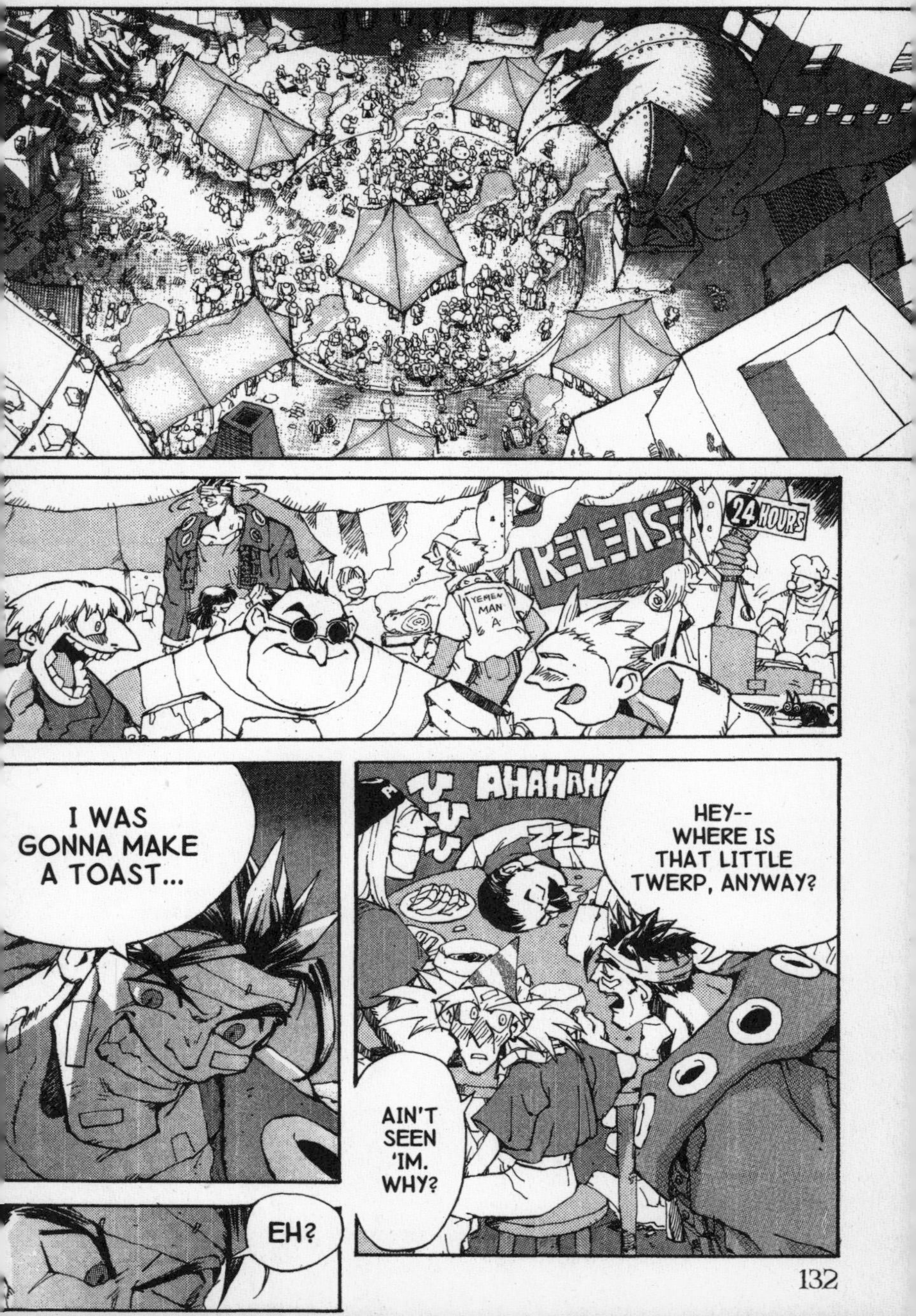
24 HOURS
RELEASE
YEMEN MAN A
HEY-- WHERE IS THAT LITTLE TWERP, ANYWAY?
AIN'T SEEN 'IM. WHY?
I WAS GONNA MAKE A TOAST...
EH?

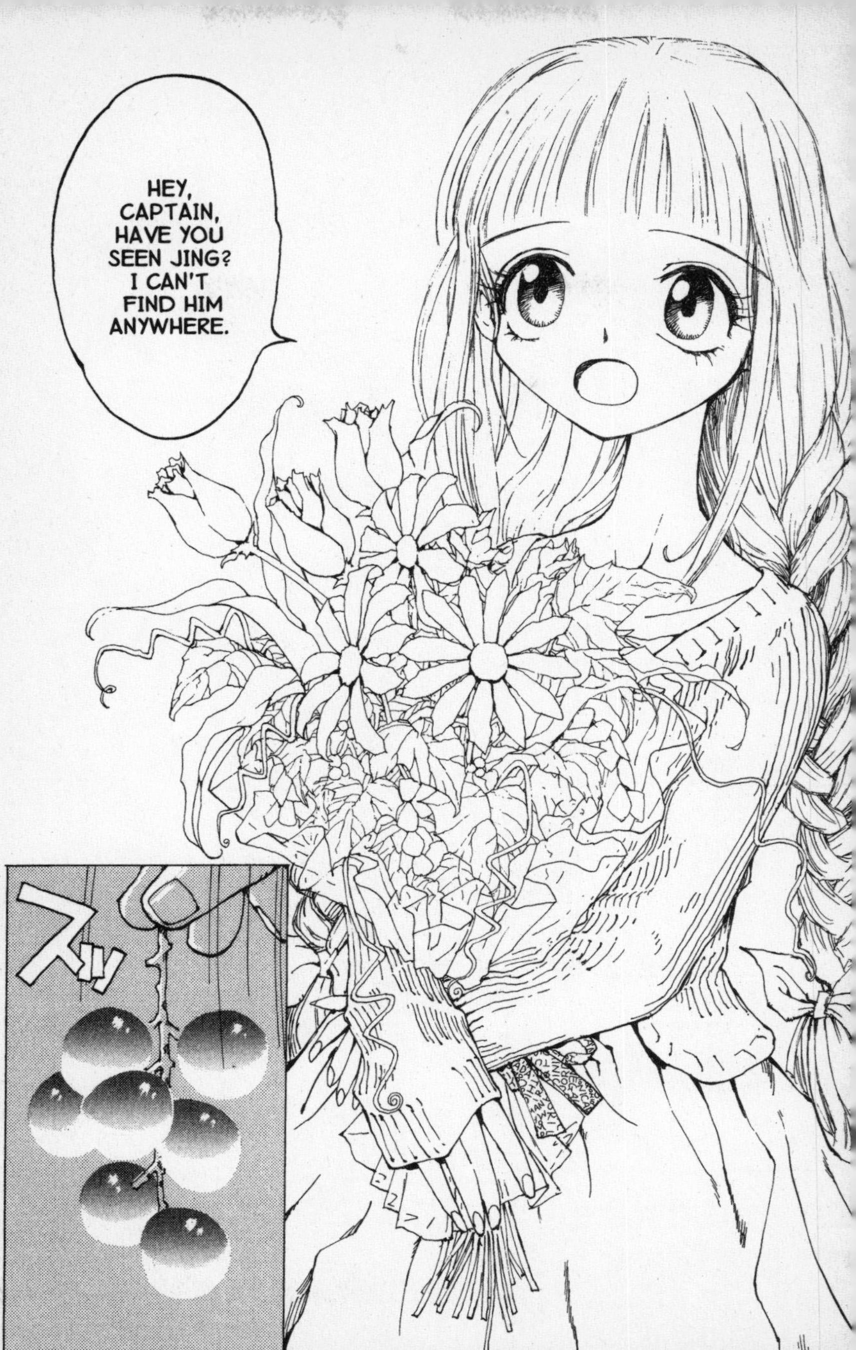
HEY, CAPTAIN, HAVE YOU SEEN JING? I CAN'T FIND HIM ANYWHERE.
スッ

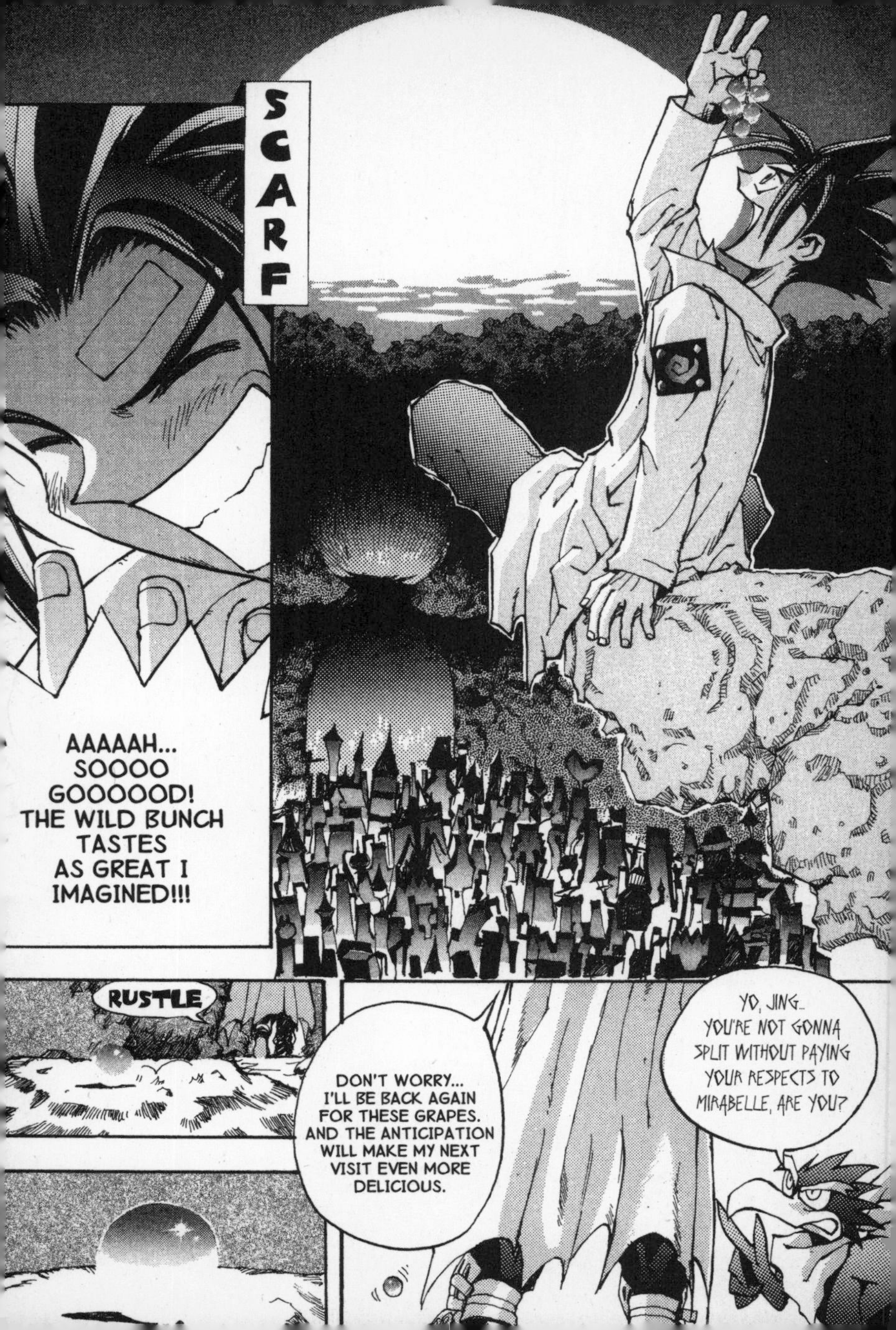
SCARF
AAAAAH... SOOOO GOOOOOD! THE WILD BUNCH TASTES AS GREAT I IMAGINED!!!
YO, JING... YOU'RE NOT GONNA SPLIT WITHOUT PAYING YOUR RESPECTS TO MIRABELLE, ARE YOU?
DON'T WORRY... I'LL BE BACK AGAIN FOR THESE GRAPES. AND THE ANTICIPATION WILL MAKE MY NEXT VISIT EVEN MORE DELICIOUS.
RUSTLE

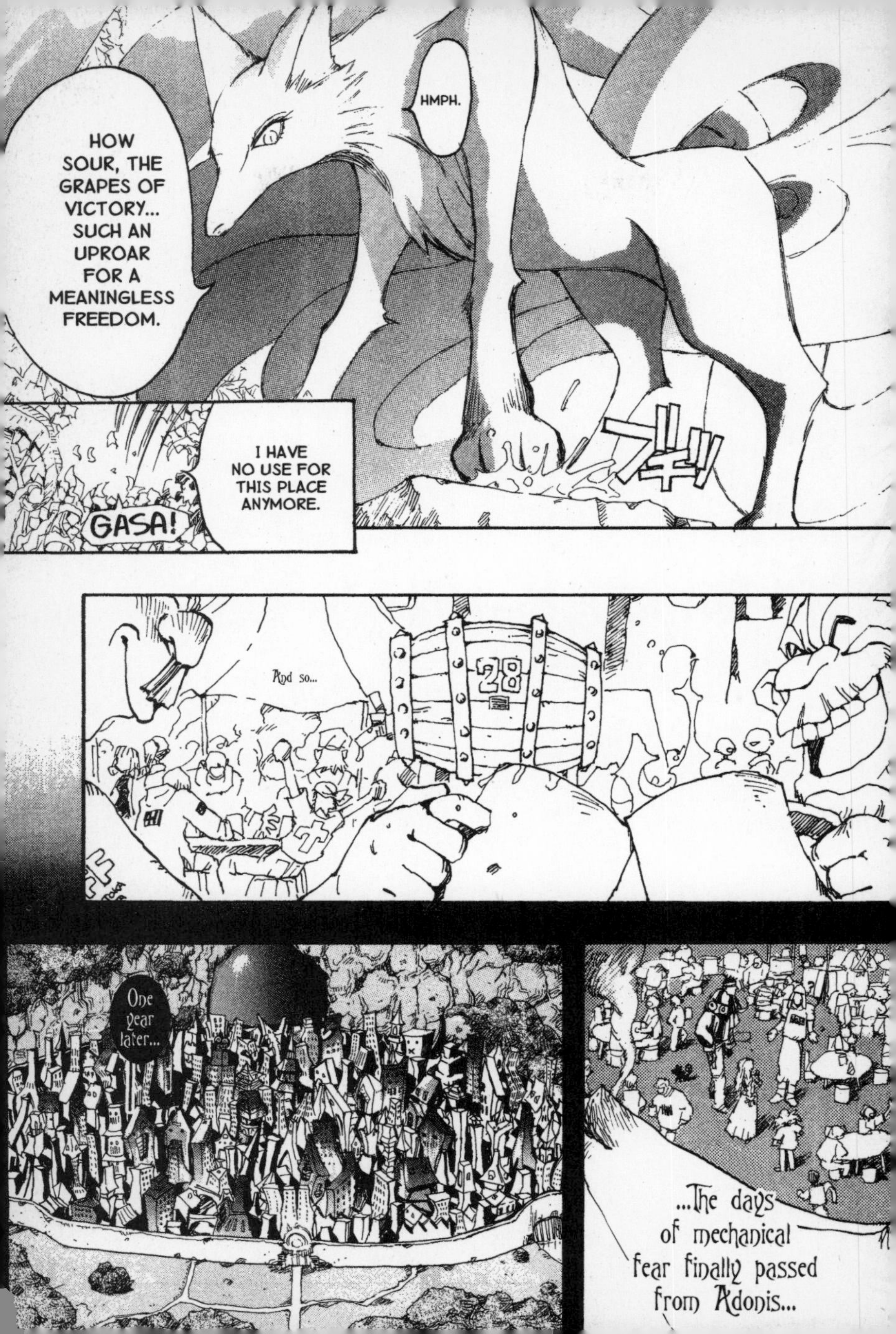
HMPH.
HOW SOUR, THE GRAPES OF VICTORY... SUCH AN UPROAR FOR A MEANINGLESS FREEDOM.
I HAVE NO USE FOR THIS PLACE ANYMORE.
GASA!
And so...
28
...The days of mechanical fear finally passed from Adonis...
One year later...

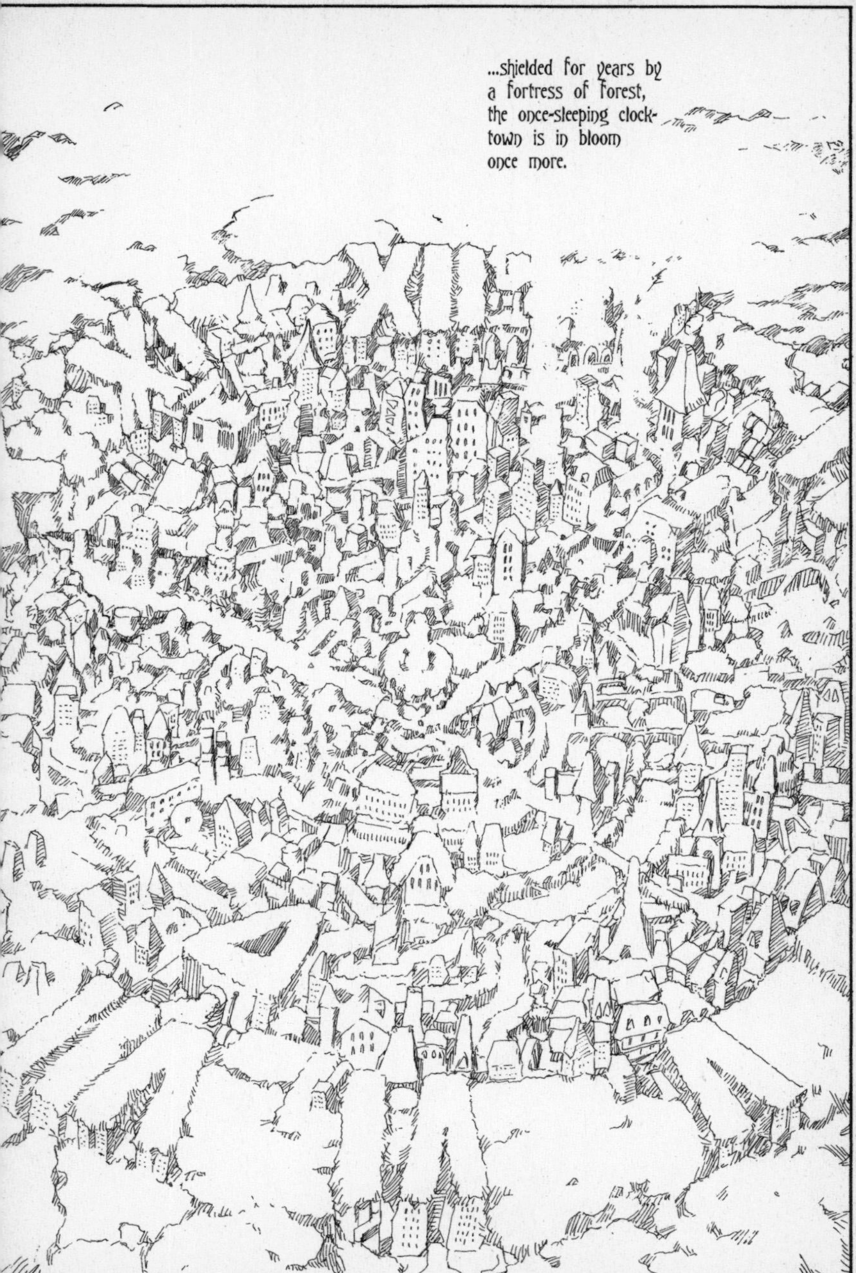
...shielded for years by a fortress of forest, the once-sleeping clock-town is in bloom once more.

For successful handling of a Porvora,
the following five points should always be heeded:

(1)

Placing the animal near fire is strictly prohibited.

(2)

If a shock vibration triggers an explosion,
move as far from the animal as possible.

(3)

Carefully earplug the animal during sleep, as accidental
explosion may occur if it is awoken by sudden noises.

(4)

Although chocolate is the animal's food of choice, all
traces of bitterness must be removed, and milk
should be added for best results.

Most importantly:

(5)
Whenever possible...
do not handle a Porvora.

(From the Authoritative Text on
Handling Dangerous Animals, Vol. 1)

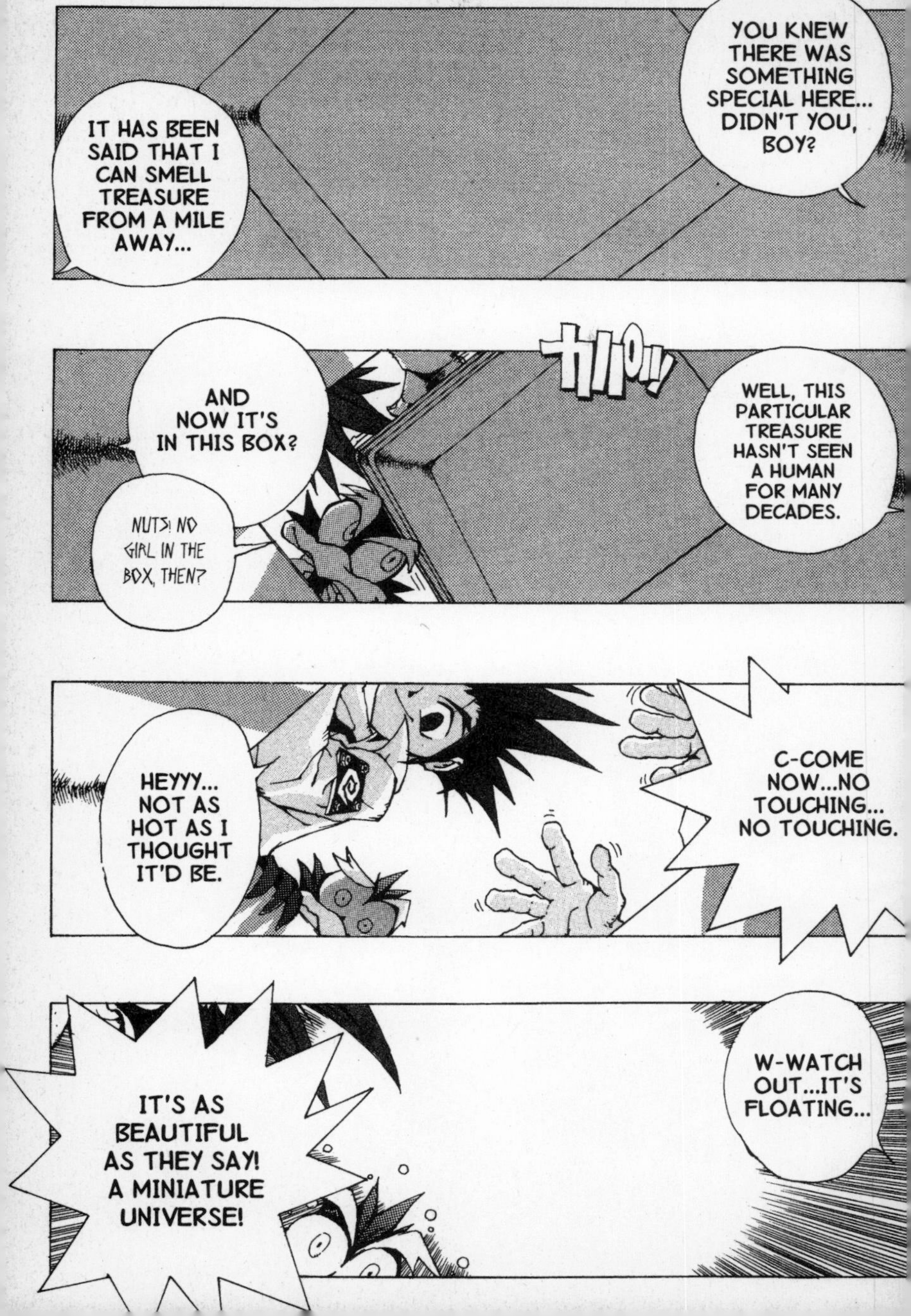
YOU KNEW THERE WAS SOMETHING SPECIAL HERE... DIDN'T YOU, BOY?
IT HAS BEEN SAID THAT I CAN SMELL TREASURE FROM A MILE AWAY...
WELL, THIS PARTICULAR TREASURE HASN'T SEEN A HUMAN FOR MANY DECADES.
AND NOW IT'S IN THIS BOX?
NUTS! NO GIRL IN THE BOX, THEN?
C-COME NOW...NO TOUCHING... NO TOUCHING.
HEYYY... NOT AS HOT AS I THOUGHT IT'D BE.
W-WATCH OUT...IT'S FLOATING...
IT'S AS BEAUTIFUL AS THEY SAY! A MINIATURE UNIVERSE!

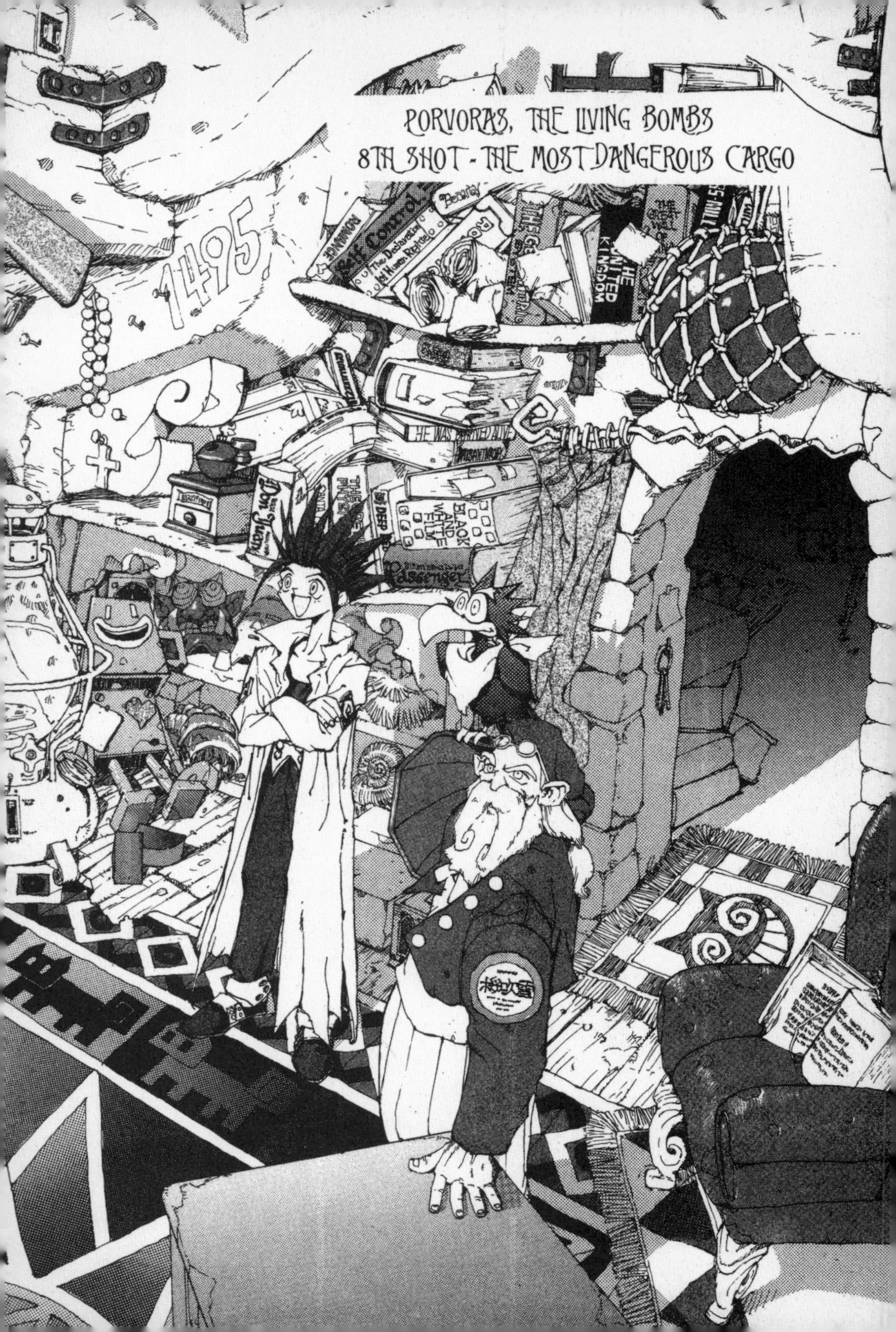
PORVORAS, THE LIVING BOMBS
8TH SHOT - THE MOST DANGEROUS CARGO
1495

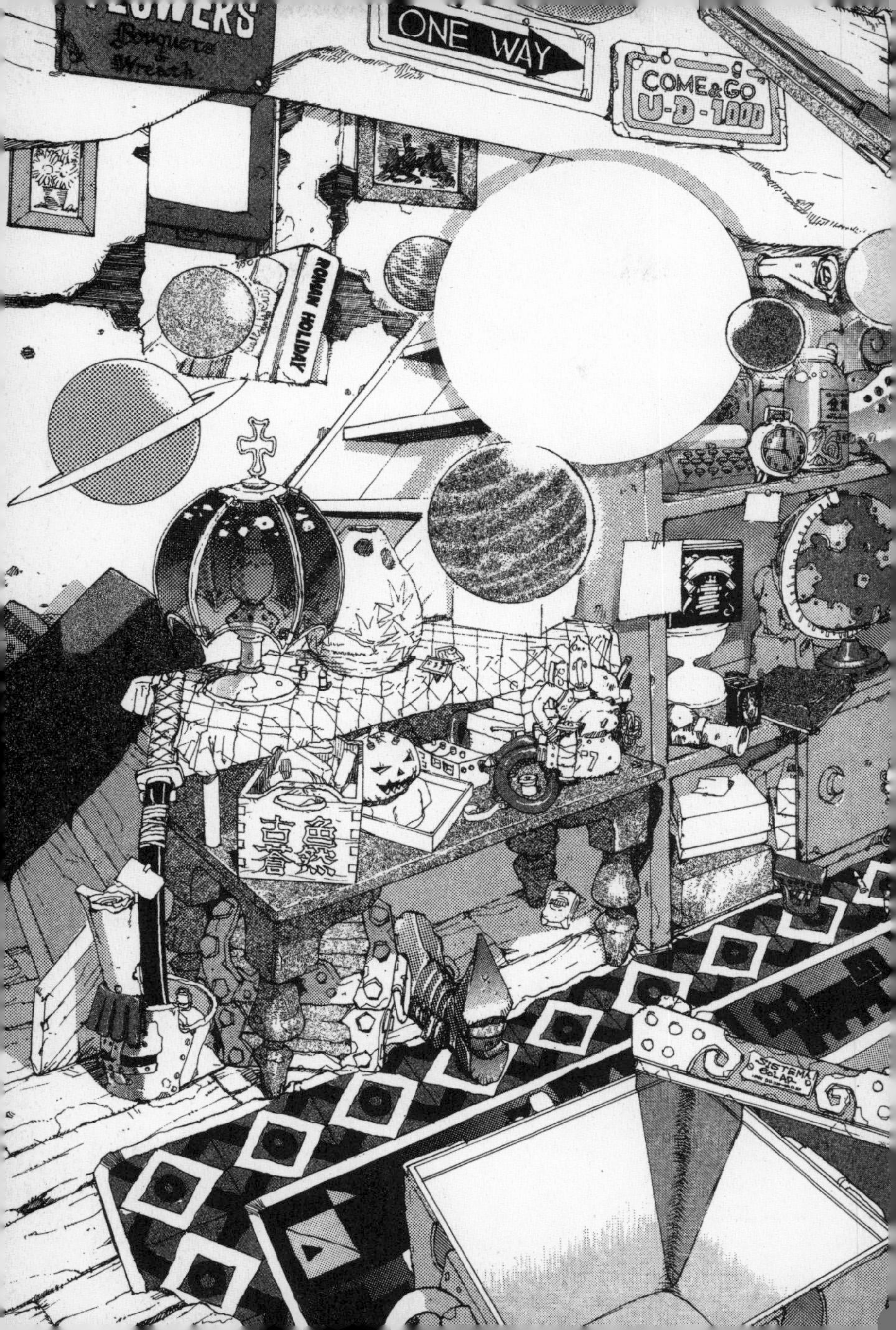
ONE WAY
COME&GO
ROMAN HOLIDAY

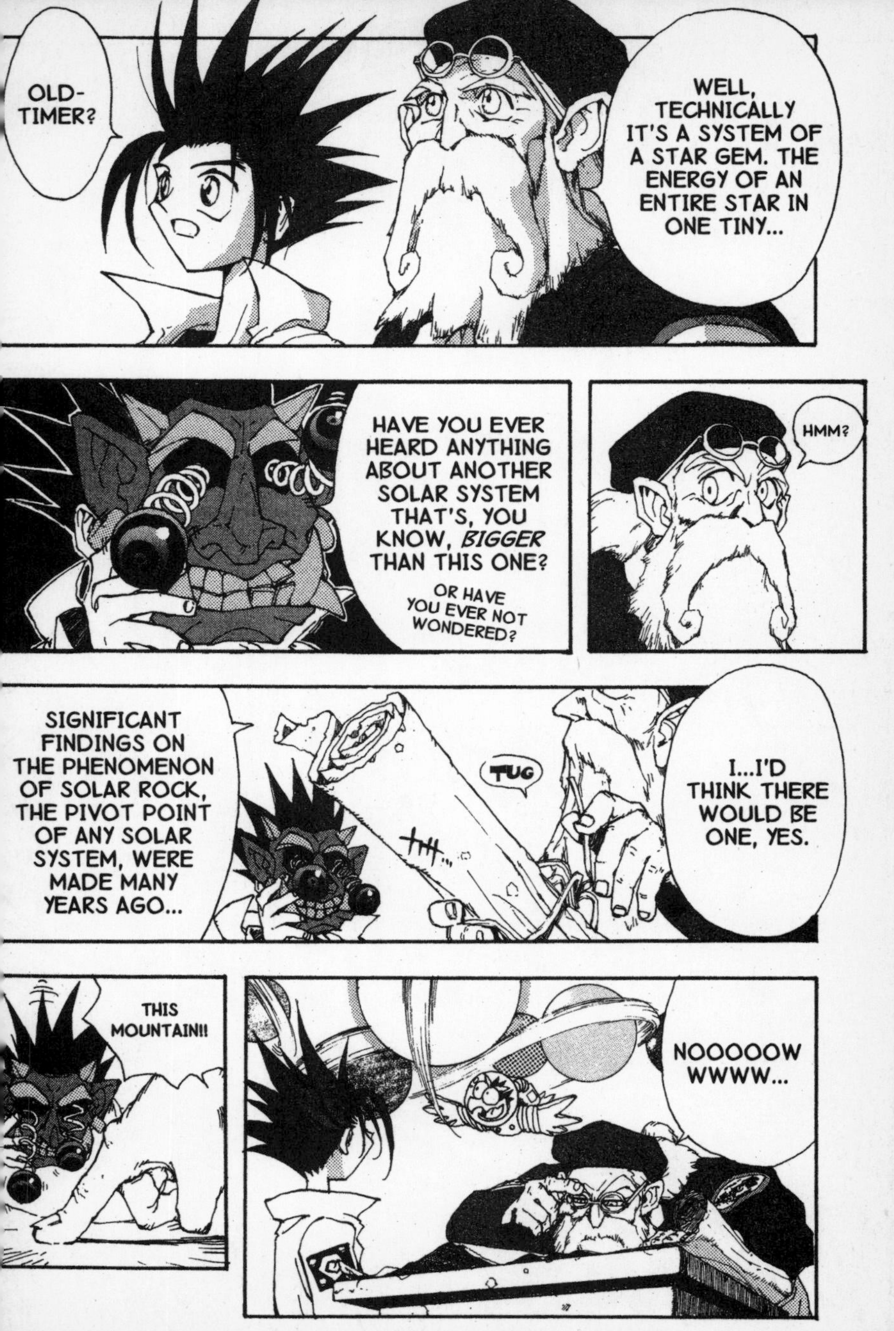
WELL, TECHNICALLY IT'S A SYSTEM OF A STAR GEM. THE ENERGY OF AN ENTIRE STAR IN ONE TINY...
OLD-TIMER?
HMM?
HAVE YOU EVER HEARD ANYTHING ABOUT ANOTHER SOLAR SYSTEM THAT'S, YOU KNOW, *BIGGER* THAN THIS ONE?
OR HAVE YOU EVER NOT WONDERED?
I...I'D THINK THERE WOULD BE ONE, YES.
TUG
SIGNIFICANT FINDINGS ON THE PHENOMENON OF SOLAR ROCK, THE PIVOT POINT OF ANY SOLAR SYSTEM, WERE MADE MANY YEARS AGO...
NOOOOOW WWWW...
THIS MOUNTAIN!!

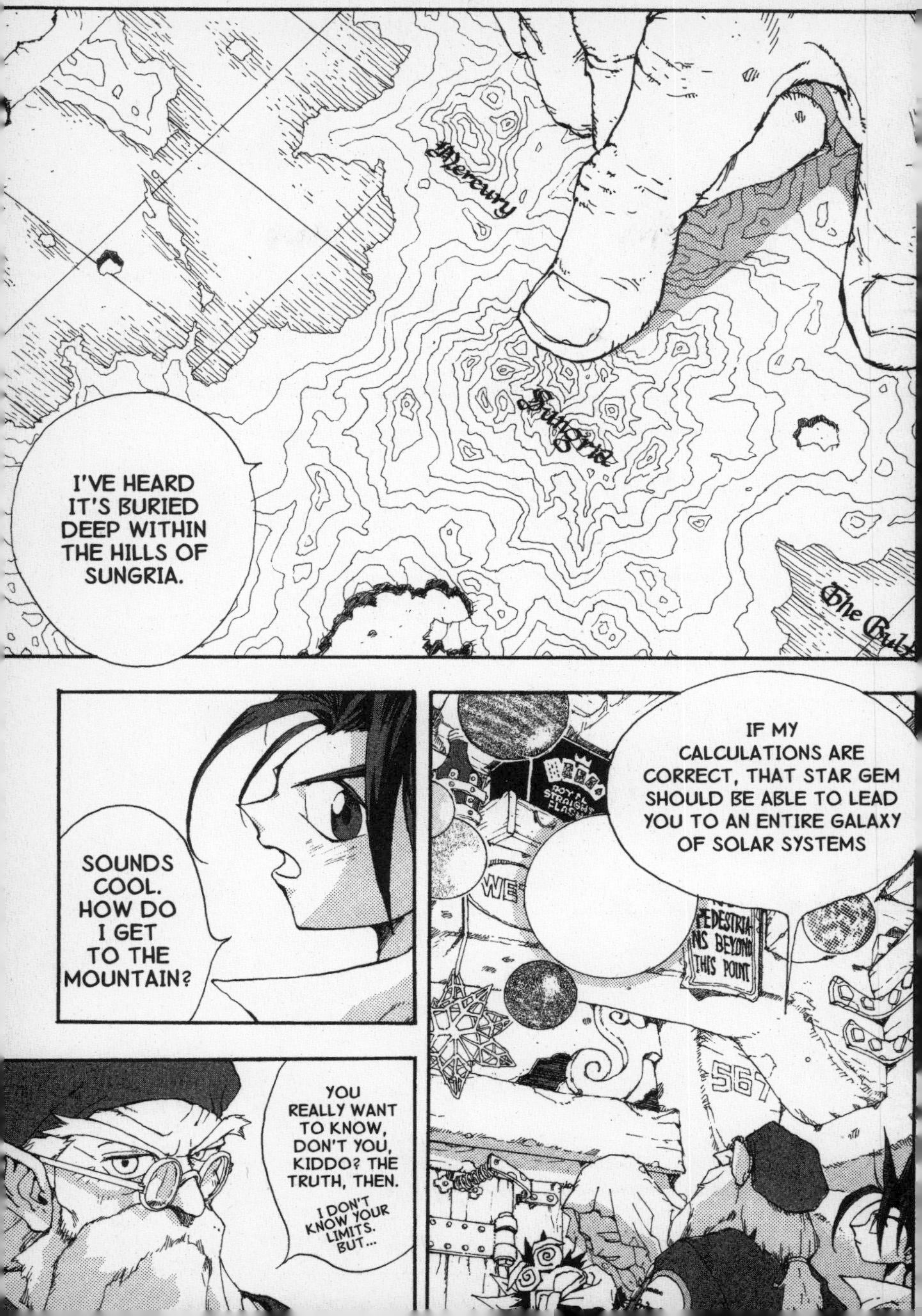
Mercury
Sungria
The Gulf
I'VE HEARD IT'S BURIED DEEP WITHIN THE HILLS OF SUNGRIA.
IF MY CALCULATIONS ARE CORRECT, THAT STAR GEM SHOULD BE ABLE TO LEAD YOU TO AN ENTIRE GALAXY OF SOLAR SYSTEMS
PEDESTRIA NS BEYOND THIS POINT
567
SOUNDS COOL. HOW DO I GET TO THE MOUNTAIN?
YOU REALLY WANT TO KNOW, DON'T YOU, KIDDO? THE TRUTH, THEN.
I DON'T KNOW YOUR LIMITS. BUT...

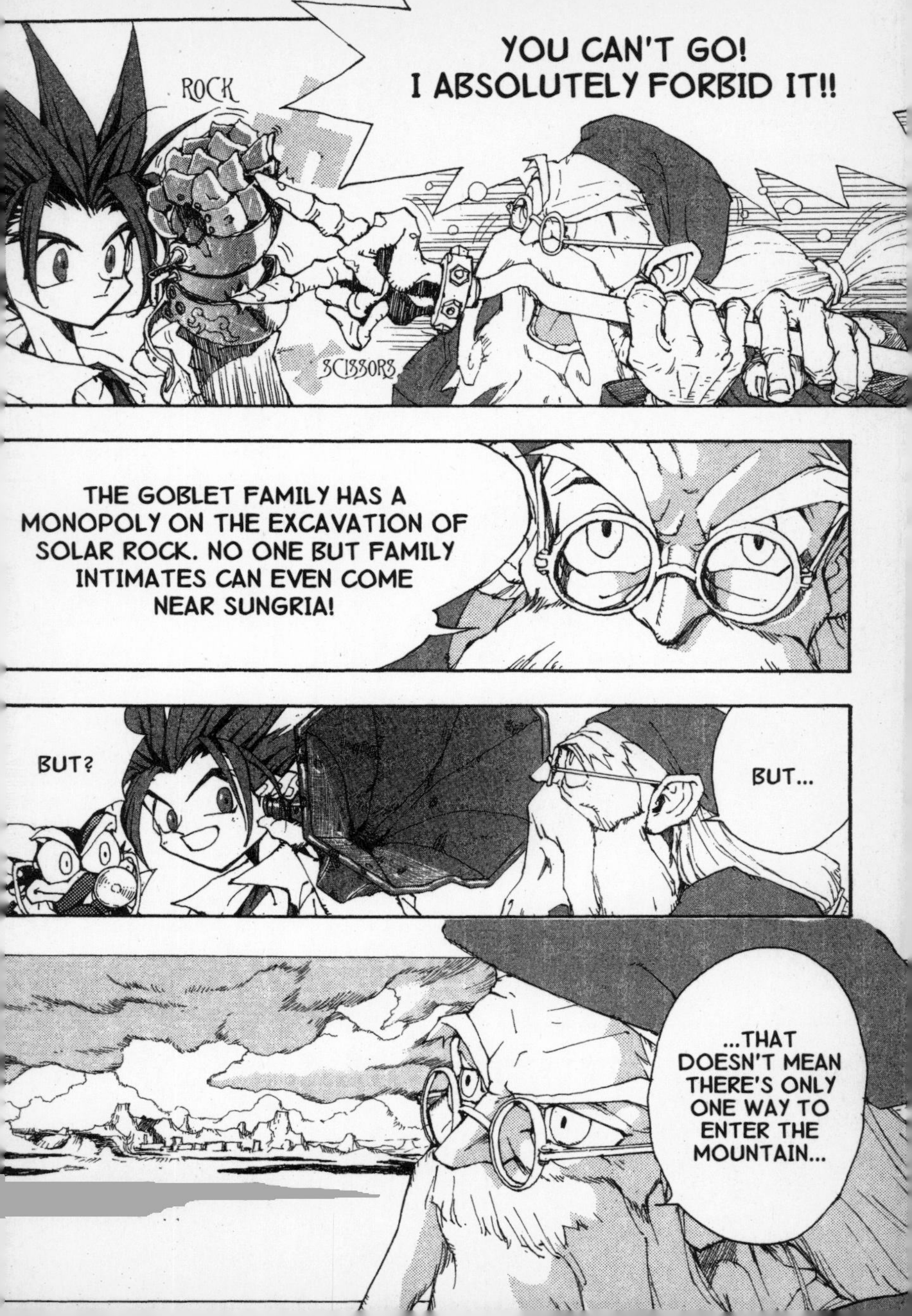
YOU CAN'T GO! I ABSOLUTELY FORBID IT!!
ROCK
SCISSORS
THE GOBLET FAMILY HAS A MONOPOLY ON THE EXCAVATION OF SOLAR ROCK. NO ONE BUT FAMILY INTIMATES CAN EVEN COME NEAR SUNGRIA!
BUT...
BUT?
...THAT DOESN'T MEAN THERE'S ONLY ONE WAY TO ENTER THE MOUNTAIN...

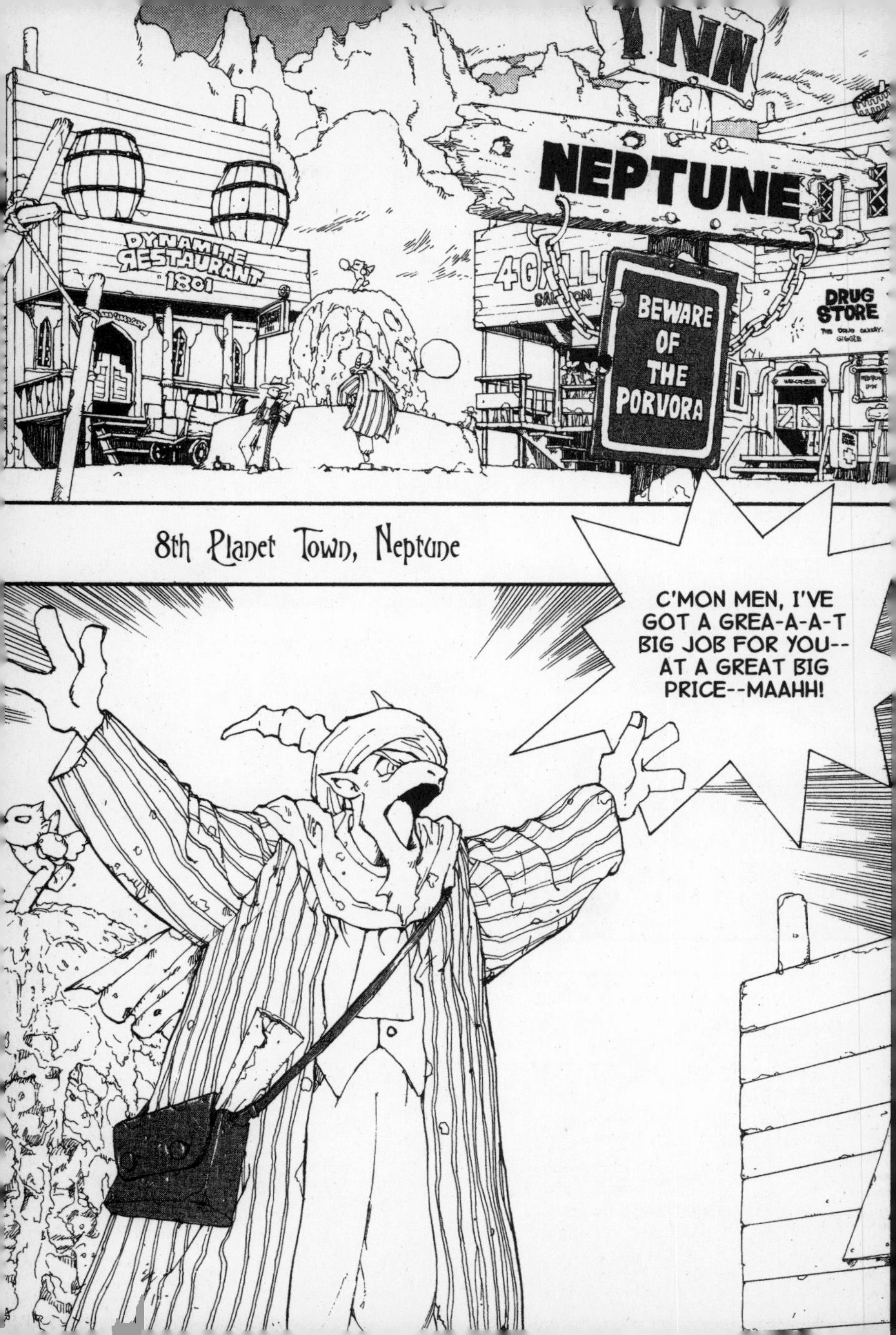
INN
NEPTUNE
BEWARE OF THE PORVORA
DRUG STORE
DYNAMITE RESTAURANT 1801
8th Planet Town, Neptune
C'MON MEN, I'VE GOT A GREA-A-A-T BIG JOB FOR YOU-- AT A GREAT BIG PRICE--MAAHH!

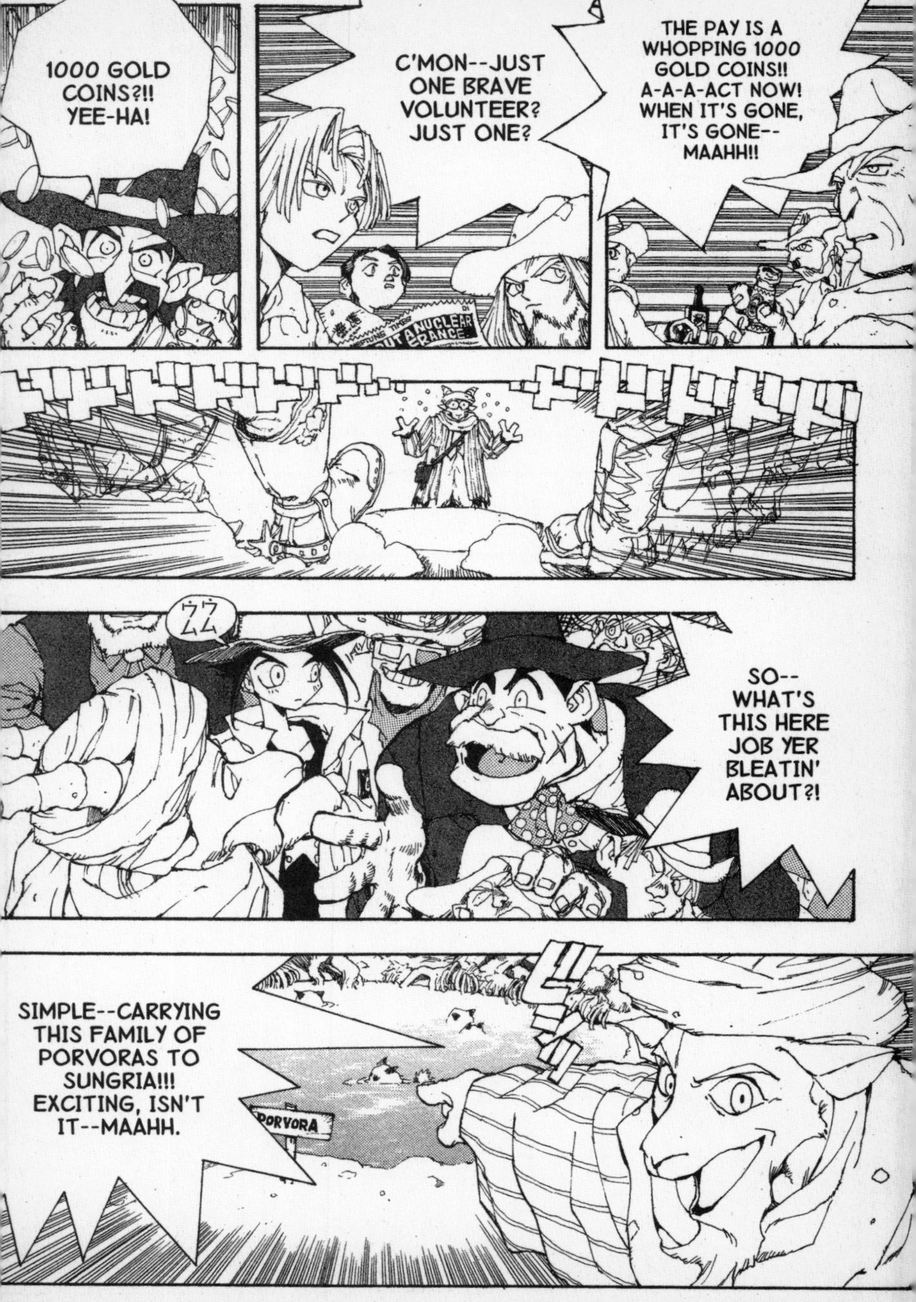
THE PAY IS A WHOPPING 1000 GOLD COINS!! A-A-A-ACT NOW! WHEN IT'S GONE, IT'S GONE--MAAHH!!
C'MON--JUST ONE BRAVE VOLUNTEER? JUST ONE?
1000 GOLD COINS?!! YEE-HA!
SO--WHAT'S THIS HERE JOB YER BLEATIN' ABOUT?!
SIMPLE--CARRYING THIS FAMILY OF PORVORAS TO SUNGRIA!!! EXCITING, ISN'T IT--MAAHH.
PORVORA

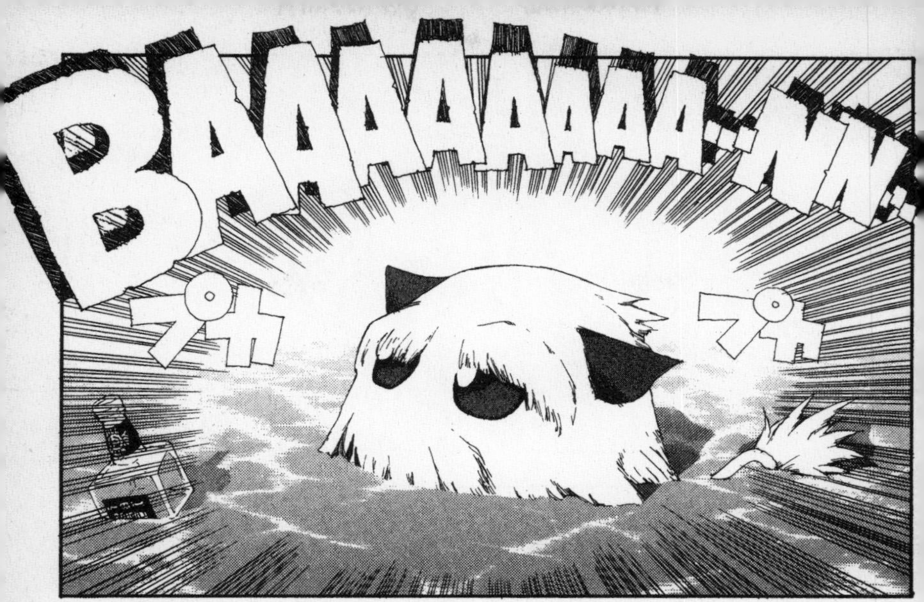
BAAAAAAA--NN...

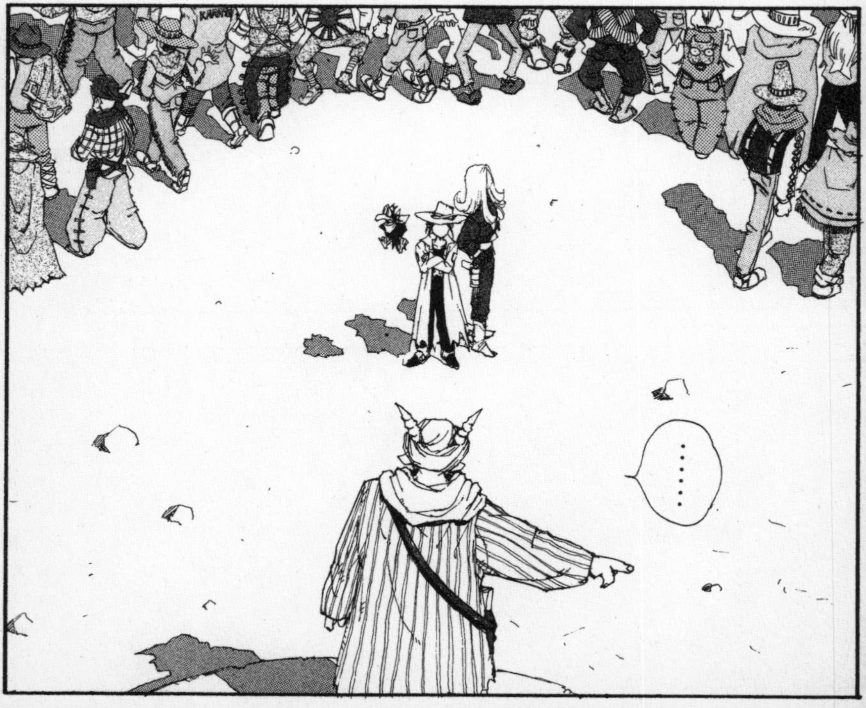
......

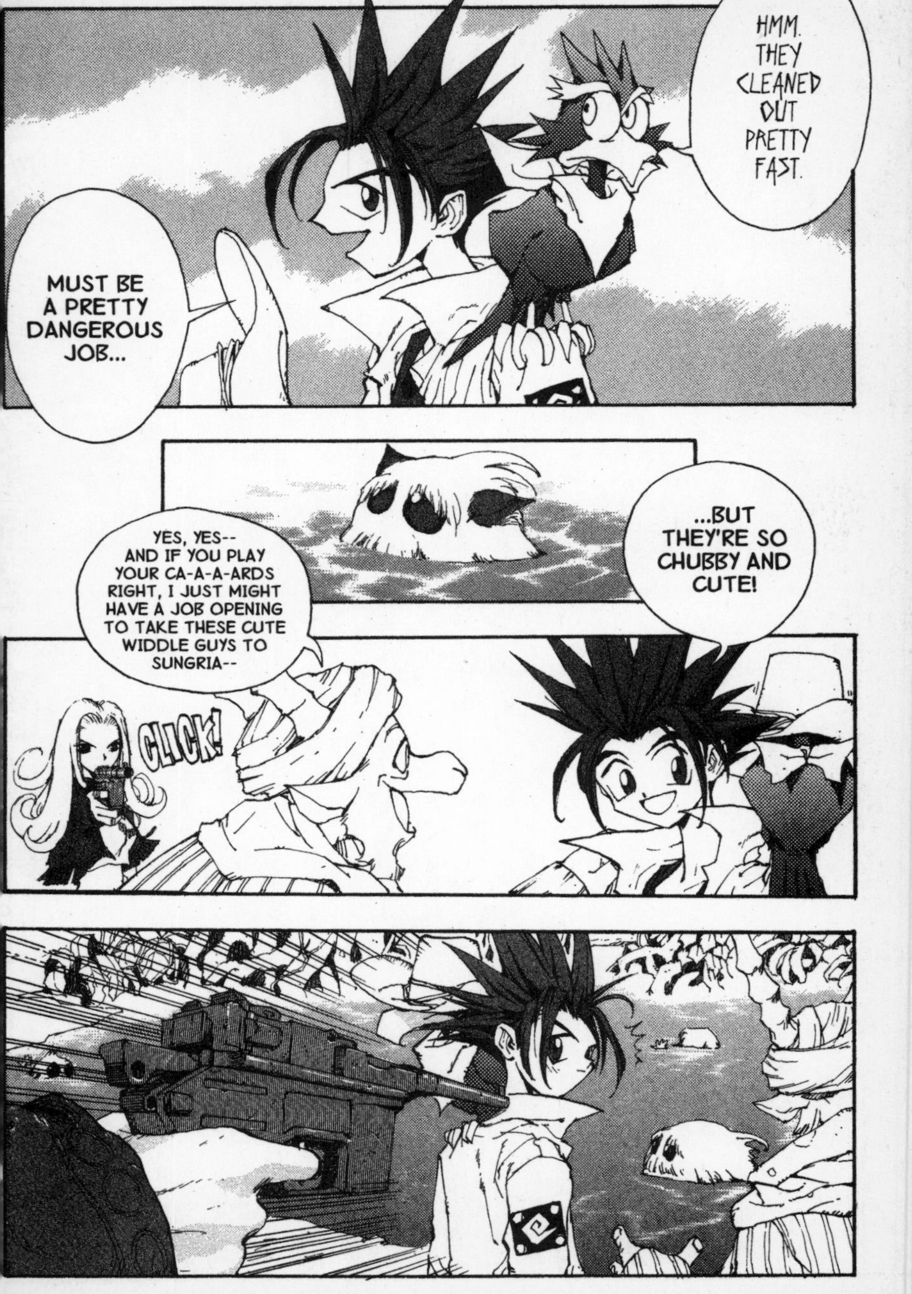
HMM. THEY CLEANED OUT PRETTY FAST.
MUST BE A PRETTY DANGEROUS JOB...
...BUT THEY'RE SO CHUBBY AND CUTE!
YES, YES-- AND IF YOU PLAY YOUR CA-A-A-ARDS RIGHT, I JUST MIGHT HAVE A JOB OPENING TO TAKE THESE CUTE WIDDLE GUYS TO SUNGRIA--
CLICK!

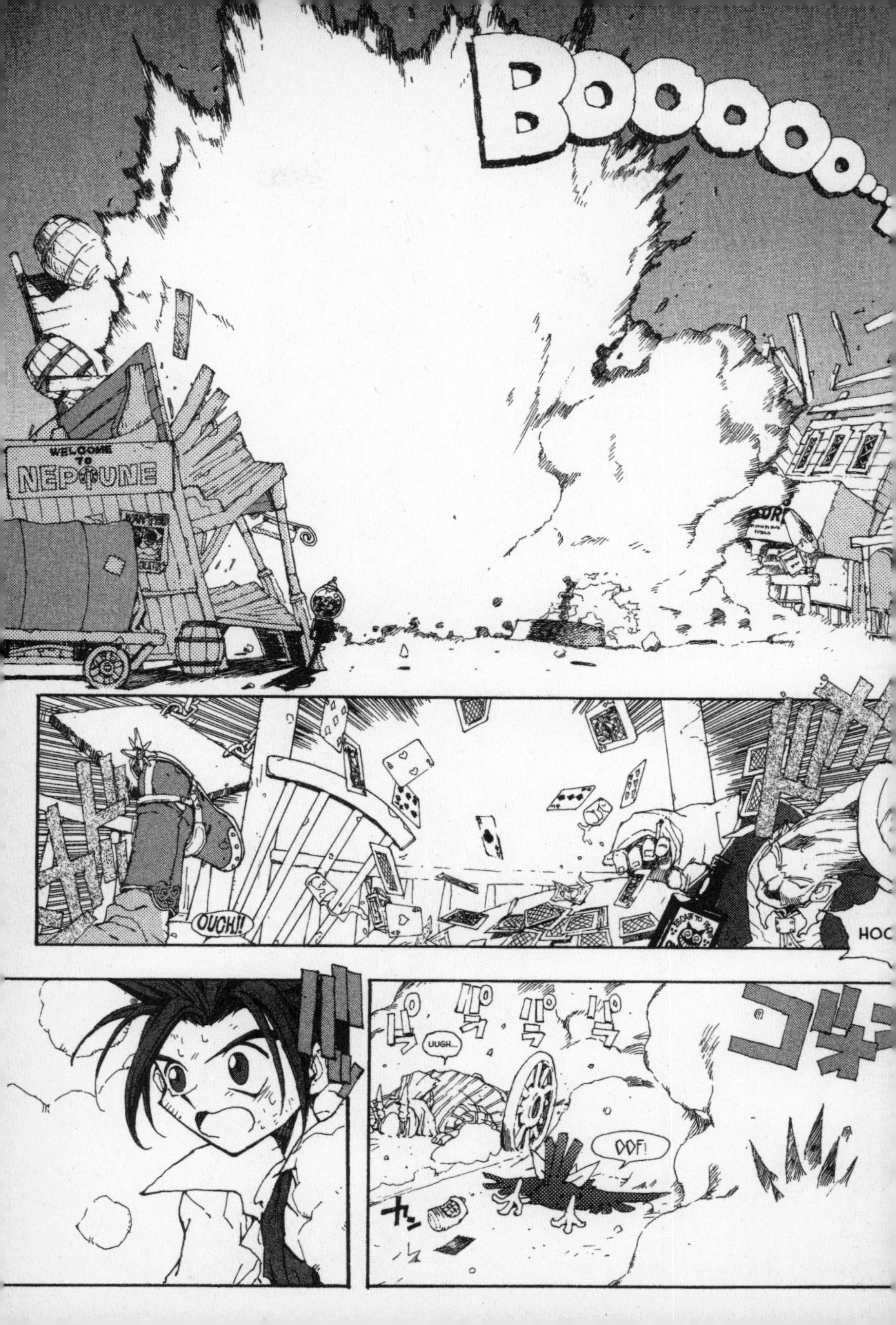
BOOOOOO...
WELCOME TO NEPTUNE
HOC
OUCH!!
UUGH...
OOF!

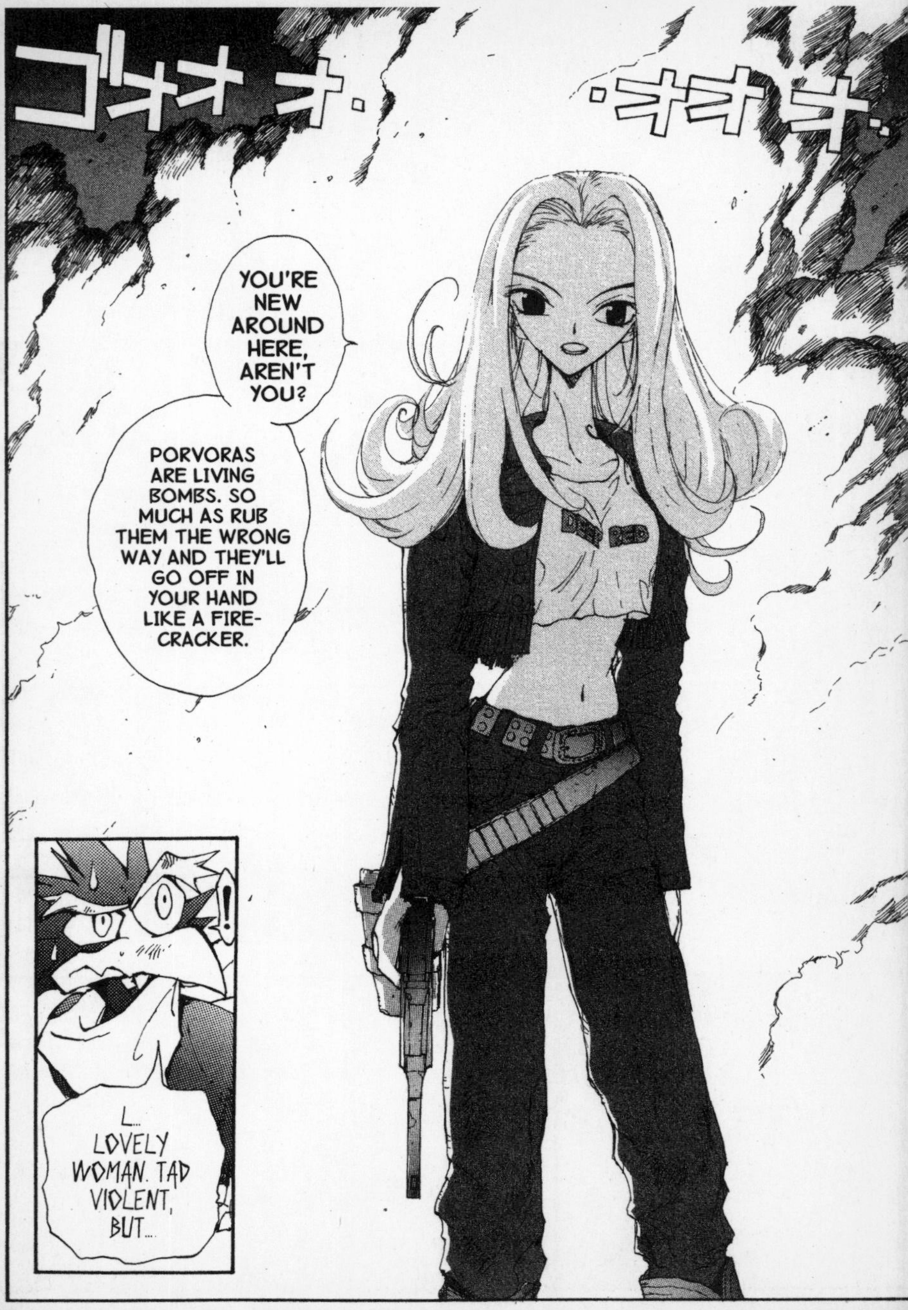
ゴォォオ・
・オオオ・・
YOU'RE NEW AROUND HERE, AREN'T YOU?
PORVORAS ARE LIVING BOMBS. SO MUCH AS RUB THEM THE WRONG WAY AND THEY'LL GO OFF IN YOUR HAND LIKE A FIRE-CRACKER.
!
L... LOVELY WOMAN. TAD VIOLENT, BUT...

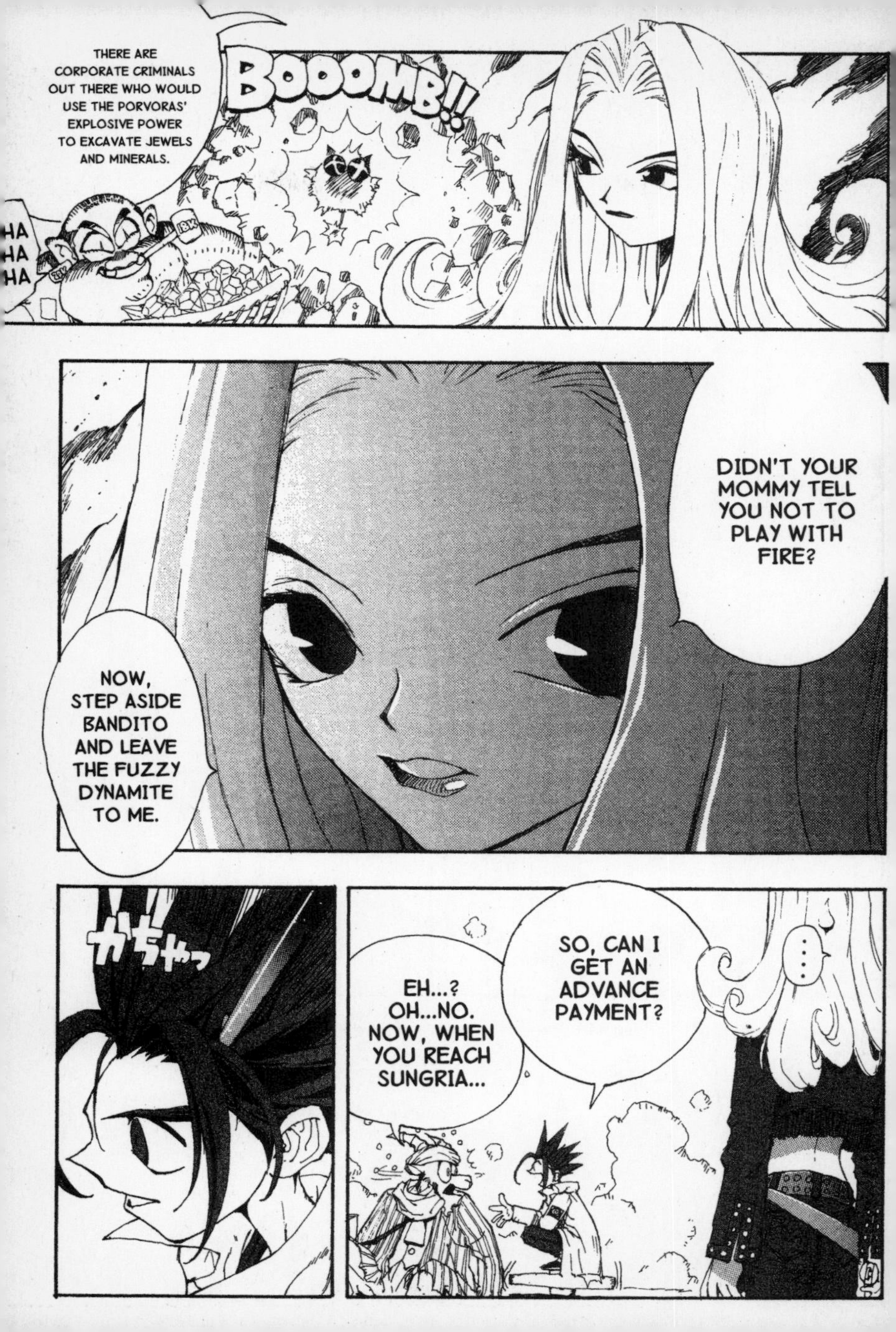
THERE ARE CORPORATE CRIMINALS OUT THERE WHO WOULD USE THE PORVORAS' EXPLOSIVE POWER TO EXCAVATE JEWELS AND MINERALS.
BOOOOMB!!
HA HA HA HA
DIDN'T YOUR MOMMY TELL YOU NOT TO PLAY WITH FIRE?
NOW, STEP ASIDE BANDITO AND LEAVE THE FUZZY DYNAMITE TO ME.
.....
SO, CAN I GET AN ADVANCE PAYMENT?
EH...? OH...NO. NOW, WHEN YOU REACH SUNGRIA...
がちゃっ

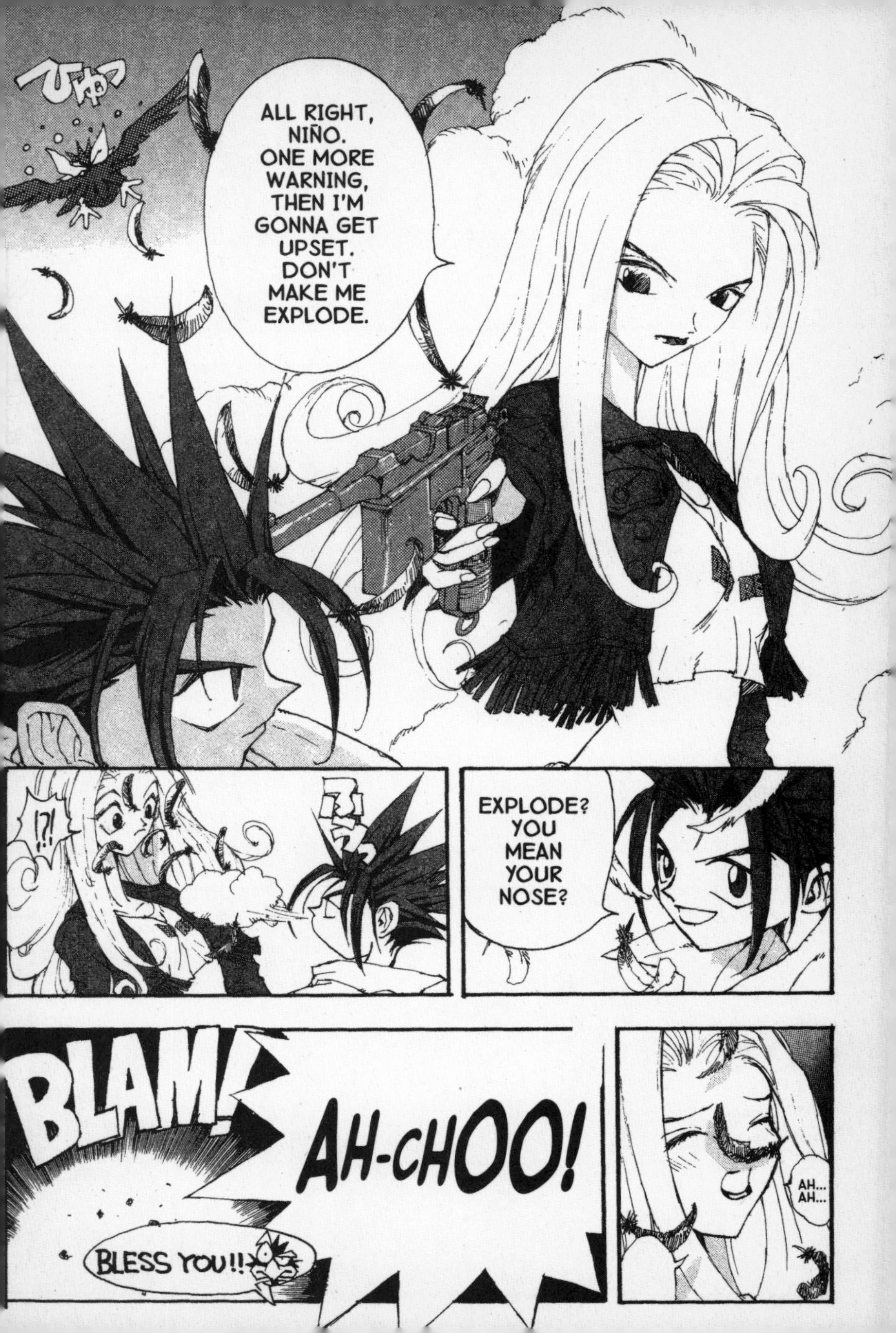
ぴゅっ
ALL RIGHT, NIÑO. ONE MORE WARNING, THEN I'M GONNA GET UPSET. DON'T MAKE ME EXPLODE.
EXPLODE? YOU MEAN YOUR NOSE?
!?!
AH... AH...
BLAM!
AH-CHOO!
BLESS YOU!!

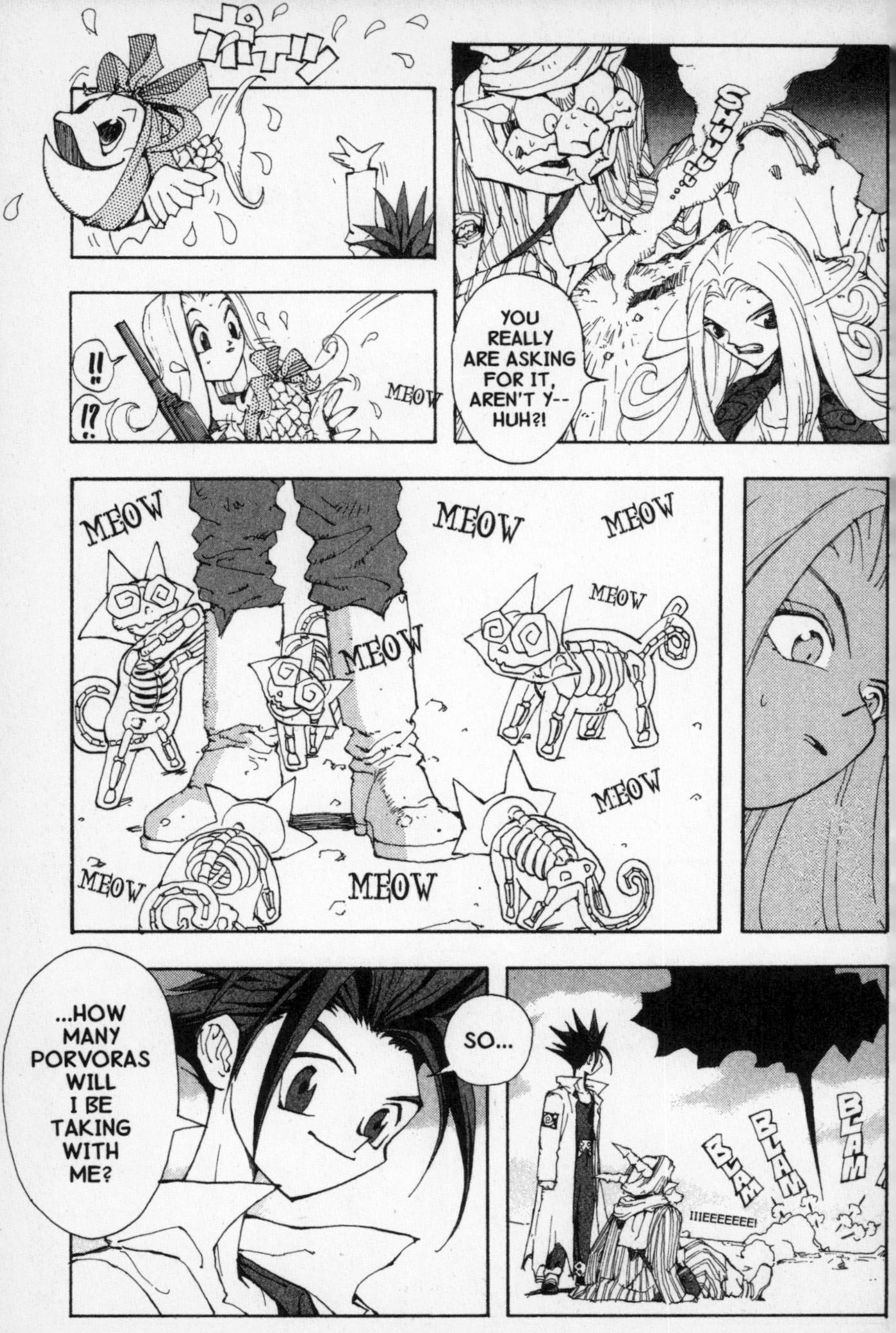
SHUUGGG...
YOU REALLY ARE ASKING FOR IT, AREN'T Y-- HUH?!
!!
!?
MEOW
MEOW
MEOW
MEOW
MEOW
MEOW
MEOW
MEOW
MEOW
BLAM
BLAM
BLAM
IIIEEEEEEE!
SO...
...HOW MANY PORVORAS WILL I BE TAKING WITH ME?

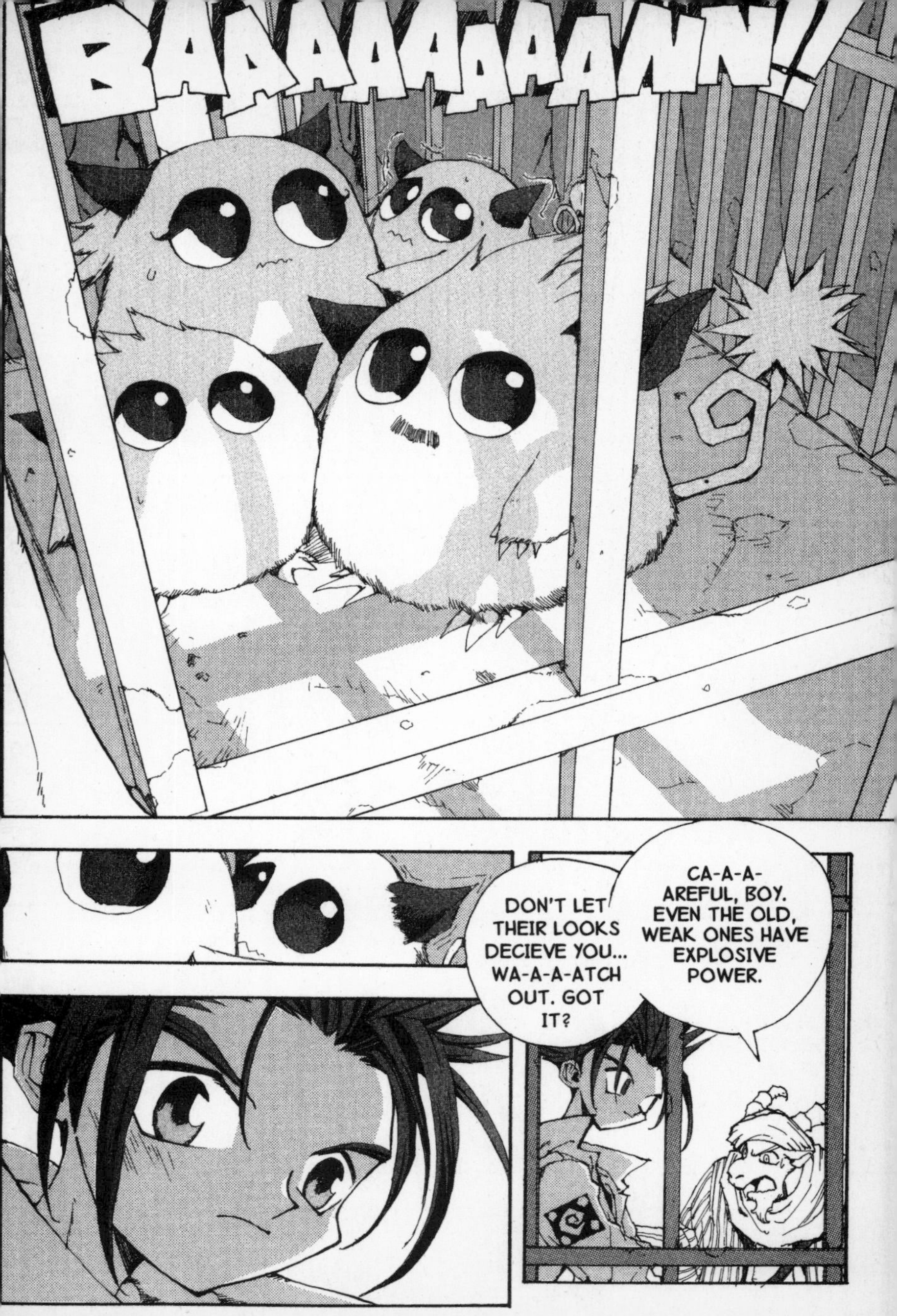
BAAAAAAAANN!!
CA-A-A-AREFUL, BOY. EVEN THE OLD, WEAK ONES HAVE EXPLOSIVE POWER.
DON'T LET THEIR LOOKS DECIEVE YOU... WA-A-A-ATCH OUT. GOT IT?

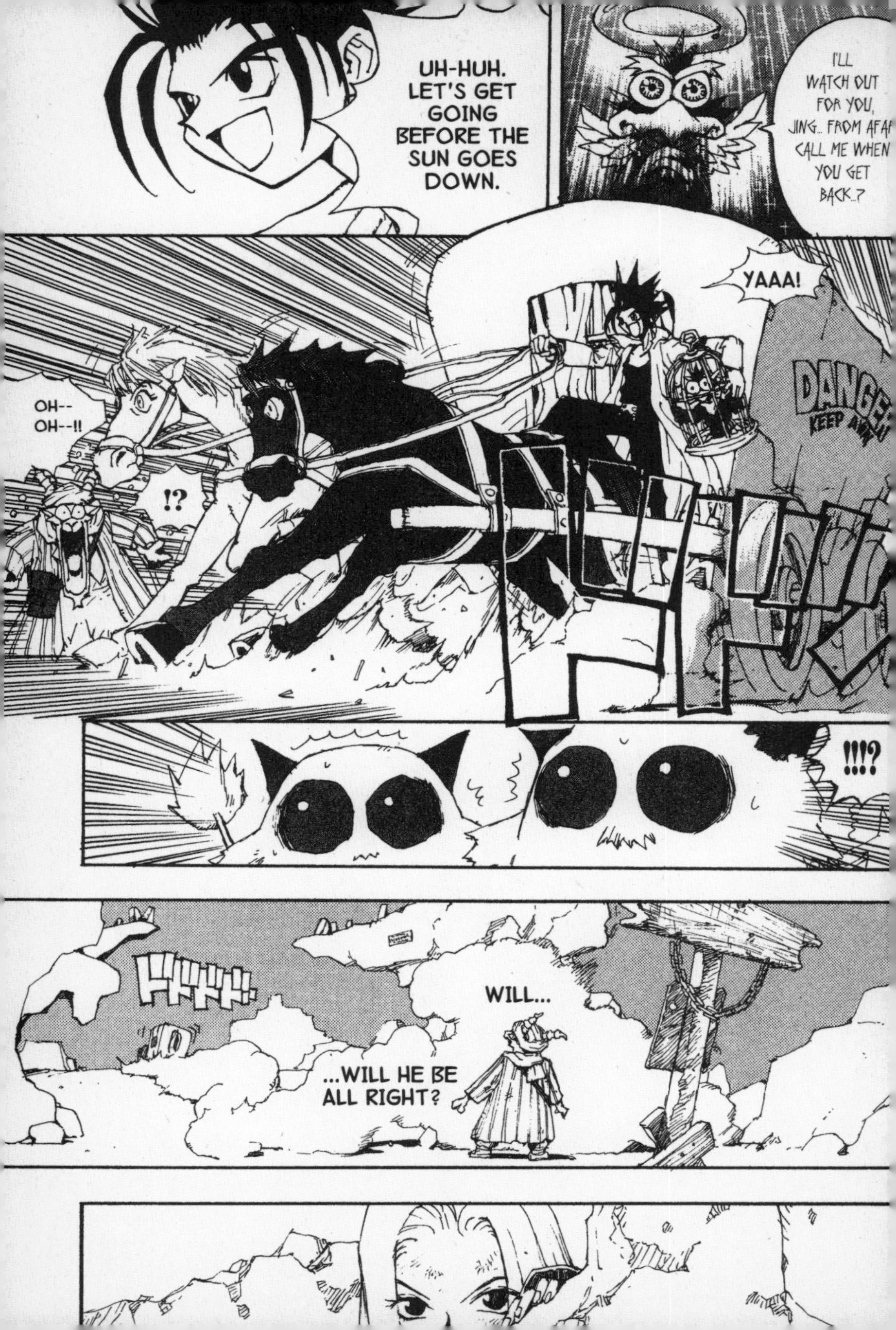
I'LL WATCH OUT FOR YOU, JING... FROM AFA
CALL ME WHEN YOU GET BACK..?
UH-HUH. LET'S GET GOING BEFORE THE SUN GOES DOWN.
YAAA!
DANGE
KEEP AWA
OH-- OH--!!
!?
!!!?
WILL...
...WILL HE BE ALL RIGHT?

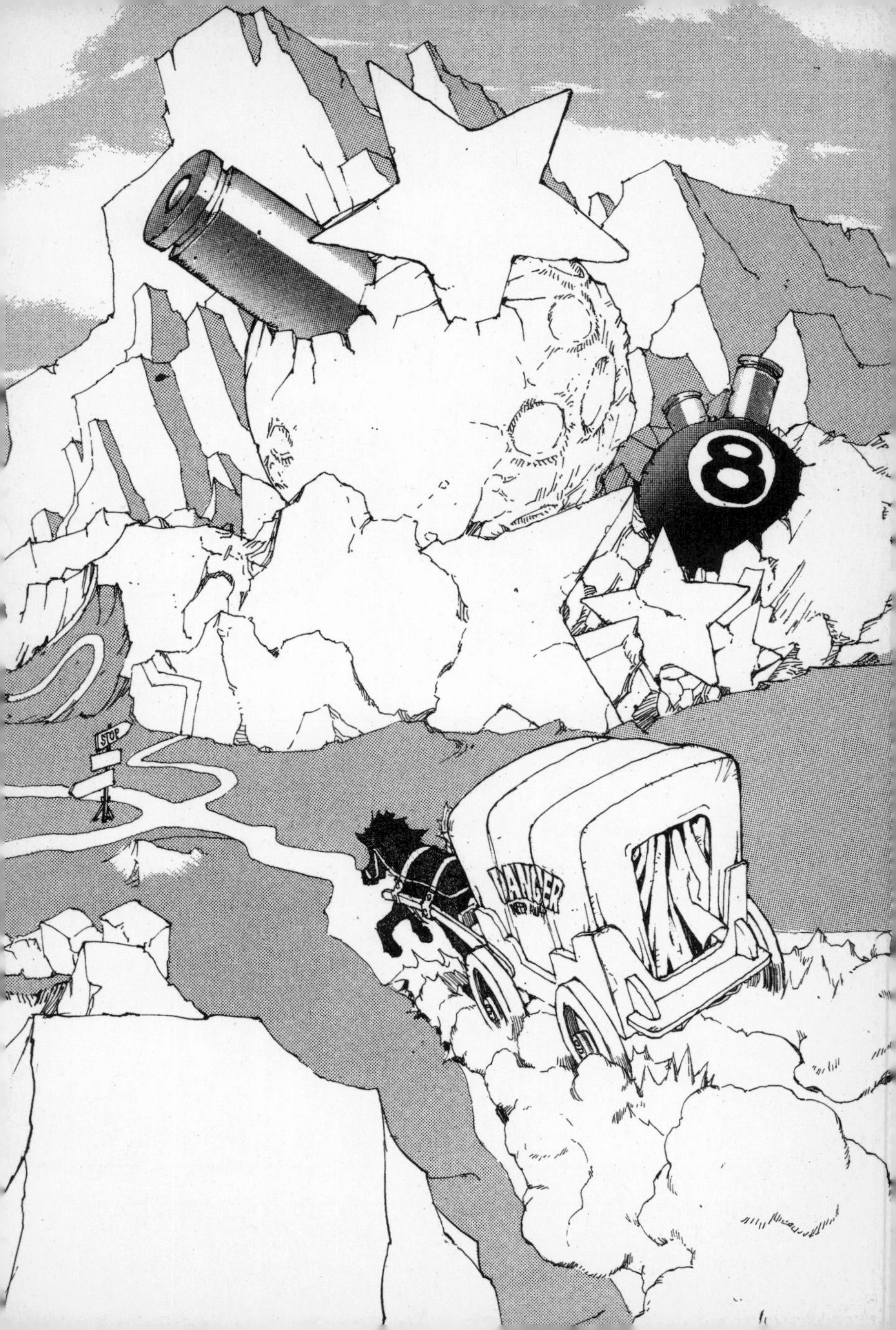
STOP
DANGER

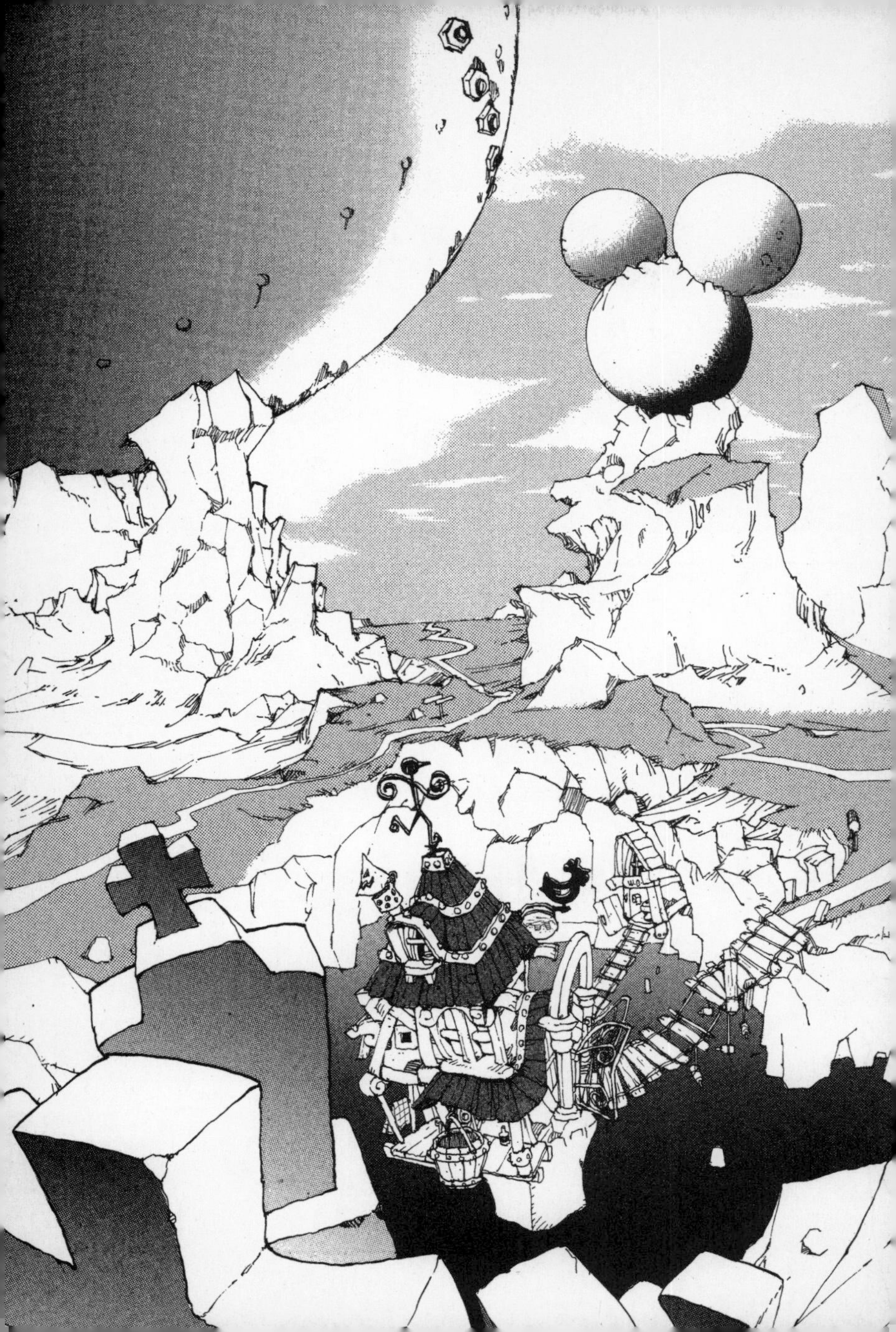

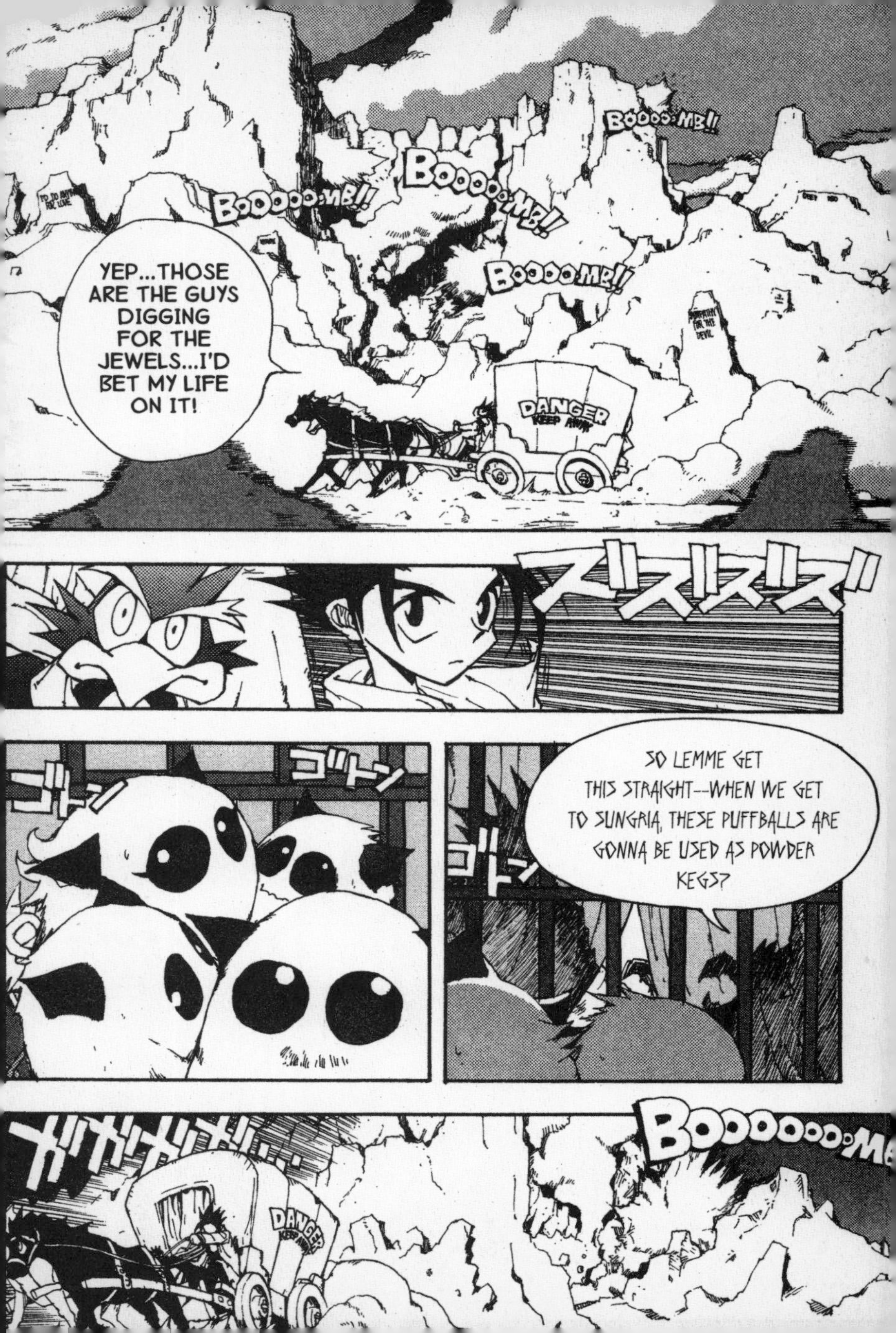
BOOOO-MB!!
BOOOOOO-MB!!
BOOOOO-MB!!
BOOOOMB!!
YEP...THOSE ARE THE GUYS DIGGING FOR THE JEWELS...I'D BET MY LIFE ON IT!
DANGER
KEEP AWAY
SO LEMME GET THIS STRAIGHT--WHEN WE GET TO SUNGRIA, THESE PUFFBALLS ARE GONNA BE USED AS POWDER KEGS?
ゴトン
ゴトン
ゴトン
BOOOOOOO-MB
DANGER
KEEP AWAY

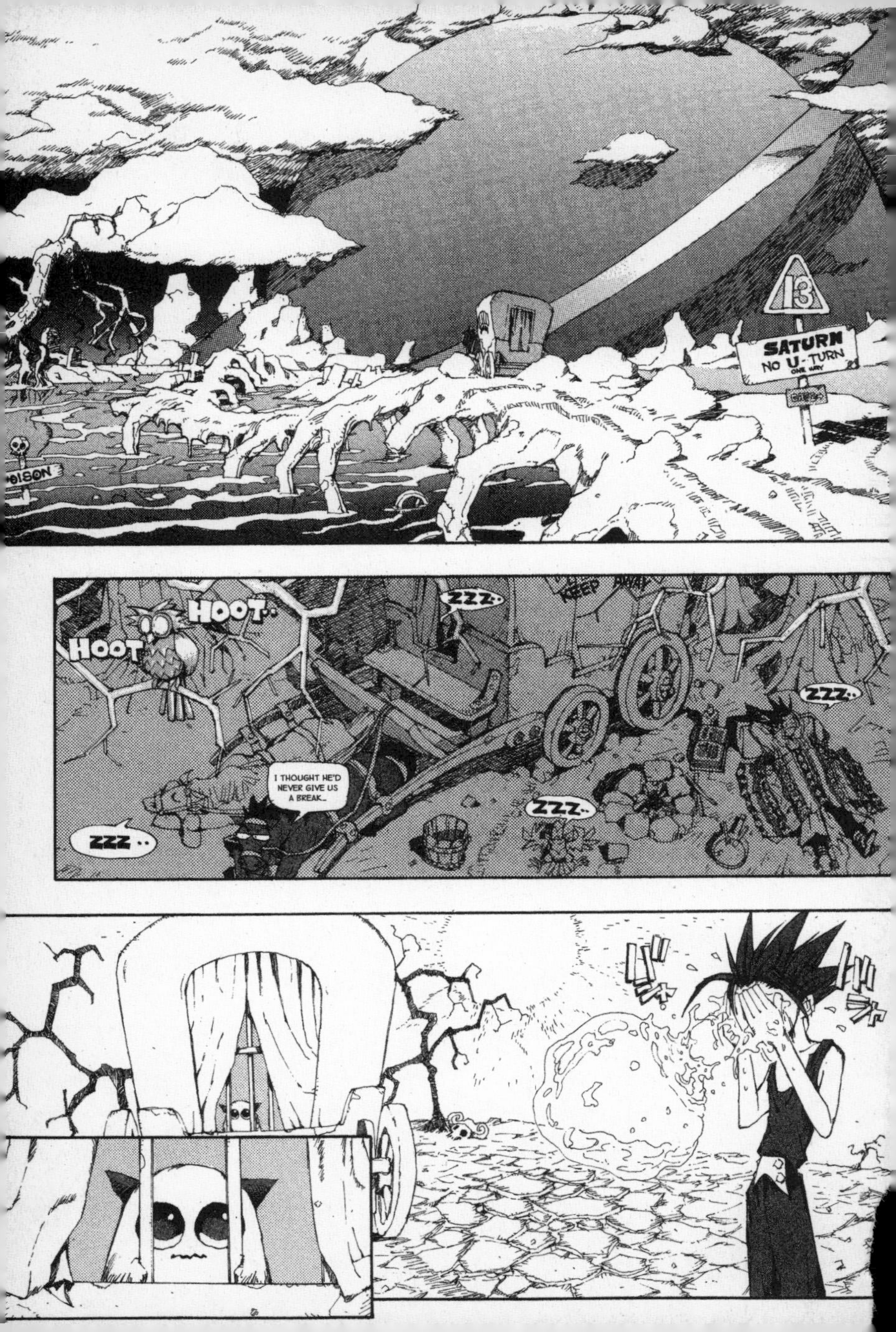
13
SATURN
NO U-TURN
ONE WAY
ZZZ..
KEEP AWAY
ZZZ..
ZZZ..
I THOUGHT HE'D NEVER GIVE US A BREAK...
HOOT..
HOOT
ZZZ..

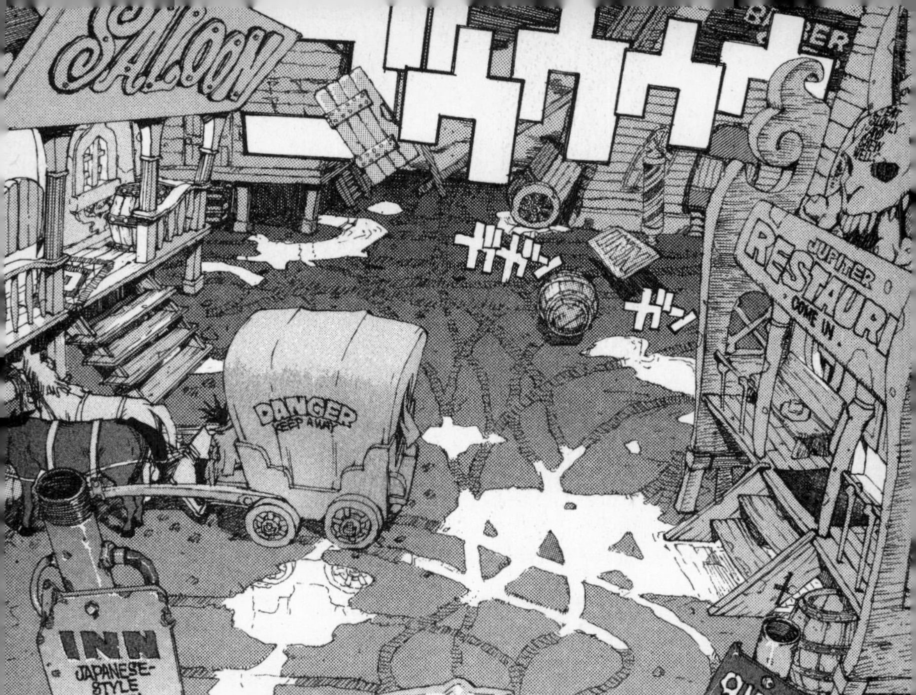
SALOON
ガン
INN
DANGER
KEEP AWAY
JUPITER
COME IN.
INN
JAPANESE-STYLE HOTEL
guack
WELCOME
JUPITER

5TH Planet Town, Jupiter

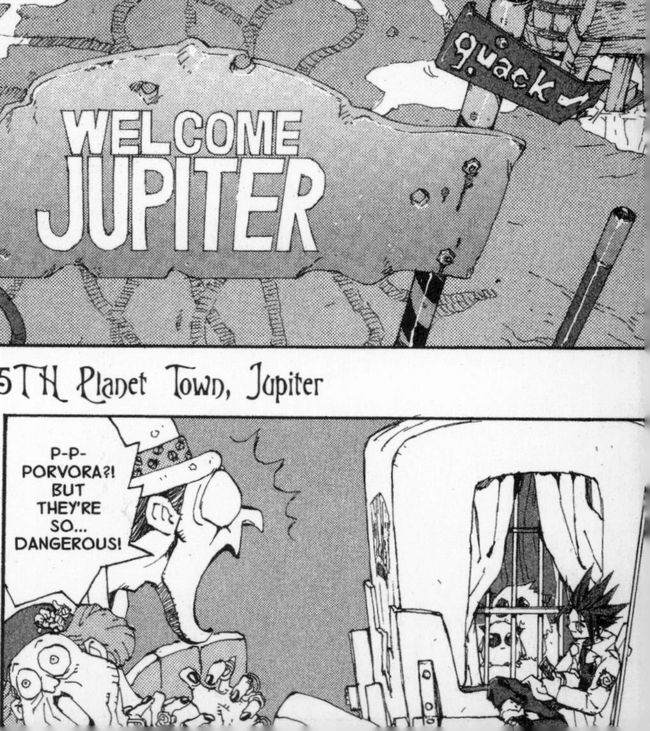
P-P-PORVORA?! BUT THEY'RE SO... DANGEROUS!

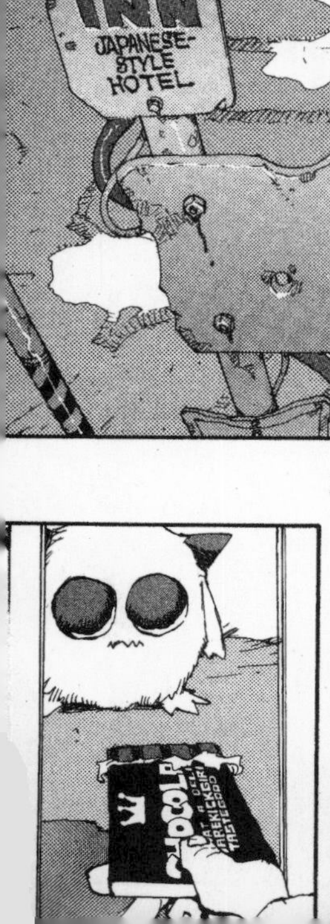

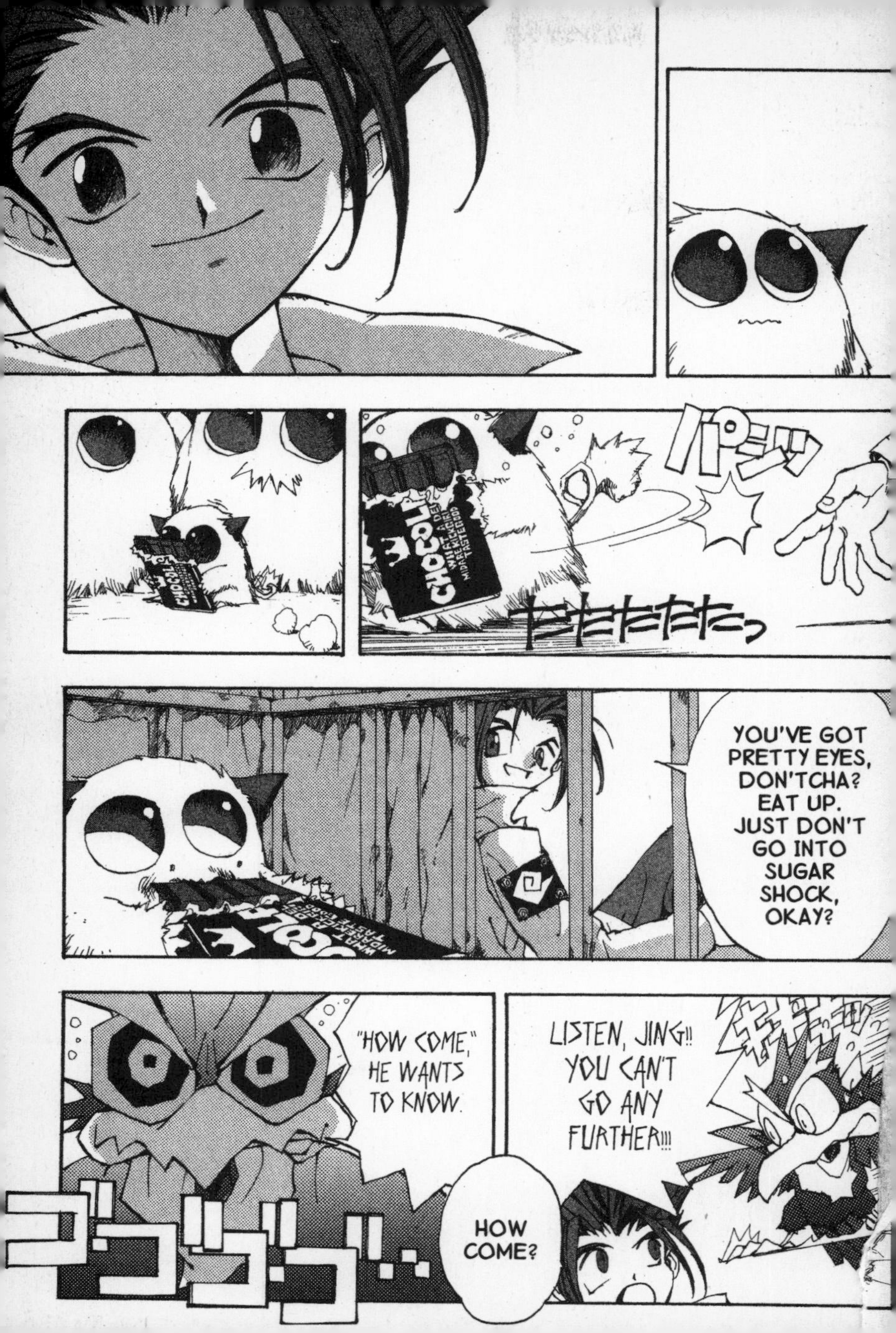
YOU'VE GOT PRETTY EYES, DON'TCHA? EAT UP. JUST DON'T GO INTO SUGAR SHOCK, OKAY?
LISTEN, JING!! YOU CAN'T GO ANY FURTHER!!!
HOW COME?
"HOW COME," HE WANTS TO KNOW.

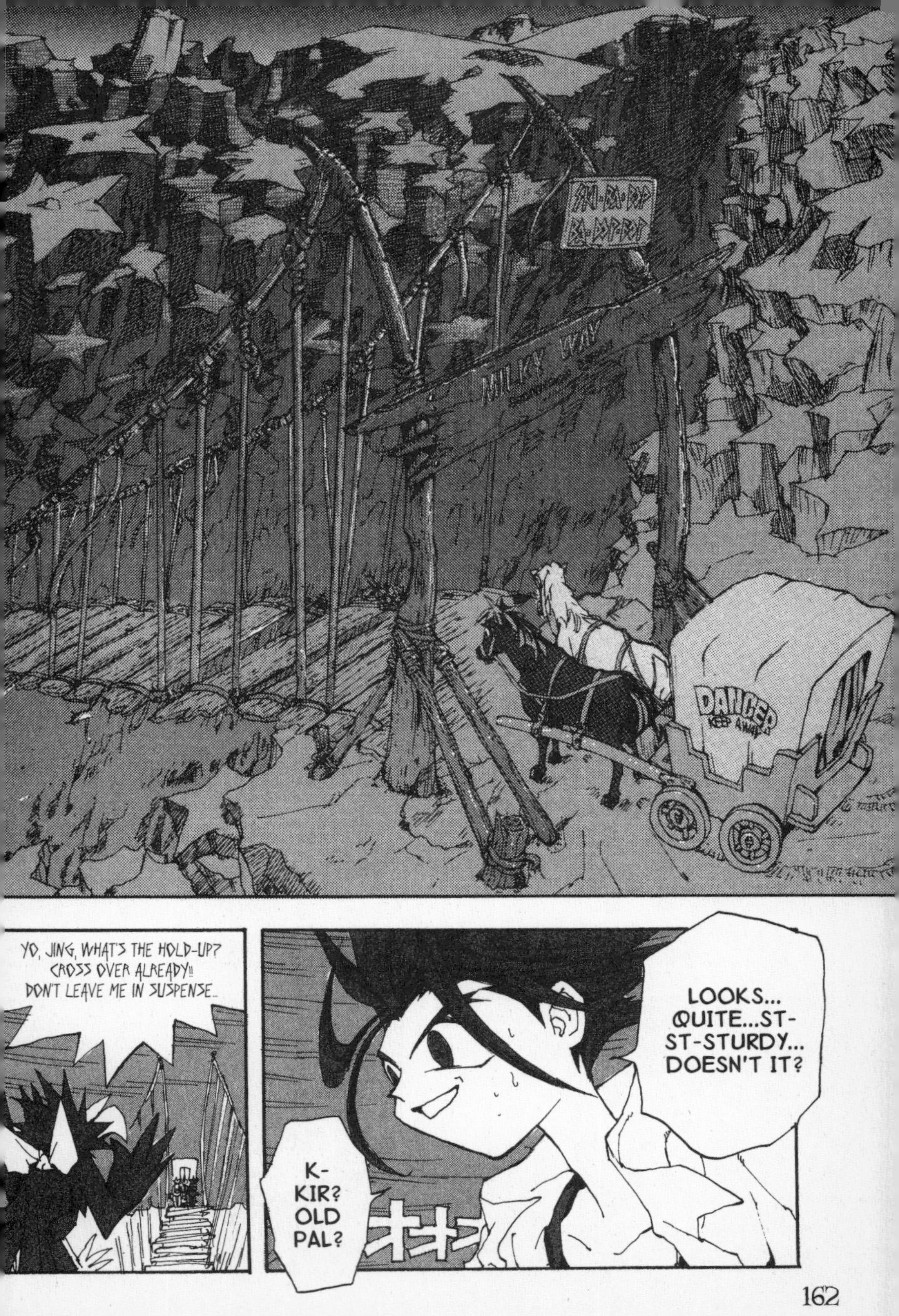
MILKY WAY
DANGER
KEEP AWAY
LOOKS... QUITE...ST- ST-STURDY... DOESN'T IT?
K- KIR? OLD PAL?
YO, JING, WHAT'S THE HOLD-UP? CROSS OVER ALREADY!! DON'T LEAVE ME IN SUSPENSE...

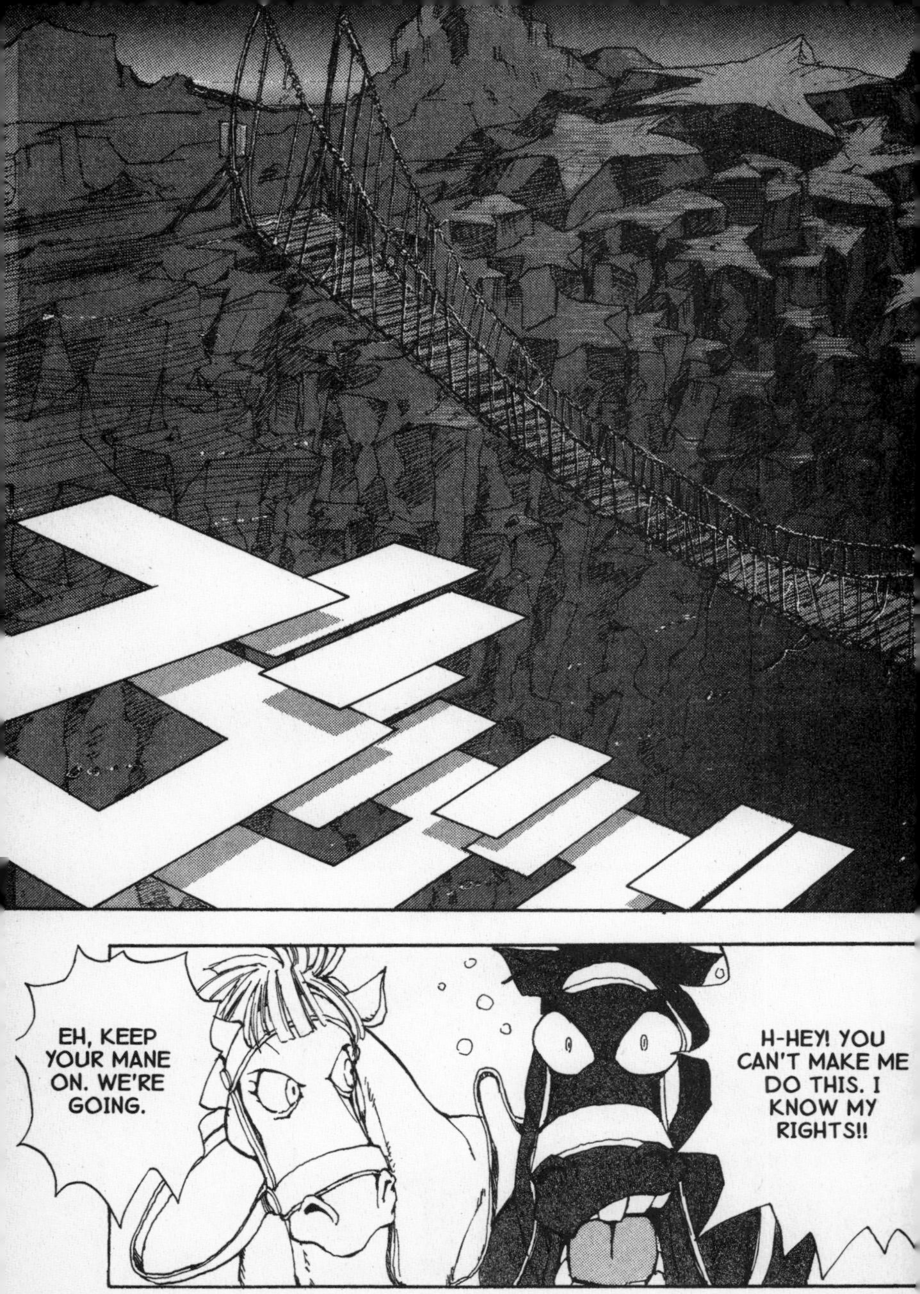
H-HEY! YOU CAN'T MAKE ME DO THIS. I KNOW MY RIGHTS!!
EH, KEEP YOUR MANE ON. WE'RE GOING.

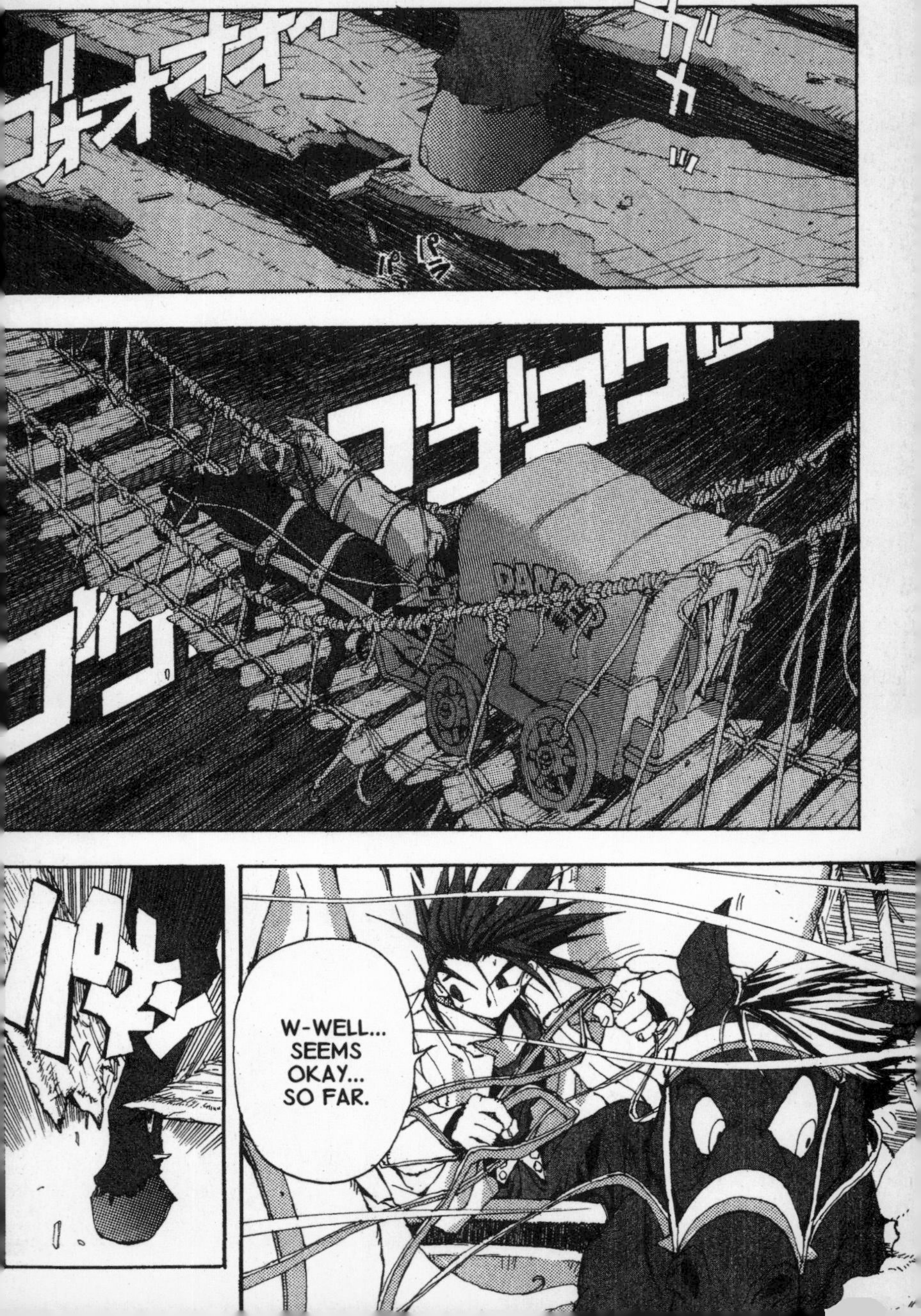
ガタッ
ゴォオオオオ
パラ パラ
ゴウンゴウン
W-WELL... SEEMS OKAY... SO FAR.
パキン

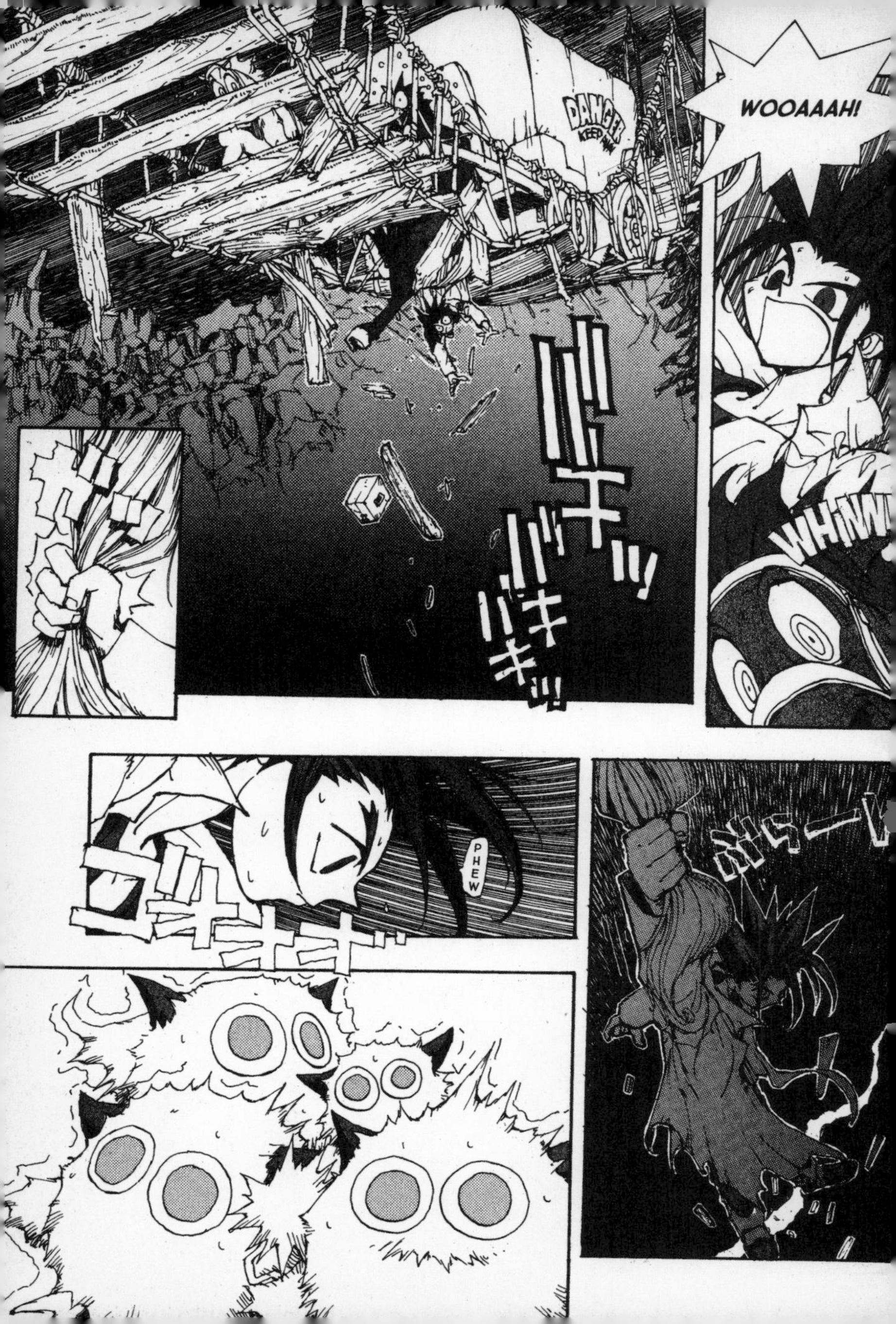
WOOAAAH!
WHINN
DANGER
KEEP
PHEW

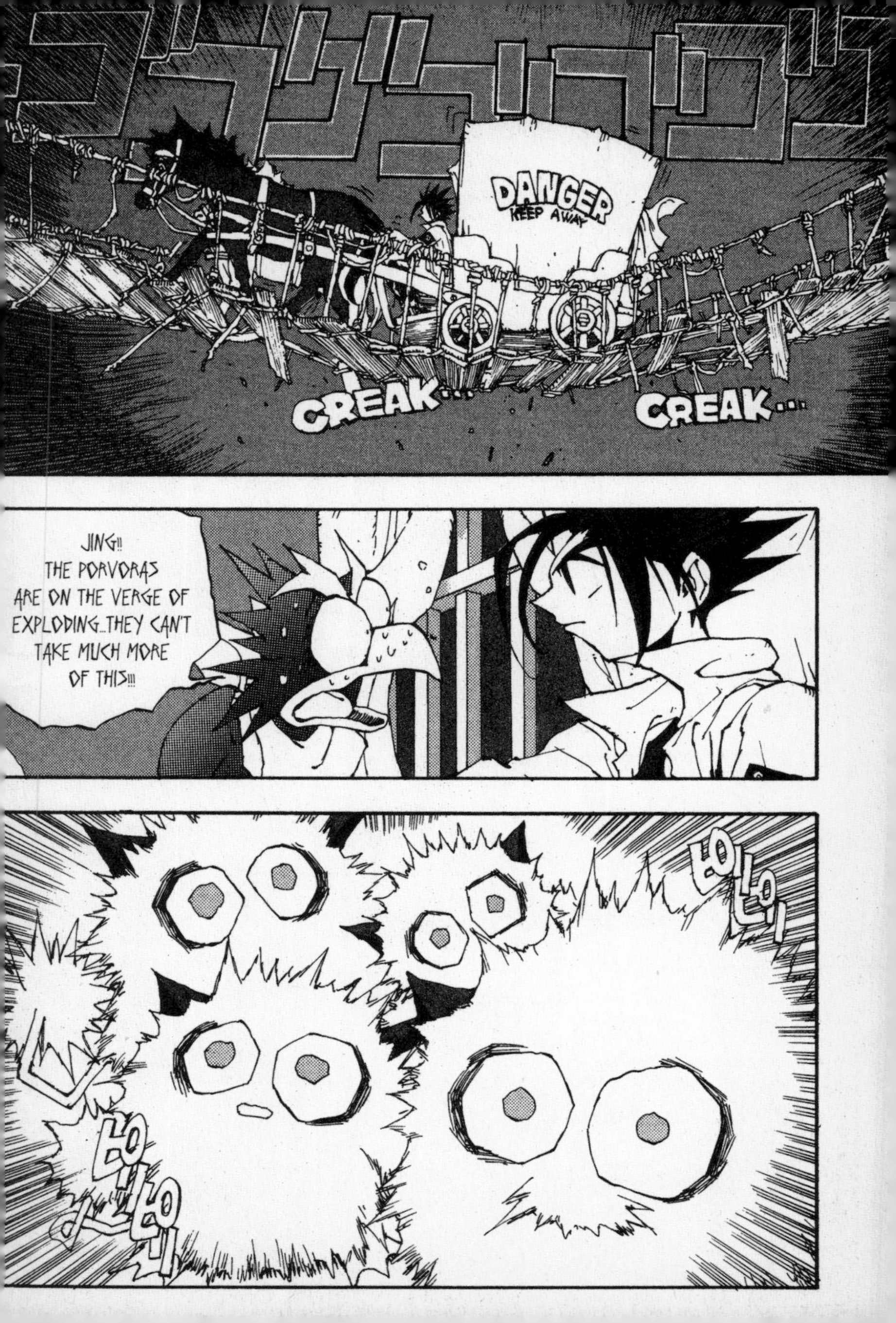
DANGER
KEEP AWAY
CREAK...
CREAK...
JING!! THE PORVORAS ARE ON THE VERGE OF EXPLODING...THEY CAN'T TAKE MUCH MORE OF THIS!!!

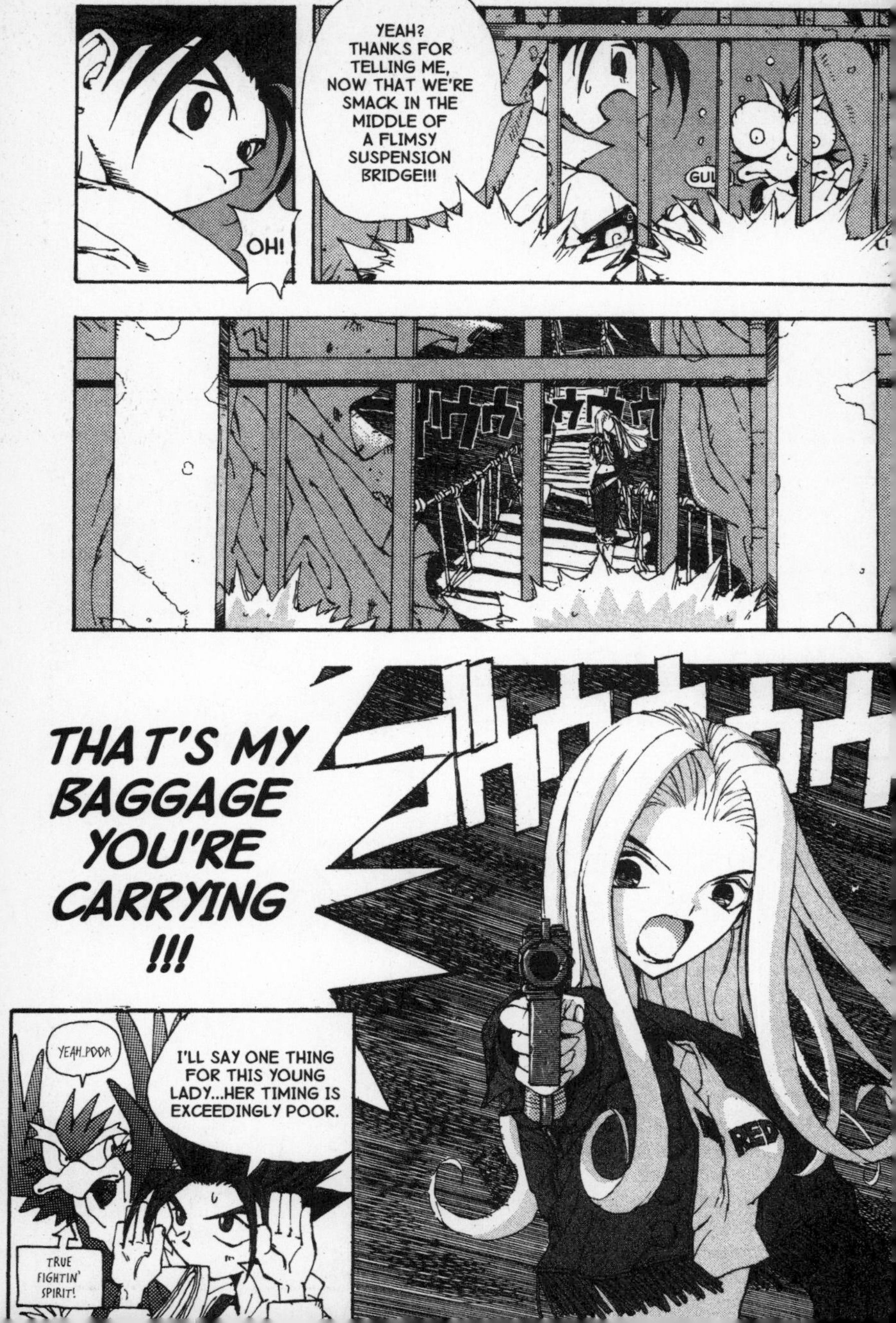
YEAH? THANKS FOR TELLING ME, NOW THAT WE'RE SMACK IN THE MIDDLE OF A FLIMSY SUSPENSION BRIDGE!!!
GUL
OH!
THAT'S MY BAGGAGE YOU'RE CARRYING!!!
I'LL SAY ONE THING FOR THIS YOUNG LADY...HER TIMING IS EXCEEDINGLY POOR.
YEAH...POOR
TRUE FIGHTIN' SPIRIT!

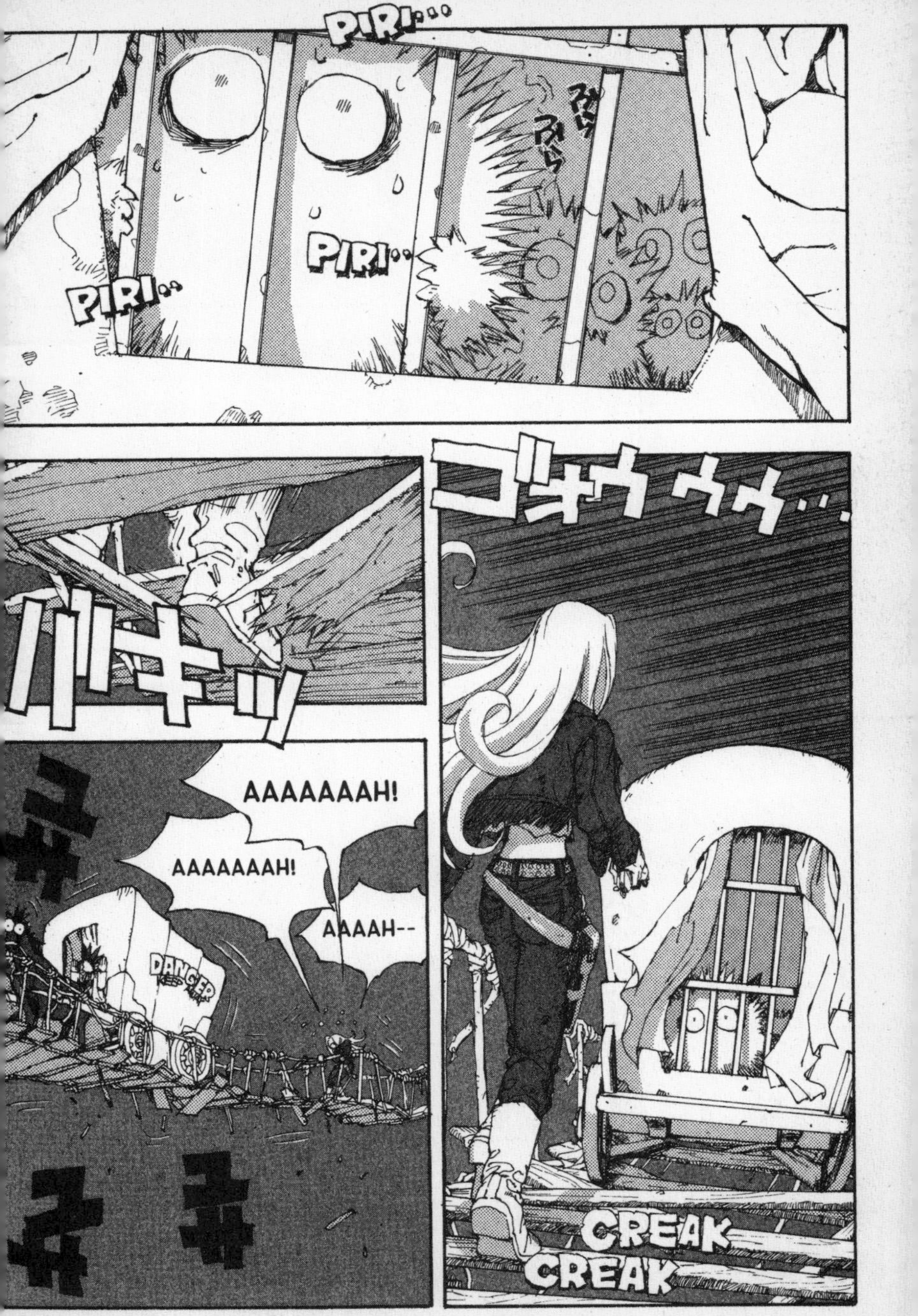
PIRI...
PIRI...
PIRI...
CREAK
CREAK
バキッ
AAAAAAAH!
AAAAAAAH!
AAAAH--

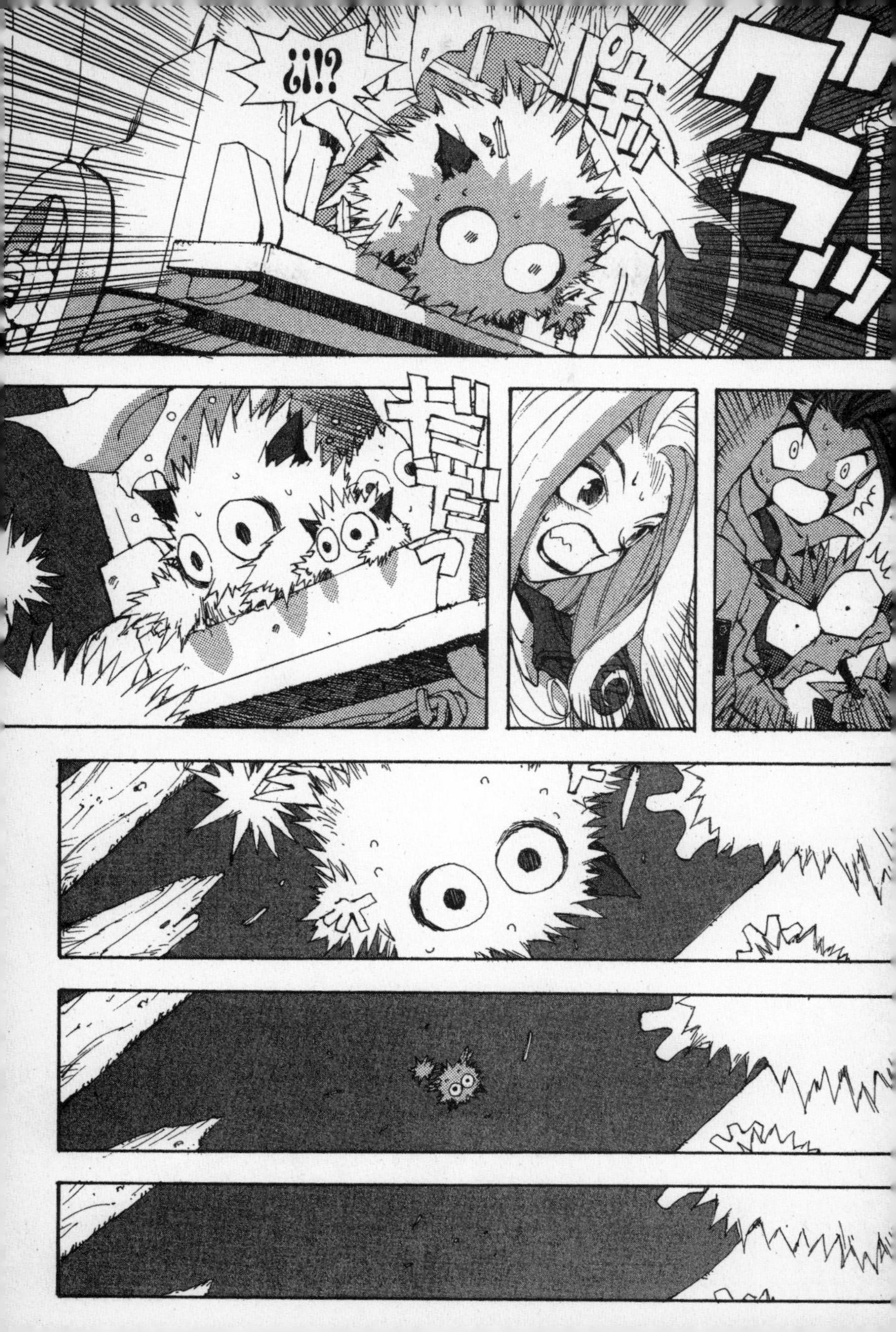
パキッ
¿¡!?

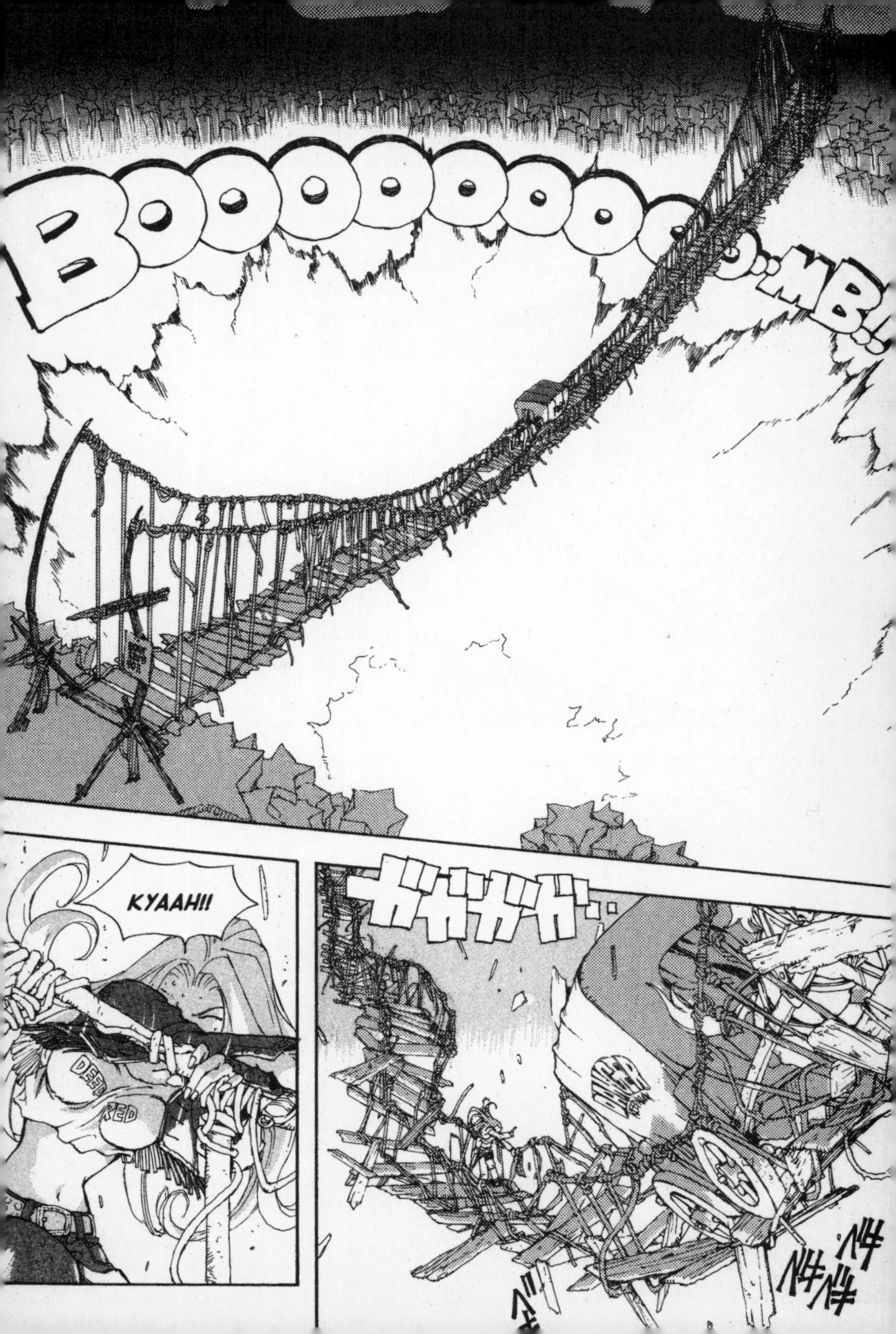
BOOOOOOOO...MB!!
KYAAH!!

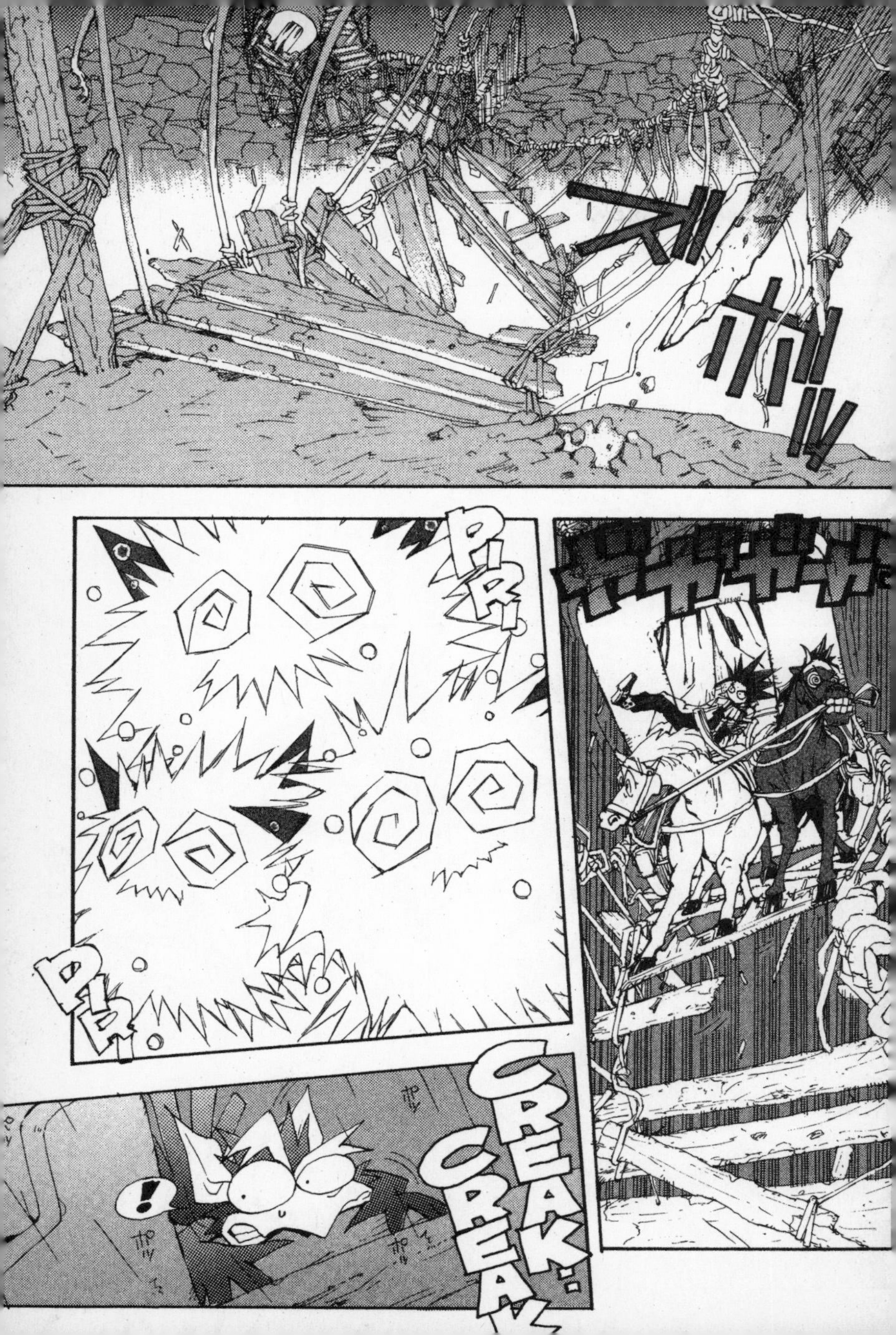
PIRI!
PIRI!
!
CREAK!
CREAK!

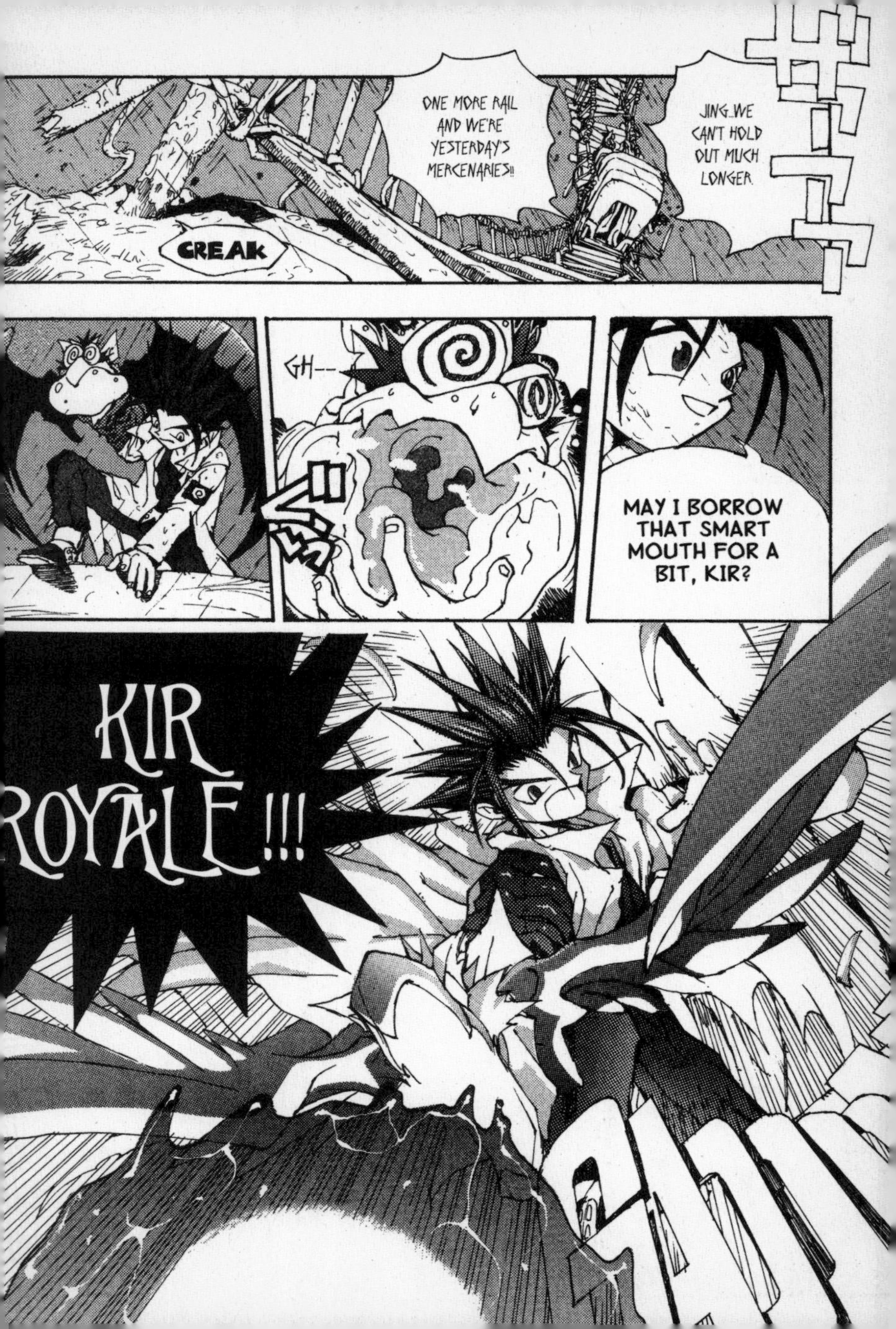
JING...WE CAN'T HOLD OUT MUCH LONGER.
ONE MORE RAIL AND WE'RE YESTERDAY'S MERCENARIES!!
CREAK
MAY I BORROW THAT SMART MOUTH FOR A BIT, KIR?
GH--
KIR ROYALE!!!

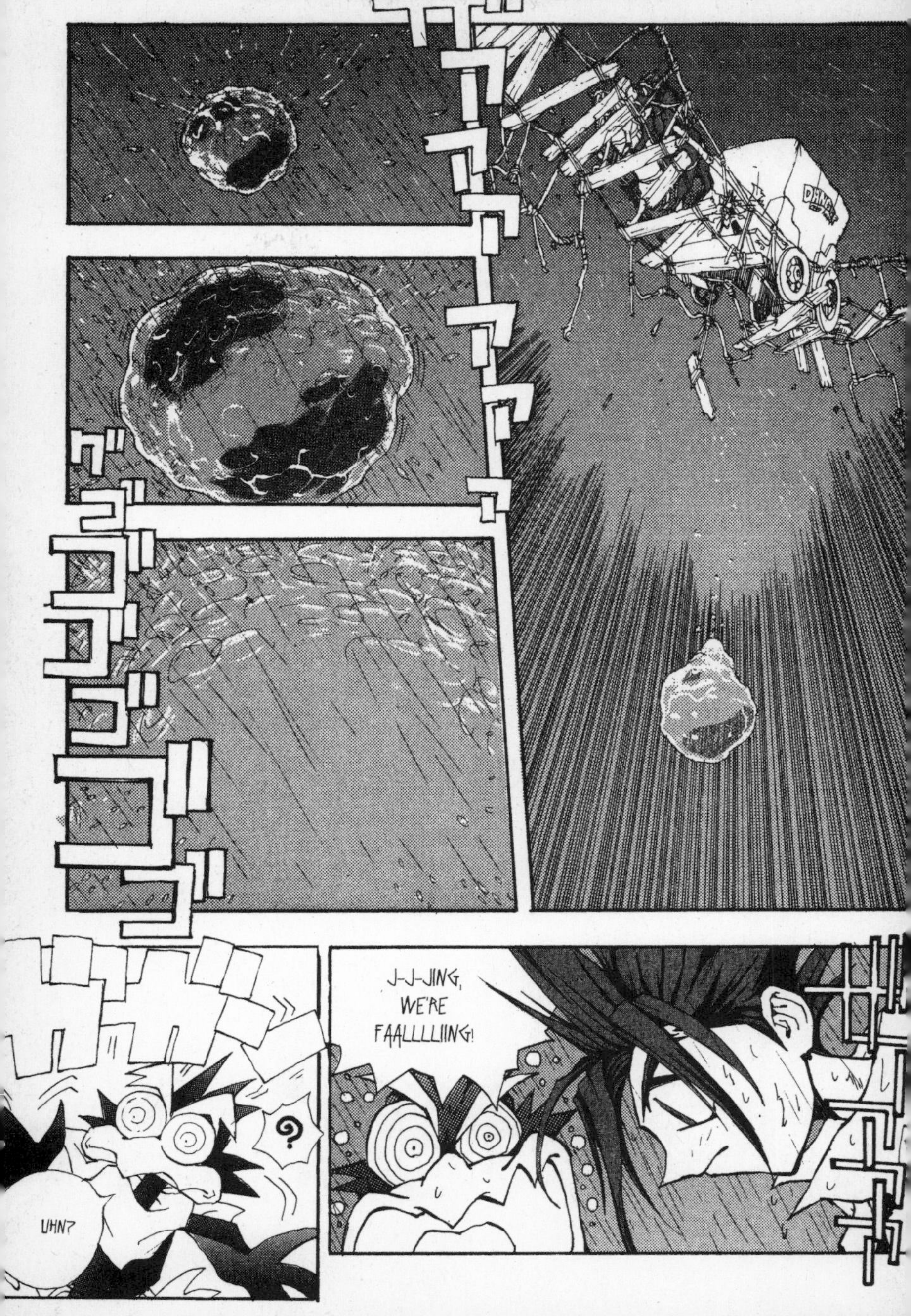
J-J-JING, WE'RE FAALLLLLIING!
UHN?

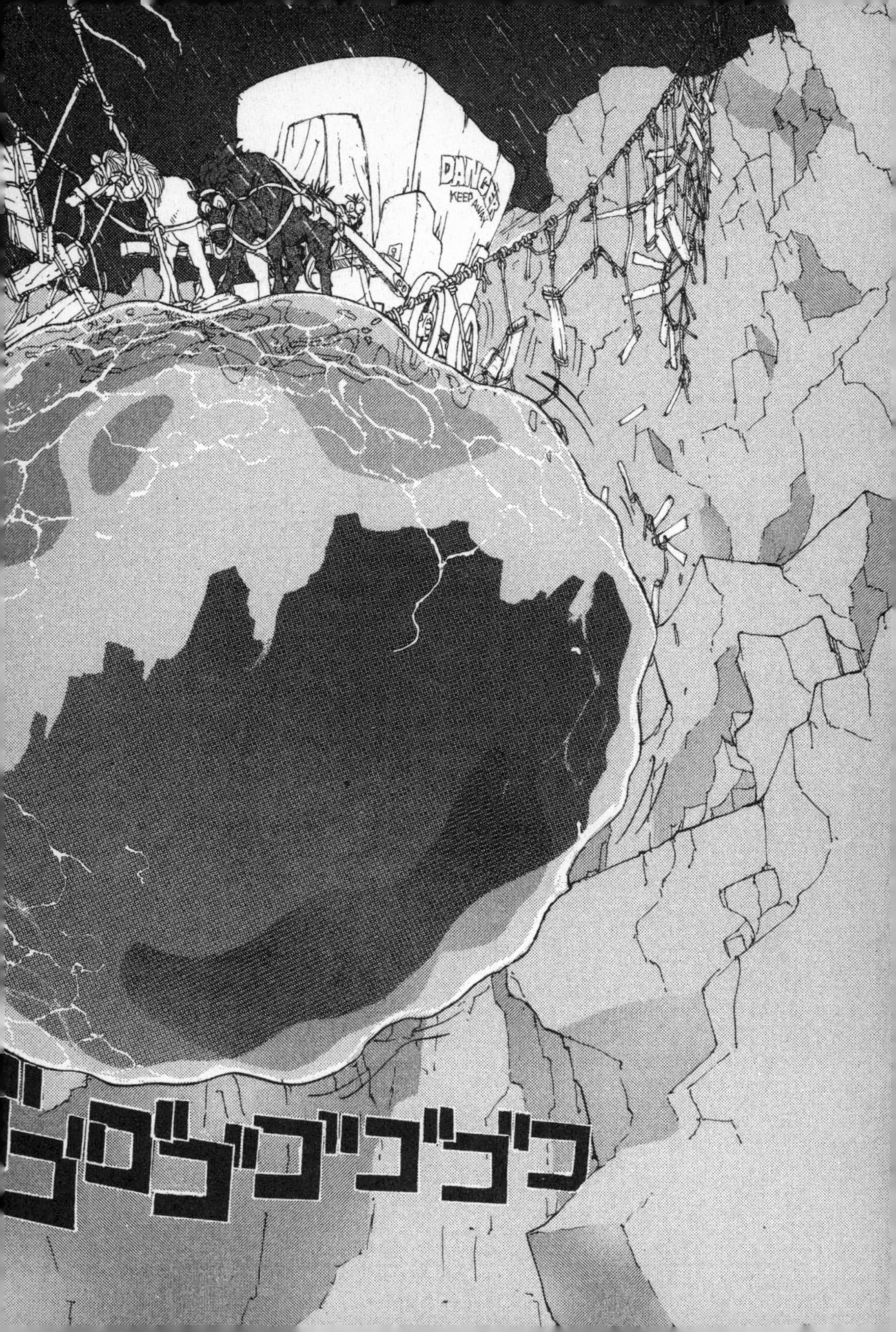
DANGER
KEEP AWAY

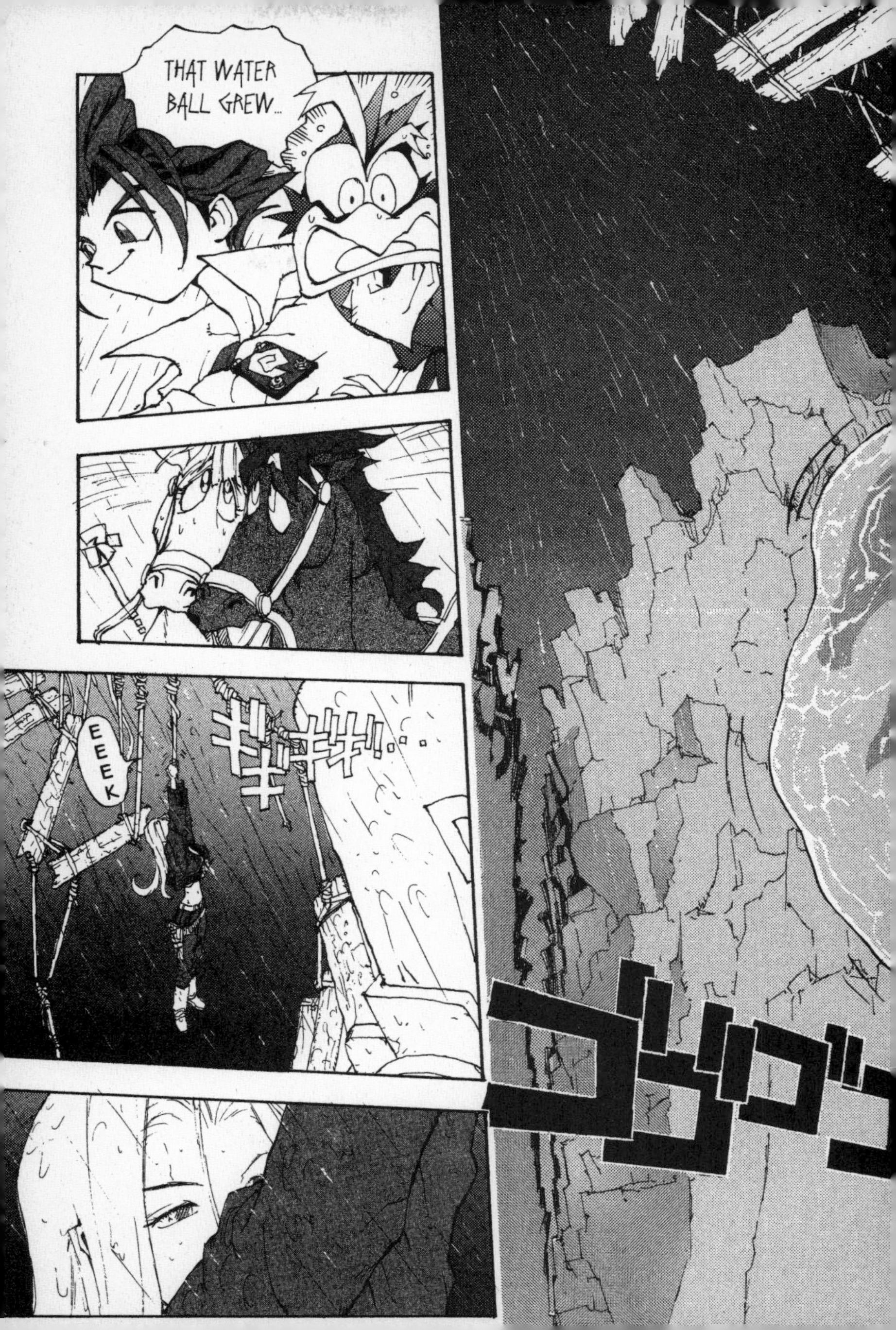
THAT WATER BALL GREW...
EEEK

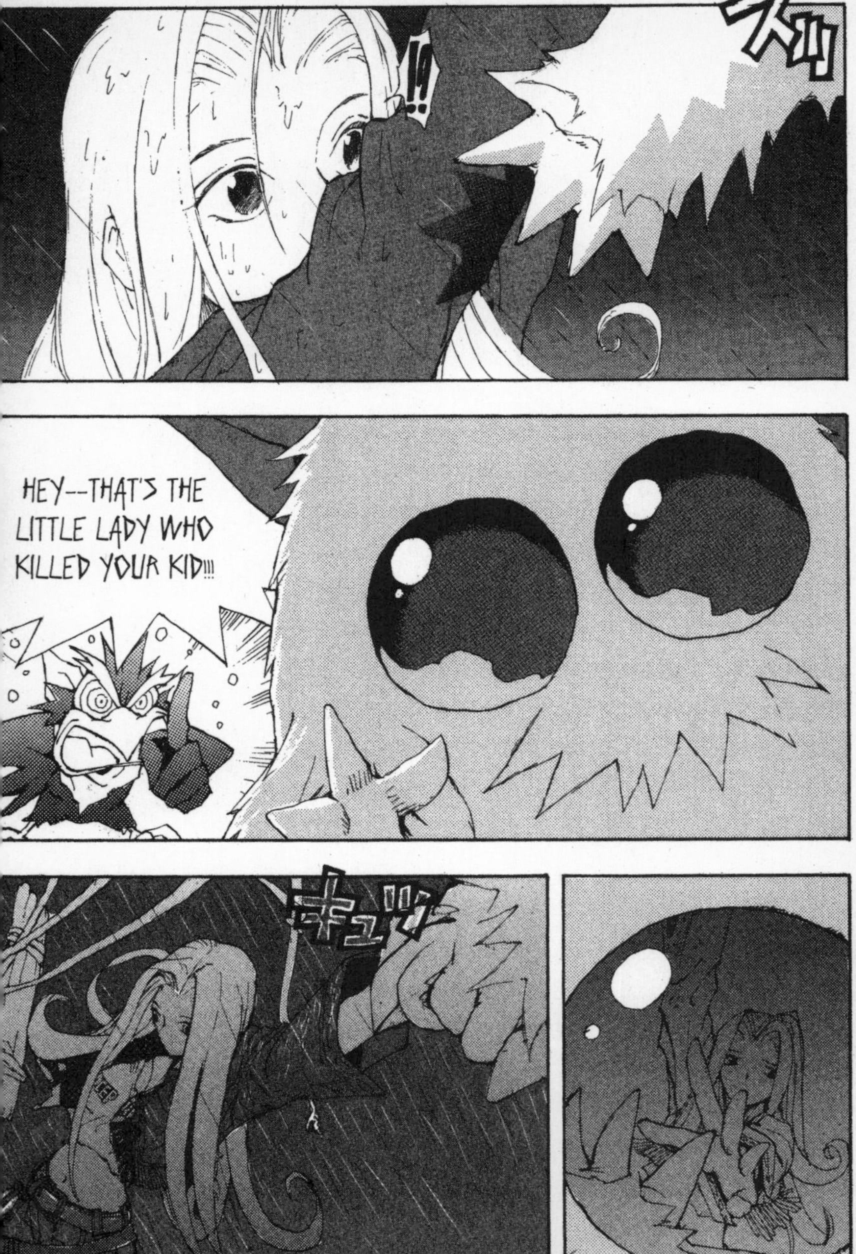
スリ
!?
HEY--THAT'S THE LITTLE LADY WHO KILLED YOUR KID!!!
ギュッ

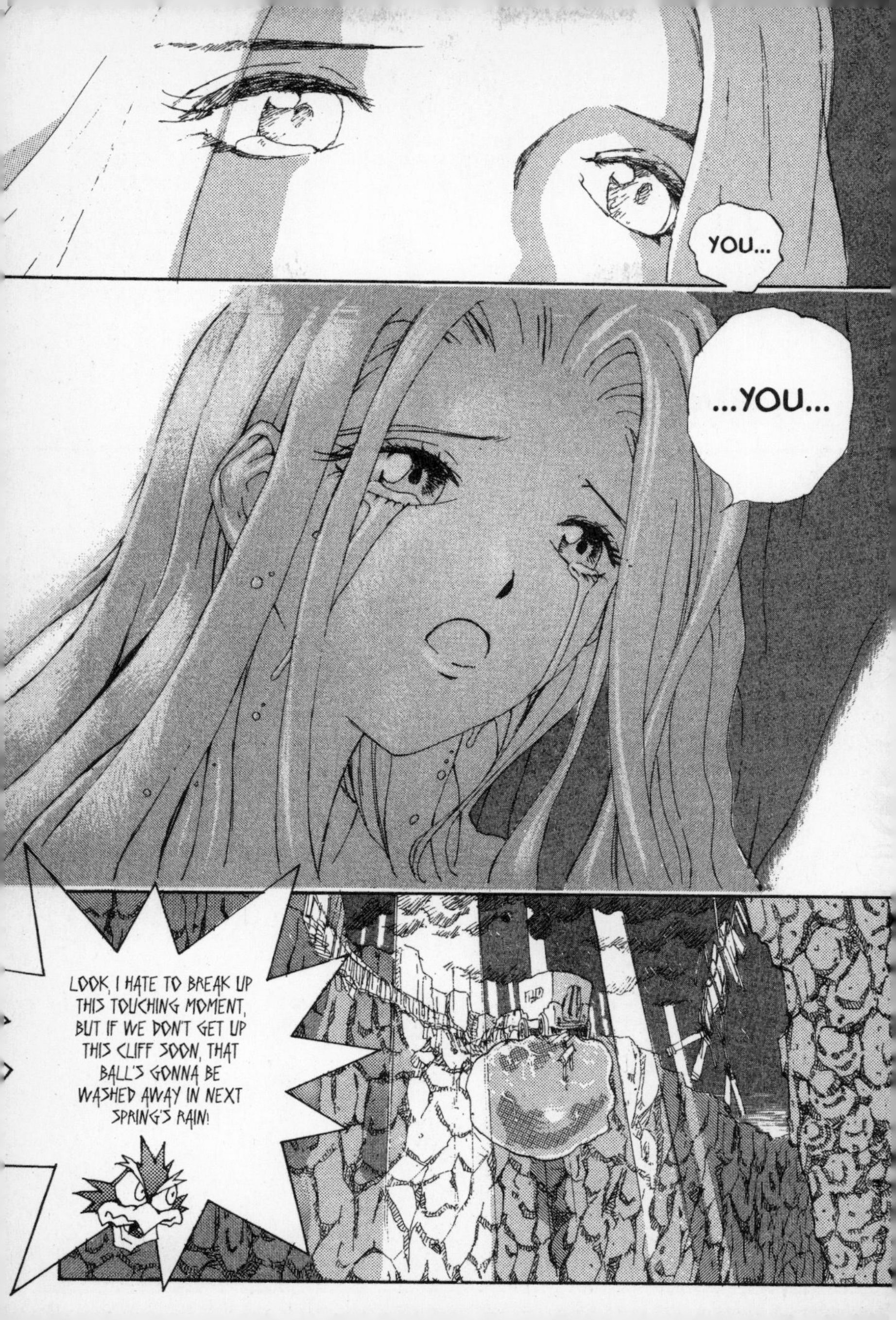
YOU...
...YOU...
LOOK, I HATE TO BREAK UP THIS TOUCHING MOMENT, BUT IF WE DON'T GET UP THIS CLIFF SOON, THAT BALL'S GONNA BE WASHED AWAY IN NEXT SPRING'S RAIN!

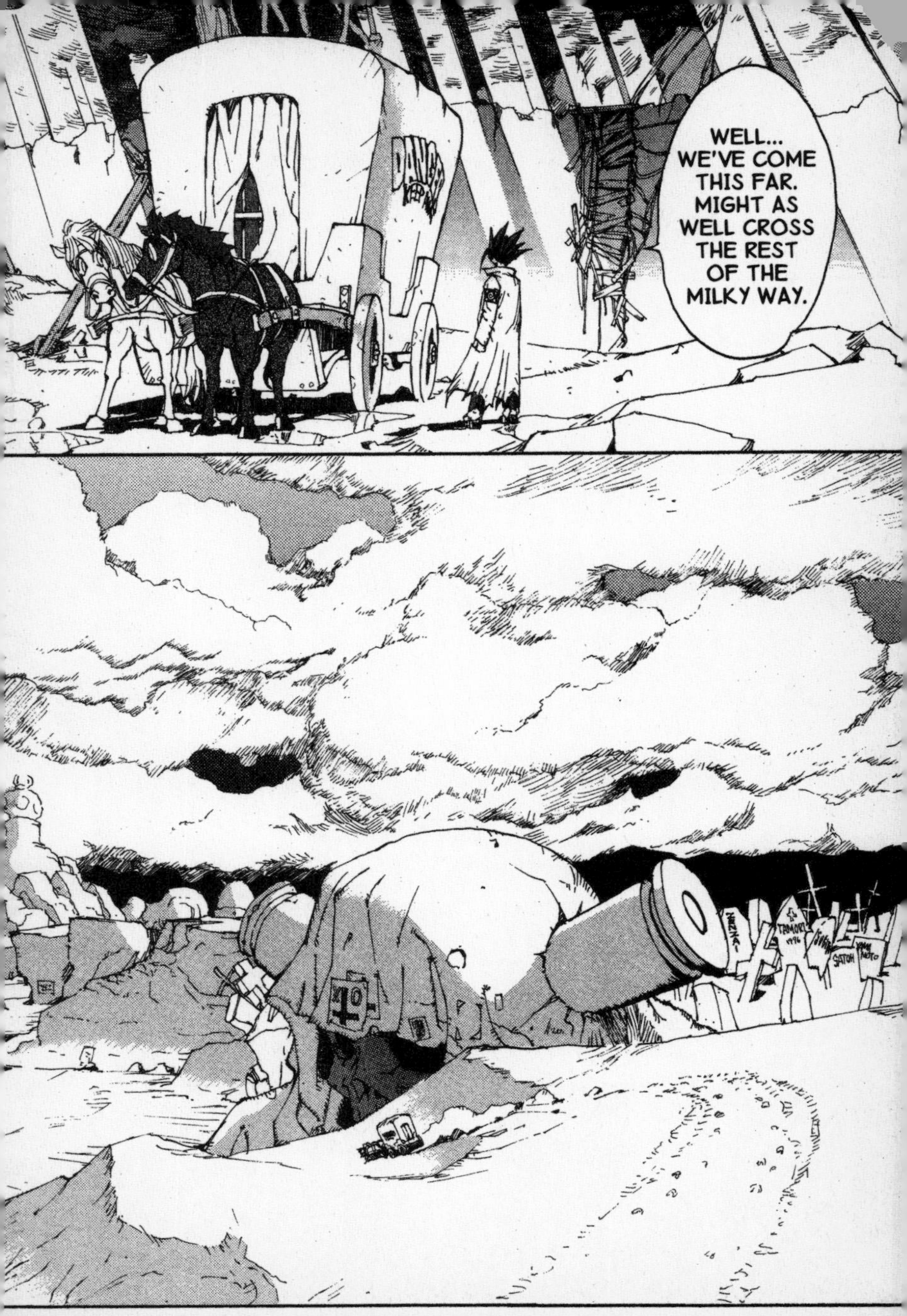
WELL... WE'VE COME THIS FAR. MIGHT AS WELL CROSS THE REST OF THE MILKY WAY.
TAMORI
SATOH

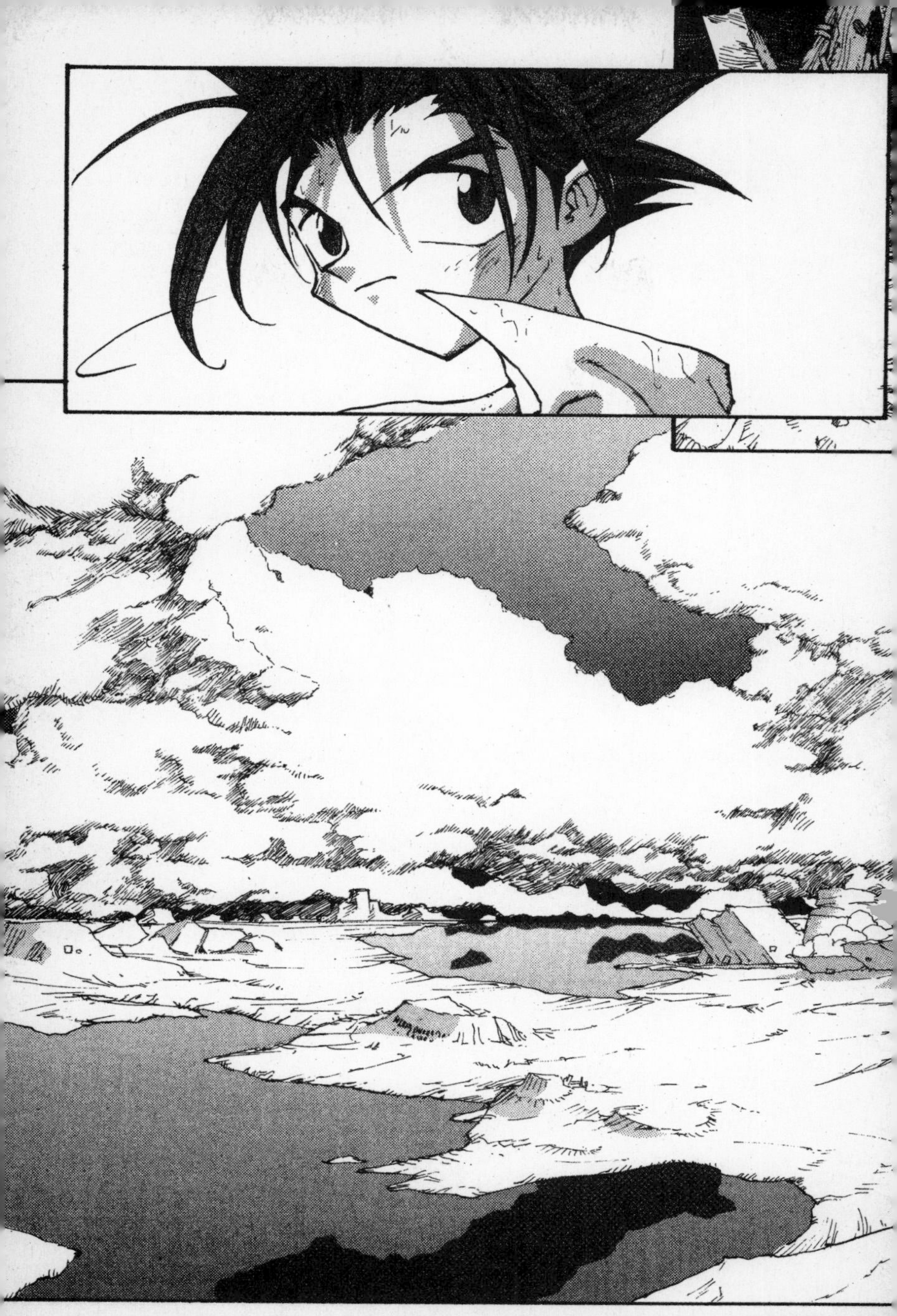

Fake is fake, after all...
It's true. I think about my dead daughter too much.
Once, my eyes and hands remembered her so well
I made a life-sized clay statue of her.
Yep... I tried. But...

In the end, it sank...
into the lava rapids...

Melted away, just like that.
I guess a cluster of gongs is still just noise after all...
Empty noise...is no substitute for what's real in the world.

Still, it's been hard to tell the difference sometimes.
That's why I've been living here like this...

Now? Now I'm content.
In fact, I'm quite happy. Because no matter what,
I'll be meeting that girl again real soon...

(Recollections of an old Europa man, living in a shack
on the outskirts of Jupiter)

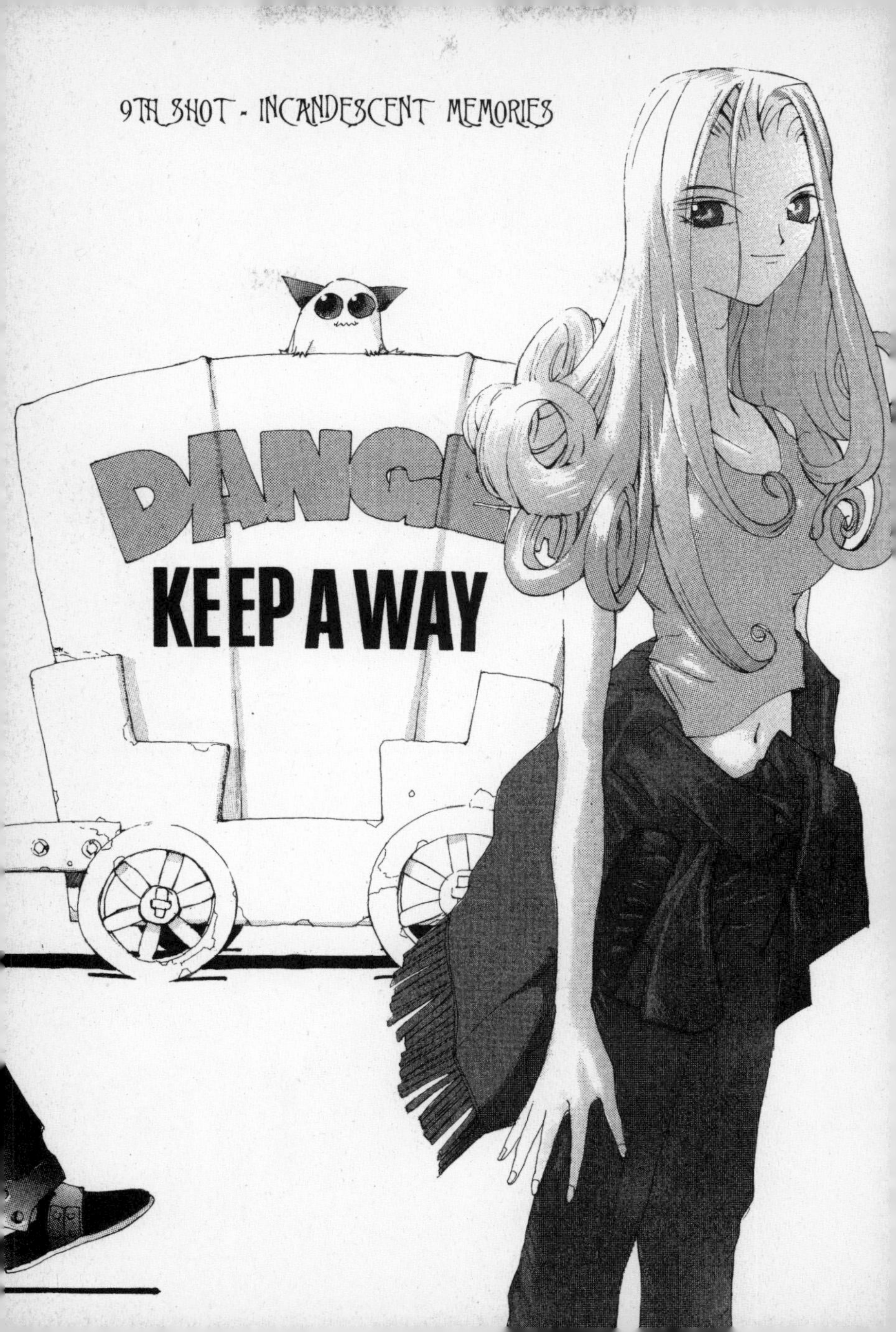
9TH SHOT - INCANDESCENT MEMORIES
DANGE
KEEP A WAY

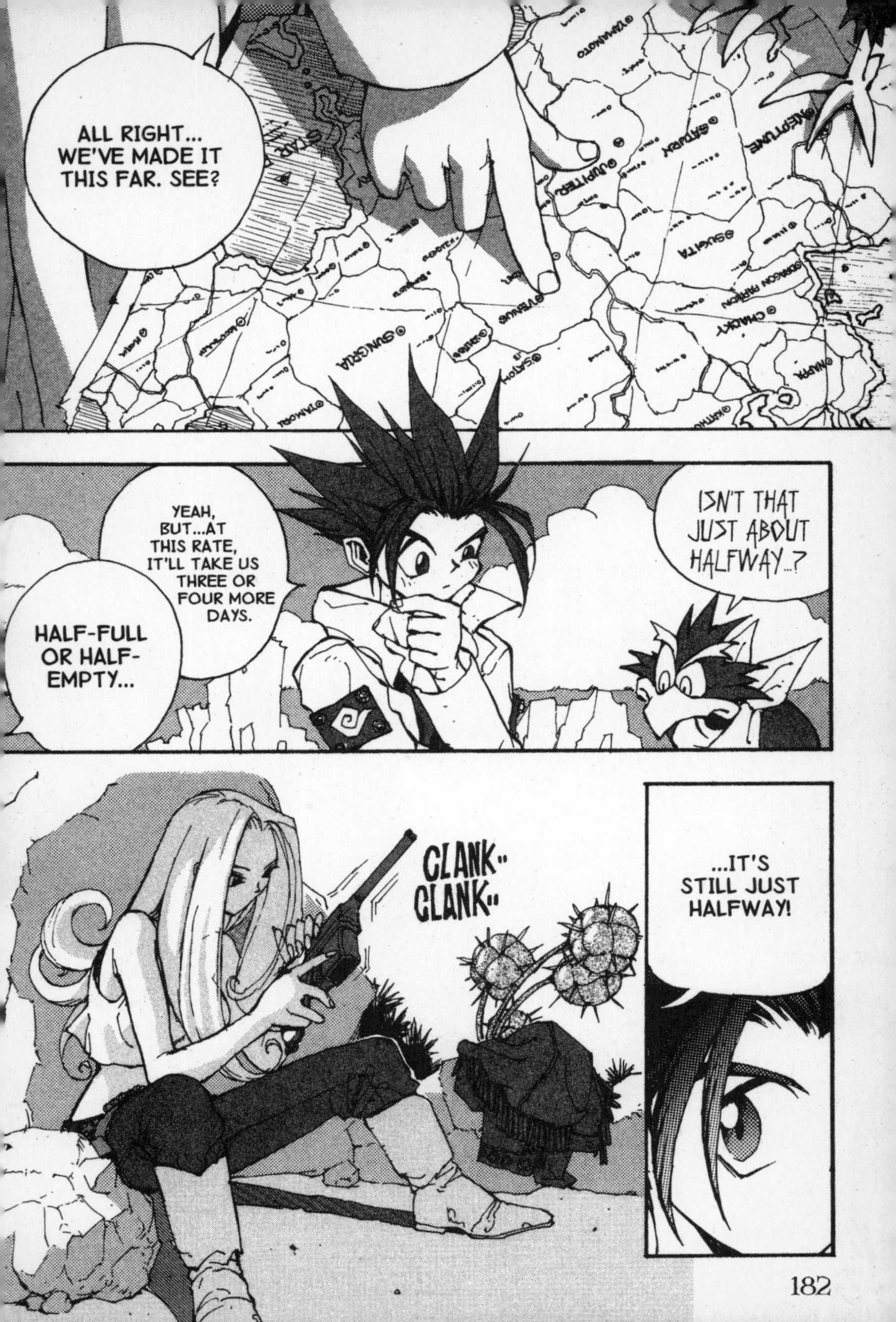
ALL RIGHT... WE'VE MADE IT THIS FAR. SEE?
ISN'T THAT JUST ABOUT HALFWAY...?
YEAH, BUT...AT THIS RATE, IT'LL TAKE US THREE OR FOUR MORE DAYS.
HALF-FULL OR HALF-EMPTY...
...IT'S STILL JUST HALFWAY!
CLANK.. CLANK..

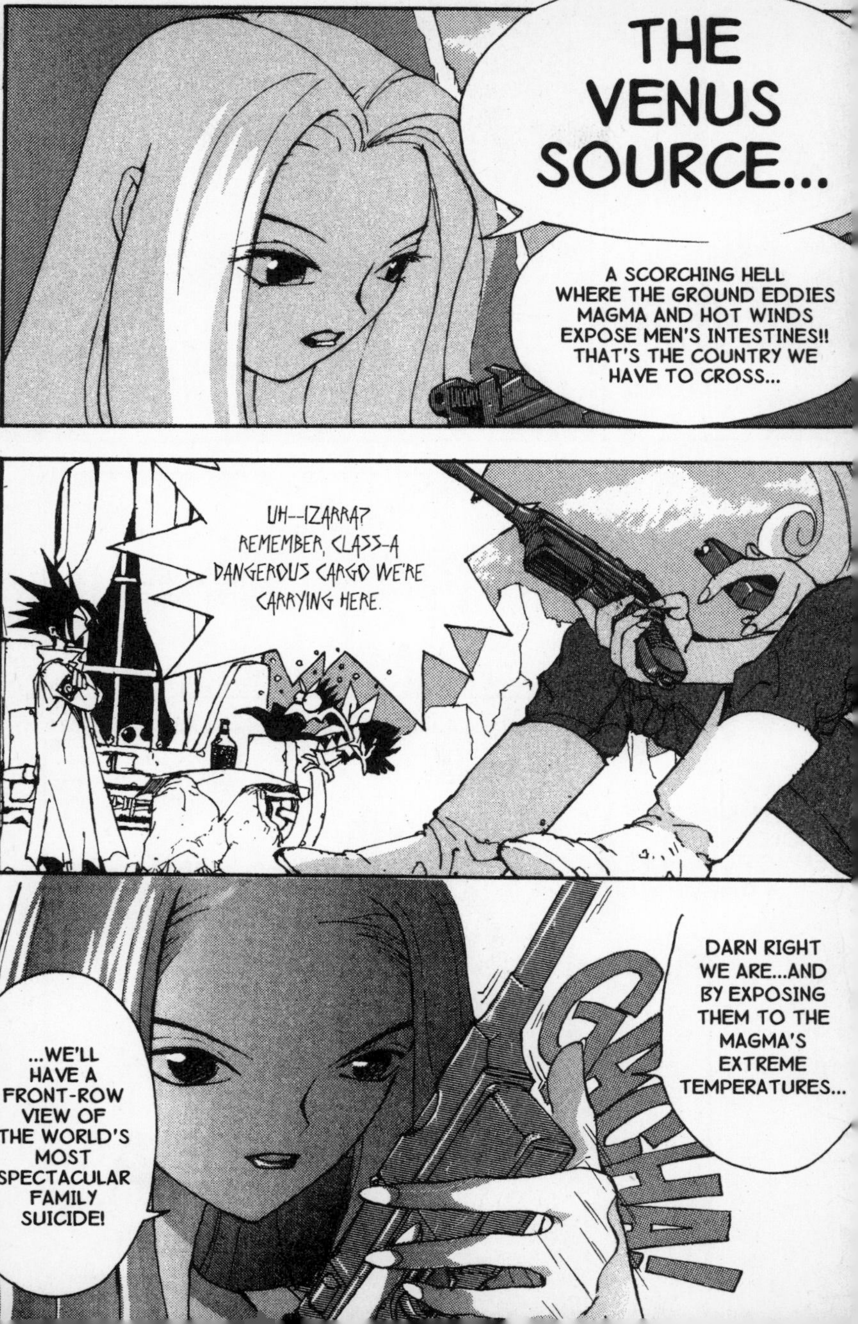

THE VENUS SOURCE...
A SCORCHING HELL WHERE THE GROUND EDDIES MAGMA AND HOT WINDS EXPOSE MEN'S INTESTINES!! THAT'S THE COUNTRY WE HAVE TO CROSS...
UH--IZARRA? REMEMBER, CLASS-A DANGEROUS CARGO WE'RE CARRYING HERE.
DARN RIGHT WE ARE...AND BY EXPOSING THEM TO THE MAGMA'S EXTREME TEMPERATURES...
...WE'LL HAVE A FRONT-ROW VIEW OF THE WORLD'S MOST SPECTACULAR FAMILY SUICIDE!

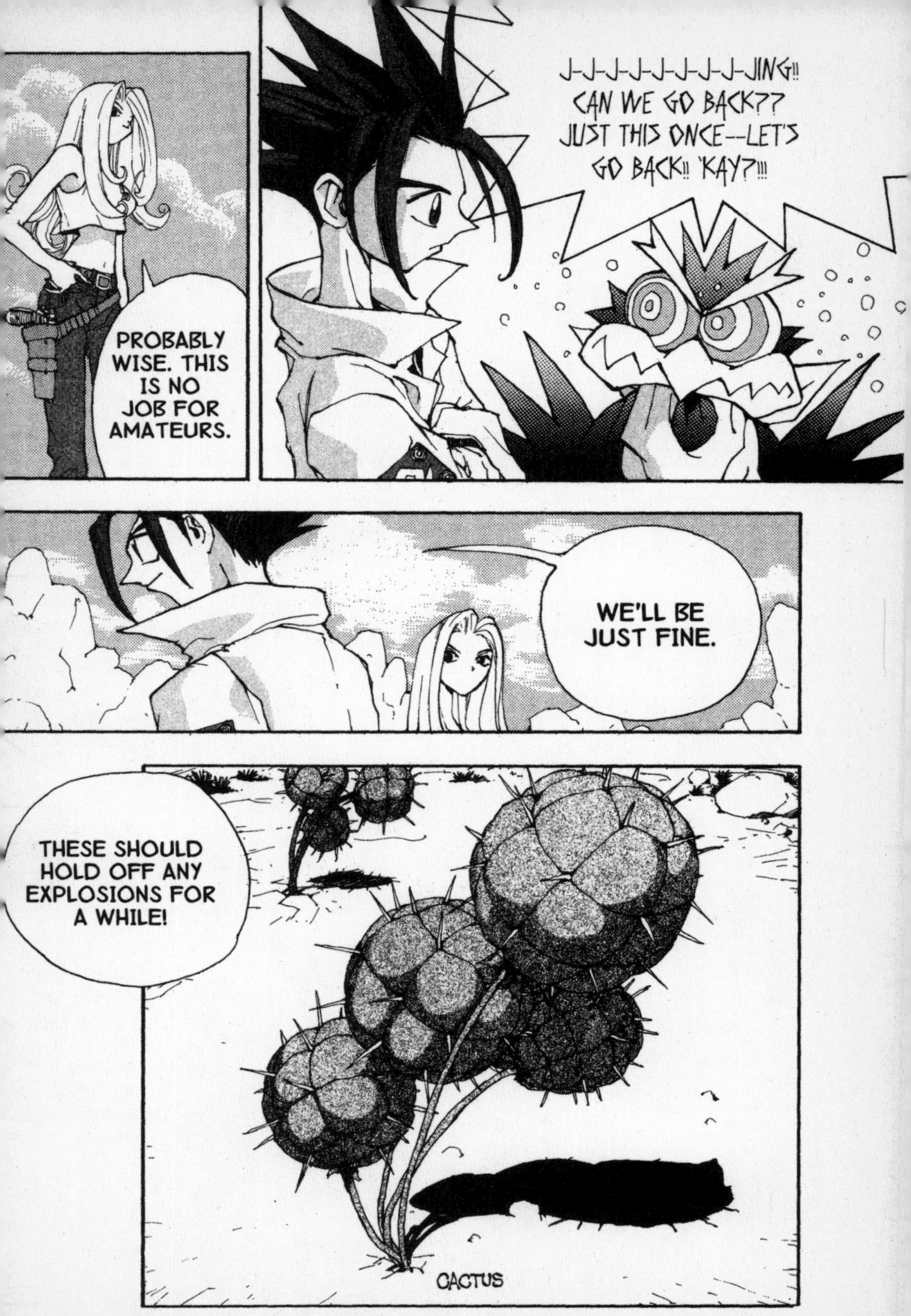
J-J-J-J-J-J-J-J-JING!! CAN WE GO BACK?? JUST THIS ONCE--LET'S GO BACK!! 'KAY?!!!
PROBABLY WISE. THIS IS NO JOB FOR AMATEURS.
WE'LL BE JUST FINE.
THESE SHOULD HOLD OFF ANY EXPLOSIONS FOR A WHILE!
CACTUS

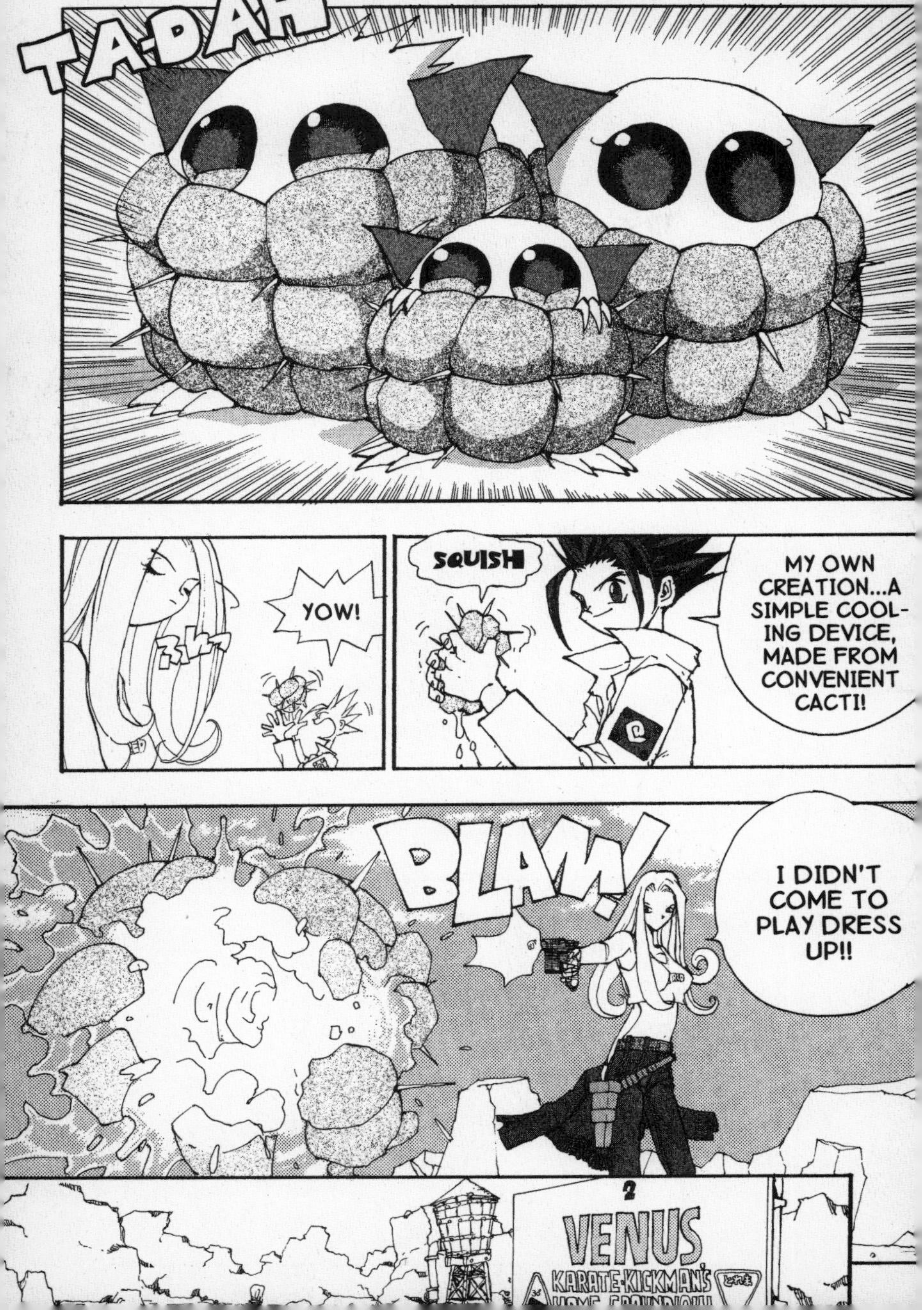
TA-DAH
MY OWN CREATION...A SIMPLE COOLING DEVICE, MADE FROM CONVENIENT CACTI!
SQUISH
YOW!
I DIDN'T COME TO PLAY DRESS UP!!
BLAM!
2
VENUS
KARATE-KICKMAN'S

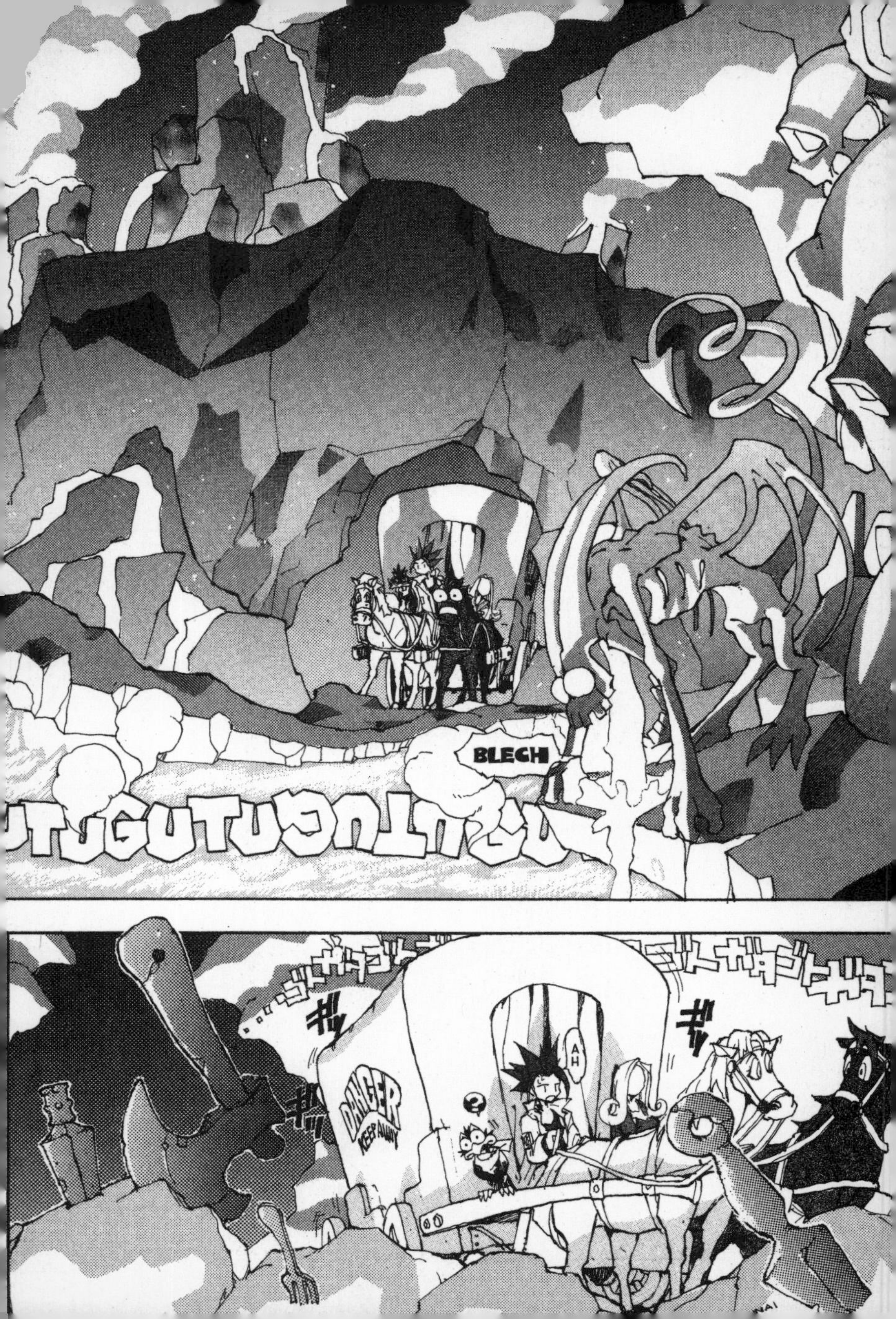
BLECH
AH
DANGER
KEEP AWAY

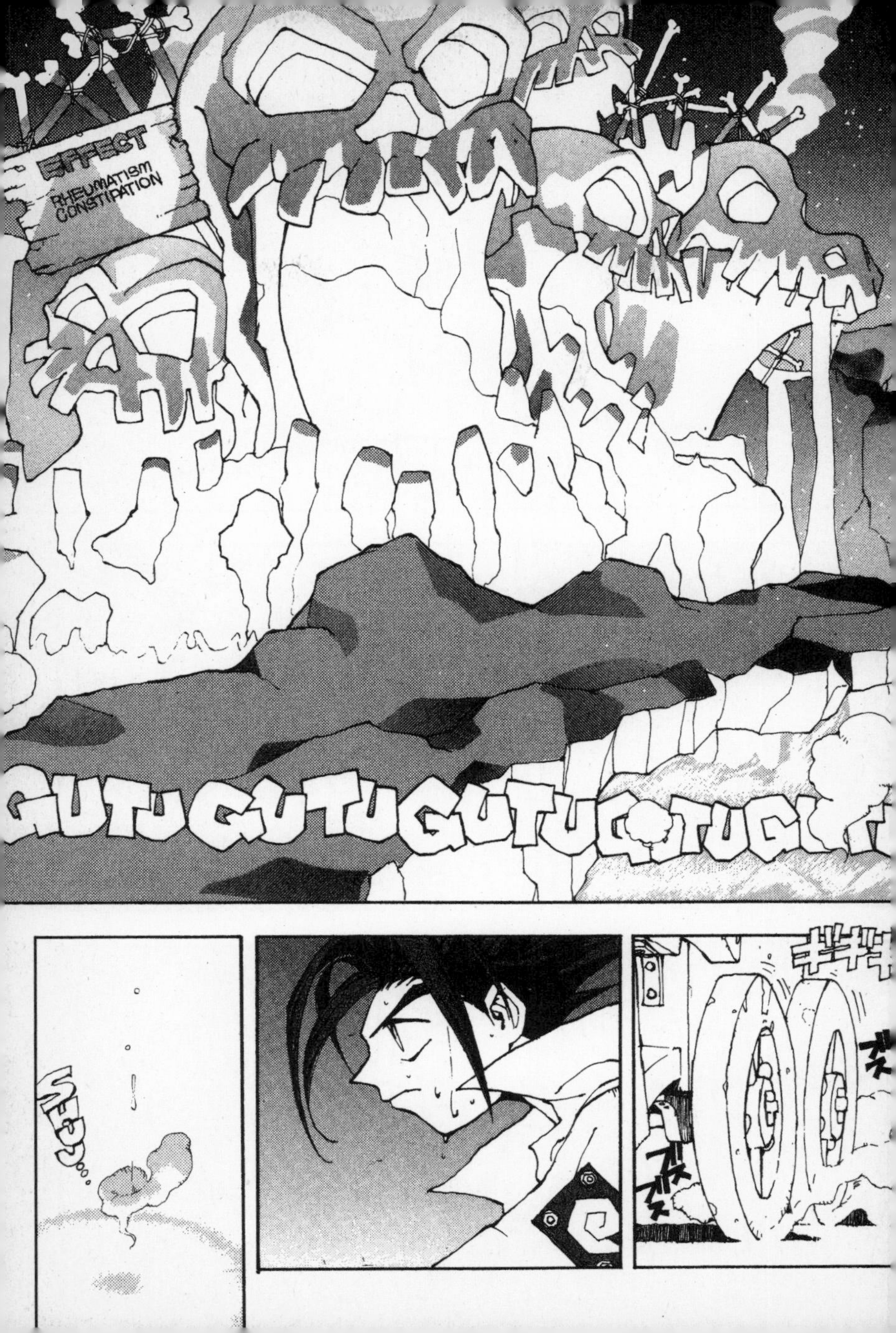
EFFECT
RHEUMATISM
CONSTIPATION
GUTUGUTUGUTU

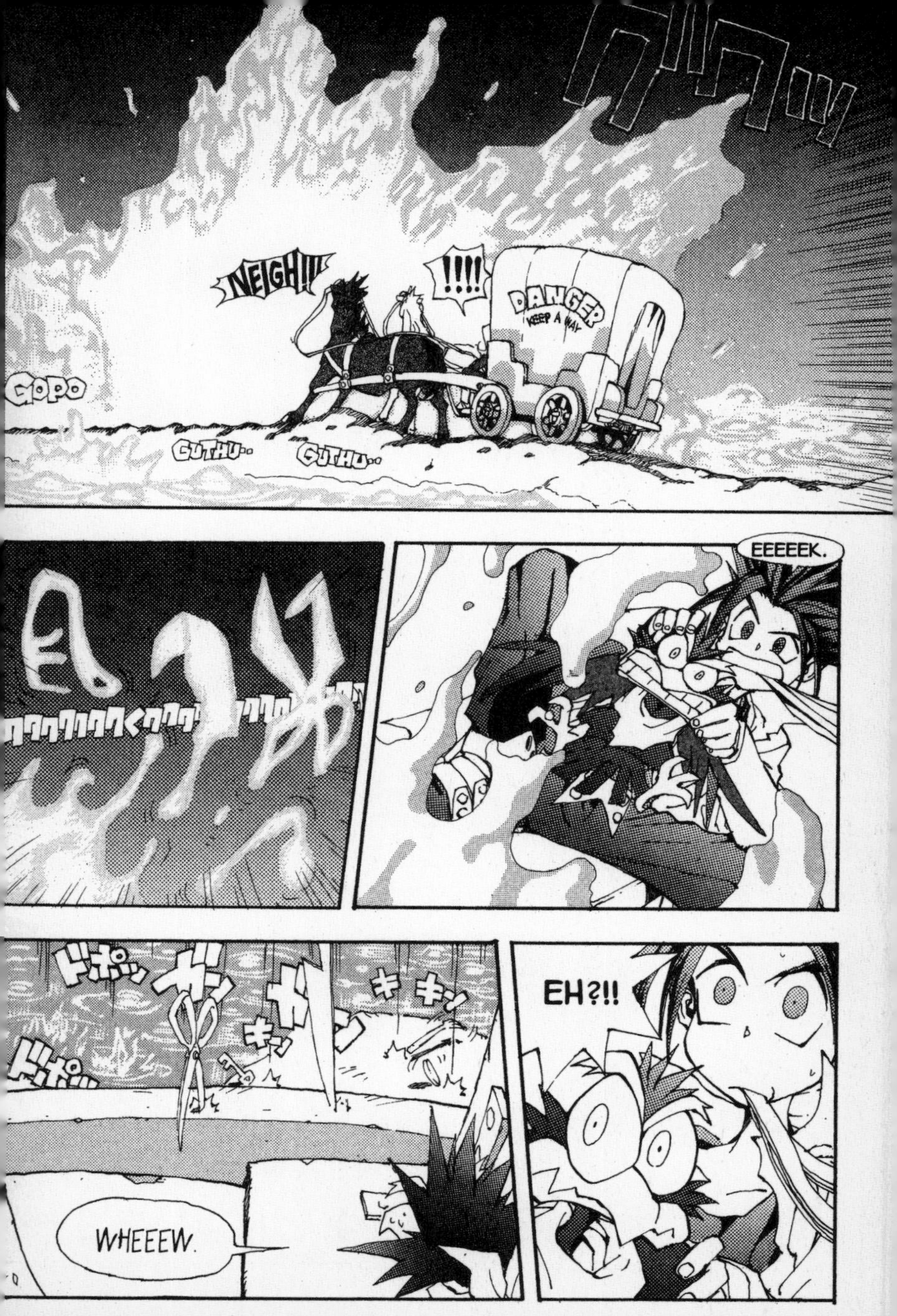
!!!!
NEIGH!!!
DANGER
KEEP A WAY
GOPO
GUTHU..
GUTHU..
EEEEEK.
EH?!!
WHEEEW.

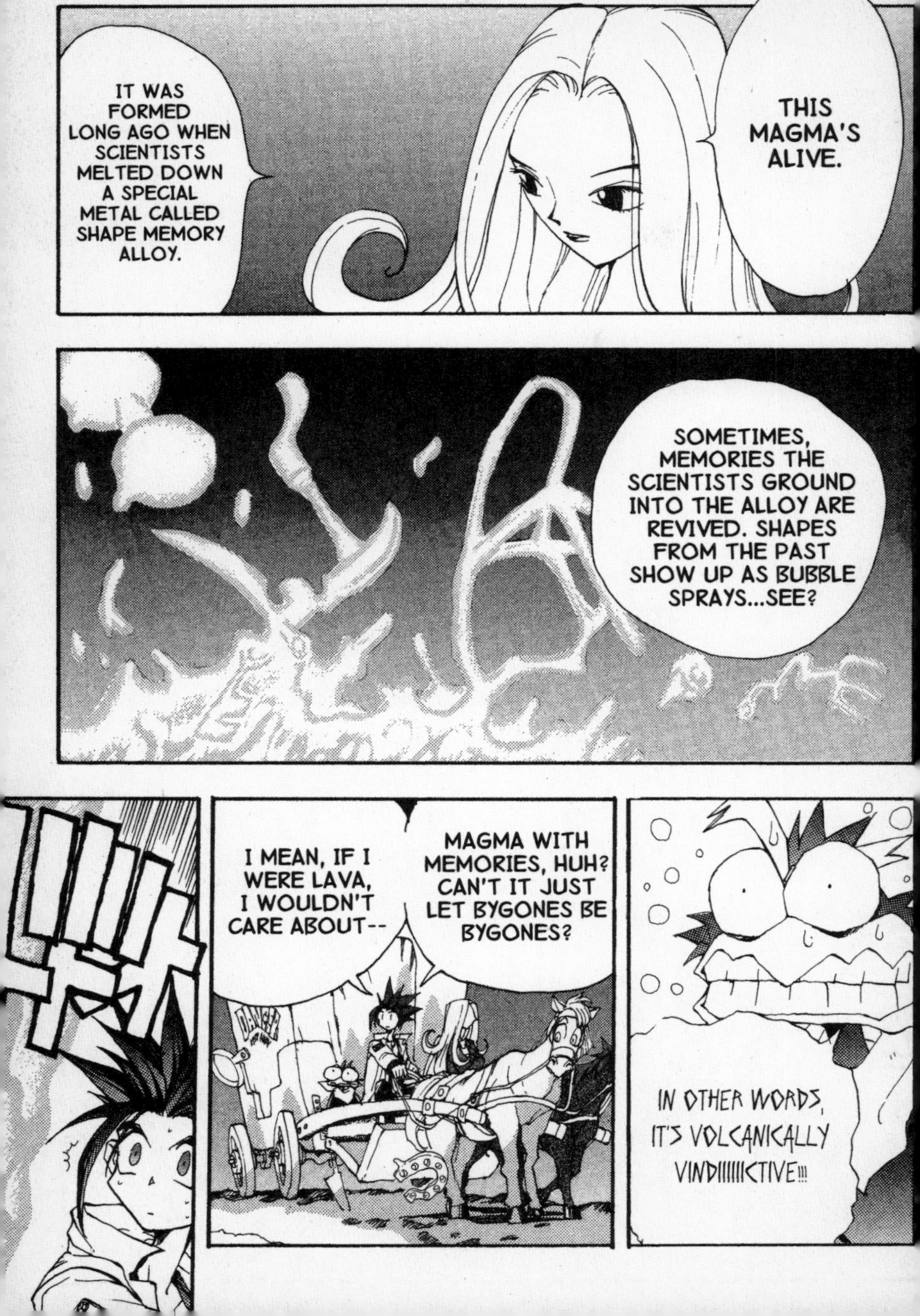
THIS MAGMA'S ALIVE.
IT WAS FORMED LONG AGO WHEN SCIENTISTS MELTED DOWN A SPECIAL METAL CALLED SHAPE MEMORY ALLOY.
SOMETIMES, MEMORIES THE SCIENTISTS GROUND INTO THE ALLOY ARE REVIVED. SHAPES FROM THE PAST SHOW UP AS BUBBLE SPRAYS...SEE?
IN OTHER WORDS, IT'S VOLCANICALLY VINDIIIIIICTIVE!!!
MAGMA WITH MEMORIES, HUH? CAN'T IT JUST LET BYGONES BE BYGONES?
I MEAN, IF I WERE LAVA, I WOULDN'T CARE ABOUT--

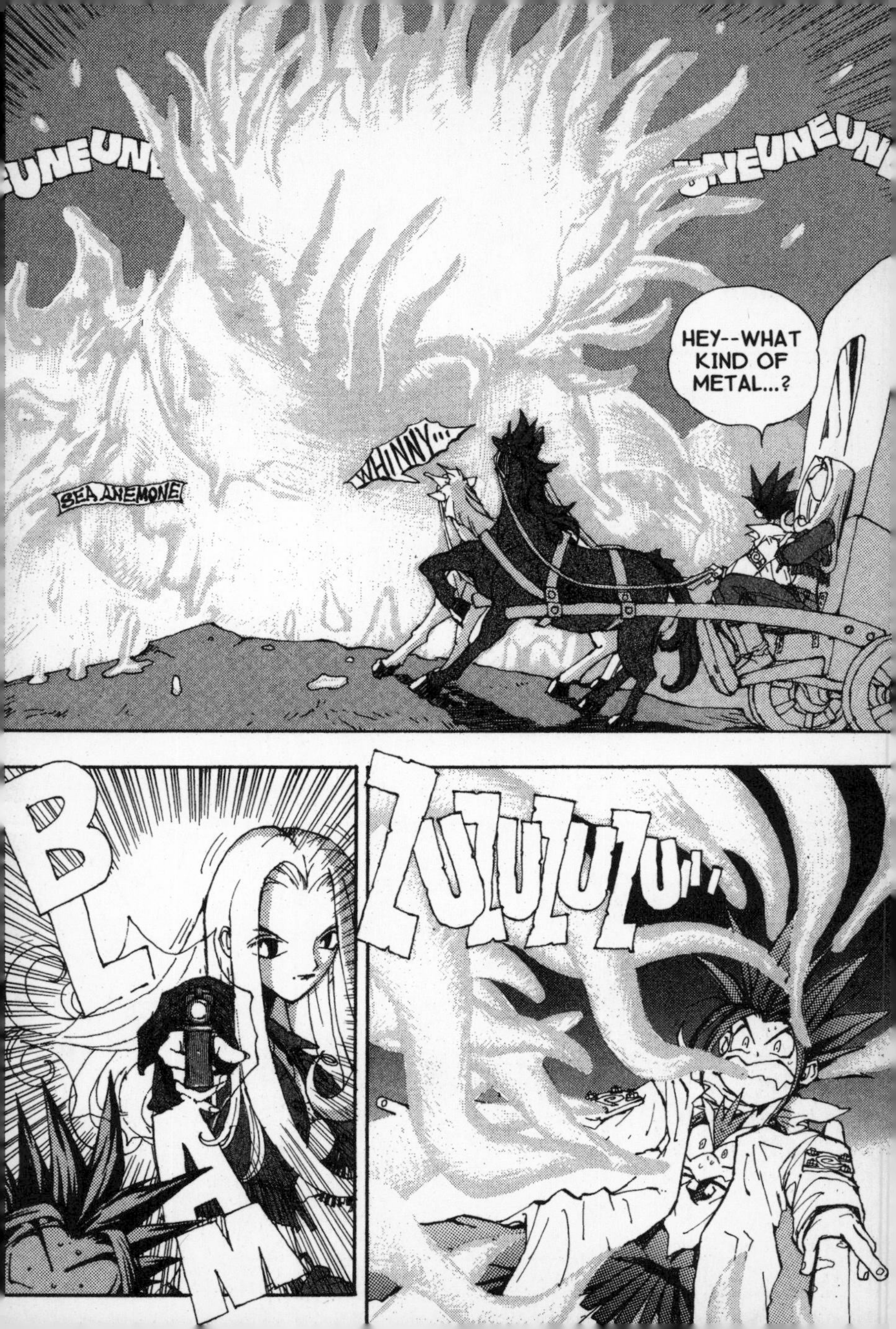

UNEUNEUN
HEY--WHAT KIND OF METAL...?
WHINNY...
SEA ANEMONE
EUNEUN
ZUZUZUZUZU...
BLAM

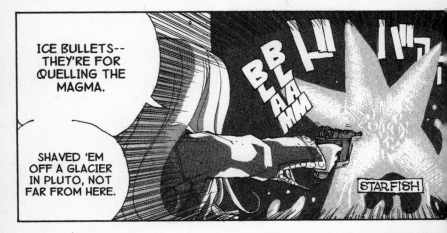

ICE BULLETS—
THEY'RE FOR
QUELLING THE
MAGMA.

SHAVED 'EM
OFF A GLACIER
IN PLUTO, NOT
FAR FROM HERE.

STARFISH

ICE
BULLET

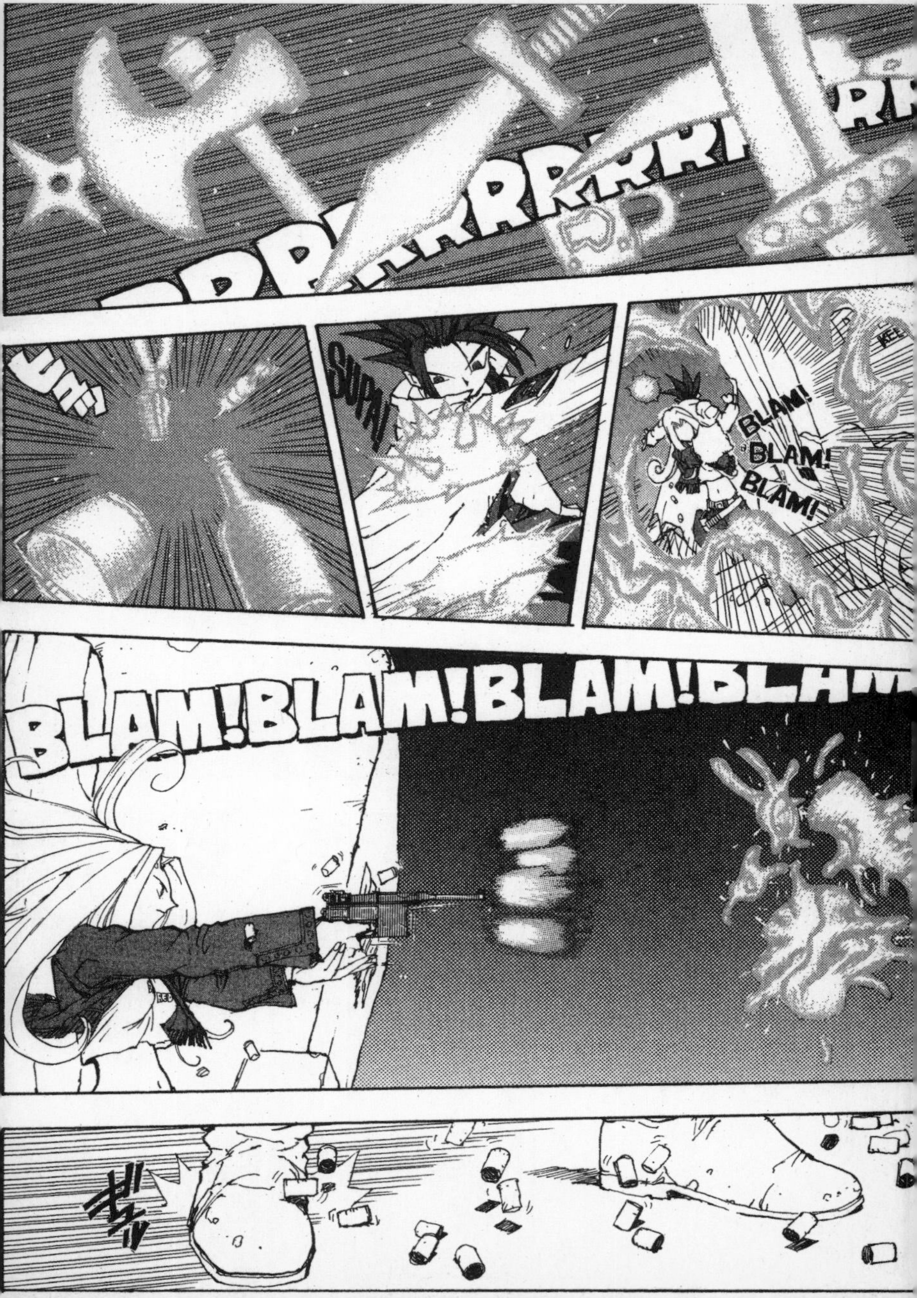

RRRRRRR
BLAM!
BLAM!
BLAM!
SUPA!
BLAM!BLAM!BLAM!

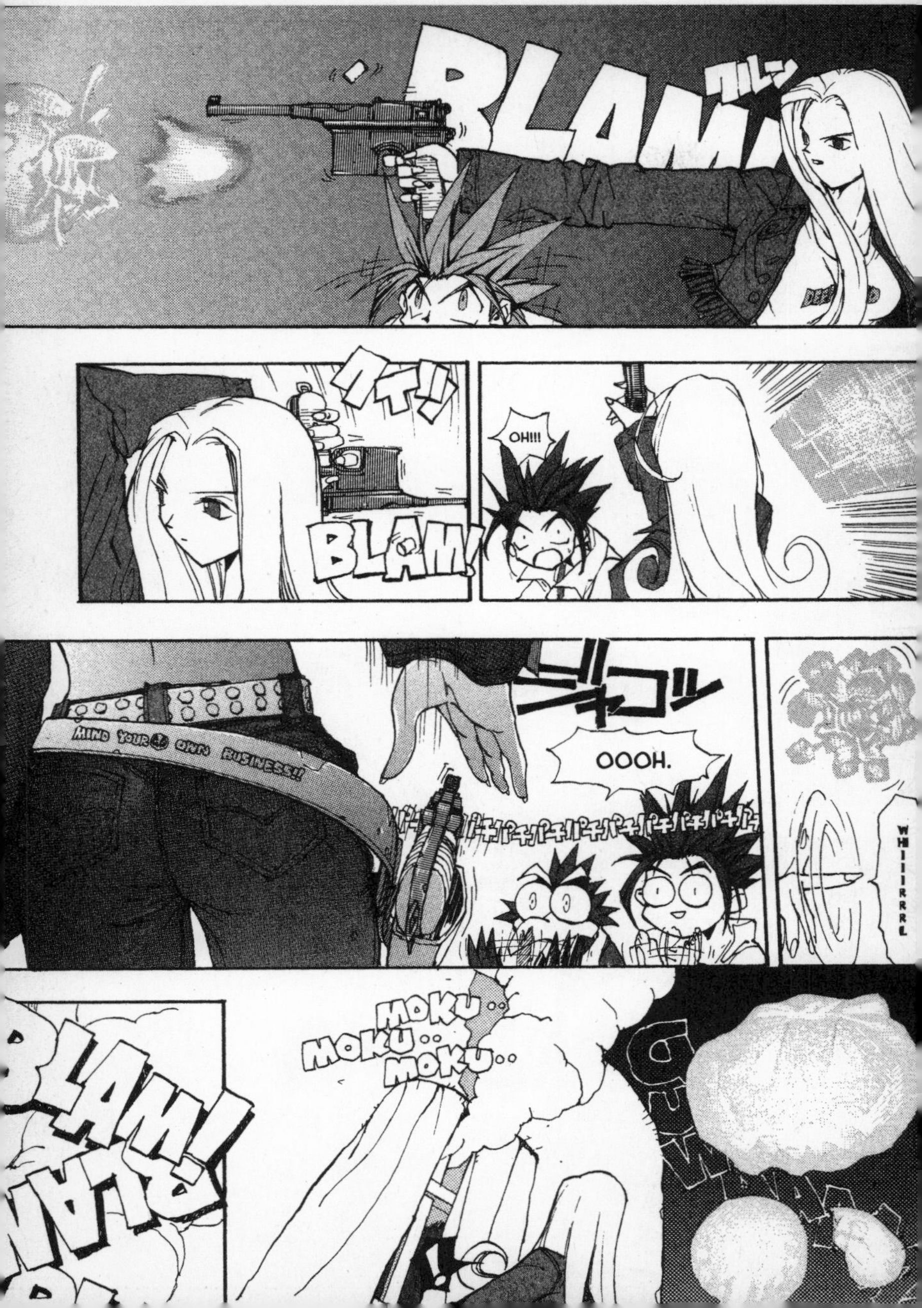
BLAM!
OH!!!
BLAM!
WHIIIIRRRL
OOOH.
MIND YOUR OWN BUSINESS!!
MOKU.. MOKU.. MOKU..
BLAM!

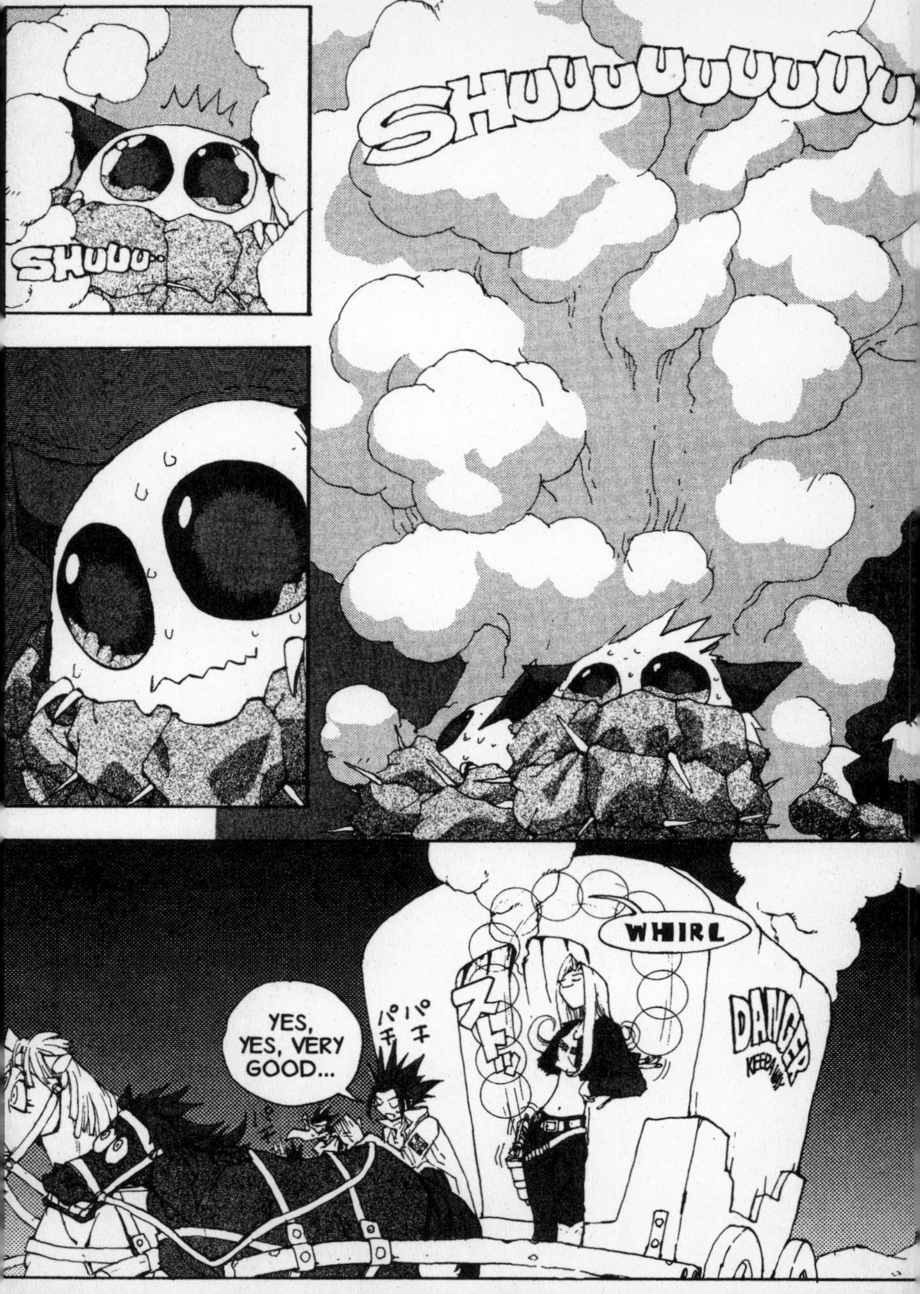
SHUUUUUUUUU
SHUUU
WHIRL
DANGER
パチ パチ
YES, YES, VERY GOOD...

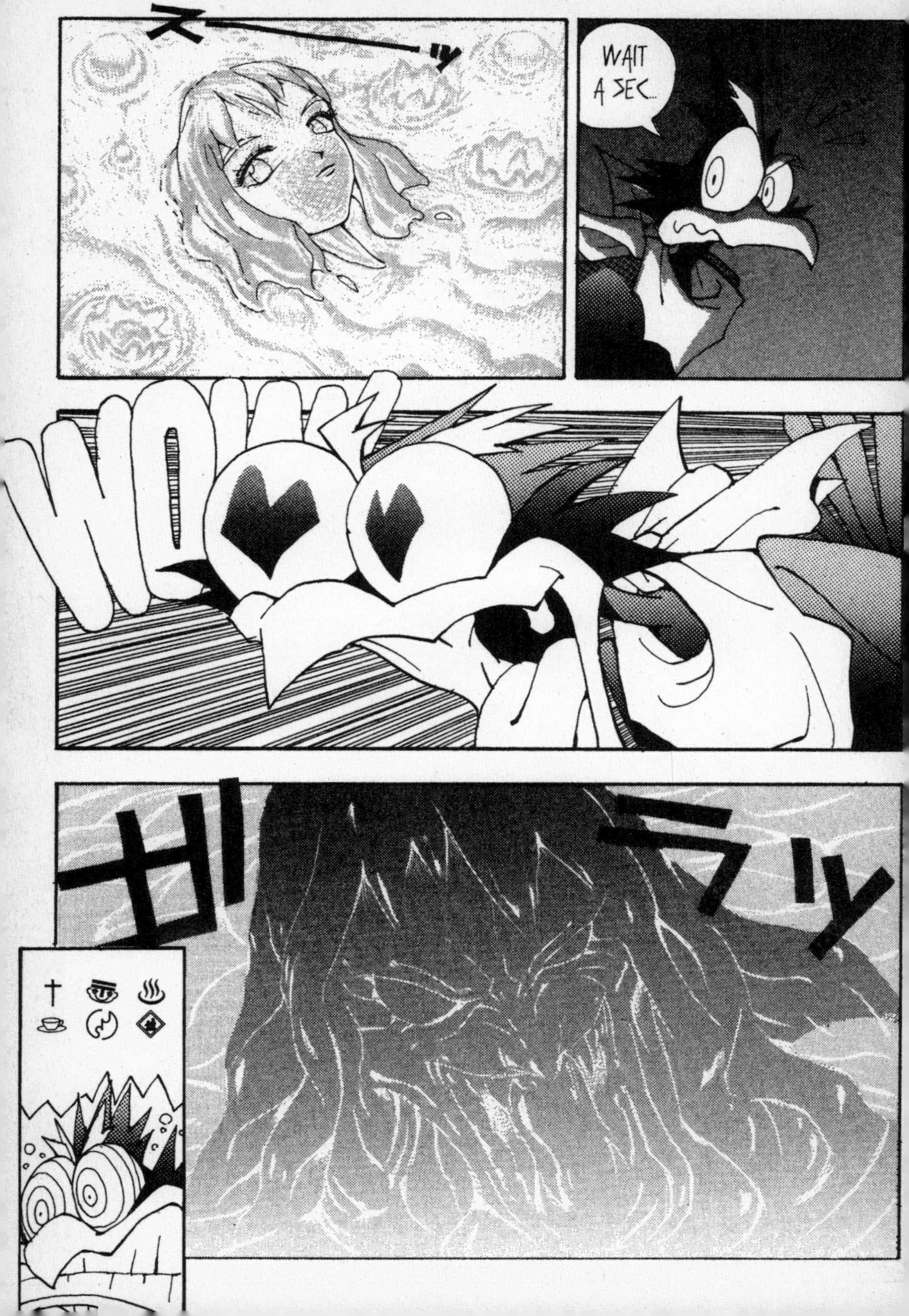
WAIT A SEC...
スーッ
WOW

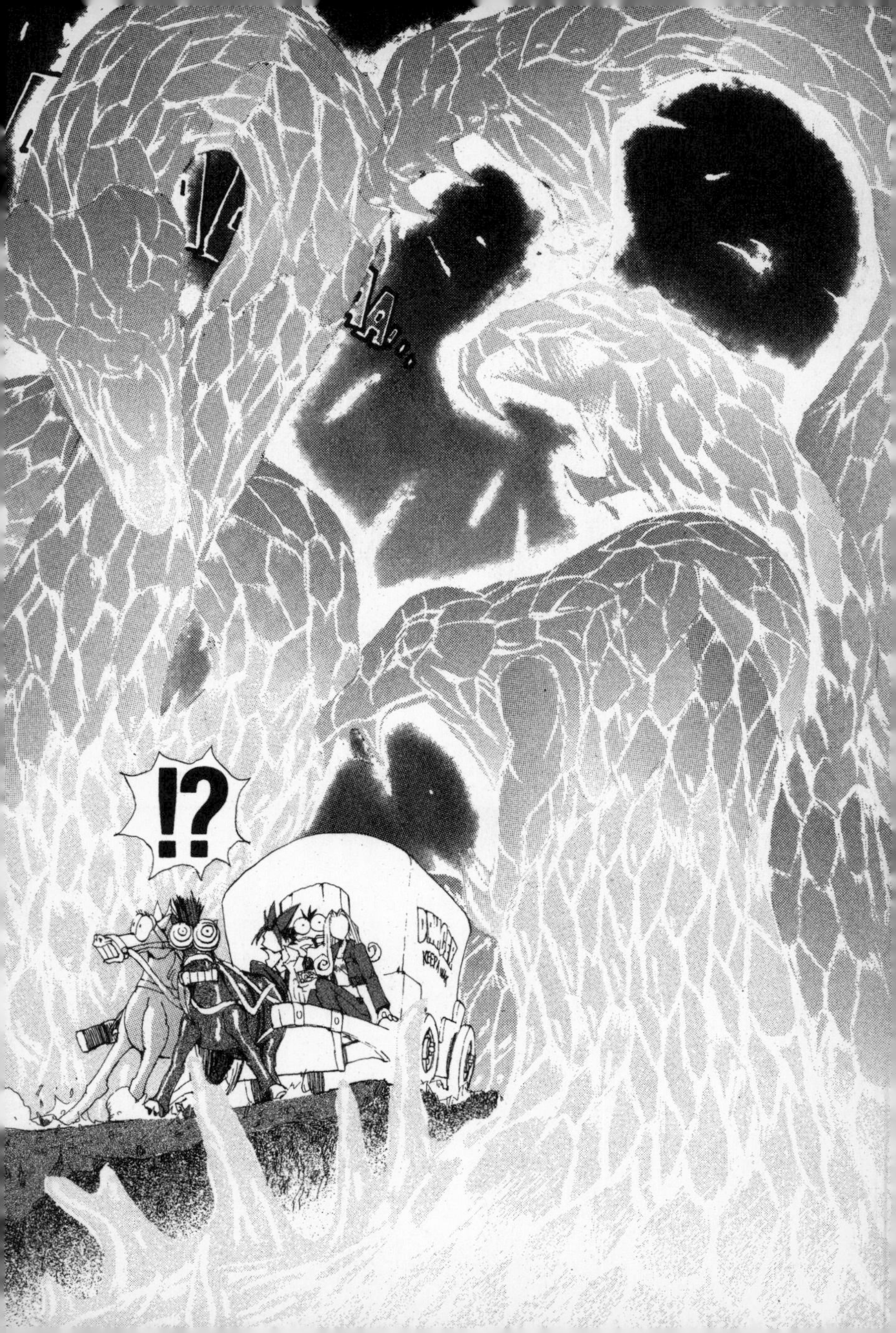!?
DANGER
KEEP A WAY

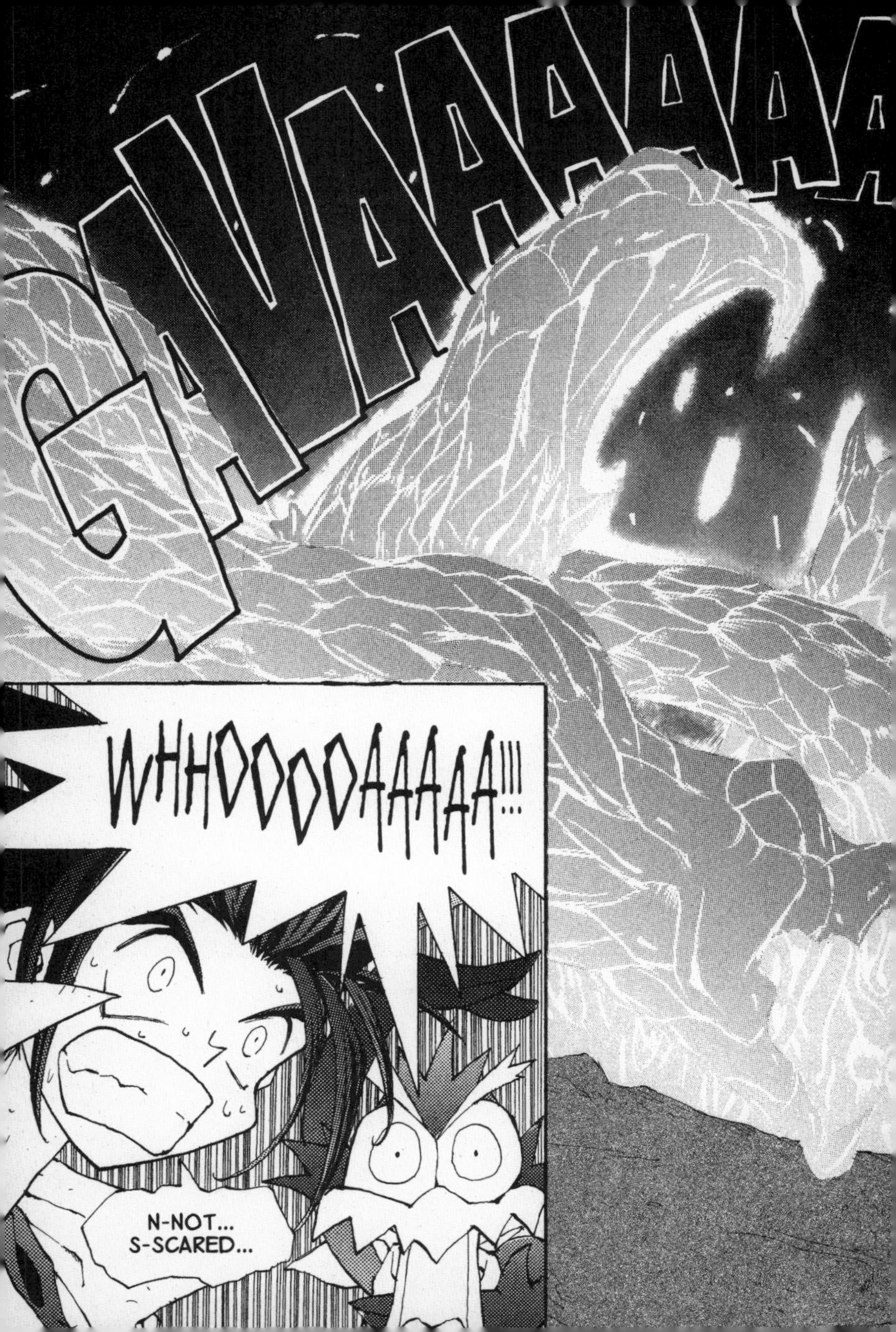
GWAAAAAA
WHHOOODAAAAA!!!
N-NOT...
S-SCARED...

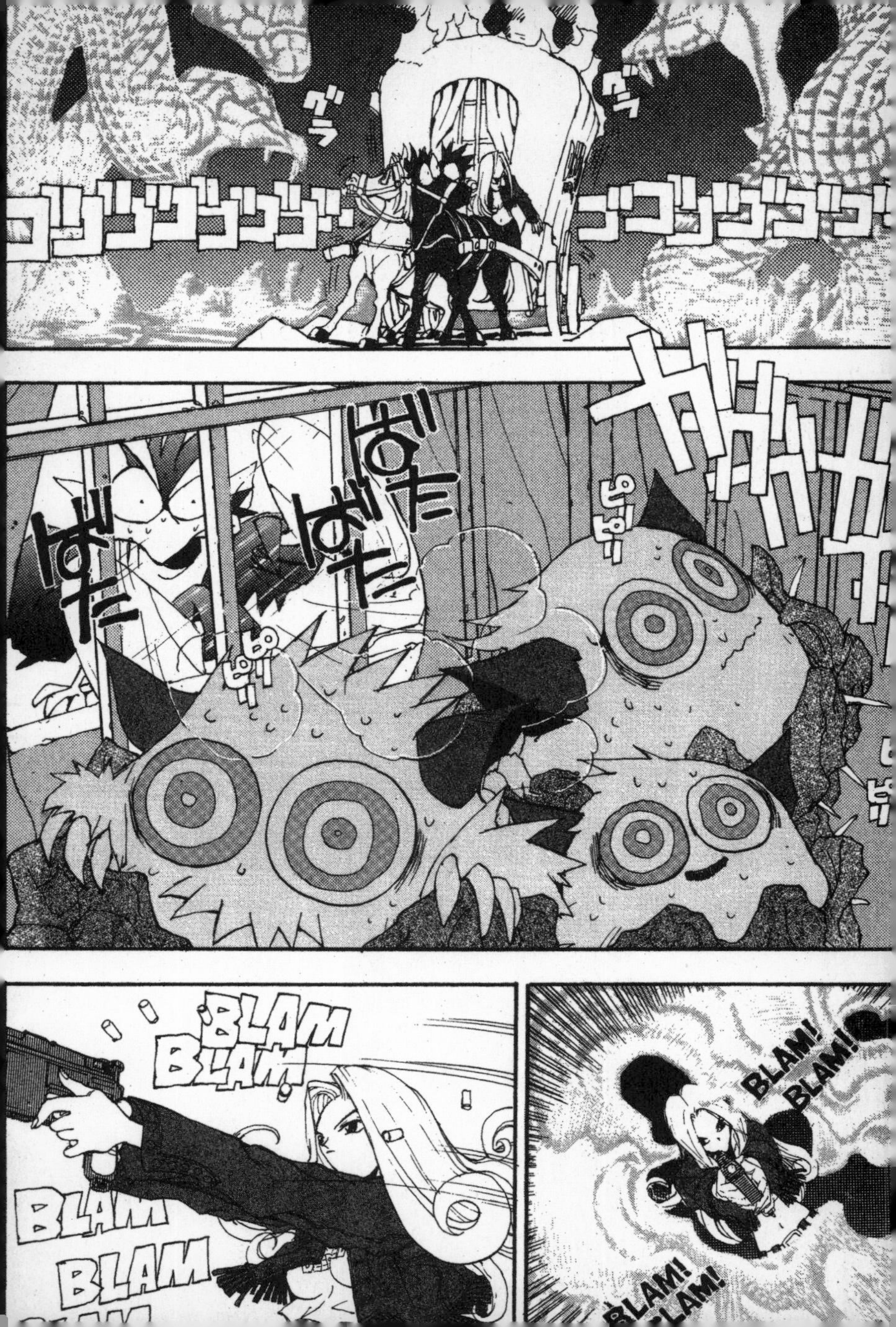
グラ
グラ
BLAM!
BLAM!
BLAM!
BLAM!
BLAM
BLAM
BLAM
BLAM

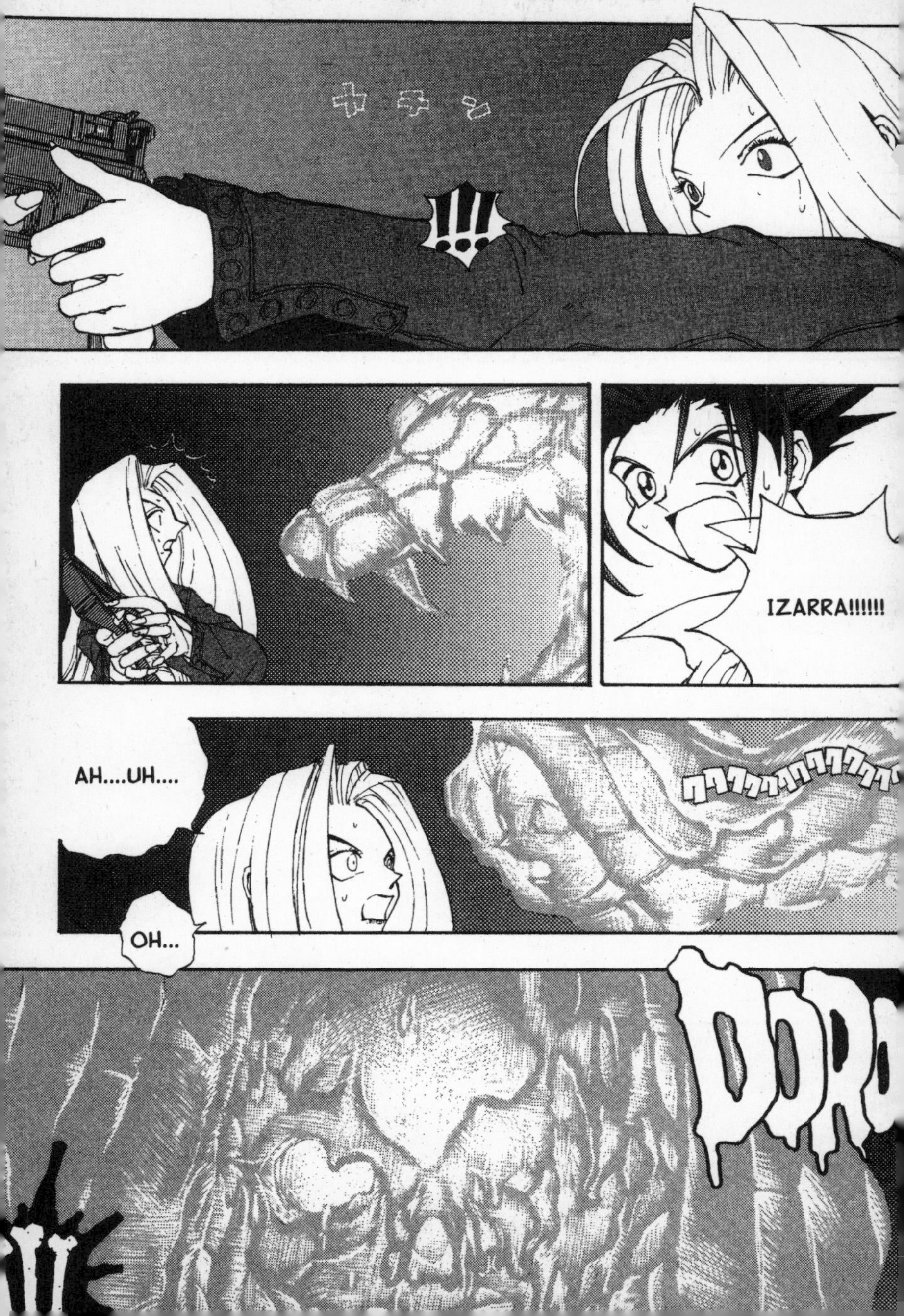
!!!
IZARRA!!!!!!
AH....UH....
OH...
DORO

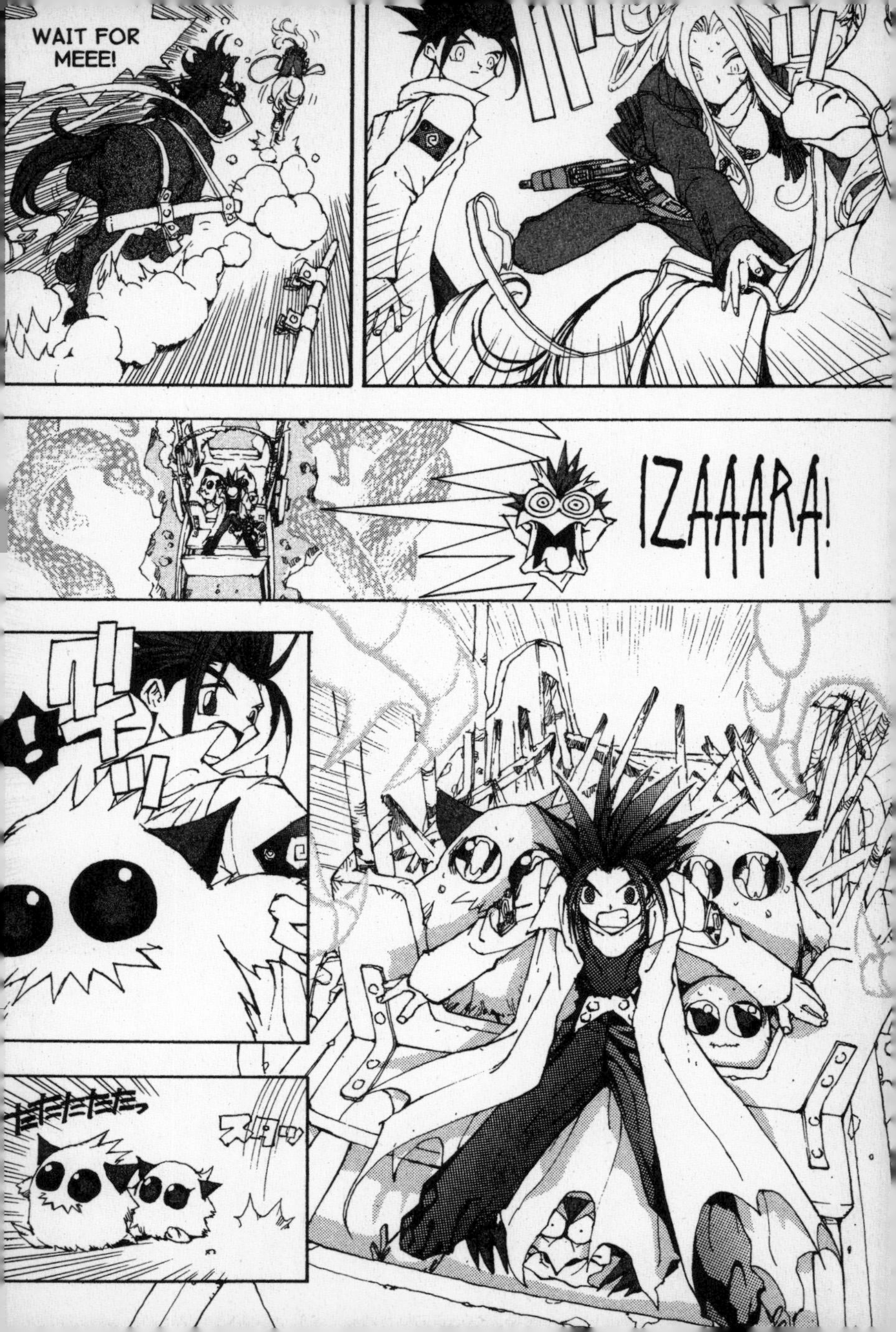
WAIT FOR MEEE!
IZAAARA!

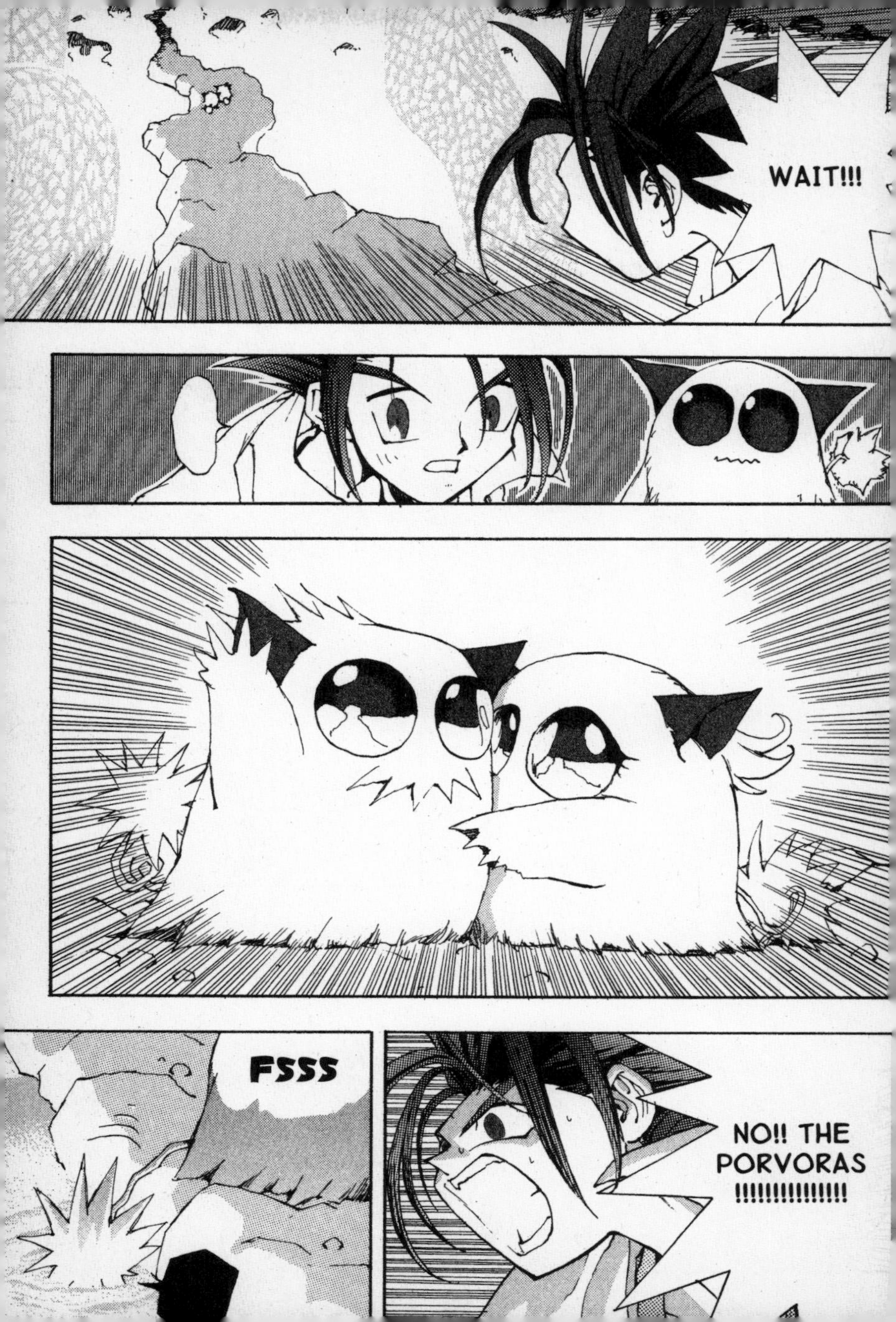
WAIT!!!
NO!! THE PORVORAS !!!!!!!!!!!!!!!
FSSS

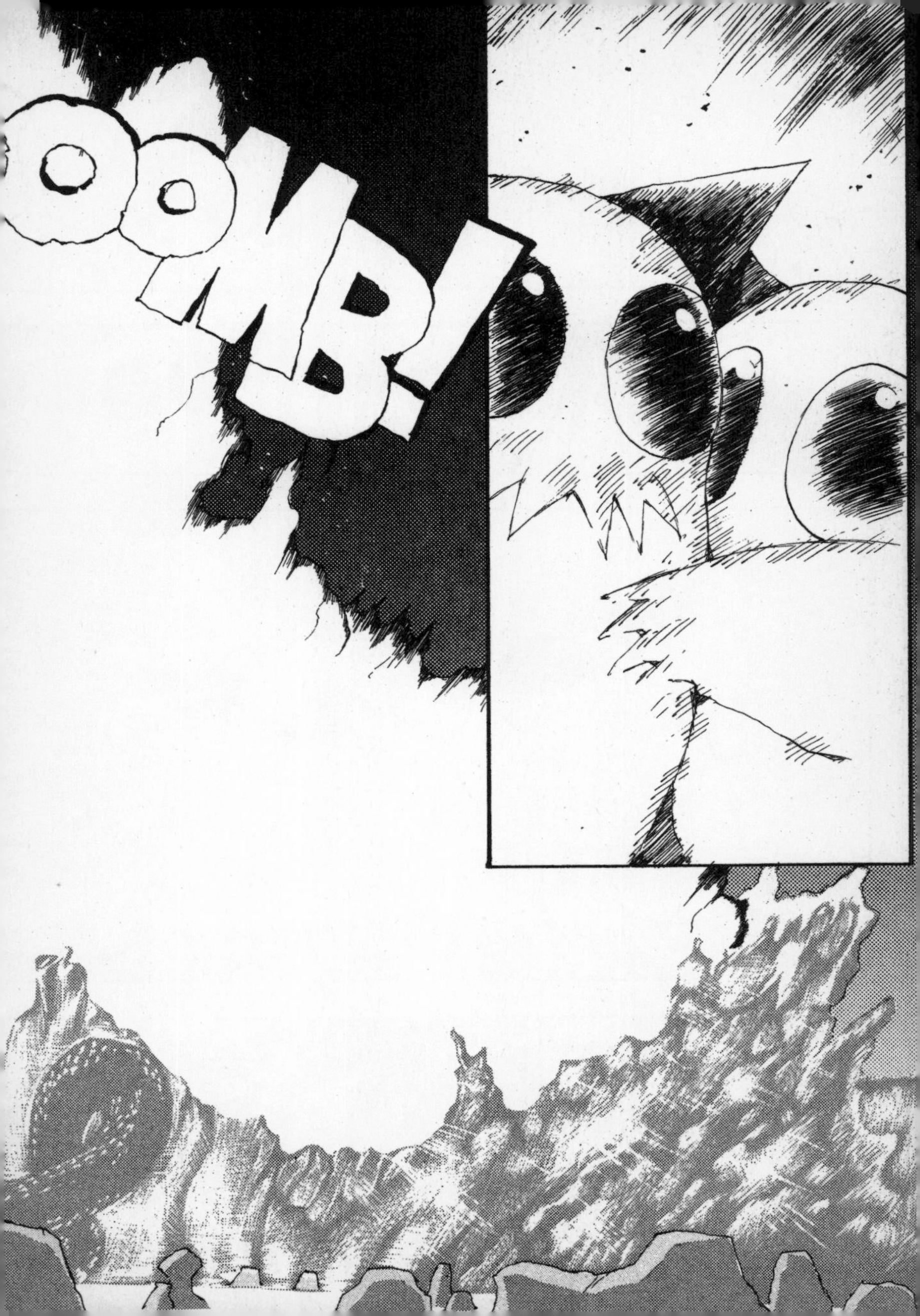
OOMB!

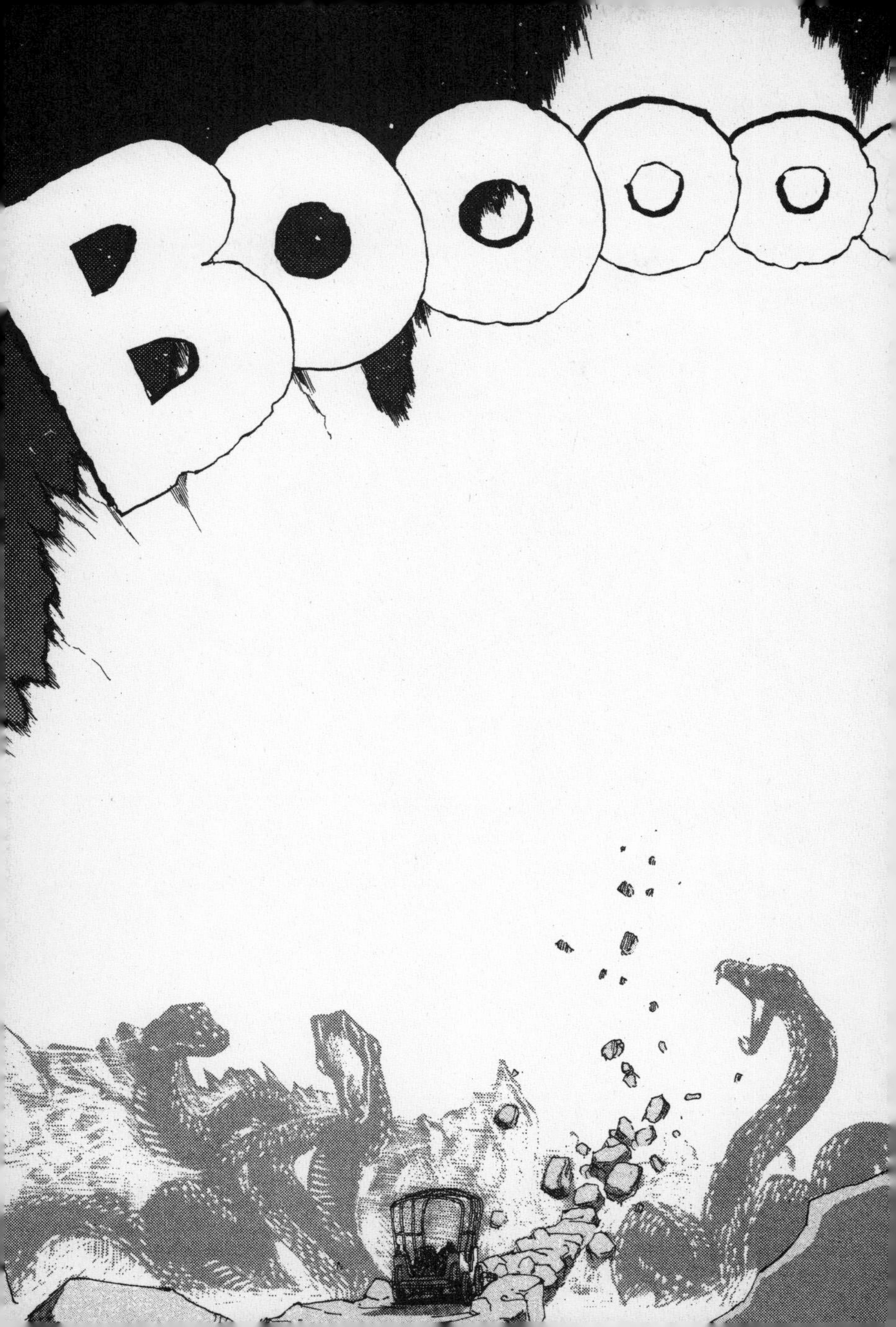
BOOOOO

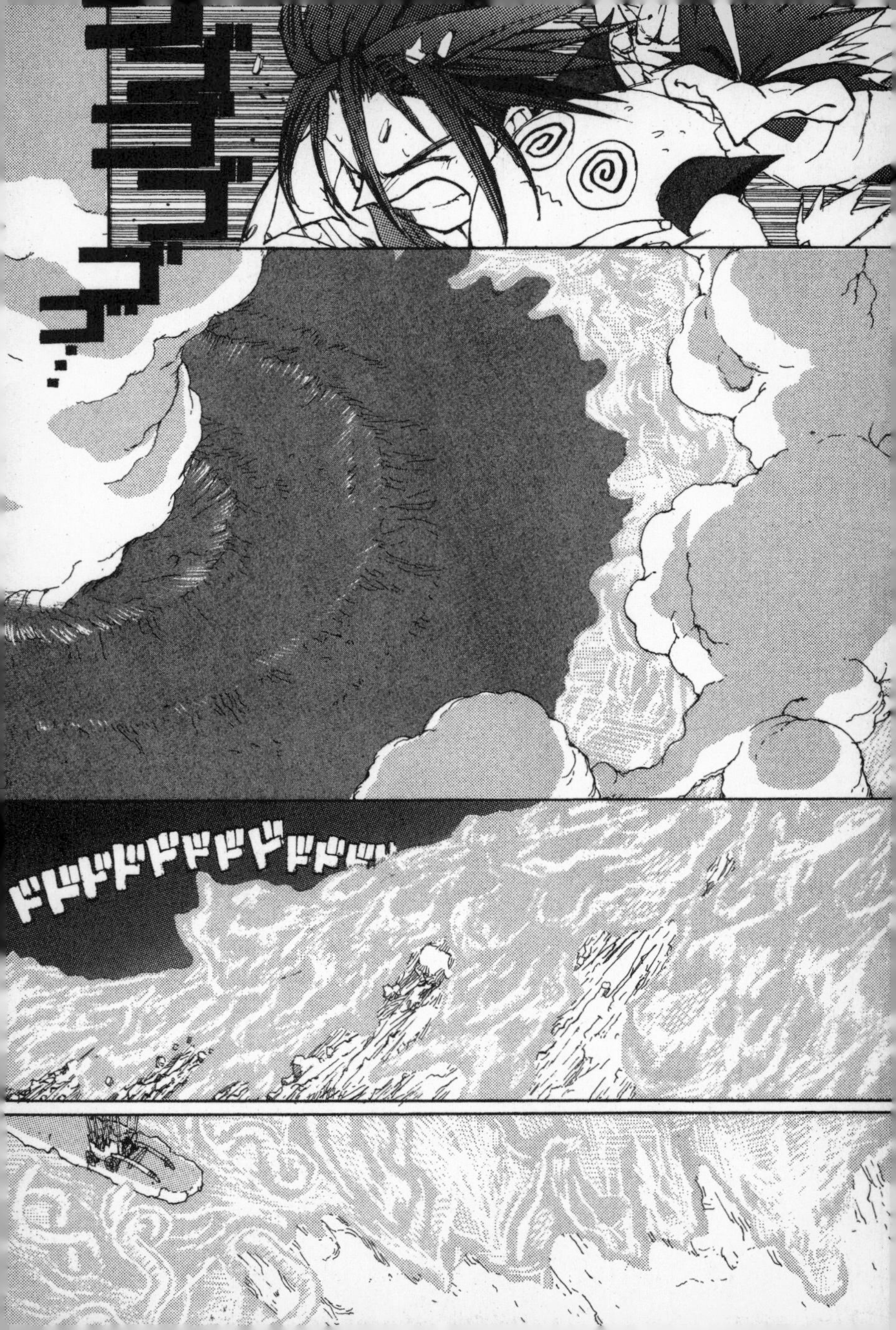
ゴゴゴゴ…
ドドドドドドドドドドド

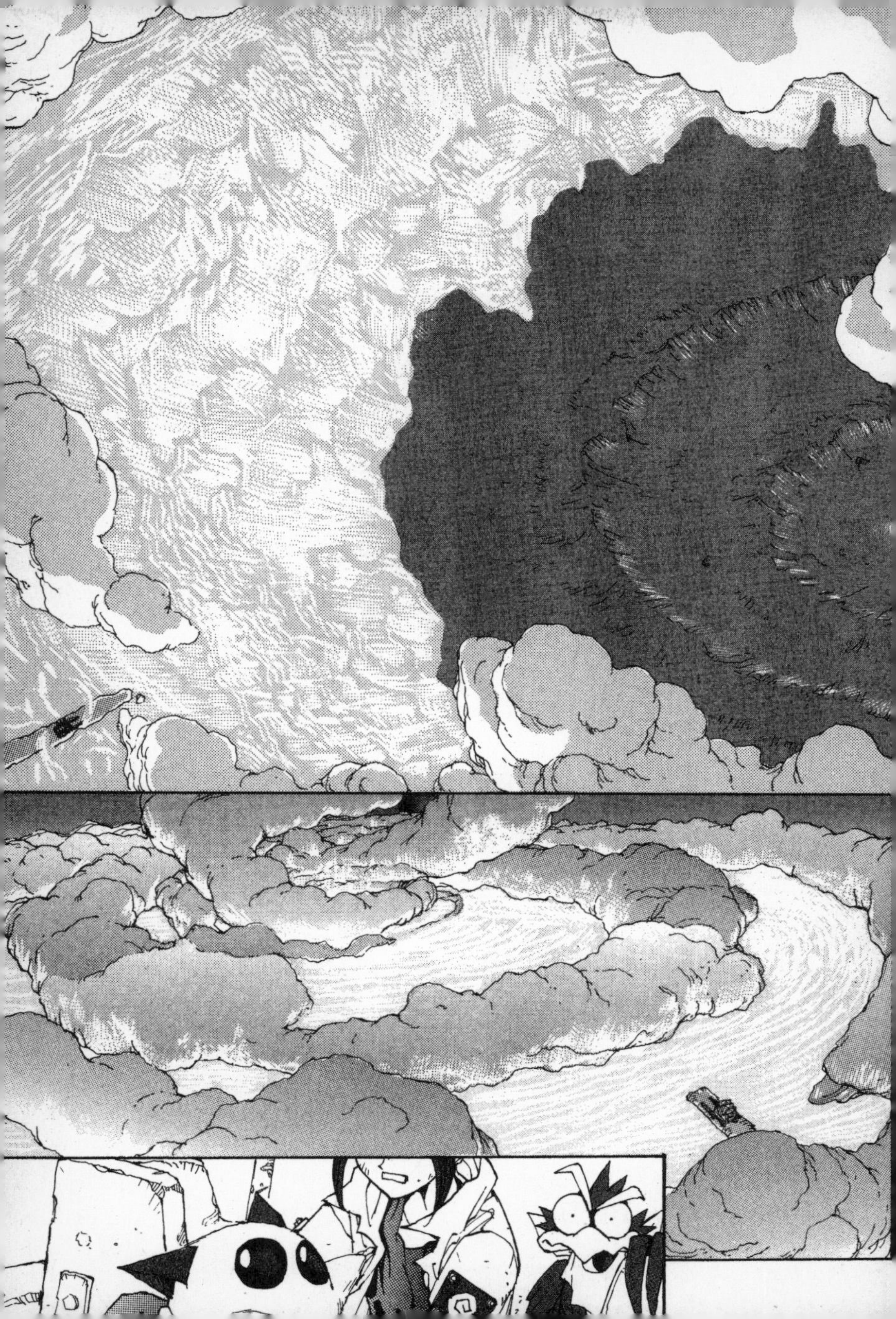

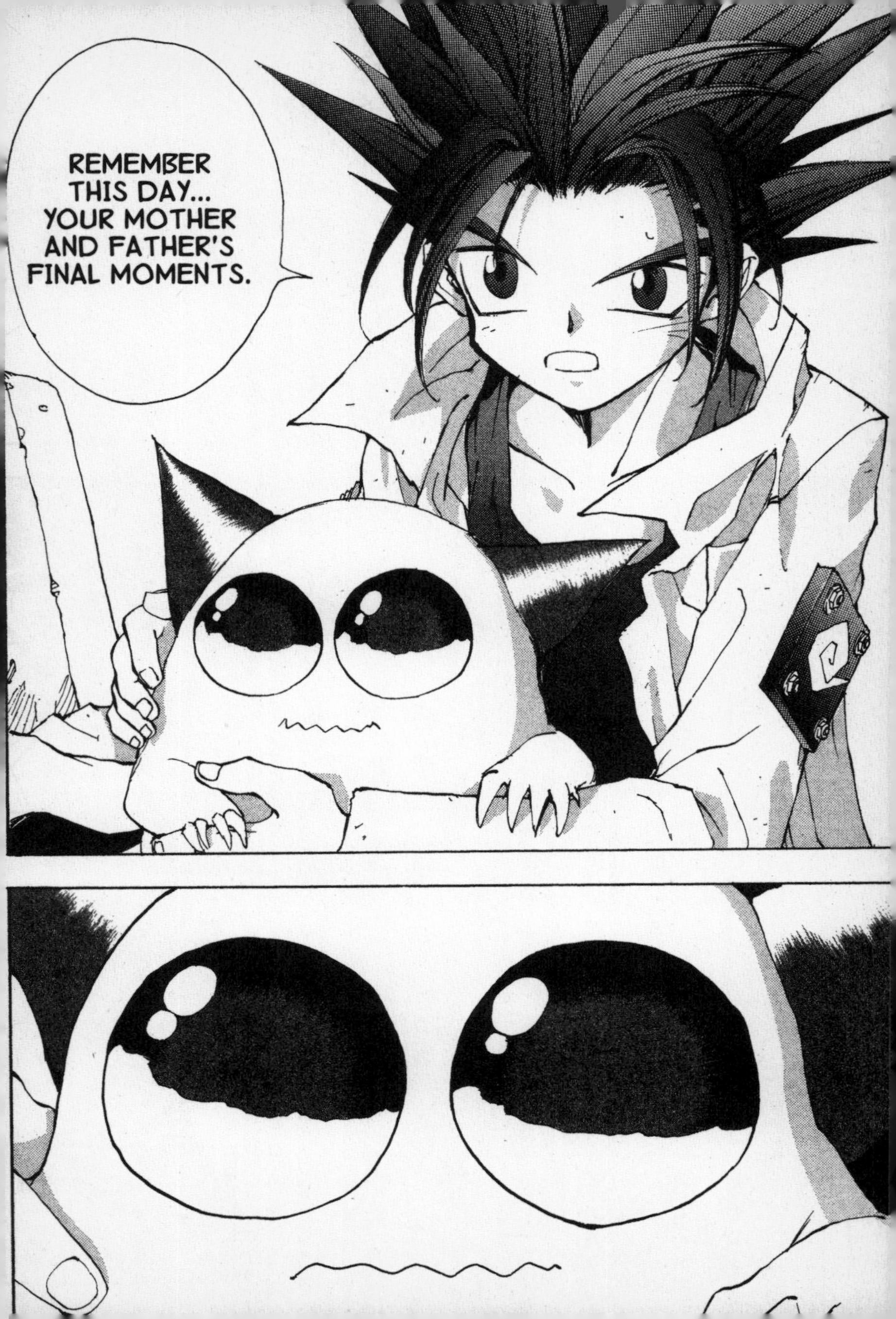
REMEMBER THIS DAY... YOUR MOTHER AND FATHER'S FINAL MOMENTS.

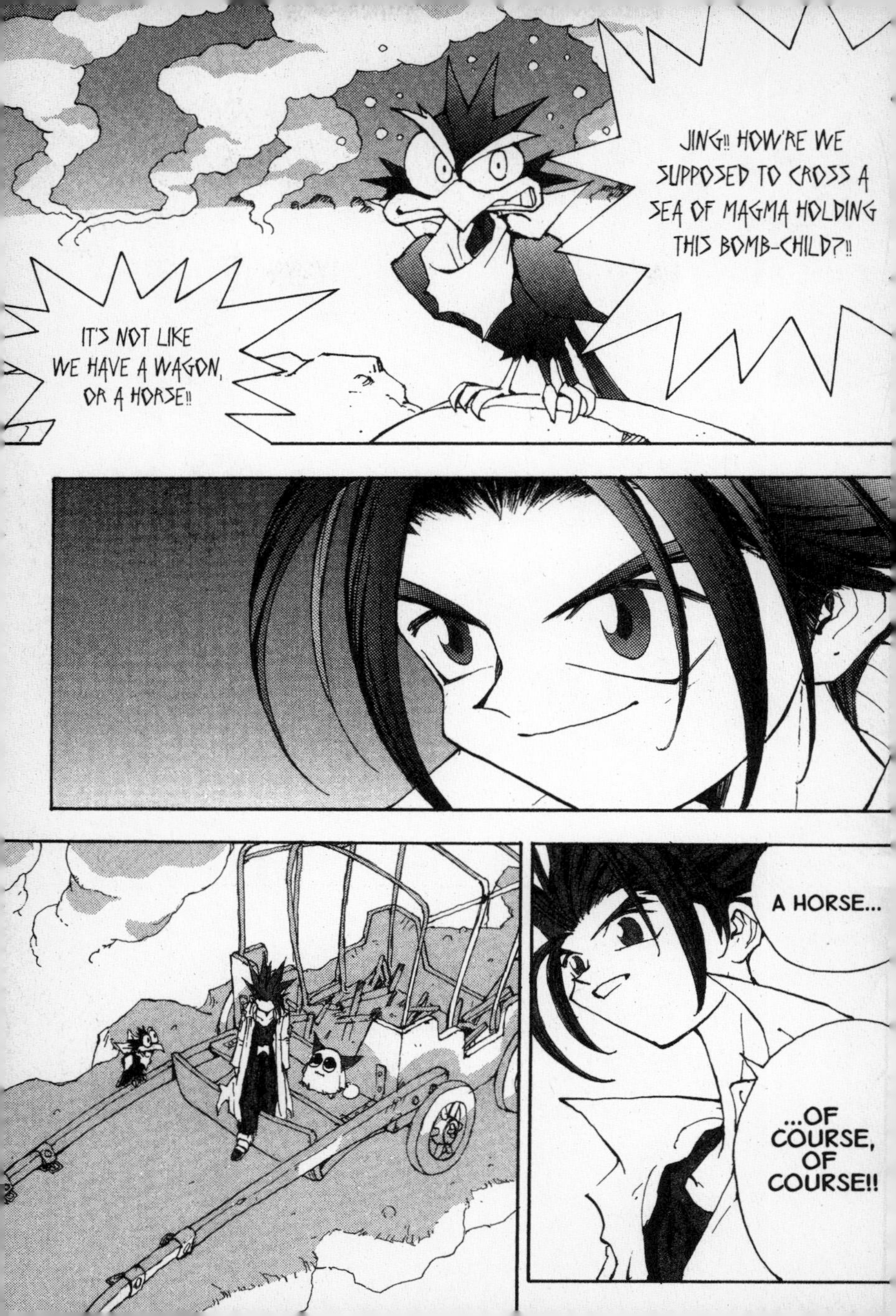
JING!! HOW'RE WE SUPPOSED TO CROSS A SEA OF MAGMA HOLDING THIS BOMB-CHILD?!!
IT'S NOT LIKE WE HAVE A WAGON, OR A HORSE!!
A HORSE...
...OF COURSE, OF COURSE!!

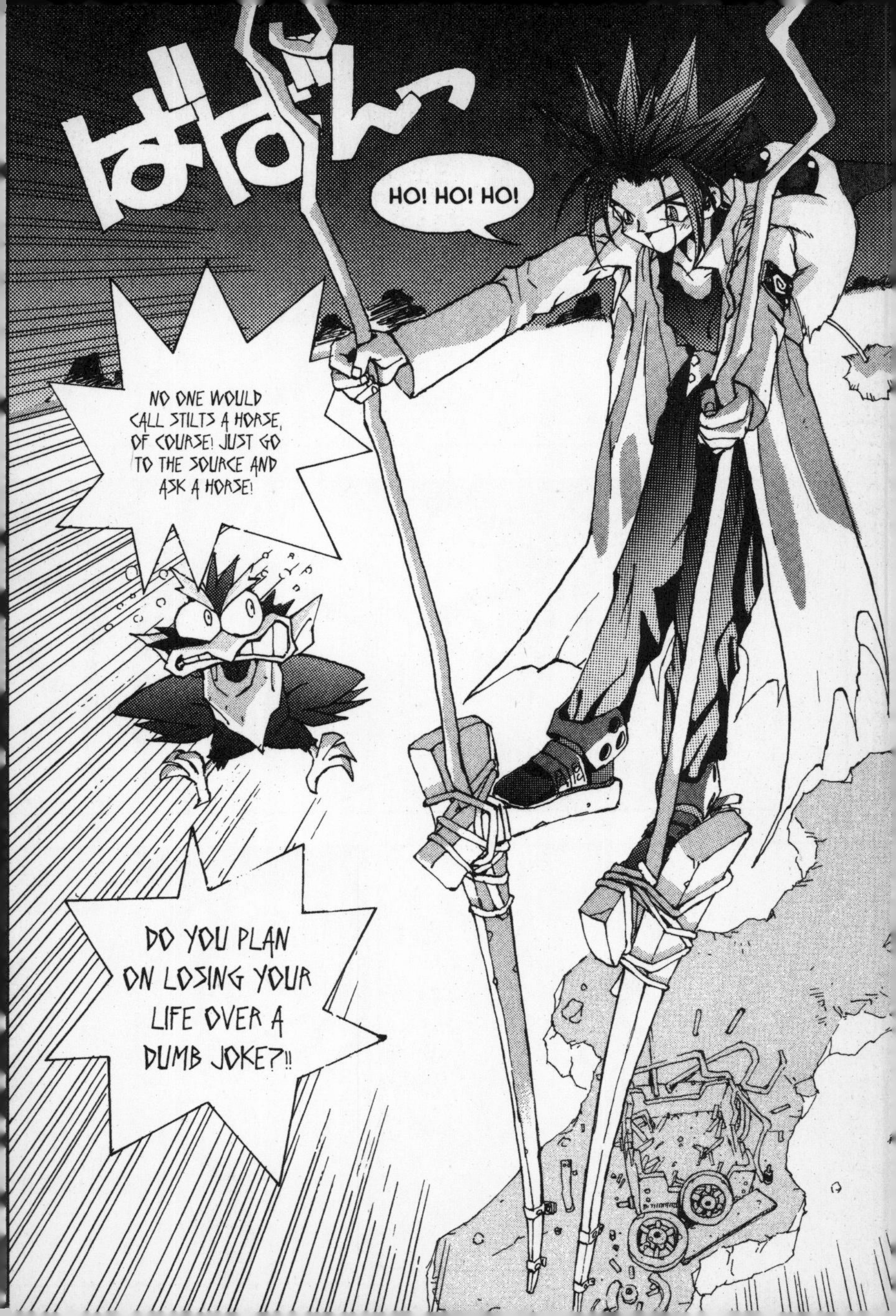
HO! HO! HO!
ばばんっ
NO ONE WOULD CALL STILTS A HORSE, OF COURSE! JUST GO TO THE SOURCE AND ASK A HORSE!
DO YOU PLAN ON LOSING YOUR LIFE OVER A DUMB JOKE?!!

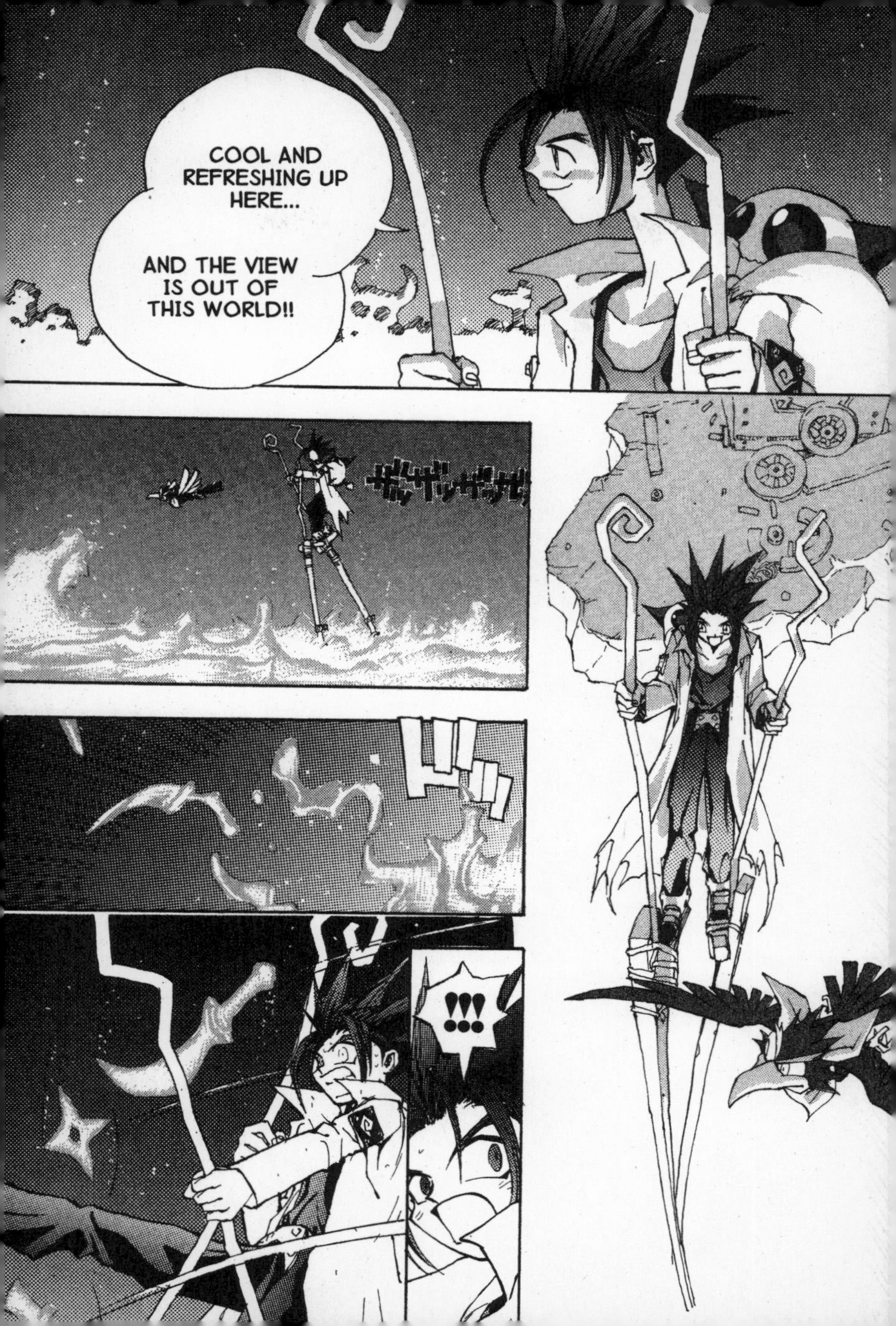
COOL AND REFRESHING UP HERE...
AND THE VIEW IS OUT OF THIS WORLD!!
!!!

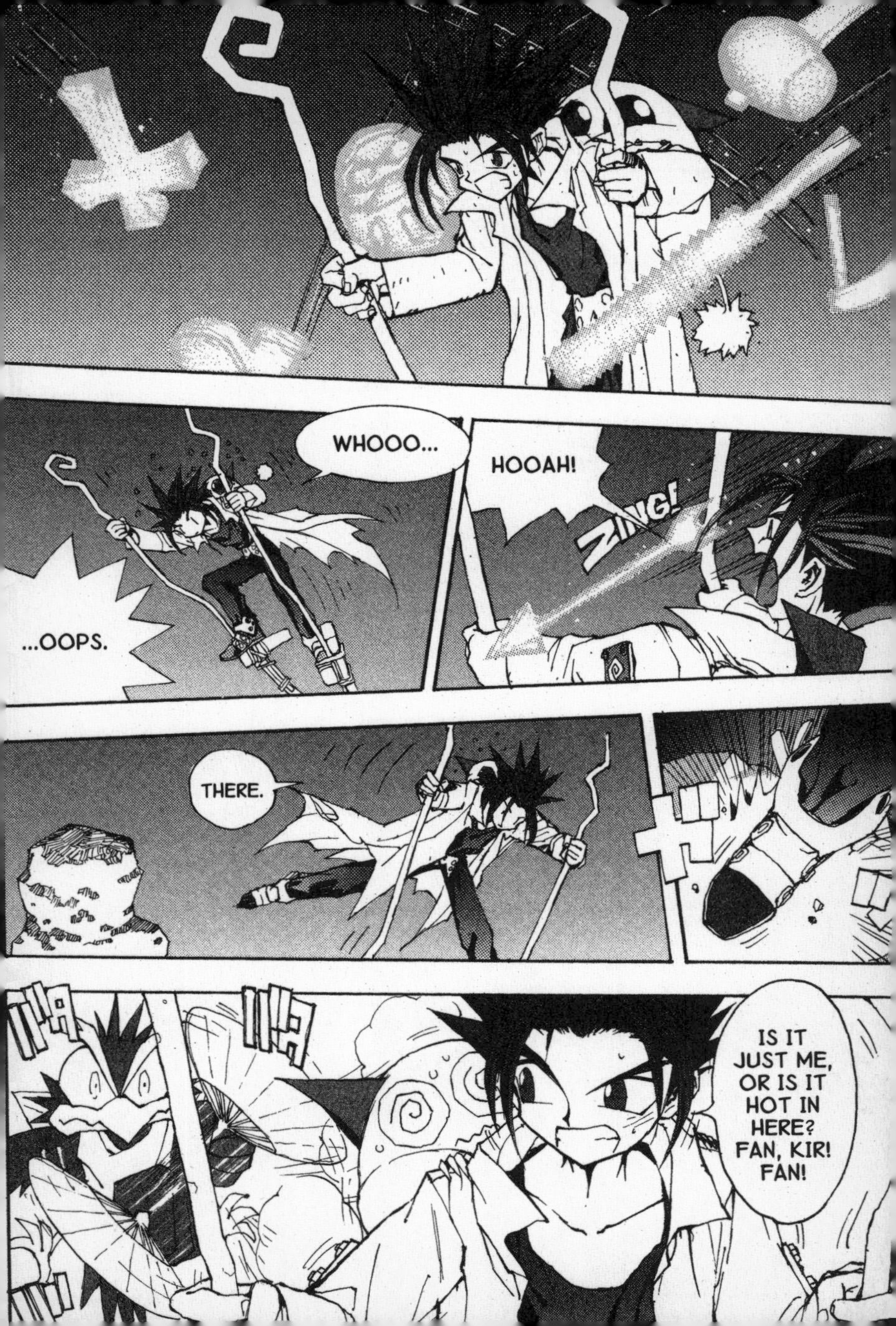
HOOAH!
ZING!
WHOOO...
...OOPS.
THERE.
IS IT JUST ME, OR IS IT HOT IN HERE? FAN, KIR! FAN!

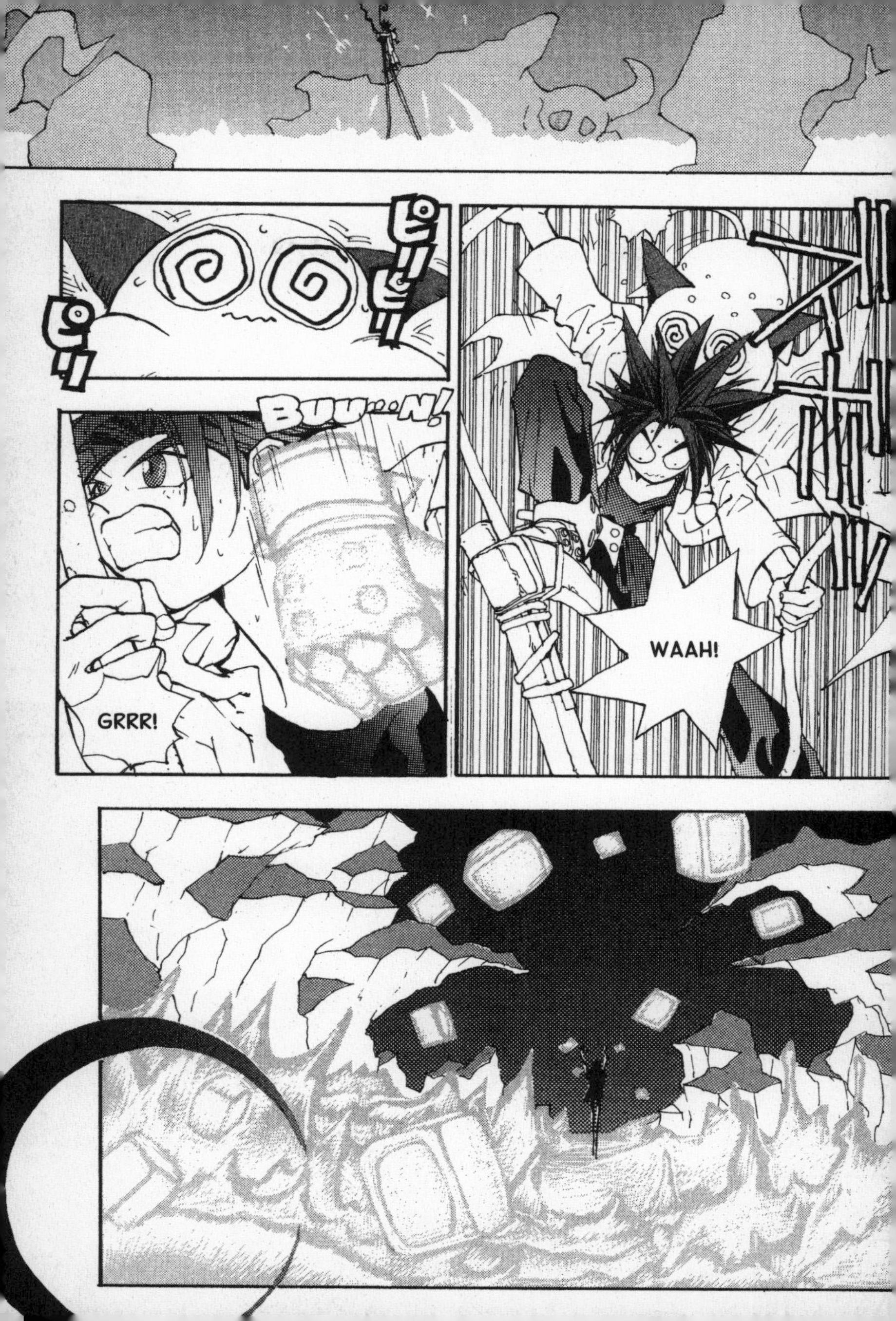
WAAH!
BUU...N!
GRRR!

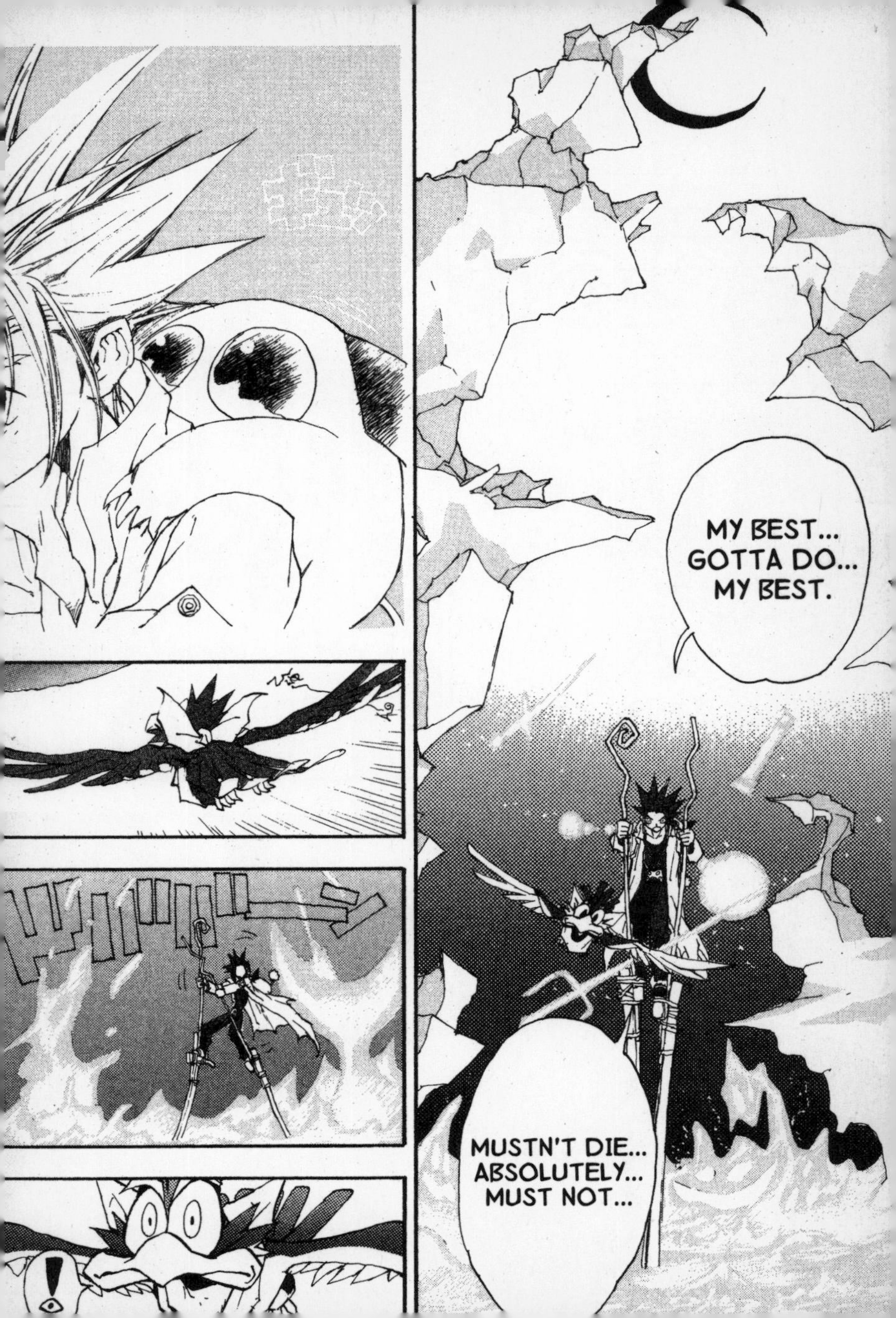
MY BEST... GOTTA DO... MY BEST.
MUSTN'T DIE... ABSOLUTELY... MUST NOT...

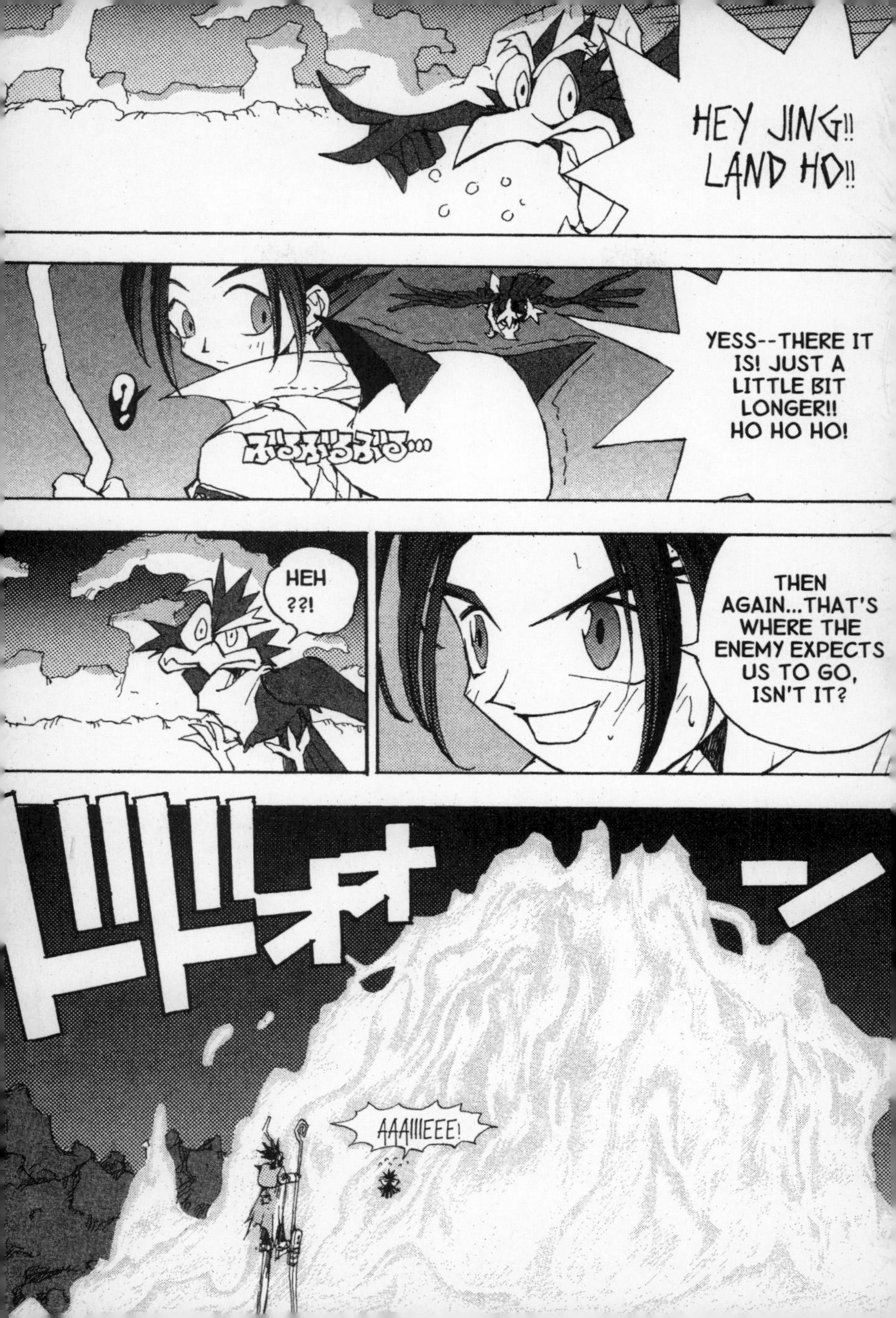
HEY JING!! LAND HO!!
YESS--THERE IT IS! JUST A LITTLE BIT LONGER!! HO HO HO!
?
THEN AGAIN...THAT'S WHERE THE ENEMY EXPECTS US TO GO, ISN'T IT?
HEH ??!
AAAIIIEEE!

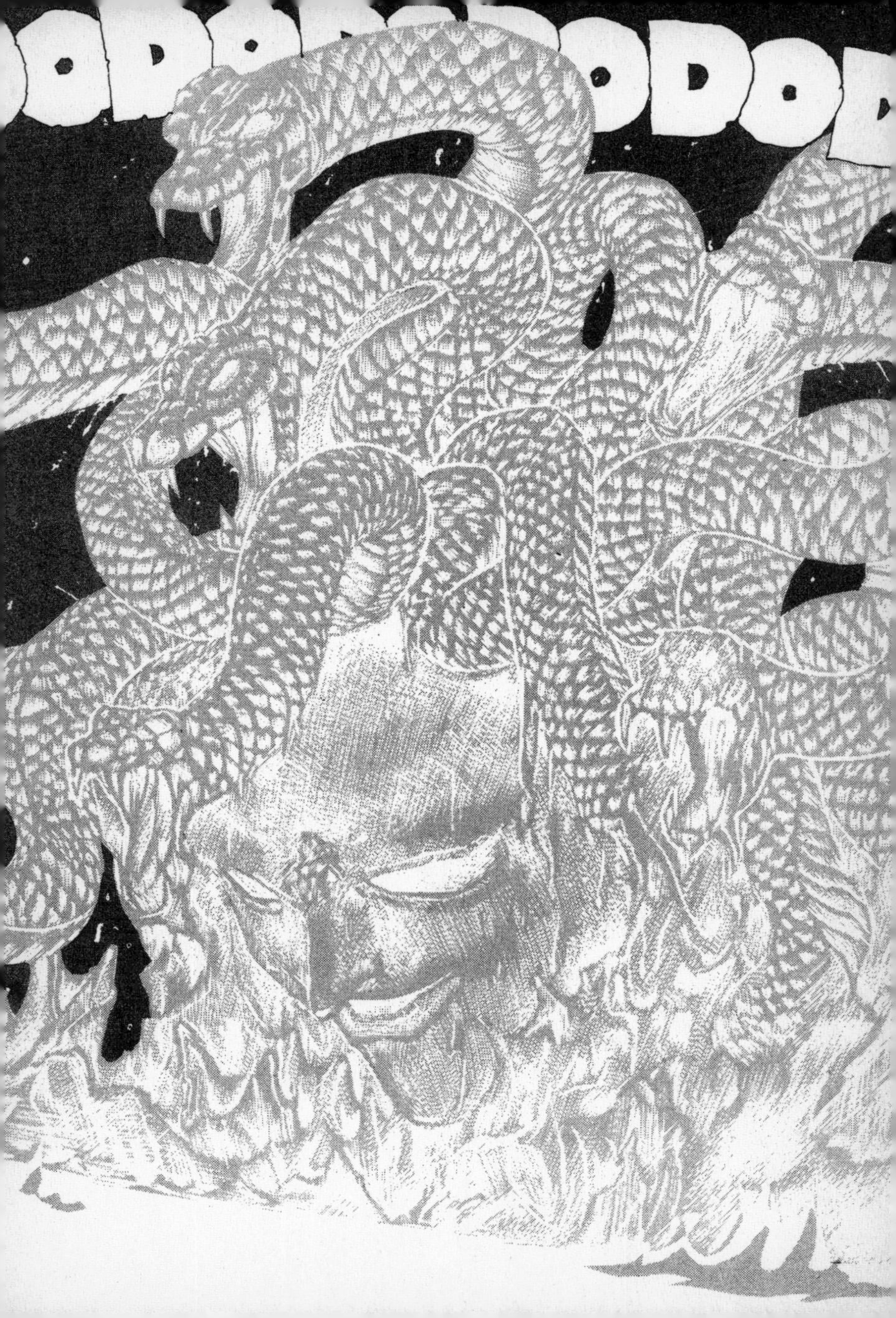

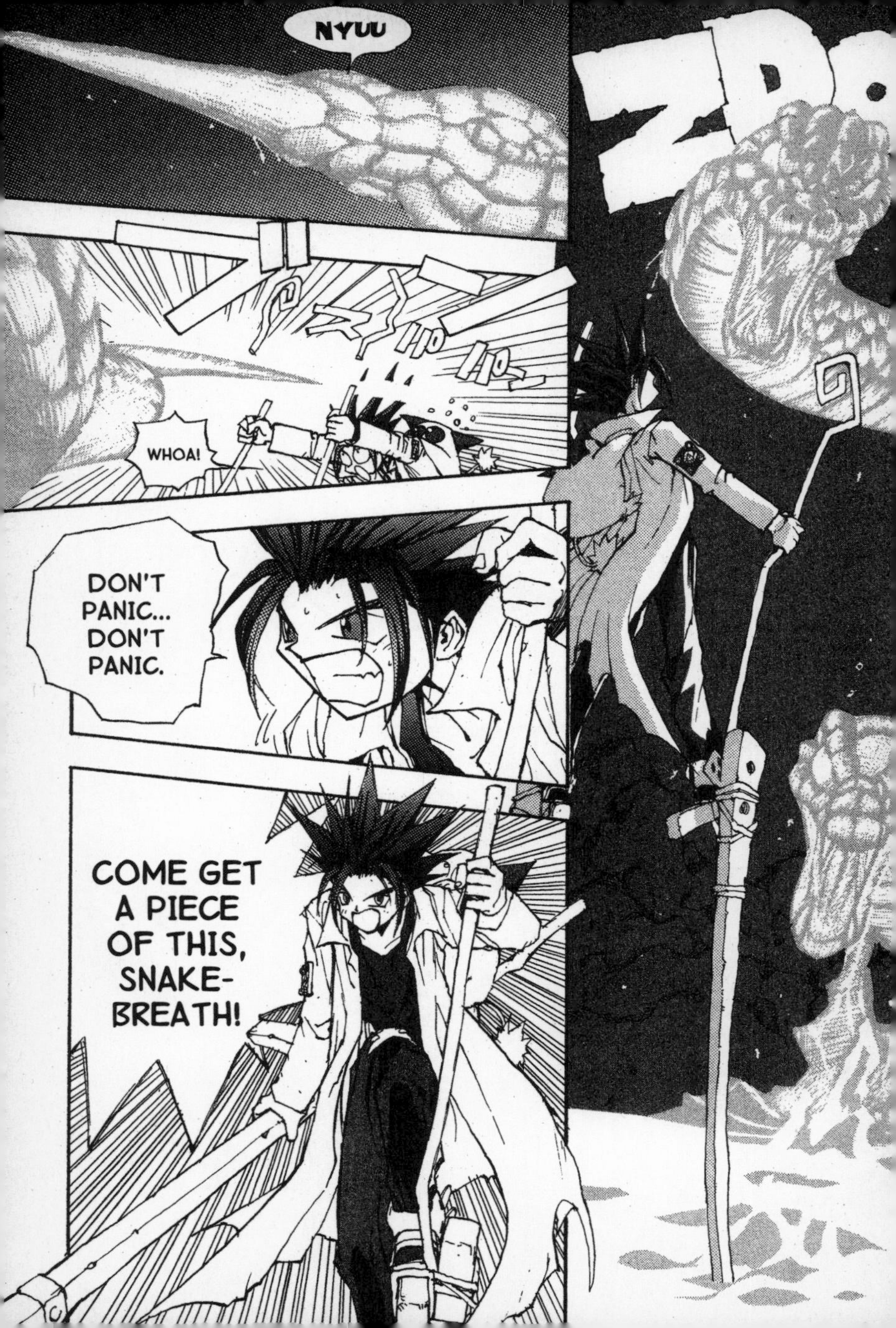
NYUU
WHOA!
DON'T PANIC... DON'T PANIC.
COME GET A PIECE OF THIS, SNAKE-BREATH!

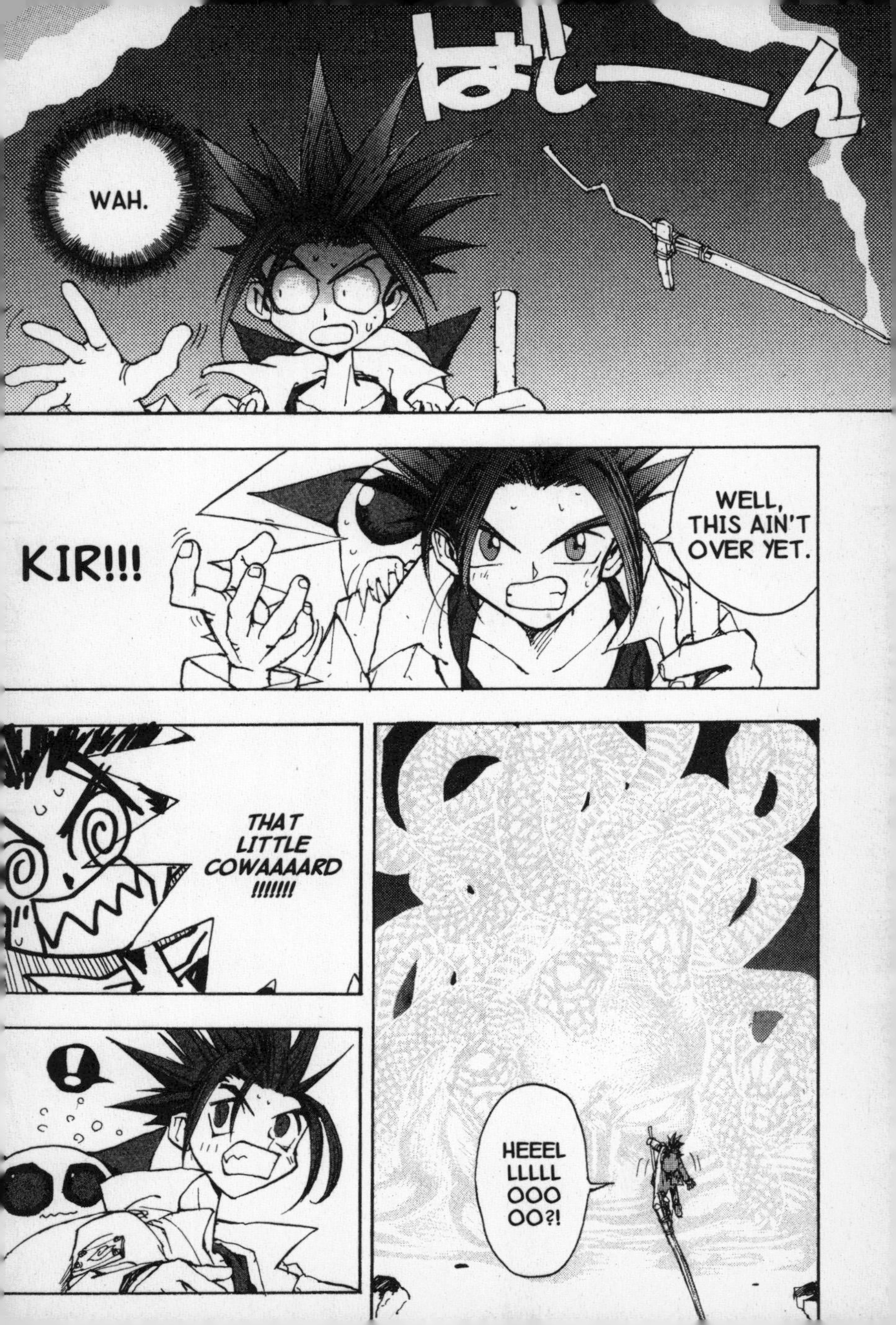
ばしーん
WAH.
WELL, THIS AIN'T OVER YET.
KIR!!!
HEEEL LLLLL OOO OO?!
THAT LITTLE COWAAAARD !!!!!!!
!

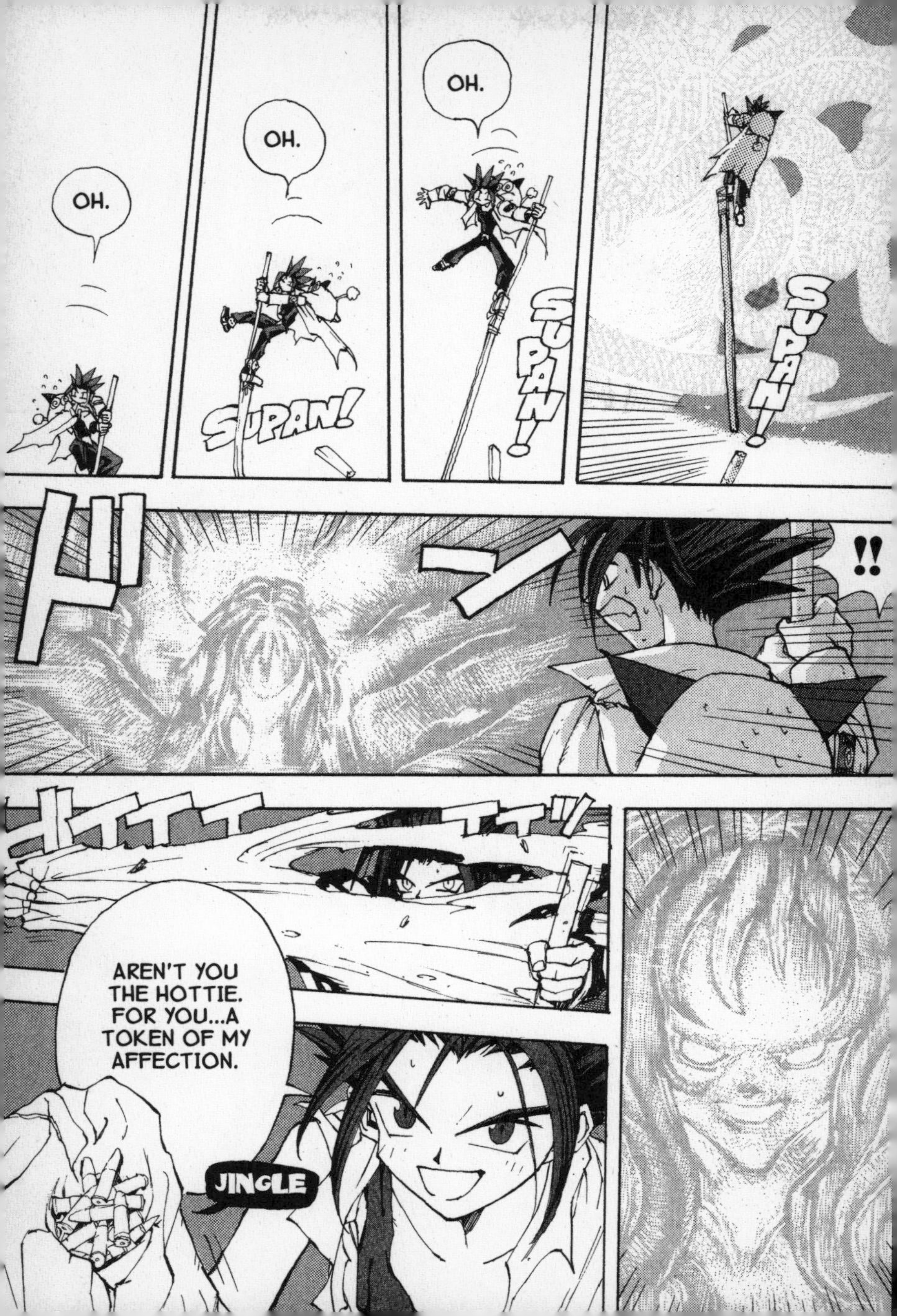
SUPAN!
OH.
SUPAN!
OH.
SUPAN!
OH.
!!
AREN'T YOU THE HOTTIE. FOR YOU...A TOKEN OF MY AFFECTION.
JINGLE

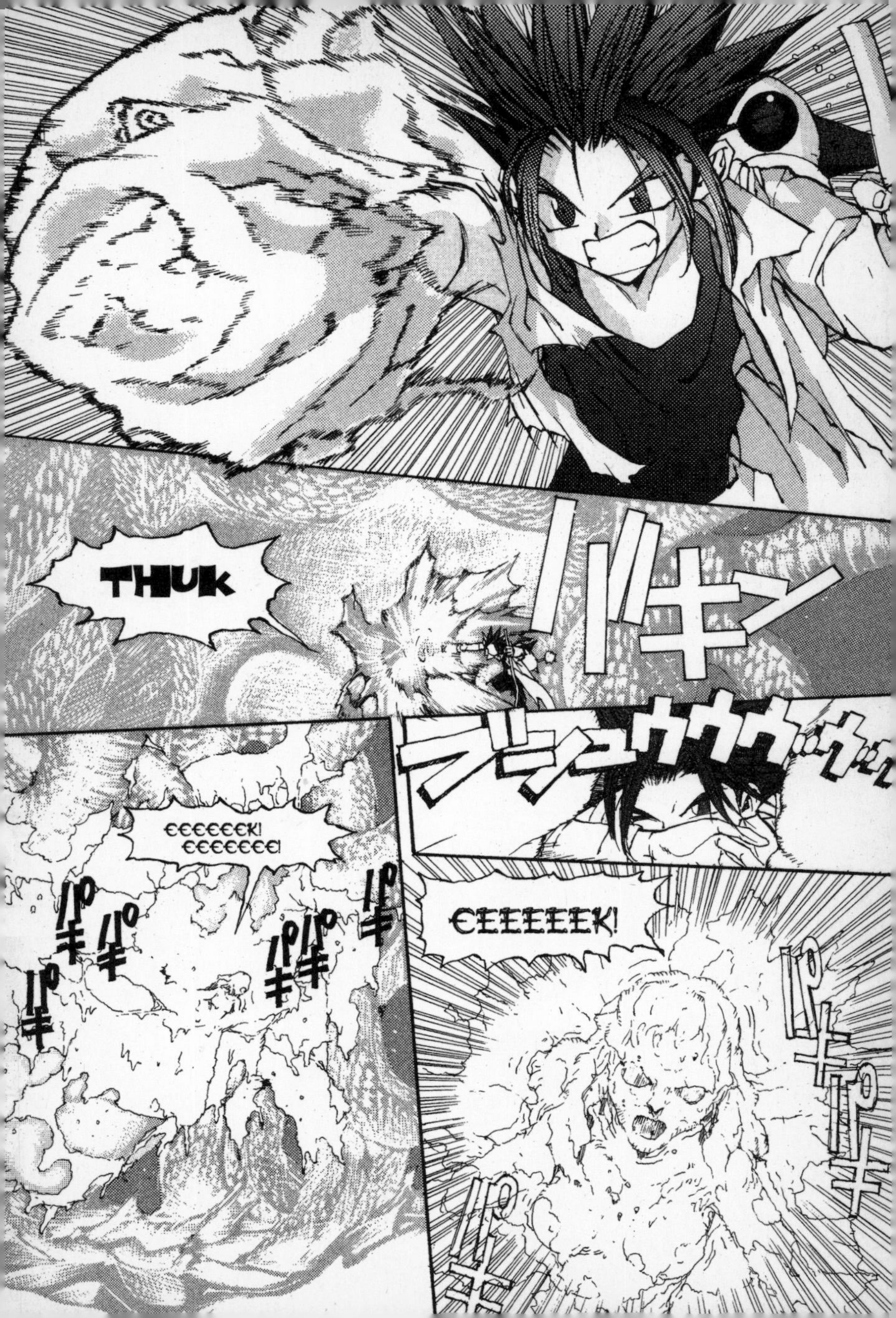
THUK
ブシュウウウ…ウ…
EEEEEEK!
パキパキ
EEEEEEK!
EEEEEEE!
パキ パキ パキ パキ パキ パキ

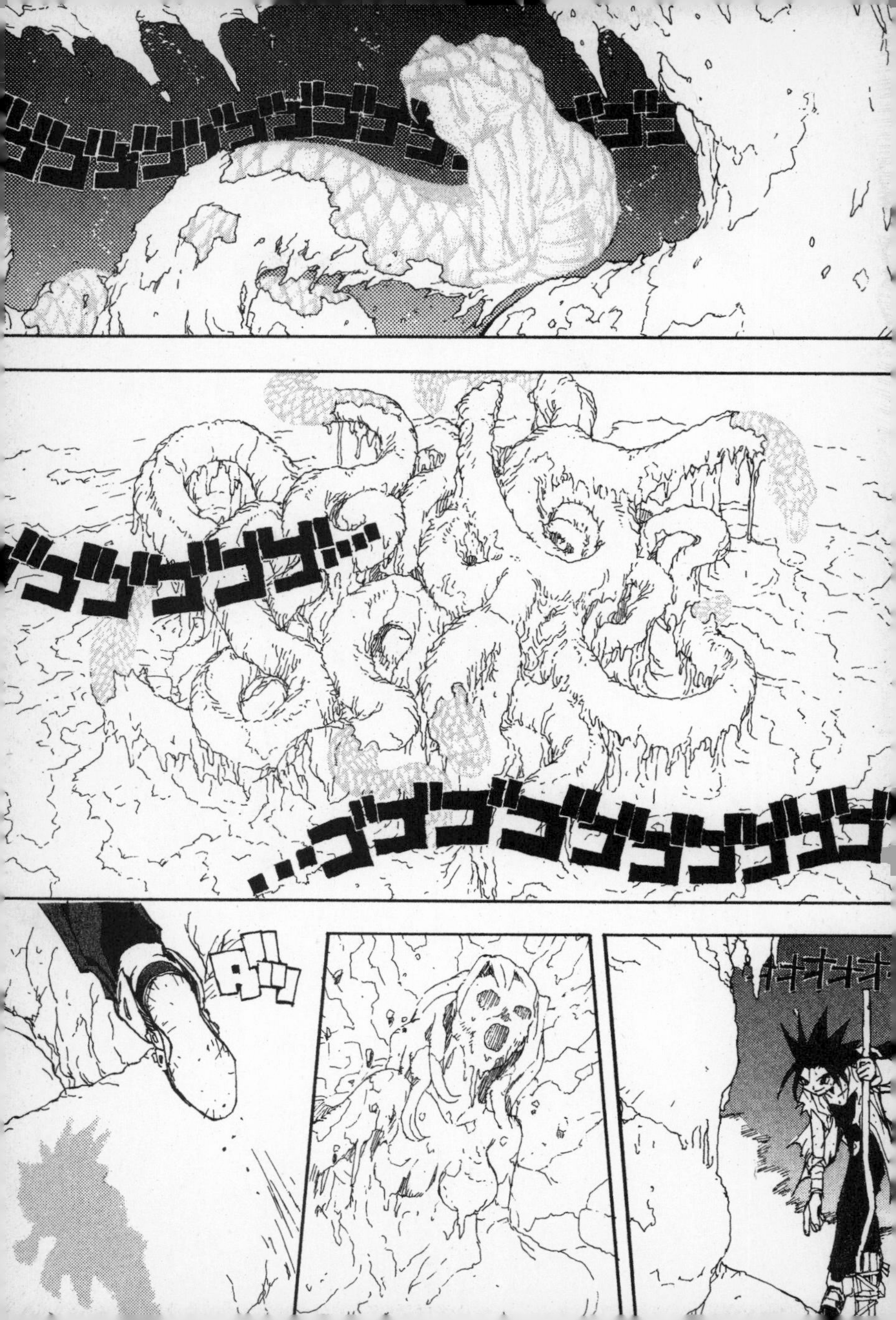
ゴゴゴゴゴゴゴゴゴ.
ゴゴ
ゴゴゴゴゴ…
…ゴゴゴゴゴゴゴゴゴ
オオオオ
ダッ

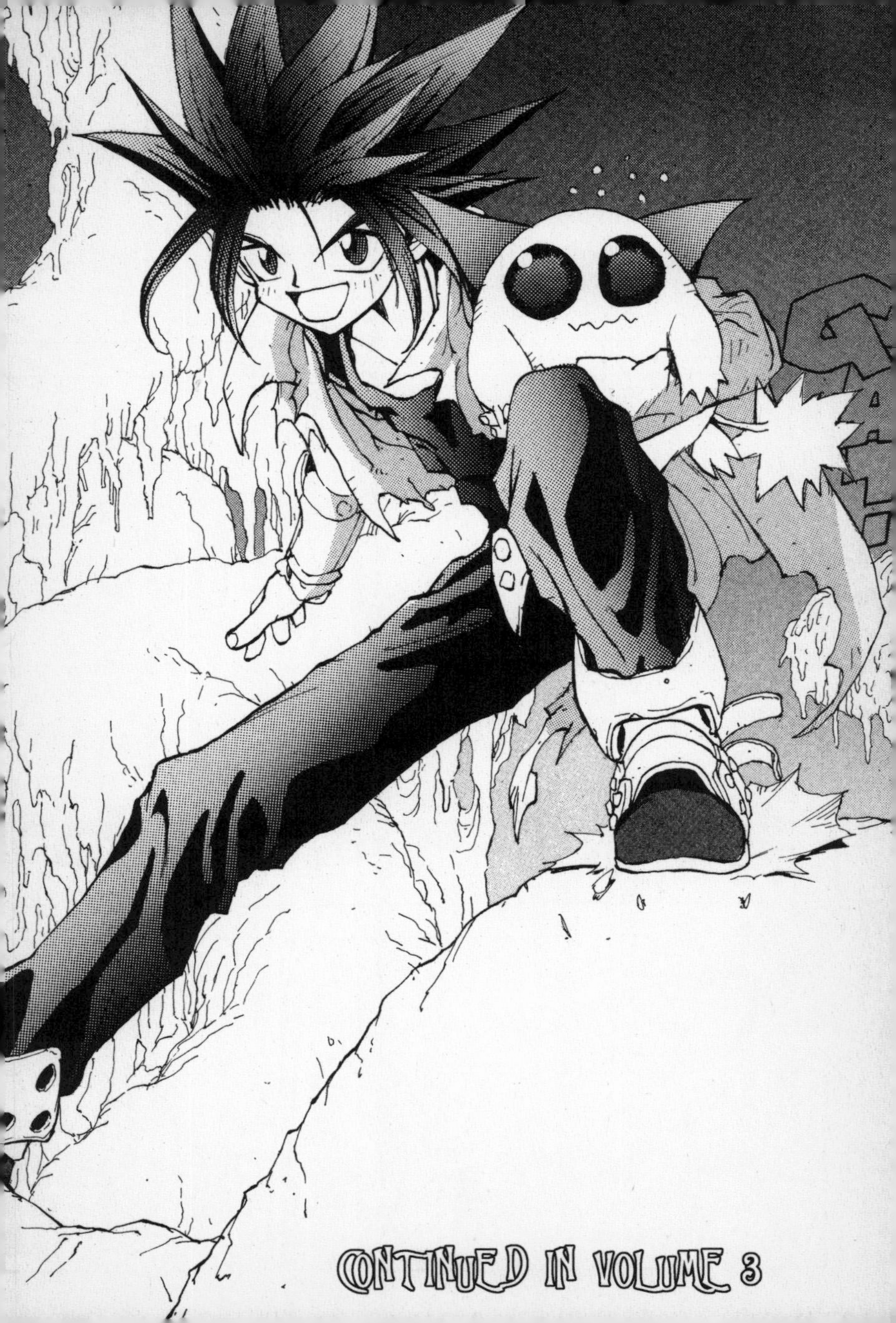

CONTINUED IN VOLUME 3

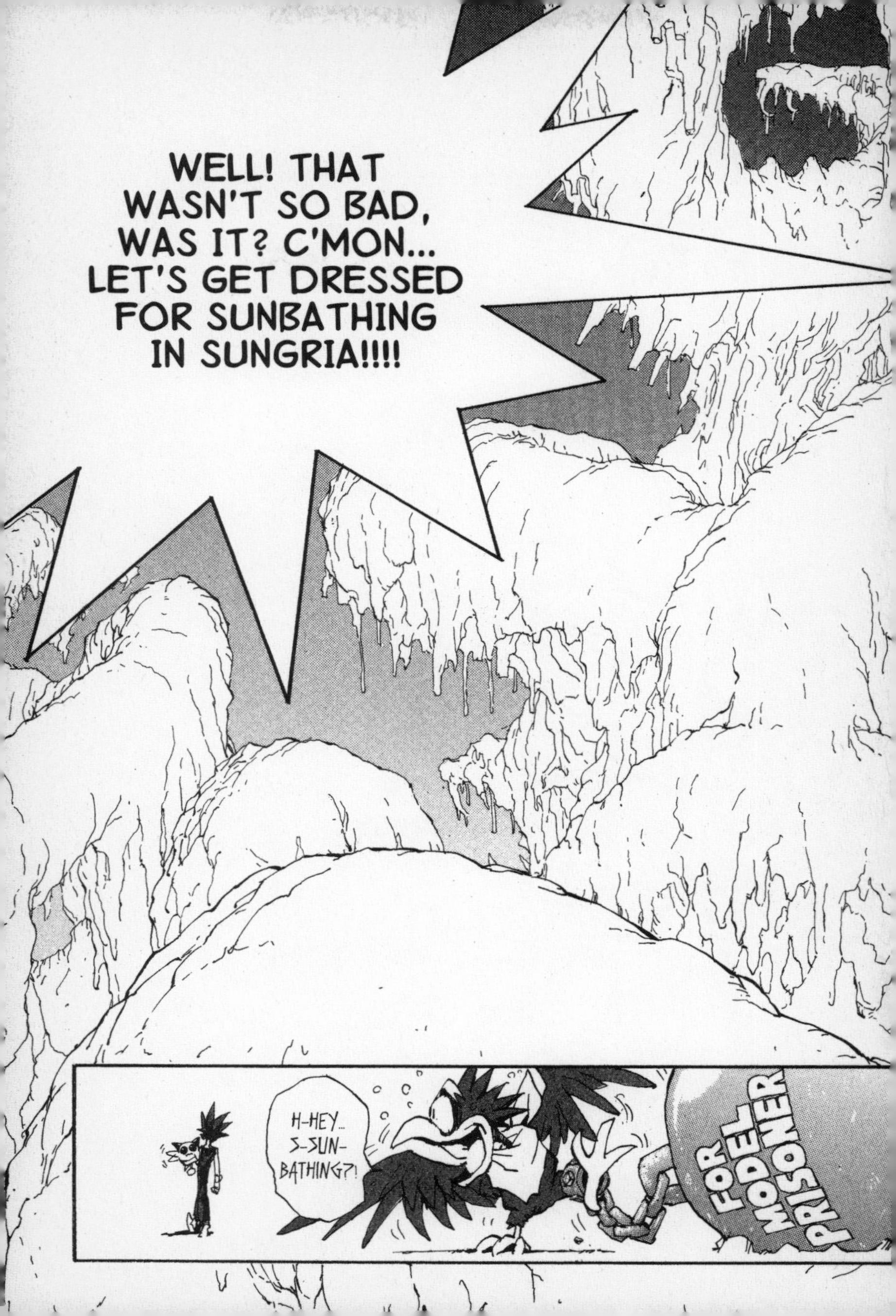
WELL! THAT WASN'T SO BAD, WAS IT? C'MON... LET'S GET DRESSED FOR SUNBATHING IN SUNGRIA!!!!
FOR FEL MODER PRISONER
H-HEY... S-SUN-BATHING?!

CITY OF THIEVES: A port city in the shape of a lighthouse, towering over an endless gorge. The design was derived from the "Tower of Babel," a masterpiece by the great Pieter Bruegel of Flanders. For the perfect touch, I set a gigantic locked gate at the bottom. This gave the city an outward appearance to incite the adventurous spirit.

KING OF BANDIT JING
INITIAL SET-UP
COLLECTION 2

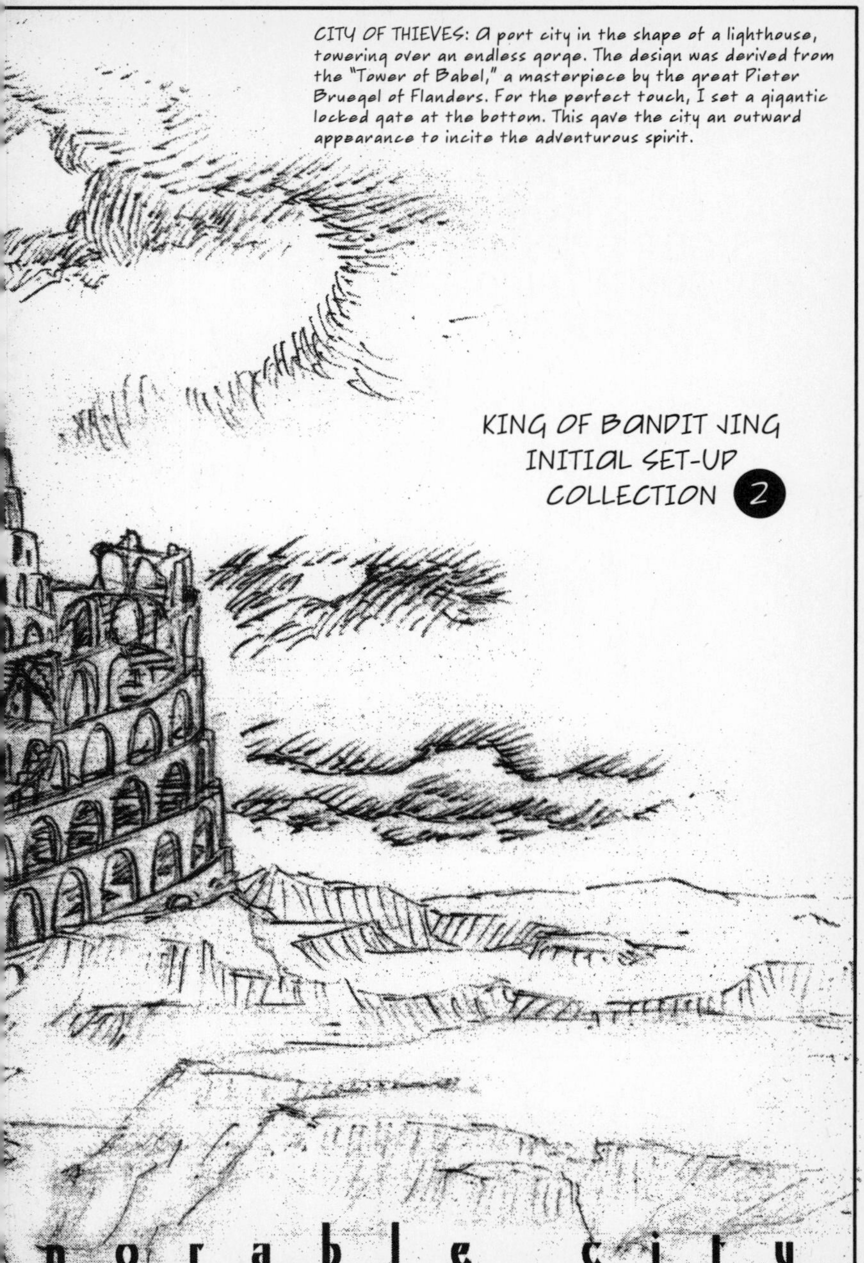
norable city

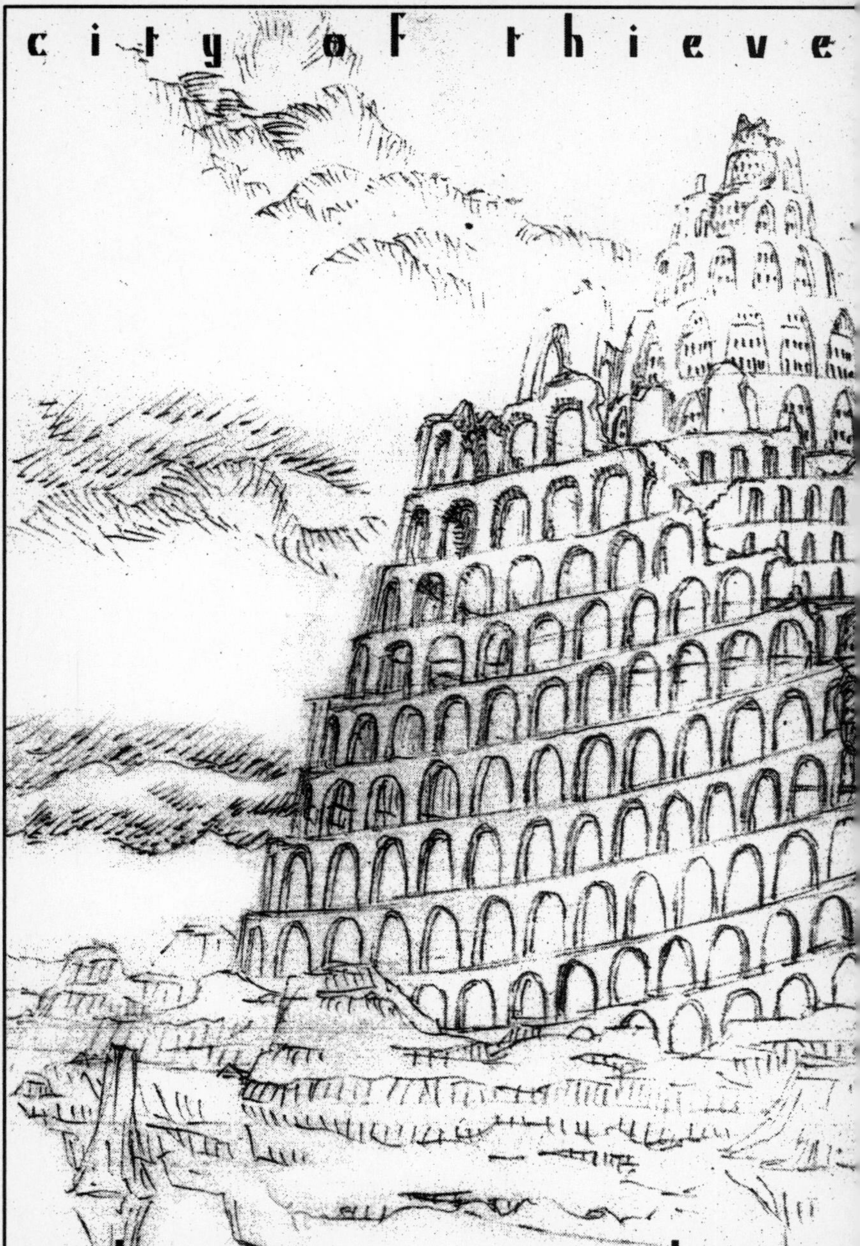
city of thieve
the most dis

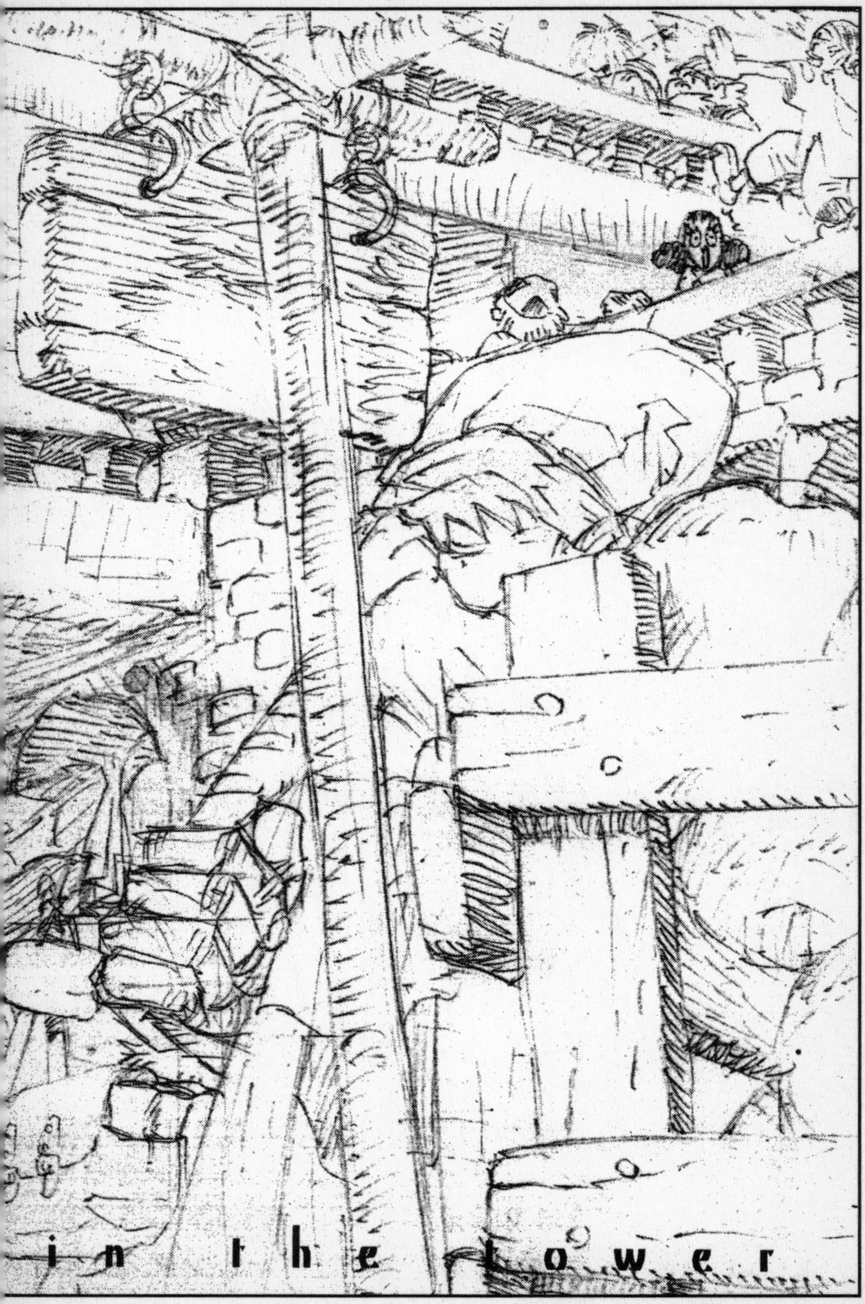
in the tower

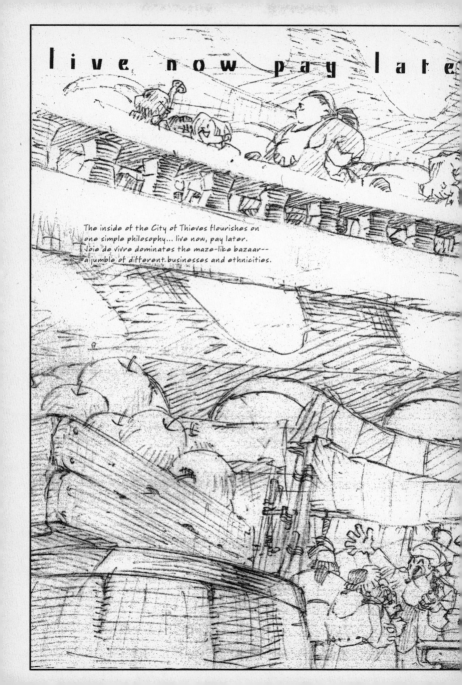

live now pay late

The inside of the City of Thieves flourishes on
one simple philosophy... live now, pay later.
Joie de vivre dominates the maze-like bazaar--
a jumble of different businesses and ethnicities.

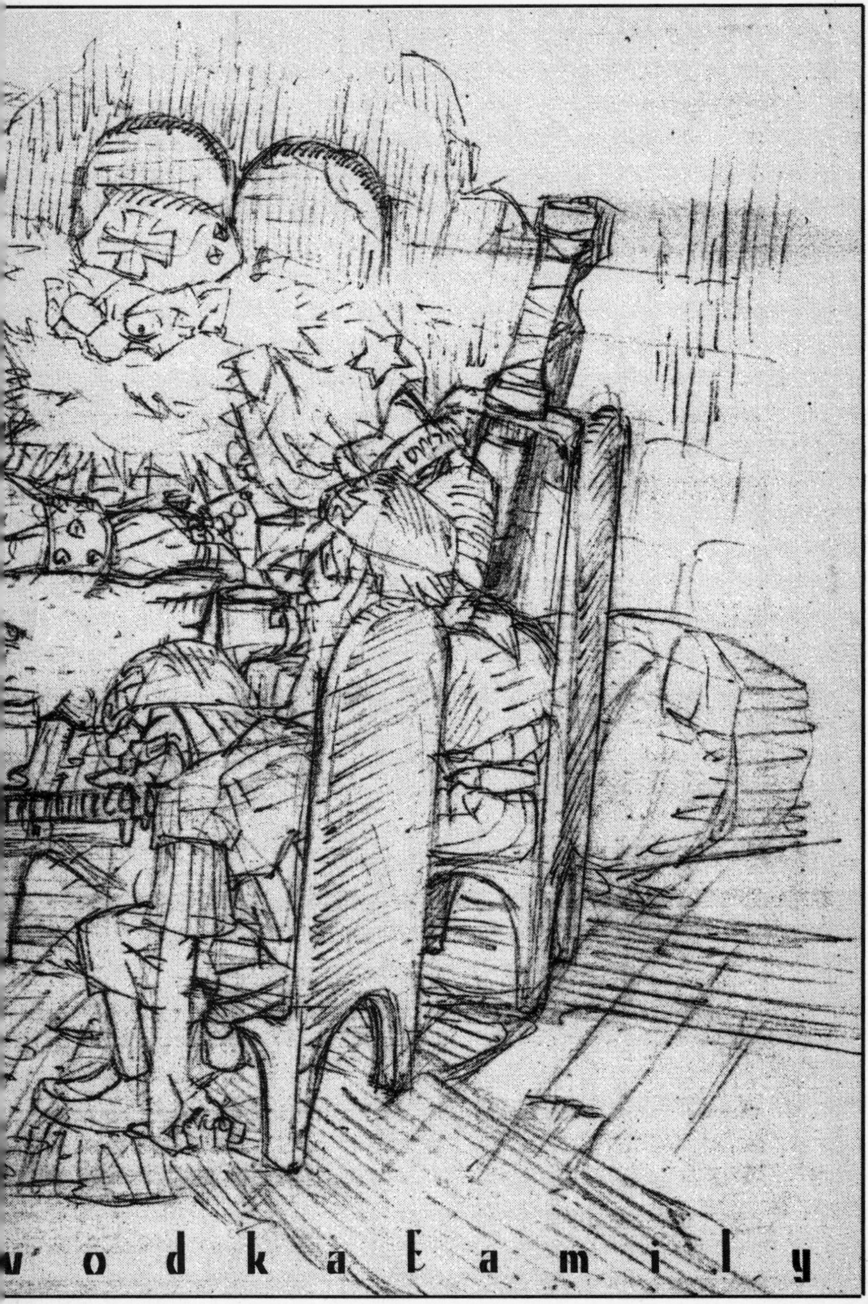
vodka family

b a n d i t s

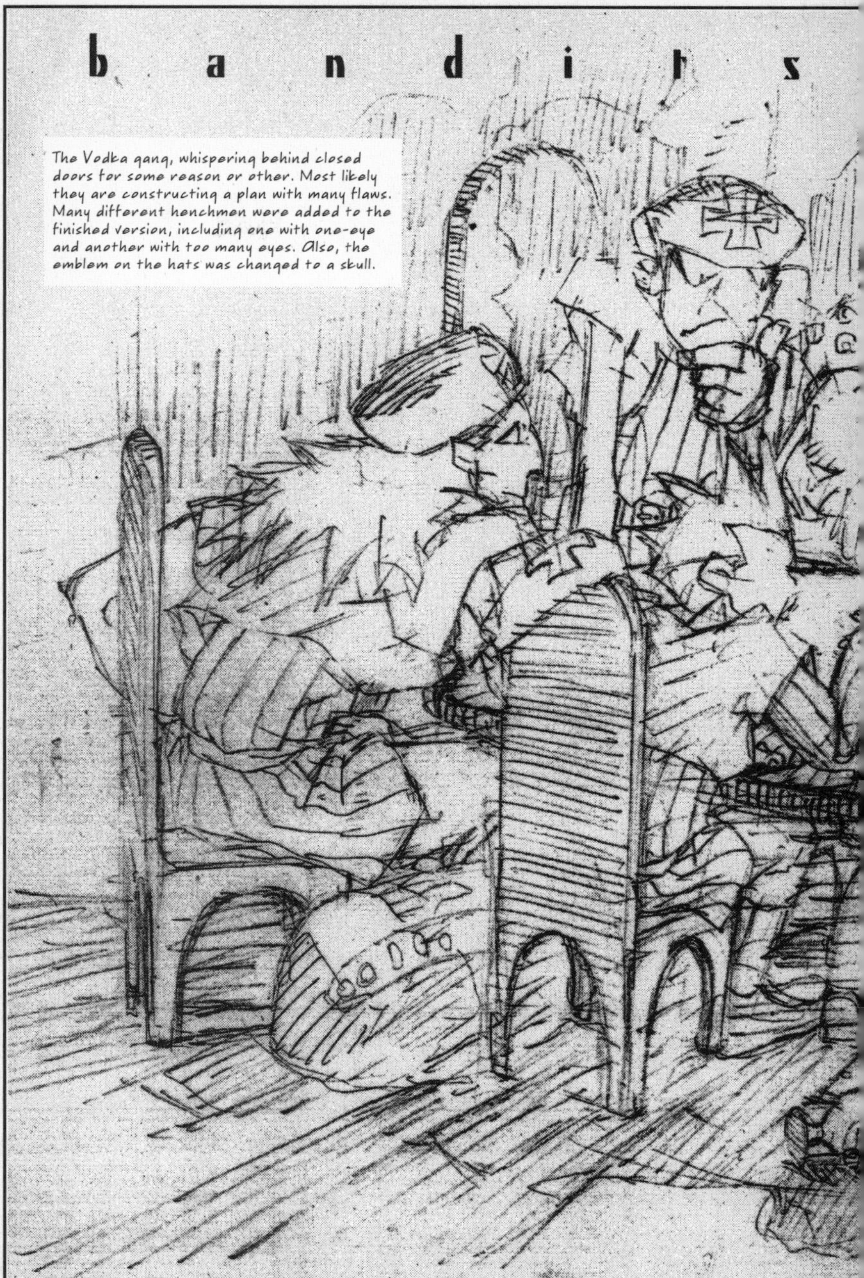

The Vodka gang, whispering behind closed doors for some reason or other. Most likely they are constructing a plan with many flaws. Many different henchmen were added to the finished version, including one with one-eye and another with too many eyes. Also, the emblem on the hats was changed to a skull.

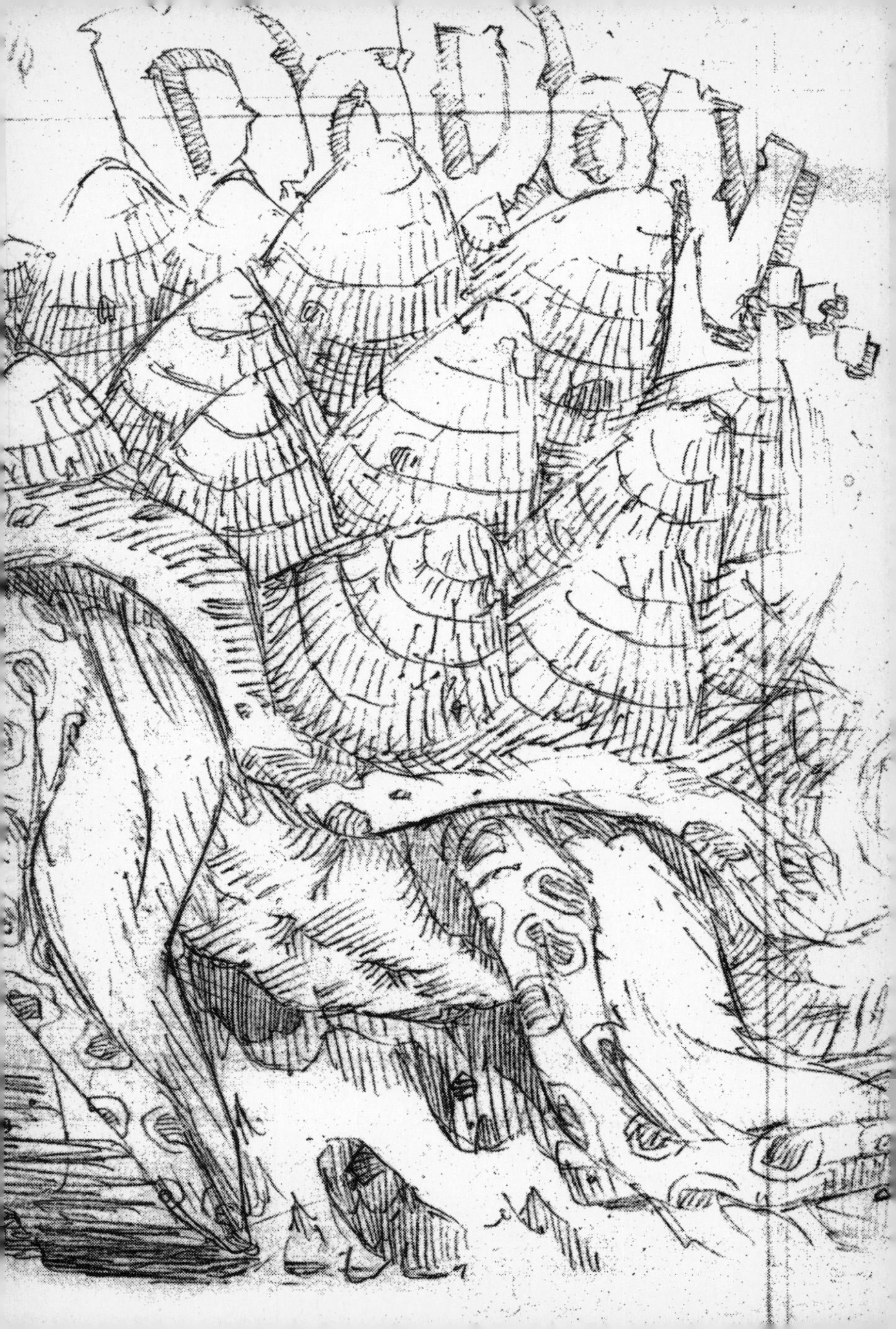

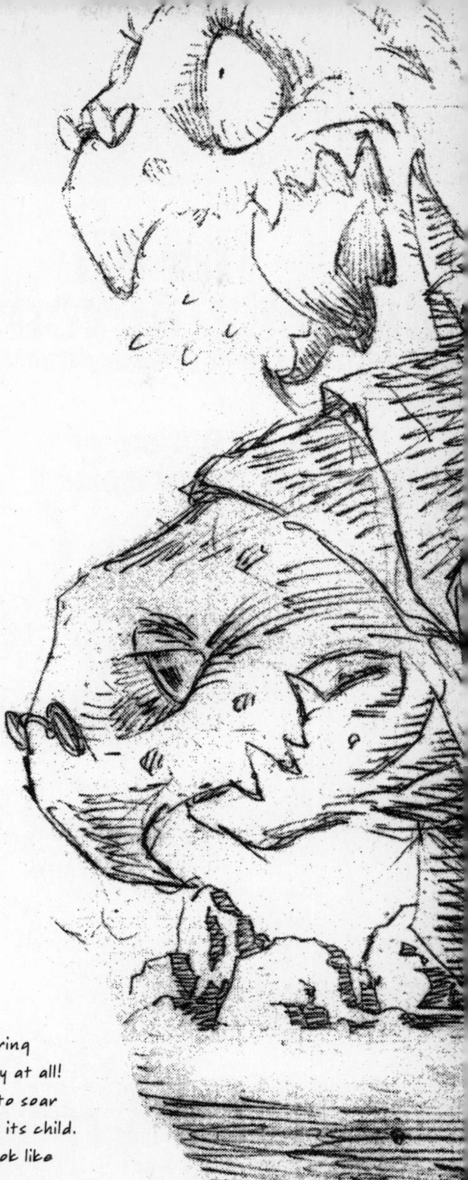

Flying turtle

It was natural to make the dragon, whose egg Jing took hostage, into a doddering turtle that didn't even seem like it could fly at all! Here's why...although it couldn't fly, it had to soar through the air in the end, for the sake of its child. The challenge was making sure it did not look like Gamera, which is why I settled on the more dinosaur-like appearance.

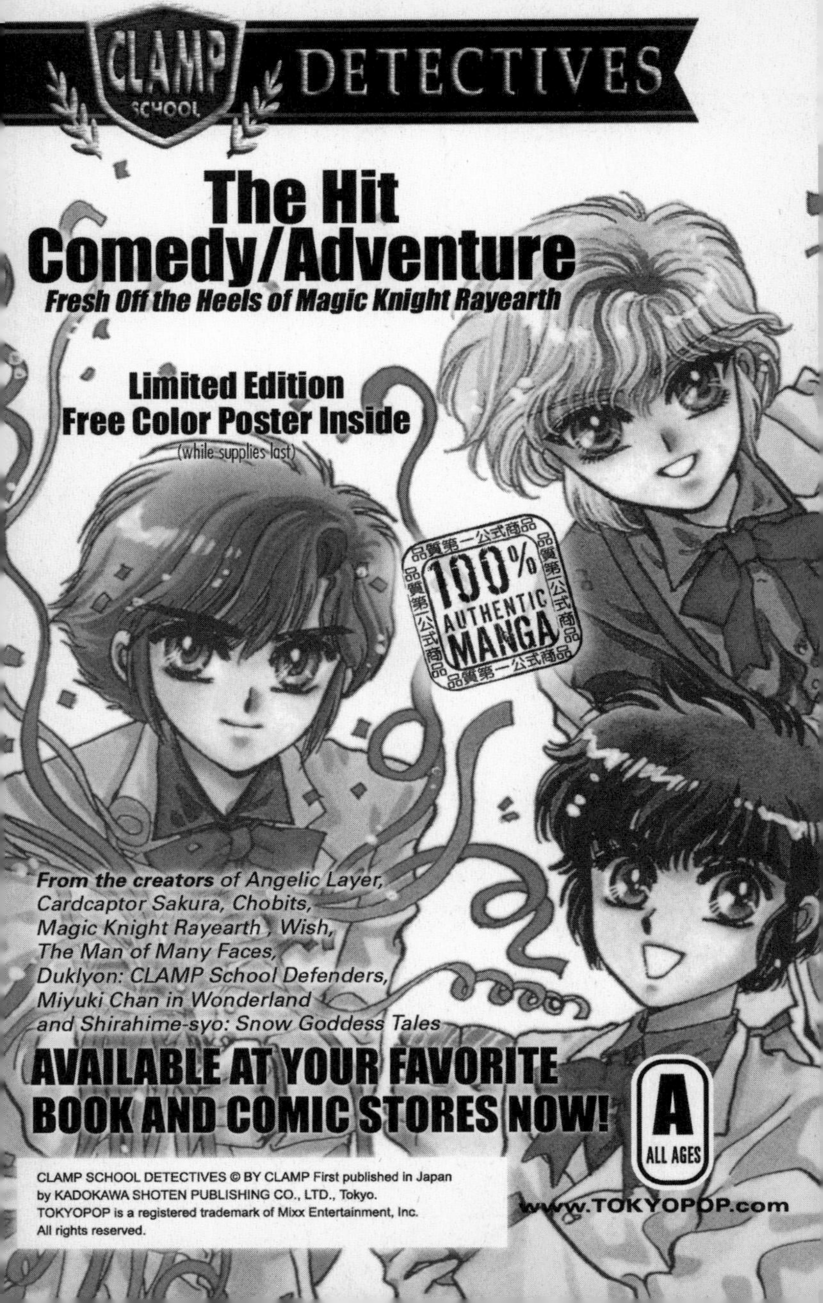
CLAMP SCHOOL
DETECTIVES
The Hit
Comedy/Adventure
Fresh Off the Heels of Magic Knight Rayearth
Limited Edition
Free Color Poster Inside
(while supplies last)
品質第一公式商品 100% AUTHENTIC MANGA
From the creators of Angelic Layer, Cardcaptor Sakura, Chobits, Magic Knight Rayearth , Wish, The Man of Many Faces, Duklyon: CLAMP School Defenders, Miyuki Chan in Wonderland and Shirahime-syo: Snow Goddess Tales
AVAILABLE AT YOUR FAVORITE BOOK AND COMIC STORES NOW!
A
ALL AGES
CLAMP SCHOOL DETECTIVES © BY CLAMP First published in Japan by KADOKAWA SHOTEN PUBLISHING CO., LTD., Tokyo. TOKYOPOP is a registered trademark of Mixx Entertainment, Inc. All rights reserved.
www.TOKYOPOP.com

STOP!

This is the back of the book.
You wouldn't want to spoil a great ending!

This book is printed "manga-style," in the authentic Japanese right-to-left format. Since none of the artwork has been flipped or altered, readers get to experience the story just as the creator intended. You've been asking for it, so TOKYOPOP® delivered: authentic, hot-off-the-press, and far more fun!

DIRECTIONS

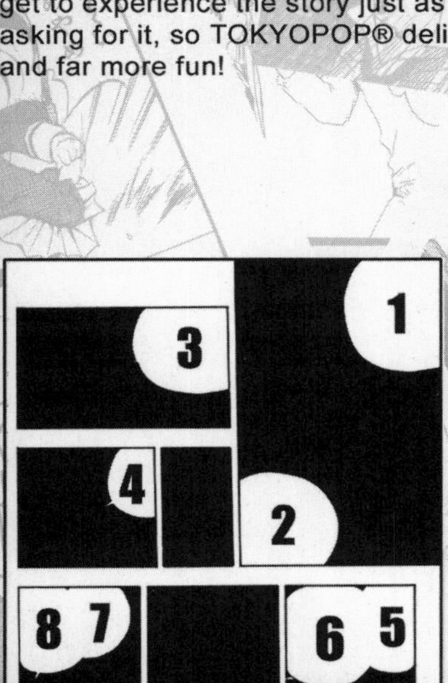
1
2
3
4
5
6
7
8
9
10

If this is your first time reading manga-style, here's a quick guide to help you understand how it works.

It's easy... just start in the top right panel and follow the numbers. Have fun, and look for more 100% authentic manga from TOKYOPOP®!

100% AUTHENTIC MANGA